Christmas 1945

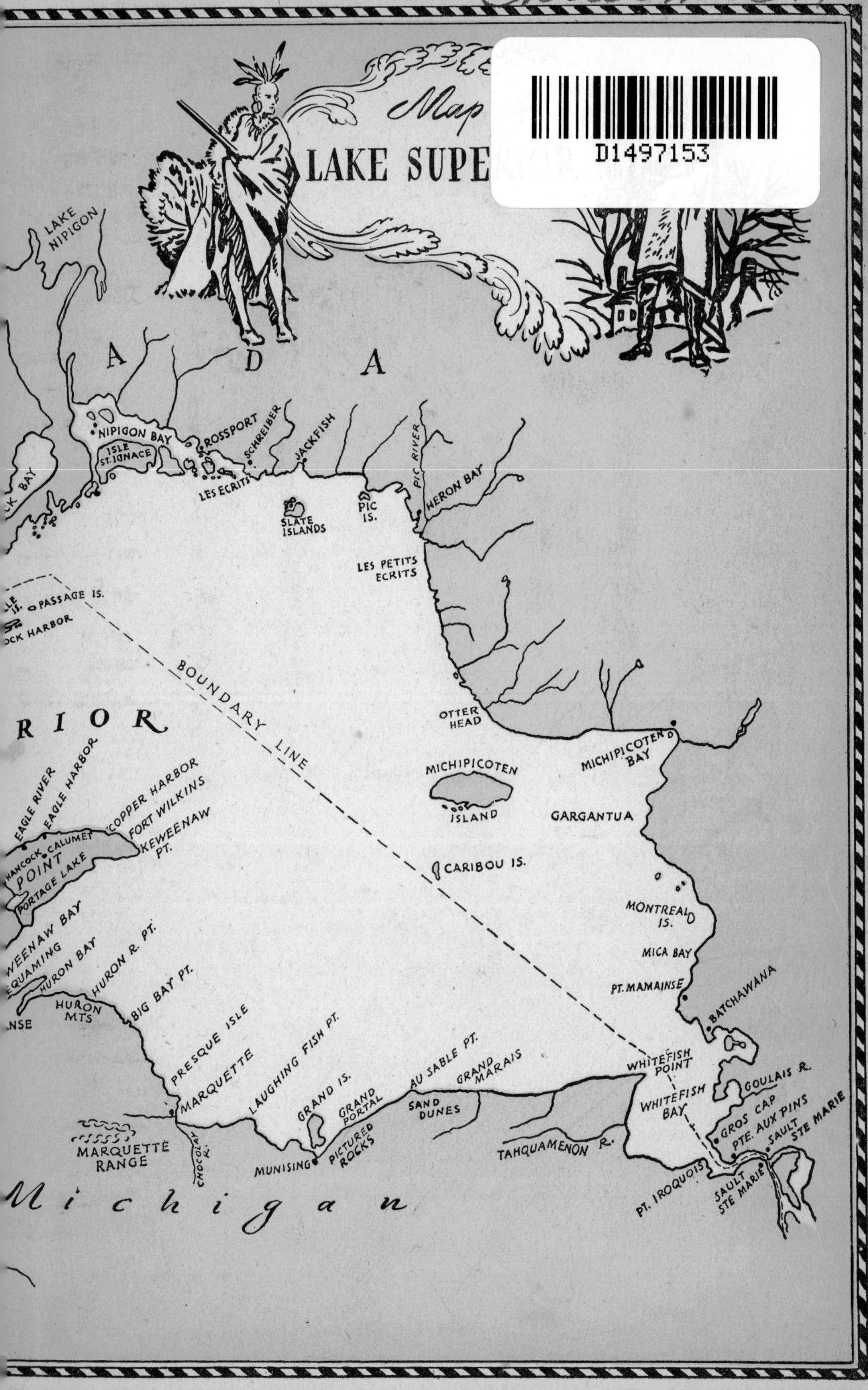

THE AMERICAN LAKES SERIES

Published:

In Preparation:

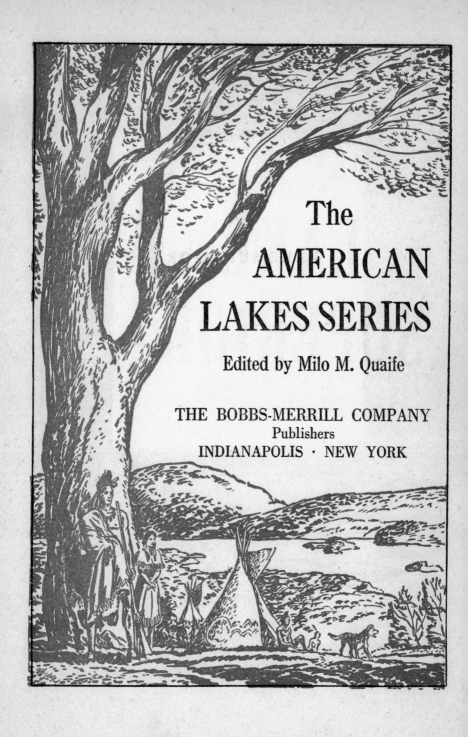

The
AMERICAN
LAKES SERIES

Edited by Milo M. Quaife

THE BOBBS-MERRILL COMPANY
Publishers
INDIANAPOLIS · NEW YORK

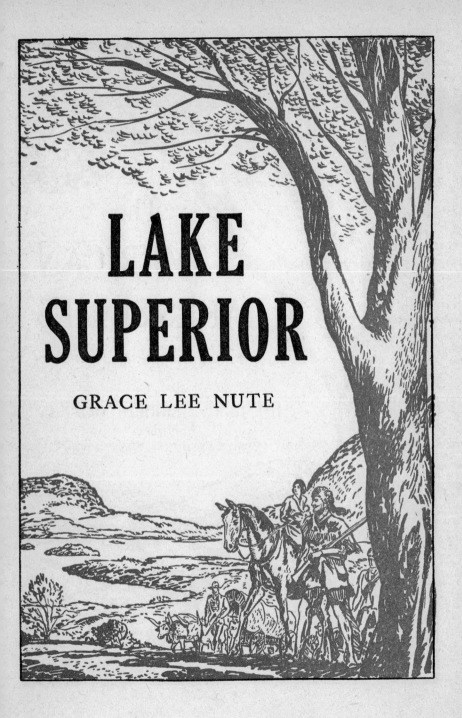

LAKE
SUPERIOR

GRACE LEE NUTE

To

THOSE WHO TRY TO KEEP THE FORESTS GREEN,
THE LAKES FULL, AND WILD LIFE
PRESENT ABOUT THE SHORES
OF LAKE SUPERIOR

EDITORIAL INTRODUCTION

On the rocky island of Malta a century and a quarter ago a British officer pored over a collection of maps and charts. Fascinated by the conception he derived from them of the St. Marys River as one of the world's great waterways, he determined that someday he would view it with his own eyes. Years passed and at length his dream came true. Resigning his commission he migrated to Canada to spend the remainder of his life beside the majestic river which conducts the waters of Lake Superior to their wedding with those of Lake Huron.

Superior's basin was still a wilderness when Major William Kingdom Rains thus succumbed to the spell of the great inland sea. Centuries earlier it had enthralled the minds of the savages who dwelt beside it, to whom its majestic shores and headlands seemed the fitting abode of gods and demons. The development of the Copper Country a century ago marked the real beginning of settlement around the lake, which even today remains sparse, save at its eastern and western extremes. Yet in curious contrast to this condition, throughout all the season of navigation a constant procession of huge ships traverses the lake from end to end, bearing in their holds the products of a commerce so vast that the figures required to express it stagger the imagination.

Yet still the earth's greatest fresh-water sea remains but little known to the world at large. "We know the Sea of Galilee better than Lake Superior, and can recite the marvels of the Lake District of England without knowing that the Lake District of America is more marvelous," was the lament a few years since of a keen observer of contemporary America. If this shall still be true in the coming years, it will not be the fault of Dr. Nute. Like Major Rains on distant Malta, she long ago was captivated by the charm and majesty of the great lake. Year after year she visited it on journeys of personal observation, while as a trained and competent scholar she has industriously mastered the writings and reports of others upon almost every aspect of its life. The results of all this study she has now summed up in the volume before the reader. In it she provides almost everything one could wish to know about Lake Superior, from its first fashioning in the workshop of Nature uncounted millions of years ago to the current year of 1944. The lake has at last found a historian capable of measuring up to the inherent majesty and grandeur of the subject.

M. M. QUAIFE,
Detroit Public Library

BIG SEA-WATER

THE mistranslation which gave Lake Superior its present name was one of those happy mistakes that occur occasionally. The first French explorers, approaching the great inland sea by way of the Ottawa River and Lake Huron and knowing nothing of the connection of that lake with Lake Erie, referred to their discovery as *"le lac supérieur."* Properly translated the expression should be "Upper Lake," that is, the lake above Lake Huron. But the English name is so apt in many ways that it would be a pity for this largest of the Great Lakes to have been named for surrounding Indian tribes.

The word "superior" suggests something a little remote, a trifle chilly, decidedly unusual and unique. Lake Superior has all of these characteristics. It is the largest body of fresh water in the world. Its geological origin has distinction and even the allure of mystery. The great basin in which it lies is unique in geological history and grand in scenic effect. The other lakes of the quintet are large and impressive; Lake Superior is awe-inspiring. Even its inhabitants—chiefly fish—are unique and quite unlike those of its neighbors, Lakes Michigan and Huron. One can become intimate with the other Great Lakes. He is a venturesome person indeed who braves the chill of Lake Superior's waters of about forty degrees' average temperature. It is a tradition that the body of a drowned person never rises to the surface of the lake, because the constant low temperature prevents decay. But on the other hand, the lake cannot be charged with inconstancy or fickleness, for she maintains that temperature, come summer or winter. Yet like all strong, aloof personalities, she has won the respect and admiration of those who have had the courage to become acquainted with her, and her admirers through the centuries have been legion: Indians of many tribes; French, British and American explorers; missionaries of numerous sects and creeds; fur traders; miners; lumbermen; sailors; and finally humble tourists.

The first recorded exploration of Lake Superior occurred early in the seventeenth century. By 1658 there was a fairly accurate map of it, and in 1672 an excellent map was published in France. Two Frenchmen spent the winter of 1659-1660 on its shores and near by. A mission station was established at Chequamegon Bay in 1665. These dates show how far back in recorded history—as American history goes—this lake almost in the center of the continent became known and, to some extent, settled. Some early French maps show it as Lac Tracy, Lac Condé, etc., but these names were never popular and disappeared early.

Fur traders and missionaries played the chief roles in the story of the lake throughout the seventeenth, eighteenth and early nineteenth centuries. Men whose names are synonymous with great daring and fame occur in the annals: Radisson, Des Groseilliers, Duluth, Le Sueur, La Vérendrye, Marin, Henry, Carver, Houghton, Thompson, Schoolcraft, Mackenzie and Pond among the traders and explorers; Allouez, Ménard, Marquette, Aulneau, Provencher, Belcourt, Evans, Taché, Baraga, Pierz, Boutwell and Hall among the missionaries. There were also humbler men whose names have been forgotten, but whose services as voyageurs to the traders and missionaries made trips into this region possible. How could anyone reach the interior except by birch-bark canoes? And who save Indians and French-Canadian voyageurs would ever dare to navigate Lake Superior's rock-bound northern shore in such cockleshells? Today it seems fantastic even to think of such hardihood, as one looks at the formidable unbroken cliffs, and realizes that there the winds have a clean sweep across some two hundred and fifty miles of open water.

By the time modern miners appeared on the lake there were sailing vessels or steamboats to convey them, though many traveled by open boat and some even by canoe. The great trading companies—the Hudson's Bay, North West, and American Fur companies—were largely responsible for this advance in transportation facilities. The North West Company had a schooner on Lake Superior by 1778; several others appeared in following years; the American Fur Company had numerous sailing craft on the lake in the 1830's both in its fur and its fishing activities; and the Hudson's Bay Company transported many of its men and goods by sail or steamboat between Fort William and Sault Ste. Marie. It was miners, however, who created the great demand for transportation after the opening of the copper mines on the south shore in the 1840's, and who insisted upon the opening of navigation between Lake Superior and the other Great Lakes. From that day to this the volume of shipping on Lake Superior has mounted almost steadily, till Duluth-Superior has become the second largest port in point of tonnage on the North American continent, despite the fact that navigation usually closes in December and does not reopen till April. Ores and minerals, cereals and their products, forest items, dairy products and fish constitute the bulk of the freight carried down the lake, with ore from Minnesota's great iron ranges leading all the rest. For if Lake Superior is rock-bound on the north and east, it is iron-clad on the west and copper-bottomed to the south.

The first fishermen were Indians. In the thirties of the last century they gave place to voyageurs, who attempted to carry out Ramsay Crooks's plan for the American Fur Company of accustoming the American palate to the trout, whitefish, herring and siscowet of this remarkably cold lake. The effects of the panic of 1837 ended the great monopoly's project, but commercial fishermen have been on the lake ever since. They give it an indescribable atmosphere, having that same extreme individualism and robust disregard for physical comfort that have made fishermen of Brittany and Norway the explorers of unknown seas and continents. Of late years many of the fishermen have come from Norway, Sweden and Finland.

The discovery of copper and iron in great quantity along the southern and western shores of Lake Superior accounts for the growth of cities and towns westward between Sault Ste. Marie and Duluth. The opening of the wheat fields of Manitoba, Alberta and Saskatchewan caused Fort William and Port Arthur to develop. There are no cities between Port Arthur and Sault Ste. Marie on the Canadian shore, and few habitations of any kind between the Pic and Sault Ste. Marie.

Lake Superior's shore line was almost completely wooded when first seen by white men. It remained so till very recent times. Noble white and red pines darkened the American north shore and ceased almost exactly at the boundary line. Beyond, on the Canadian north and east shores, the forest still presents almost the same picture that met Agassiz' eyes in 1849: spruce, poplar and birch for the most part. Magnificent hardwood forests graced the south shore. A remnant may still be seen in the Porcupine Mountains of the Michigan shore. There were also white and red pine forests on the south shore. These were cut in the period between 1850 and 1890. Then the Maine and Canuck lumberjacks of that shore moved over to the American north shore and denuded that stretch in the years between 1890 and 1925. Today there are few pine trees left. Poplars grew after fires swept the slashings, but these are still very young—and very lovely in their dress of autumn gold against the almost Mediterranean blue of the lake in October.

TABLE OF CONTENTS

TABLE OF CONTENTS—*Continued*

Part V

RED AND WHITE ART

LIST OF ILLUSTRATIONS

Part I

FOOTPRINTS ON THE SANDS OF TIME

Chapter 1

Under the Golden Lilies

Vexilla regis proderunt,
Fulget crucis mysterium.
The Royal Banners forward go,
The Cross shines forth in mystic glow.
—VEXILLA REGIS

THE FIRST white men ever to dip paddle in the clear water of Lake Superior seem to have been Etienne Brulé and a young man named Grenoble, whose first name is unknown. Brulé was one of Samuel de Champlain's interpreters, whom he sent to live among the Indians, learn their ways and languages, and report on the country. By 1623 missionaries among the Huron Indians had learned from these two men and possibly others that there was "another very great lake," above Lake Huron, into which it poured by rapids already bearing the name of the king's brother, the Sault de Gaston. This lake and the connection with Lake Huron are shown on Champlain's published map of 1632. Brulé and Grenoble had visited a place on Lake Superior from which the Indians were taking copper. Historians are inclined to believe that they had been to Isle Royale, though possibly only to the copper mines of the south shore. There, bearing Brulé's name to this day, is a stream famous for its scenery and trout and for being the northern half of a canoe route into the interior.

For more than two hundred years after Brulé's death in 1633 the river carried explorers, traders, missionaries and travelers from Lake Superior to the Mississippi and back by way of a portage and the scenic St. Croix. Rivers of this part of the continent were often named for the men who first opened a main thoroughfare thereby, and probably Brule River in northwestern Wisconsin is no exception. It is more than likely that Etienne Brulé opened up this trade route

19

for the whites and that the honor for that event therefore does not belong to Daniel Greysolon, Sieur Duluth, as usually claimed.

Oddly enough, Lake Superior was thus discovered and explored before Lakes Michigan, Erie and Ontario. The reason for such a strange occurrence was the enmity between the Iroquois Indians and the tribes to the west and north of them. As the French of the lower St. Lawrence were allies of some of these tribes, they, too, became targets for the enmity of the Iroquois. It became necessary to take a safer route to the interior than was afforded by the St. Lawrence and the lower Great Lakes. Moreover, the trade route up the Ottawa, through Lake Nipissing, and down French River into Georgian Bay, was preferable in some other respects to the apparently easier route. There was no such waterfall as Niagara to portage around, though there were thirty-six portages and many *décharges** on the customary route. In addition, birch-bark canoes were the vehicles for transportation, and such fragile craft are not at their best in great lakes like Ontario and Erie. To be sure, the trade route eventually skirted the largest of the lakes, but that was of necessity, not by choice. There was no route other than the lake itself for arriving at the west end of Lake Superior.

In 1641 two Jesuit missionaries, Charles Raymbault and Isaac Jogues, visited the rapids between Lake Superior and Lake Huron and changed the name to Sault de Ste. Marie in honor of the Virgin Mary. There they also learned of a new tribe of Indians who dwelt about the western end of Lake Superior—the Dakota, or Sioux—eighteen days' journey to the west. To reach them, wrote the missionaries:

"The first nine days are occupied in crossing another great lake that commences above the Sault; during the last nine days one has to ascend a river that traverses those lands. These people till the soil in the manner of our Hurons, and harvest Indian corn and tobacco."

Gradually Lake Superior was becoming known. At first the maps all represented its eastern end correctly but left the western end open as an indication that its complete shape was still unknown.

---

* Places where the canoe could remain in the water but without its human cargo.

Sometime before 1658, however, a map was drawn that delineated the entire lake fairly accurately. Who drew this manuscript map, now in Paris archives, is unknown, but on it he pens in French, "Some people have told me of having gone for twenty days about Lake Superior without having circumnavigated half of it." By the time this map was drawn, four of the Great Lakes had become known, but no connection is shown on it between Lake Huron and Lake Erie.

The first dated piece to mention the largest lake as "Supérieur" or "Superior," is the Jesuit *Relation* of 1647-1648:

"Other Algonkins [live] still farther away, on the shores of another lake, larger than Lake Huron [*La mer douce*], into which it discharges by a very large and very rapid river; the latter before mingling its waters with those of our mer douce, rolls over a fall [*sault*] that gives its name to these peoples [Saulteurs or Ojibwa], who come there during the fishing season. This superior lake extends toward the Northwest,—that is, between the West and North."

The first men known to have traveled on Lake Superior and to have recorded their experiences in any detail were Médard Chouart, Sieur des Groseilliers, and his young brother-in-law, Pierre Esprit Radisson. The latter wrote out his reminiscences for court and scientific men in England while he was spending the winter of 1668-1669 in London, but the trip had taken place just a decade earlier and is mentioned in the Jesuit *Relation* of 1660. Des Groseilliers had been in the West on earlier occasions. Radisson had been twice a captive among the Iroquois, who had subjected him to all the refinements of torture that they knew so well how to employ on hapless men, women and children. His pluck and endurance had won their admiration and he had finally escaped to Manhattan and thence to Europe in 1654. Later he returned among them and spent a winter at a new Jesuit mission south of Lake Ontario, close to the site of modern Syracuse. On the trip to Lake Superior the two men refused to allow the Governor of New France to send his agents nor would they allow certain eager Jesuits to accompany them. For this recalcitrance they suffered neglect and even worse upon their return in the summer of 1660 with cargoes of furs that saved Canada from economic ruin. Though they tried to show officials in France and New France that the great store of beaver furs lay to the north and west of Lake Superior, and that the best route to those regions lay through Hudson Bay and not through Lake Superior, they were given no support. Accordingly, they carried their knowledge and experience to England, where they were heeded, and the result was the founding of the Hudson's Bay Company in 1670.

Radisson's narrative of his Lake Superior experiences was preserved by Samuel Pepys, the famous diarist, and a translation of it now reposes in the Bodleian Library in Oxford, England. It lay unknown to historians till almost the end of the nineteenth century. When it was discovered and published, it opened a whole new chapter of knowledge concerning Lake Superior. Radisson describes the Sault de Ste. Marie and its fisheries, the Pictured Rocks, Keweenaw Peninsula, across which he portaged, the gulls ("goilants") of the lake, and Chequamegon Bay, where he and Des Groseilliers built the first known dwelling of white men on the lake. The winter of 1659-1660 was spent on a little inland lake, probably Lac Court Oreilles in Sawyer County, Wisconsin, to which a trail led long after these men were dead and gone. Later they returned to the bay, crossed to the north shore, and probably explored the age-old trail to the interior which begins at the mouth of the Pigeon River, now on the international boundary. As late as the American Revolution this river bore Des Groseilliers' name. Even today a river on the north shore carries a translation of his name, the Gooseberry River. Careless cartographers of the seventeenth and eighteenth centuries moved the river up and down the shore line at will on their maps, and eventually the name became attached to a stream that is exquisite in its beauty but impossible of navigation.

All that remains of Radisson's narrative is a contemporaneous translation couched in quaint, middle-class English of the seventeenth century. It was prepared for the Hudson's Bay Company in 1669 and five pounds sterling was paid to the translator for it. With all its deficiencies it is still a most interesting and appealing document. Even though it is a poor translation, it shows the man Radisson reveling in the beauty and wonders of Lake Superior. Its shores were "most delightfull and wounderous." On the south shore is a bank of rocks "like a great Portall, by reason of the beating of the waves. The lower part of that oppening is as bigg as a tower." In winter "the snow stoocke to those trees that are there so ruffe, being deal trees, prusse cedars, and thorns, that caused y^t darknesse upon ye earth that it is believed that the sun was eclipsed them 2 months." The pelicans interested him greatly; and so did the "staggs, buffs, elands and castors [deer, buffalo, elk and beaver]." He describes the Indians, their domestic arts, their customs, dress and organization. His delight in all that he saw was summed up in a phrase: "We weare Cesars being nobody to contradict us."

After Radisson and Des Groseilliers, explorers and traders came thick and fast. The prime beaver pelts that the brothers-in-law took to Montreal and Quebec excited the cupidity of many persons from the Governor on down. Jesuit missionaries and seven traders returned in 1660 with Radisson's and Des Groseilliers' recent Indian companions. Neither of the two missionaries, Father René Ménard nor his lay assistant, Jean Guérin, survived the trip. Ménard was feeble at the start and felt that he was badly treated on the arduous canoe trip up the Ottawa River and down the French River to Georgian Bay. Probably he had no more to endure than anyone who made such a trip, for it demanded great strength and endurance at best. In Lake Superior he had the misfortune to be in a canoe that was struck by a falling tree. The accident delayed the occupants of that canoe several days, but they eventually reached Keweenaw Bay on Ste. Therese's day, October 15. The missionary accordingly named that body of water Ste. Therese's Bay. Here he and his canoemates spent the winter, though the remainder of the party went on to winter at Chequamegon Bay, where the Ottawa Indians from Lac Court Oreilles had begun a village even before Radisson and Des Groseilliers left. It was a mild winter and the missionary did not suffer unduly. In the spring he went to Chequamegon Bay, named by this time the Bay of the Holy Ghost (*Saint Esprit*). From this point he later undertook a journey by way of the trail to Lac Court Oreilles and down the Chippewa River. He wandered away from his companions, however, and was never heard from again. Guérin also lost his life on his Lake Superior trip, having been shot accidentally by one of his companions.

The village at the foot of Chequamegon Bay now became the focus of attention of French trading interests until 1668. To it went the seven men already mentioned, who left the lower St. Lawrence soon after Radisson and Des Groseilliers appeared with their treasure-trove of furs. These seven traders were well-known men of their communities. Among them was Louis Jolliet's elder brother, Adrien. They expected to return the following year, but it actually was three years before they again saw the island of Montreal and the spires of Quebec. A Jesuit narrator has left for us a graphic account of their experiences as they fished in Chequamegon Bay:

"It was a sight to arouse pity to see poor Frenchmen in a Canoe, amid rain and snow, borne hither and thither by whirlwinds in these great Lakes, which often show waves as high as those of the Sea. The men frequently found their hands and feet frozen upon their return, while occasionally they were overtaken by so thick a fall of powdery snow, driven against them by a violent wind, that the one steering the Canoe could not see his companion in the bow. How then gain the port? Verily as often as they reached the land, their doing so seemed a little miracle. Whenever their fishing was successful, they laid by a little store which they smoked and used for provision when fishing was over, or the season no longer admitted of fishing."

Troubles with the Sioux prevented a trip down to Quebec in 1661; in 1662 the Iroquois reached Lake Superior, intending to attack the party on its way down to the French settlements. However, a band of Chippewa, or Saulteurs, as they were then called, aided by Ottawa, Nipissing and Beaver tribesmen, fell upon the invaders and defeated them at the spot on the south shore that still bears the commemorative name, Iroquois Point.

So it was only in 1663 that the traders reached their homes again. They took with them much knowledge of the Lake Superior country and its inhabitants, some copper, but not enough furs to make their venture financially profitable.

In 1664 the great interpreter and trader Nicolas Perrot was probably with the canoes from Lake Superior that came to a dramatic and pageantlike halt at the little settlement of Three Rivers, halfway between Montreal and Quebec. He and his Indian companions had beaten off two attacking parties of the Iroquois, and their canoes were piled high with furs. So it is small wonder that they sang songs of victory, shot off their guns, and otherwise impressed four companies of soldiers just arriving for the first time from France. When the Indians returned to their homes, a cultured and vigorous Jesuit missionary accompanied them, Father Claude Jean Allouez. He made his way to the foot of Chequamegon Bay, where seven different tribes were then living in a little settlement. There he built a bark chapel and a hut for himself. He worked long and hard, and without too much success. In the spring of 1667 he decided to visit the Nipissing tribe, then in the area north of Lake Nipigon. To do so he skirted the entire shore of Lake Superior in a small bark canoe propelled by two Indian guides. Later, with the help of Father Jacques Marquette, he prepared a map of the lake, which was one of the finest and most accurate of all the maps drawn until very recent times. It was published in the Jesuit *Relation* of 1670-1671, which appeared in 1672 in book form. Another map, drawn about 1680 and showing all the mission posts in the West, has crosses wherever mission work had occurred. It is interesting to note on it crosses at Keweenaw Bay, at Chequamegon Bay, at the site of modern Duluth, on the southeast shore of Lake Nipigon and at Sault Ste. Marie. Thus, at last, the great lake had been circumnavigated by a white man and accurately delineated on a chart. At this same period Allouez also learned from Illinois Indians who came to him at his station that there was a great river to the southwest called the "Messipi." This is the first known reference to that river by that name.

Allouez left his post in 1667 long enough to return to Quebec and get another priest for his mission. This was Father Louis Nicolas, who turned out a great disappointment to Allouez. With them went the last trading company of this period to Lake Superior. It consisted of Adrien Jolliet and eight companions, who were outfitted by the Péré firm of La Rochelle. Jean Péré, who with his brother made up the firm, soon found his way to Lake Superior and in time became one of the most traveled explorers of northern North America. French and even English maps long carried his name as the designation of the Albany River, which he was apparently the first white man to explore. This occurred in 1684.

Jolliet's company of traders met with some accident and only three survived. Another group that went out the same year included Perrot and Toussaint Baudry, who spent the winter on Lake Superior, probably at Chequamegon Bay. There they met a delegation of Potawatomi Indians from Green Bay, who invited them to the shores of Lake Michigan. This move now became possible because of the peace which the new intendant of New France, Jean Talon, made with the Iroquois in 1667. It was no longer necessary for the western tribes to wander far afield on the shores of Lake Superior because they dared not remain at home within reach of their ruthless enemies. So, after 1668, the center of trading operations in the West shifted from Lake Superior to Green Bay.

Allouez returned to his mission in 1667, having been at Quebec two days between trips. His zeal was unflagging but he became despondent over results and determined to remove the mission to Sault Ste. Marie, where the Chippewa offered more prospects of success and where French traders were usually to be found in some numbers. The Ottawa of Chequamegon, fearing to lose all contact with white men and the chance to get greatly prized weapons and kettles, hastily had a change of heart and were baptized en masse. So Father Allouez stayed yet a little longer at Chequamegon. In 1669 he returned to the lower St. Lawrence, and in his place Father Marquette was sent to the Mission of Saint Esprit on Chequamegon Bay. Marquette had already established the Sault Ste. Marie mission in 1668 and had met Allouez there in the spring of 1669. It was at this post that he also met Louis Jolliet, who had been sent out by Talon in 1669 with provisions and reinforcements for Péré. The latter had gone out in 1668 on a three-year tour of exploration. A few years later Marquette and Jolliet were to win for themselves the honor of being the first white explorers known to have been on the upper reaches of that "Messipi" River reported by Allouez. Péré meantime made a thorough exploration of Lake Superior and found a copper mine.

Marquette remained at his post on Chequamegon Bay until the summer of 1671. Then he went to Mackinac with the entire body of Huron and Ottawa, when they fled the wrath of the Sioux. They had picked a quarrel with these formidable neighbors and were unable to endure the results. So ended the first mission on Lake Superior.

When Marquette left the Sault, his place was taken by Father Claude Dablon in 1669, who was succeeded by Father Gabriel Dreuillettes in 1670. Dreuillettes remained there for the next nine years. Both men were present at a famous pageant which took place at the Sault on June 14, 1671, when a young French nobleman, François Daumont, Sieur de Saint Lusson, took possession of all interior North America, including the Lake Superior basin, for France and its Sun King, Louis XIV. The results of Radisson's and Des Groseilliers' defection to the English were beginning to be felt. Talon saw quickly that to forestall an English encirclement of New France from Hudson Bay and the colonies along the Atlantic seaboard it was necessary to claim possession of a vast hinterland. Colbert, prime minister of Louis XIV, to whom the proposal was referred, was opposed to distant expeditions from the centers of New France, but when the mineral resources of Lake Superior were pointed out to him, he acceded promptly. De Saint Lusson and Perrot were dispatched, the former to explore for mines of copper on Lake Superior, the latter to gather in the distant tribes to a ceremony at Sault Ste. Marie. When the natives arrived, they represented seventeen tribes, including all of those on the shores of Lake Superior and immediately beyond: Chippewa, Cree, Monsoni, Ottawa, Huron, Assiniboin, Menominee, Winnebago, Potawatomi and Nipissing.

The ceremony took place on the southwest shore of the rapids near the palisaded mission and the native village. The gates of the mission opened and out came black-robed Jesuits, traders in gay sashes, Perrot the interpreter, and De Saint Lusson, the personal representative of the King, in the bright uniform of a French officer. From his helmet fluttered the royal ensign, gold lilies on a field of white. The priests' crucifixes were held aloft as a Latin hymn was sung en route to the little hill where the Indians stood impassive in all the finery beloved of them.

De Saint Lusson beckoned the natives to approach. Perrot interpreted, telling them that the Great Father beyond the sea was now their father and that he had sent them tokens of his concern for them. At this point bales of presents were opened and distributed among the Indians. In return they presented the King with furs. Then the standard bearing the royal arms was set up, while the *Exaudiat* was sung and Latin prayers were chanted. Finally, as part of an old feudal custom, De Saint Lusson bent, broke off a bit of sod, and holding it aloft proclaimed in a loud voice:

"In the name of the Most High, Most Mighty, and most Redoubtable Monarch Louis the Fourteenth, Most Christian King of France and Navarre, we take possession of the said place Sainte Marie du Sault, as also of Lake Huron and Superior, the island of Manitoulin and all the other countries, rivers, lakes, and their tributaries contiguous and adjacent thereto, those discovered and to be discovered, bounded on one side by the Northern and Western seas, and on the other by the South Sea, this land in all its length and breadth."

All this he repeated three times while the French priests and traders exclaimed *"Vive le Roi"* and the traders and Indians shot off their muskets. The chiefs signed the record, as did four missionaries and fourteen traders. The grand old hymn, *Vexilla regis,* chanted at the close of these performances, ended this stirring and symbolic ceremony, the first of many similar events in various parts of the continent. Duluth took possession of the Sioux country in 1679 by the same device; La Salle in 1682 followed the same pattern at the mouth of the Mississippi; Perrot on the shores of Lake Pepin in 1689 claimed all the region of the upper Mississippi for France by a similar method; and minor *prises de possession* were enacted on Hudson Bay and in the interior.

Not much is known of Lake Superior for a few years after 1668. A celebrated engineer, Hugues Randin, was sent thither in 1676, and though we have no account of his trip, we know something of his experiences and the places he visited because of a manuscript map which he made and which is still in existence. It is an excellent delineation of Lake Superior, but it has never been published. Geographical knowledge grew considerably during the seventies, though it is impossible now to say who were the men who went exploring in the West, and when. It is more than likely that Robert Cavelier, Sieur de la Salle, was in the general vicinity of Lake Superior, if not actually on its waters or shores, just prior to 1678. Another famous man was certainly there in the late seventies and early eighties. This was Daniel Greysolon, Sieur du Lhut, more often known as Sieur Duluth. It was he who reopened Lake Superior to trade and traders after years of warfare between the Sioux on the one hand and the Chippewa, Huron and Ottawa on the other. We have already seen the origin of the struggle at Chequamegon Bay in 1671.

Duluth spent the winter of 1678-1679 among the Chippewa near Sault Ste. Marie and then started to the West to make an enduring peace between the tribes, so that trade might be reopened. Among the young and adventurous men who accompanied him were two brothers by the name of Pépin, for whom it is supposed that Lake Pepin on the Mississippi River was named. A meeting had been arranged in advance at the west end of Lake Superior, probably within the radius of present-day Duluth. Well does that interesting city constitute an enduring memorial to the young nobleman who took his life in his hands on this mission of peace.

When peace had been made between the great tribes, Duluth went inland to the headquarters of one group of the Sioux on the headwaters of the Mississippi, and as he departed he sent out some of his men to explore even farther inland. Just where they went is not known, but probably not farther than the limits of western Minnesota of today. Duluth himself was unable to go with these explorers because he had designated a rendezvous with the Assiniboin and Sioux on Lake Superior, where another peace was to be attempted.

This meeting was held on September 15, but the exact spot is unknown further than that it occurred at the head of the lake (Fond du Lac). Since spring found him opening the old route via the Brule River, it is more than likely that he had spent the winter in the vicinity either of Chequamegon Bay or Fond du Lac. He ascended the river with some difficulty, cutting away more than a hundred beaver dams, portaged over the watershed between the turbulent waters of the Brule and those of placid Lake St. Croix, and descended the picturesque St. Croix River, through all its foaming rapids, to its junction with the Mississippi. There he learned of the captivity of Father Louis Hennepin and two other Frenchmen among the very Sioux whom he had visited the preceding summer. Realizing the gravity of the situation, he straightway went in search of the Frenchmen, recovered them, called a council of the Sioux, berated them soundly for their breach of faith, and returned by the route across Lake Michigan to Mackinac to spend the winter.

Duluth's purpose on Lake Superior had been that of reopening trade there and of going on yet farther to the West to discover the Sea of the West and the Northwest Passage. He had now sacrificed one year of that projected trip to ensure the safety of Father Hennepin's party. Then the reopening of the Iroquois wars in the East prevented him from returning immediately to his task. In 1683 he was back at Mackinac ready to go on with his project. To his dismay he found that much of his work would have to be done over again. During his absence the western tribes had got out of hand again and it was once more unsafe for traders to go through Lake Superior to the regions beyond. So he reached the great upper lake by a circuitous route—up the Fox River, down the Wisconsin, and up the Mississippi to the mouth of the St. Croix. In that region he once more won the Sioux to a French allegiance and pushed up the St. Croix. At the portage he probably built a wintering or supply post, near the site of modern Solon Springs, Wisconsin. Then he continued his journey down the Brule to Lake Superior and across that body of water to the mouth of the Kaministikwia River, where Fort William is located today. Here he built another supply post and made an alliance with the Assiniboin and Cree with the help of his

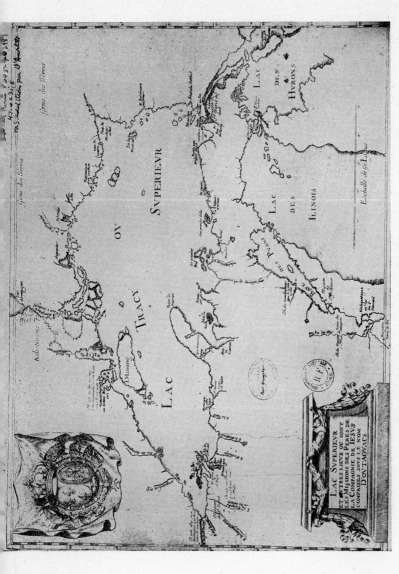

ONE OF THE EARLIEST MAPS OF LAKE SUPERIOR

Probably this manuscript map was the draft from which the printed form of the Jesuit map of 1672 was made. A photographic copy of the original in Paris is owned by the Minnesota Historical Society.

H.M.S. "THE NANCY"

This type of early sailing vessel was seen on all the Great Lakes.

younger brother, Claude Greysolon, Sieur de la Tourette. This young man established his post on Lake Nipigon, which commanded the trade route between Lake Superior and Hudson Bay. It was his aim to regain for the French the trade of those tribes who had been going of recent years to the English Hudson's Bay Company forts on James Bay.

Again, just as Duluth was about to leave Lake Superior to go westward on his explorations, he felt it necessary to discipline some of the Indians, this time because of the murder of two Frenchmen at Keweenaw Bay. Jean Péré, now trading on the lake, assisted him, and the two carried the murderers under guard to Mackinac for trial and punishment. Once again it was safe for white men on Lake Superior —but Duluth was now still another year behind his schedule for finding the Western Sea. He returned to the mouth of the Kaministikwia, only to be summoned again to the East to take part in another expedition against the Iroquois. This was his third and last attempt to penetrate beyond Lake Superior into the far West. Other duties, followed by illness, kept him in the East or on the lower Great Lakes until his death in 1710. His was a life of thwarted purpose, but he had served the Lake Superior region well and he deserves all the remembrance that has come to him through his namesake, the city at the Fond du Lac.

The opening of formal war between Great Britain and France in 1689 spelled doom to the fur trade of Lake Superior for many years. The Iroquois, allied with the English, began their attacks once more, and only prompt action by the governor of New France, Count Frontenac, prevented the western tribes from also joining forces against the French. The English traders had penetrated as far as Mackinac by this time and were offering many inducements to the western Indians to change their allegiance. Thus it became very dangerous for French traders to get furs and still more dangerous to transport them to Montreal and Quebec. For three years after Frontenac's return to the governorship in 1689 not a trade canoe came down from the West. Then he sent word to the western traders to bring down their furs at any hazard.

So in 1693 a great fleet of canoes swept down the St. Lawrence loaded with furs, much to the joy of the Canadians, who depended for their existence on this harvest of the woodlands. When the canoes returned to the interior, Pierre Le Sueur was with the tribesmen as the appointed successor of Duluth to command in the Lake Superior region. He had been a trader there much earlier, but more recently he had been trading on a river that long bore his name, Rivière St. Pierre, now the Minnesota River. He had been present at the colorful pageantry on Lake Pepin in 1689 when Perrot took possession of the north country for France in imitation of that other ceremony at the Sault seventeen years before. Now his orders were to reopen the trade routes between Lake Superior and the Mississippi and to bring the Sioux into alliance with the French. Therefore, in 1693, he built his post on the south shore of Madeline Island at Chequamegon Bay, close to the spot believed to be the site of Radisson's and Des Groseilliers' cabin of 1660. As time went on, this island, known as La Pointe because of the long point that reaches out near by from the mainland, became more and more the trading center of Lake Superior. The tradition of the Chippewa still points to this area as the "home" of the tribe, and until the middle of the nineteenth century it certainly was their headquarters. Here also missionaries placed their main station in the 1830's, and the American Fur Company made it the central depot for its northern fur-trading and fishing operations after 1834. The members of the little tourist colony there today revel not only in the beauty of their surroundings of cliff, green islands and limpid water, but also in the historical associations left by three centuries of almost continuous occupation by whites, and many more by Indians.

The next year Le Sueur established a post at the mouth of the St. Croix River and for still another year continued to operate on Lake Superior. Then in 1695 he succeeded in taking a Sioux chief down to New France with him and presented him to the great Onontio, the Indian name for Frontenac. Ostensibly the fierce warriors that the chief represented were at last allies of New France.

But Duluth, Perrot and Le Sueur had done their work too well. There were too many furs. Prices sank ruinously. On May 21, 1696,

Louis XIV of France issued a royal ordinance revoking all fur-trade licenses and prohibiting all colonials from taking any goods to the western country. The Indians were to be obliged to resort to their original custom of taking all their furs to Canada to trade.

This policy, if persisted in, meant ruin to the fur trade and to the traders, and the loss of a western empire to France. The Upper Country was deserted for over a decade. A few *coureurs de bois* lingered in out-of-the-way Indian villages, and a few Jesuit missionaries appeared now and then, but the age of exploration and the great explorers was almost at an end as far as France was concerned. France was gradually giving way to England, though the complete surrender would not occur for more than a half-century yet. Nevertheless, the old vigor and hardihood were waning, and the rot that was to eat away the root of monarchy in France was already commencing to break France's hold on the tribes about Lake Superior and elsewhere in the American West.

In 1713 peace was made at Utrecht between Great Britain and France. By the terms of the treaty the trade of Hudson Bay, where fighting for trade supremacy had been going on since 1683, was yielded by France to the Hudson's Bay Company. France had come to realize too late that her great explorers, Radisson and Des Groseilliers, had been right in advocating that the chief trade route to the interior of North America should go by way of Hudson Bay rather than through the Great Lakes. Now it was more necessary than ever that French posts should be maintained on Lake Superior in order to keep a hold on the trade of the interior, even by means of an inferior route. So, in line with the new French policy of acknowledging that withdrawal from the interior in 1696 had been a mistake, three new posts were established on or near Lake Superior.

In 1717 the Sieur de la Noue re-established Fort Kaministikwia at the mouth of the river of that name. Here he remained, operating very successfully, for four years. In 1721 his place was taken by Captain Deschaillons. Other men, some very able, commanded at this post in ensuing years, which was given up only when the Seven Years' War brought a detachment of English troops there and forced the garrison to yield. Thereafter this old French route to the interior was practically forgotten for thirty years and more, while an easier way via Grand Portage, about forty miles to the southwest, was utilized.

The second post was at La Pointe, which was re-established in 1718. Its importance lay primarily in the fact that it commanded many important trails and canoe routes into the interior. It was fitting that the command should go to a grandson of Jean Nicolet, the first known white man whose exploration of the Upper Lakes is recorded in any detail. Paul Le Gardeur, Sieur de St. Pierre, was one of three famous brothers, all native Canadians and all officers in the royal armies. Le Gardeur had been in the West before—he had been dispatched by Frontenac to Mackinac in 1691, when it was extremely dangerous to travel in the Great Lakes area; and again in 1707 he had been a courier to the western Indians. Now he took to Chequamegon Bay his youngest son, Jacques, who was destined to play a leading role in the colonial wars. Life among Indians and experience with the navigation of Lake Superior and the busy life of its wilderness shores prepared the young man for his career of later years, which included the reception of George Washington at Venango in 1753.

The second of the commanders at La Pointe was another scion of a famous Canadian family, René Godefroy, Sieur de Lintot (Linctot in many documents). The Godefroys had already been connected with the history of Three Rivers for almost a century when this member of the family took over the command of Chequamegon in 1720 and remained for six years at a post well known to his family since the days of Radisson and Des Groseilliers. The latter's wife had lived long in the household of the first seigneur of Lintot.

The third post to be established after the Treaty of Utrecht was the successor of Duluth's and La Tourette's post on Lake Nipigon. Here in 1726 the last famous explorer of the French period learned of routes to the Sea of the West and resolved to follow out Duluth's original plan of reaching it. This was another son of that prolific mother of explorers, Three Rivers. His name was Pierre Gautier de Varennes, Sieur de la Vérendrye. One of his Indians, Ochagac, drew for him a map of the route he should follow to the Sea of the West.

It showed the waterways from Lake Superior up the Pigeon River, via Grand Portage, to the height of land near Gunflint Lake, thence down rivers flowing toward Hudson Bay through Rainy Lake and River to Lake of the Woods and Lake Winnipeg, and even suggests that a great river (the Saskatchewan) from the West enters Lake Winnipeg and forms a flowing highway to the Sea of the West. The map itself, drawn originally on a piece of birch bark and now available only in contemporary copies, depicted the route to Lake of the Woods as looking like nothing so much as the human spine, with the many lakes of the North Country constituting its vertebrae. Following that bit of bark, La Vérendrye and his hardy sons and a nephew were to advance the French flag far toward the Rocky Mountains and open up the plains fur trade to the French in competition with the posts of the Hudson's Bay Company, now thoroughly enjoying their monopoly of a much easier route to the Canadian West by way of ships to Hudson Bay.

In 1731 La Vérendrye and other members of his family started on the Grand Portage route, having already advanced through Lake Superior to the mouth of the Pigeon River. There a threatened mutiny kept the senior La Vérendrye at the Kaministikwia post for the winter, but his nephew, La Jémerais, proceeded along the waterways to establish Fort St. Pierre on Rainy Lake. This post and its successors were to last right down to the end of the last century. The next season the party reunited to found Fort St. Charles on the Lake of the Woods. From that time till the end of the French regime there was much passing back and forth over Lake Superior to supply these and more westerly posts with men, provisions and equipment. Even the names of many of the voyageurs have been preserved in the licenses still extant in archives in Ottawa.

During the French and Indian wars the little garrisons in the West, including especially the one at La Pointe, sent their quota of officers, men and Indian adherents to fight the battles of France against General Braddock, Robert Rogers, George Washington, and others who represented the new order for the North American continent. But all to no avail. Louis Le Gardeur, Sieur de Repentigny from the Sault, Pierre Hertel de Beaubassin from La Pointe, Joseph

Marin from Green Bay, La Pointe and the upper Mississippi, and Jacques Le Gardeur, Marin's predecessor on Lake Pepin and recently returned from following up La Vérendrye's occupation of the valley of the Saskatchewan—all served notably under the golden lilies on many a battlefield in the Ohio Valley and along the lower Great Lakes. They could not cope with the graft and moral decay in high places in New France. Indeed, men like Marin had instigated much of it through corrupt trade methods. La Pointe yielded up her last French garrison in 1759, leaving only Detroit, Mackinac and Green Bay to guard the Northwest. These capitulated shortly, and New France became a memory.

Chapter 2

Peddlers, Potties and Packs

So dat's de reason I drink tonight
To de man of de Grand Nor' Wes',
For hees heart was young, an' hees heart was light
So long as he's leevin' dere—
I'm proud of de sam' blood in my vein
I'm a son of de Nort' Win' wance again—
So we'll fill her up till de bottle's drain
An' drink to de Voyageur.
                    —WILLIAM HENRY DRUMMOND

ROM 1763 to 1783 the lake was wholly British. Thereafter for a time it remained in effect British, though nominally a boundary line had been drawn through it, dividing British territory to the north and the new United States to the south. Just where that line lay was a question that was not completely answered until 1842. Should it run to the north or the south of Isle Royale? Should it end at the mouth of the Kaministikwia, the Pigeon, or the St. Louis River? Was the Grand Portage on British or American soil, or was it common ground? These were the larger issues, but there were scores of lesser ones.

Meantime the fur trade on the lake reached its peak. It was almost entirely in the hands of British traders, mostly Scotsmen or colonials, until 1817. Then a competitor appeared who very quickly and effectively made the south shore, and the north shore between Fond du Lac and Grand Portage, his hunting preserves. This was the immigrant from the Rhine Valley, the capable, canny and Midas-like John Jacob Astor of New York, the head of the American Fur Company from 1808 until 1834. Largely through his influence, an act was passed by the American Congress in 1816 prohibiting foreigners from trading in American territory. Then for the first time the

Union Jack ceased to fly over important trading posts near to and on the shores of Lake Superior south of the international boundary line.

The last quarter of the eighteenth and the first quarter of the nineteenth century formed the heyday of the North West Company. Just before the end of the American Revolution it was founded as a loose combination of trading and supply concerns, mostly in Montreal. It shortly became the chief competitor of the Hudson's Bay Company of London. The older concern called the new traders "Pedlars" in derision, but they obliged the London company to establish itself on Lake Superior and elsewhere in the fur country. Since the Treaty of Utrecht in 1713 the Hudson's Bay Company had had undisputed control of the cheaper and easier trade route to interior North America by way of Hudson Bay, and had been content to restrict its posts pretty well to the shores of that bay. The Montreal company fell heir, so to speak, to the old French route through the Great Lakes, which brought to the height of their long and faithful service a class of men who knew Lake Superior better than any others have ever known it. These were the French-Canadian voyageurs, who in 1763 brought to their new masters the great navigating skill and profound knowledge of geography that they had acquired during generations of trading under the French traders. For almost a century they put that knowledge and skill at the command of others, first of the North West Company, then of the American Fur Company, and finally of the Hudson's Bay Company for a brief time. There were voyageurs on all the Great Lakes, but Lake Superior knew them better and more frequently than any of the others. They navigated both its southern and its northern shore lines, and established many posts along its entire periphery. There is hardly a cove or the mouth of a river on the entire lake, not to mention its islands, that has not at some time held a trading post. Present-day names of capes, points, coves, bays and streams are usually the ones given them by the voyageurs, or else translations of those names.

From the conquest of Canada until 1767 it was the British Government's policy to restrict trade in America to a few larger posts. For the Lake Superior fur trade that meant the fort at Mackinac. Throughout the British regime and late into the American, Mackinac remained a post of first importance. In 1765, however, Alexander Henry, a British colonial who had escaped miraculously from the clutches of Pontiac's conspirators at Mackinac, was given by the commandant at Mackinac the exclusive right to the trade about Lake Superior. To develop this right, he built a post on Chequamegon Bay in the fall of that year, and sent one of his clerks to trade with the Chippewa at the Fond du Lac. He was able to do this because he was already in the West when the Indian troubles of Pontiac's rebellion began, and he could thus get his supplies at Mackinac without having to put himself under the restrictions imposed on traders in the East. So for three years he had the advantage and he made great use of it. The second winter he spent at the Sault; the third and fourth at Michipicoten, on the east side of Lake Superior, close to what the Chippewa regarded as the tomb of the Great Hare. This is the translation of the name of one of their chief deities, Nanabazhoo. Under the name of Hiawatha, he is the hero of Longfellow's well-known poem.

All this while Henry was learning of the great lake on which he was trading, especially about its geography, its natives and its mineral resources. He did not fail to hear about La Ronde's earlier copper-mining ventures on the south shore,* nor himself to visit the great rock of copper on the Ontonagon River. Later he explored extensively for ore bodies near his Michipicoten post and finally began a mining company, which was organized in England in 1770 and which built a barge and a sloop of forty tons at Pointe aux Pins. Shafts were sunk at Ontonagon and operatives were left there for the winter of 1771-1772. The venture was a failure, and a similar undertaking, begun in the summer of 1772 at Michipicoten, also failed, though some copper was actually shipped to England. The spring of 1775 saw Henry once more leaving the Sault with a brigade of canoes and skirting the north shore to the Grand Portage. This time he was bound for the far interior, and his life on Lake Superior was practically over.

Alexander Henry and Jonathan Carver, another colonial, are the first to leave good descriptions of Lake Superior. Both visited it just before the Revolution and both published accounts of their experi-

---

* See page 161.

ences, though Henry's did not appear until 1809. Carver, meantime, published his first edition in 1778, and other editions followed quickly. Thus Lake Superior was introduced to the English-speaking world by the brief account of a shrewd Massachusetts colonial. His route of exploration had taken him to the valley of the present Minnesota River, to Prairie du Chien and then to Lake Superior, partly at least by Brulé's and Duluth's old route down the Brule River. He then navigated the north shore of the lake from the Fond du Lac to Grand Portage in the spring of 1767. Here he had expected to find reinforcements and necessary provisions for the exploratory trip he was to make under Captain James Tute and James Stanley Goddard to find the "Ouragan" River on the Pacific Coast. This was Robert Rogers' scheme, well known today to readers of a novel called *Northwest Passage*. Rogers was the commandant at the fort at Mackinac, and had great ideas for the fur trade of the West and for the advancement of Robert Rogers. One of his plans was to erect a new British colony covering all of modern Wisconsin and some adjacent territory. Of this new colony bordering on Lake Superior, he, of course, was to be the governor.

Rogers fell on evil days while Carver was absent in the Mississippi Valley and on Lake Superior. Therefore he could not send the reinforcements and provisions that the expedition had to have to proceed beyond Grand Portage. Carver and the others left that place and returned along the north shore to the Sault and Mackinac. Unfortunately, he gives very little account of his trip from Grand Portage to the Sault. He does describe the rocky shores, mentions the largest rivers, admires the clearness of the water, and marvels at its coldness even in summer. He also describes some of the fish, refers to Indian superstitions and legends about its islands, and tells something of its flora.

Carver mentions the Grand Portage and traders in the West so casually that it is obvious that fur traders were already plunging into the Far West from that spot. Indeed, traders had been plundered at Rainy Lake in 1765 and 1766. Henry in 1775 writes that he "found the traders in a state of extreme reciprocal hostility, each pursuing his interests in such a manner as might most injure his neighbor. The consequences were very hurtful to the morals of the Indians." The year 1767 saw the fur-trade policy of Canada altered and the trade thrown open. Carver must have met some of the men who were taking advantage of the new regulations. That year Henry is listed as sending five canoes "by Lake Superior" with goods valued at £2,600; Alexander Baxter as having eight canoes "by Lake Superior" bound for "Fort Daphne [Dauphin?] & La Pierce," valued at £3,200; Forrest Oakes as sending three canoes to Lake Nipigon; Thomas Curry as going with two canoes to "Caministiquia"; and Benjamin Frobisher as dispatching two canoes "by Lake Superior to Petit Ouinipique." Little Lake Winnipeg, it may be added, was an early name for Lake Winnibigoshish near the source of the Mississippi River. In all, eighteen canoes went that year to Lake Superior, and fourteen others by Lake Superior to the Northwest.

Henry found it advantageous from the start to enter into partnership with an experienced man from the older French period, Jean Baptiste Cadotte, of Sault Ste. Marie. They maintained that partnership for many years. Others soon duplicated Henry's experience, for all found it advantageous to have a French Canadian, if possible, as a means of keeping on the best possible terms with Indian customers and neighbors, who were distinctly hostile at first to all British traders. In addition, the traders found that one person could not undertake alone the great financial risks of the trade. Thus it came about that by 1770 there were four partnerships in the trade centering at Mackinac; in 1773 there were six; and in 1775 there were seven. These included the men whose names are most famous in the later North West Company: Benjamin and Joseph Frobisher, Todd and McNeall, Henry and Cadotte, James and John McGill, Paterson and Kay, Finlay and Gregory, and Dunn, Grant and Porteous. Out of the ruinous competition and lack of co-operation of which Henry complained at the Grand Portage grew the realization finally that a union must be made or all would ruin one another. So the North West Company came gradually and unostentatiously into existence— never a corporation like its chief rival, the great Hudson's Bay Company, but rather a loose grouping of partners and firms, with outfitting companies and headquarters at Montreal, but always with many partners actively in the trade in the interior, where Grand Portage became the chief gathering place.

One of the earliest posts to be re-established after the Conquest was Grand Portage. Carver does not mention a post when he was there in 1767, but in 1768, we know from records in the General Register House in Edinburgh, a clearing was made near the site of an earlier French post there. John Askin of Mackinac seems to have been responsible for the clearing and probably also for the immediate erection of a post. It was the natural gathering place for men from the East and the West. Large canoes could proceed to that point and no farther. A different type of canoe had to be used in the smaller lakes and streams beyond. So a big canoe yard was developed there. Men could paddle their canoes to that point and return to Montreal in one season of open water.

Frequently over a thousand traders and voyageurs assembled there in July in some sixteen buildings within the stockade of cedar posts, under canvas tents, or sheltered from the elements only by their overturned canoes. It was a lively scene, one that has become famous through Washington Irving's description of similar scenes at the successor post, Fort William. After 1802 it seemed wise to the men of the company to anticipate an expected arrival of American customs officers at Grand Portage. So they withdrew their post about forty miles to the northeast, to land that was British without question. The boundary dispute still made it uncertain which country had possession of Grand Portage.

The North West Company men had Lake Superior practically to themselves for a number of years. The Hudson's Bay Company was busy elsewhere and did not completely realize the competition that was rising against it. John Jacob Astor, arriving in the United States from the Rhine Valley and selling cakes and musical instruments in New York, was beginning his fur-trading ventures only in a small way. He would not organize his competition with the North West Company until 1808, and then ostensibly as a sort of partner. So the *bourgeois* had things pretty much their own way for some time.

They erected their great post at Grand Portage. They built their first schooners for carrying goods, furs and a few men between Grand Portage and Sault Ste. Marie. They sent their traders farther and farther into the West, until eventually Alexander Mackenzie discovered a magnificent river that he called River Disappointment, because he had expected to find the Pacific Ocean at its mouth but found the Arctic instead. We of today call the river by the explorer's own name.

The North West Company had in its employ several thousand voyageurs, or canoemen, besides the guides, interpreters and clerks that it employed. The voyageurs have the distinction of being one of the few classes of men in American and Canadian history who have been unique on this continent, not only in their origin as a class, but also in their manner of life, customs, language and dress. They came from the Canadian-French settlements along the lower St. Lawrence, where the traditions of voyaging into the Indian country had been handed down from father to son for several generations. It was considered the proper social step in those communities for young men to go into the *pays d'en haut,* the upper country, on trading expeditions in the employ of some *bourgeois.* To take this step one made an engagement with an agent of the trading company, which specified the wages and other terms of the contract. In May an expedition would set out from Montreal—several canoes organized into a "brigade." The vessels of this flotilla were birch-bark canoes, but not of the simple Indian style. They were about forty feet long and had to be carried on the portages by several men, where an Indian canoe could be portaged by one man.

The voyageurs had their final fling in Montreal, said their emotional farewells, assembled at the pier of the North West Company above the Lachine Rapids clad in their plumes and best regalia, heard their last Mass at St. Anne's, and pushed off to the strains of one of their paddling songs. They were renowned for those songs. The Irish poet, Thomas Moore, heard them singing on a trip, and was so impressed that he wrote a famous poem in imitation of one of their best-loved songs. The words of the first stanza are:

Faintly as tolls the evening chime
Our voices keep tune and our oars keep time.
Soon as the woods on shore look dim,
We'll sing at St. Ann's our parting hymn,
Row brothers, row, the stream runs fast,
The rapids are near, and the daylight's past.

The voyageur route led up the Ottawa, through Lake Nipissing, down French River into Georgian Bay, across the top of Lake Huron, and around the falls at Sault Ste. Marie into Lake Superior. There they had a choice of routes. If they were going into modern Michigan, Wisconsin or Minnesota, they pushed along the south shore; but if they were bound for the West, they took the great arc of the lake on the north shore and arrived after several days of hard and dangerous paddling at Grand Portage.

En route from Montreal they had some thirty-six portages to make before reaching Grand Portage. Because of the large amount of freight which they carried in their cockleshell barks, they devised very efficient ways of loading, landing, portaging and packing. The outward freight was blankets and other trade goods for the Indians; the inward freight was furs and skins. The exchange was effected at Grand Portage, where the men from the East in Montreal, or *maître* canoes, met the North men, or winterers, from the western posts, in their North canoes. Those who came from Montreal were "pork-eaters" in voyageurs' parlance. They merely ferried goods and furs between the two points, and all in one season. The North men, or Nor'westers, as they were frequently called, had lived for at least one winter at a trading post in the interior, and had passed over the divide between Lake Superior and Hudson Bay or the Mississippi River. An initiation ceremony took place at that spot. They were the only ones entitled to wear plumes in their hats. All voyageurs, however, wore sashes, the celebrated *ceintures flèchées,* yards long, of bright hues, and made by a special hand-weaving method.

These men were renowned for their strength, docility and cheery dispositions. They were almost invariably courteous. They were proud of their race, their origin, their language and their *métier*. The highest praise a voyageur could give of anyone was, "That is a voyageur!" Ten to fifteen of them manned a Montreal canoe; six to ten a North canoe. Their packs, whether of trade goods or furs, almost invariably weighed ninety pounds. Two of these packs were the usual burden for a voyageur in making a portage. Some boasted of carrying many more, however. They loved to pull the long bow, especially about their own exploits, and though Paul Bunyan seems to be a very modern mythological hero of uncertain parentage, his prototype was every voyageur's conception of himself.

When they arrived at Grand Portage, it was with flag flying proudly from the stern of the canoe, the *bouts* (end paddlers) standing in great state in the high, painted ends of the craft, twelve or so red-bladed paddles puncturing the water of Lake Superior in unison to the tune of a lively song, and every voyageur clad in his best array. There they would stay for many days, while *bourgeois* conferred and decided weighty business in their great hall. Then, after many nights under their overturned canoes, the voyageurs loaded them with packs of furs, and in full song pushed off for Montreal.

The voyageur is known best for his songs and blithe spirits, for his sashes and capotes, and for the naming of topographical features clear across the continent. He was much at home on the shores of Lake Superior, and his descendants are still to be recognized with ease as one prowls about the lake—at the Sault, at Rossport, at the twin ports, at Grand Portage, Grand Marais, Duluth, Superior and many places on the south shore, including La Pointe. It will be noted that every one of those places is named by voyageur terminology, or for a French explorer, with the exception of Rossport and Port Arthur. The Indians of the region call the lake their own, Ojibwa Kitche Gammi (the great lake of the Ojibwa), but it might equally well be termed Voyageur Kitche Gammi.

The North West Company established its posts at Sault Ste. Marie, Michipicoten, the Pic, the Pays Plat, the Nipigon country and Fort William, all on the present Canadian shore; and at Grand Portage, Grand Marais, Fond du Lac, La Pointe, Ontonagon, L'Anse and some other places on the American side. For one, at the Pic, we have dimensions and other detailed data, which we lack for all the others. We know some things about the Fond du Lac fort and about the one at Grand Portage, but nothing in detail. It is only in the last few years that the material relating to the Pic post has come to light.

Generally speaking, the company's posts were palisaded enclosures. The stockade stood ten to fifteen feet above ground. There were bastions and both large and small gates in the fences at the larger posts. On Lake Superior many of the posts were of sawed lumber, the logs having been made into lumber at the company's sawmill at the Sault. In the interior and at smaller forts, both squared timbers and round, unpeeled logs were common. The voyageurs constructed these forts and so they often showed the usual voyageur type of architecture, *i.e.*, two posts at every corner, with logs slipped into a slot in each of them, one above the other, and thus held in place without nails. The ridgepole rested on a high pole placed upright in the middle of each gable end, outside the log wall. The roofing was made of pieces of bark from the white cedar tree. Fireplaces and chimneys were constructed of mud, or of mud and stones.

The post at the Pic is described in a document probably dating from early in the nineteenth century. It shows an establishment built by three different persons or groups. One, the Coté fort, consisted of a piece of cleared ground about one arpent* broad and three-fourths of an arpent deep, enclosed in pickets nine feet above ground. In that enclosure stood two buildings of Coté's. One was a warehouse thirty-six feet by twelve, made of round cedar logs laid horizontally in voyageur fashion, roofed with cedar bark, with two little glassed sashes that opened and closed. The other was the residence, thirty feet by twenty, of similar construction to the warehouse, divided into two rooms, and having two little windows of the same type as the other building. The furnishings included tin plates, tin kettles, a copper kettle, eight crystal goblets, a frying pan, two large wooden platters, twelve chairs, two little poplar tables, a desk of the same wood, and two "miserable" bedsteads.

The buildings belonging to the "old firm" consisted of a shed twenty-four feet by fifteen, of horizontal logs, on posts, and with a bark roof; a "big house" forty feet by twenty-one, of squared logs

---

* The arpent, or acre, was a measure of slightly less than 193 feet.

laid horizontally, and roofed with boards, divided into five rooms, with eight windows and eight glassed sashes, and with a fireplace; and a stable about fifteen feet by eight, of horizontal logs, with a window, and holding tools, all of which are carefully listed.

The buildings of the "new firm" consisted of a warehouse forty-eight feet by eighteen; a "big house" forty feet by about nineteen, still being erected, for it lacked a roof; a little shop for the forge (fifteen feet by twelve); and a cellar serving as a powder magazine.

Some of the famous factors and men of the North West Company at Lake Superior posts or near by were Dr. John McLoughlin, the subsequent "Father of Oregon," at Grand Portage; Charles Oakes Ermatinger at the Canadian Sault; Jean Bte. Perrault and William Morrison at the Fond du Lac post; John Johnston at the Sault, on the American side; Duncan Cameron in the Nipigon country; David Thompson, the Company's surveyor and map maker, who was often on the lake, though never actually stationed at a lake post; John Macdonell, who passed through Lake Superior and Grand Portage in 1793 and has left one of our best accounts of the lake, the post and the voyageurs of the trade; Daniel Harmon, a Vermont trader who lived in the vicinity of the lake for a time and kept a diary that has been published; Alexander Henry, Jr., a nephew of the first English trader known on the lake, who also has left us a diary telling of his visits to Grand Portage and of life at posts dependent upon it; and the Mackenzies, Alexander and Roderick.

At the end of the century Alexander Mackenzie became associated with the Little Company, an offshoot of the "Big Company." In French the smaller concern was called "Les Petits," which was soon corrupted to "Potties," and by that name they were known throughout the fur country. The rivalry between the old and the new companies was keen around Lake Superior. A reunion was effected in 1804, however, just in time to bring the full force of a united company to bear on the struggle, then beginning to be intense, between the Hudson's Bay Company and its rival. In the 1790's the Bay Company began to build a post in the Rainy Lake country. It would not be long before it would try to establish itself on Lake Superior. Nothing effectual was accomplished, however, until the two companies coalesced in 1821. Thereafter the posts on the Canadian shore of the lake belonged to the Hudson's Bay Company. That company also operated between 1833 and 1847 along the American North Shore, but solely by reason of a special agreement between Ramsay Crooks, president of the American Fur Company, and the governor of the Hudson's Bay territories, George Simpson, soon to be Sir George Simpson.

For some forty years the North West Company used Lake Superior as part of its fluid highway to the fur country. To its men in large part we owe the lake's many trading posts as well as the first sailing vessels on it. They also wrote narratives and diaries which mention the lake and the life about and on it.

It is impossible even to list all of the men who wrote diaries or reminiscences of their experiences on Lake Superior. Besides those already mentioned there were those whose writings were gathered up by L. R. Masson and published in two volumes as *Les bourgeois de la compagnie du Nord-Ouest.* These accounts throw a flood of light on Lake Superior's history and Indians. Charles M. Gates has published another collection of similar writings under the title, *Five Fur Traders of the Northwest.*

One of the men thus preserved to posterity's gaze through the products of his own pen was the Irishman, John Johnston. At Roderick Mackenzie's request, he wrote about 1807 "An Account of Lake Superior, 1792-1807." Masson includes it in his volumes and writes of the author:

"The descendant of a highly connected Irish family, he was, at the age of twenty, and through some unfortunate circumstances which blasted his hopes and expectations in the Old World, induced to emigrate to Canada, where high protections and numerous recommendations obtained for him a cordial reception. Lord Dorchester was himself foremost in his protections and introduced him to the Partners of the North-West Company, who were then already at the head of the society in Montreal. . . . He selected *La Pointe,* on the south shore of Lake Superior, as his first winter home, purchased goods, engaged men and, in the spring of 1792, began in earnest his new life as a fur trader. Endowed with that high spirit of religion which bore him successfully through life, a melancholic turn of mind and a considerable share of elevated and refined sentiments, the severe and sublime grandeur of our American scenery, whose stern beauties are so lavishly displayed along the shores of Lake Superior, made him cherish his solitude."

There he met and loved the daughter of the local chief, Wabogish, or White Fisher, and asked for her hand in marriage. But the old chief had seen other white men take Indian women to their beds and boards and knew that frequently it was not a permanent arrangement. So he replied that he understood Johnston was planning to return to his home on business; that upon his return to La Pointe, if he still wanted to marry the Indian girl, she should then be his. Johnston went on his trip, arranged his business matters, returned to La Pointe, and claimed his wife. The arrangement was permanent. The Johnstons settled at Sault Ste. Marie, where they raised a numerous family, nearly all of whom are well known in American history. Jane became the wife of Henry R. Schoolcraft, and is described by many discriminating travelers who visited her home as a woman of singular charm and beauty. George, who was a well-known trader about Lake Superior, became the government subagent at La Pointe, and ran the boundary line in 1835 between the Chippewa and Sioux in Minnesota. William was a trader of the opposition at Leech Lake in the 1830's. His letters of that period will repay readers who have access to volume 37 of the *Michigan Pioneer and Historical Collections*—incidentally, the volume which includes a translation of Jean Baptiste Perrault's reminiscences of his life about Lake Superior. In John Johnston's reminiscences there are several mentions of Perrault.

Johnston's account of his Lake Superior experiences is a classic. Mainly it is a description of the lake itself as it looked to the young Irishman in 1792. He starts at the Sault, describes the village as "pleasing and romantic," and marvels at the slight outlet of such an immense body of water. He then describes the manner of portaging trade goods around the rapids:

"The goods are carried over the portage, which is half a mile in length, and deposited in a store from whence they are conveyed in *bateaux* to the vessel which transports them to Caminitisquia, their chief settlement on the north-western extremity of the lake.—The meaning of the word in the Chipeway language is 'River of difficult entrance.'—It is about one hundred leagues from St. Mary's."

His description goes on with Pointe aux Pins, where "is a sand bank of several miles ... covered with red and white pine, the best of which have been cut down and used by the North-West Company for building their vessels." He compares the view from the portal rocks at the entrance of Lake Superior to that seen from the Pillars of Hercules:

"Lake Superior washes the base of these, its strong and natural barriers, from the summit of which the view is grand, extensive, reminding us at once of Calpe and Ceuta, and only wanting a poet to erect them into 'Pillars' and make them the boundary of some hero's travels."

Occasionally he pauses in his minute description of the lake to make a generalization such as this one:

"It is very remarkable that all the rivers on the south side of the lake have their waters tinged as black as if their source was from turf bogs. The leaves and other vegetable matter which fall into them are not a sufficient cause for this, but I fancy the soil in land has actually acquired the nature of peat from the accumulation of vegetable matter in the course of ages. There are many advantages which should induce farmers to settle here; the soil is excellent, very little under wood and large improvable meadows."

When he reaches the famous sand dunes, which he calls the Sandy Mountain, he is "struck with wonder" on finding himself "on a sandy plain several leagues in extent, the side of which, fronting the lake, is from one hundred to two hundred feet high, and nearly perpendicular. . . . The Indians have many superstitions with respect to this mountain which, with every other remarkable or dangerous place on the borders of the lake or interior country, has its Genii, to whom they never fail to make a speech, accompanied with a present of tobacco and sometimes their silver ornaments, whenever they pass. The Negouwatchi, or Sandy Mountain, is the scene of many of their fairy tales, some of which are very pretty and attended with a moral, and others equally absurd and childish, but all tending to prove their Tartar or Arabian origin, especially those relating to the creation and deluge."

At this point—in describing how voyageurs are saved from disaster in doubling the terminating point of Sandy Mountain, with its submerged rocks close to the surface, by the crystal clearness of the water—he rhapsodizes on the great lake:

"There is not perhaps on the globe a body of water so pure and so light as that of Lake Superior. It appears as if conscious of its innate excellence: the innumerable tainted streams which pour into it are forced to creep merely along the beach without once being able to make an impression on its unstained bosom. There is no better proof of its lightness than the manner in which it becomes ruffled by the slightest wind. When a gale blows from the opposite shore, it has been known to raise the water several feet some hours before its arrival."

He next describes the Pictured Rocks and their approaches.

"The rock is white freestone, perfectly perpendicular, and, in a distance of three leagues, has three little bays nearly at equal distance, and as if placed by the hand of Providence to ensure safety on a coast otherwise not to be attempted in hardly any season.... [A little waterfall] breaks from amongst the trees and tumbles in foam down the side of the rock for about sixty feet. The projection then becomes greater, and about twelve to fifteen feet from the base, collecting its scattered force, it pours the contents of its little urn perpendicularly into the lake. I once passed here in the month of May, immediately after a gale of wind which had continued for four days, with severe frost and snow from the north. The effect on the fall was beautiful. It was frozen up entirely except a little gutter in the middle, not more than a foot wide. The sides resembled pillars variously fluted; the shrubs at the mouth of the rivulet were perfect figures in ice, which appeared like Corinthian capitals. A young pine about thirty feet high which grew in the middle of its bed, and sparkling like a conical pillar of crystal sculptured in fret work, crowned the brilliant perspective."

He does not fail to do justice to the Pictured Rocks, ending with:

"The base of this point is curious from the manner it is perforated, which resembles bowls turned down and others set upon their bottom, the interstices giving you the idea of porches and gothic windows, the water rushing in and regorging from them in a manner that by no means invites to close inspection, except when the wind is off the shore, or else during a dead calm."

Miner's Bay recalls to Johnston the story of Alexander Henry's mining venture there. Then he continues:

"After you leave Miner's Bay you double a point nearly similar to the last described, except that there is a little natural arch through which you can pass in a small canoe. Grand Island is now opposite to you; it stretches almost due north into the lake, and is about nine leagues in circumference. The soil is excellent and the timber chiefly beech and maple. Grand Island is the summer residence of a small band of Indians, who cultivate maize, potatoes and pumpkins."

The next bay reminds him of Milton's "shade above shade a woody theatre," which, he says, if ever realized, is here. In the bay the Indians of Grand Island went fishing every calm night with *flambeaux*. "They take as fine trout and white fish as are found in any part of the lake." Like Carver and others, who have described the lake in the early days, he notes the many small rivers flowing into the lake and what is still true, namely that they are "choked at the entrance with banks of sand thrown up by the lake" and "are seldom navigable more than three or four leagues, even for small canoes."

Next Johnston describes Presque Isle, "the peninsula which projects northeast and is curious from being one half freestone and the other basalt."

"The Indians find in the fissures of this last a black substance not unlike limestone, which, when pounded, they put in a small bag and boil with any stuff they wish to dye black; the colour, however, is not bright, though lasting; the same quantity will serve many times without any apparent diminution of strength."

Here, then, may be the source of the black dyes so much used by the Chippewa and other Algonquian tribes in making their moccasins and other pieces of apparel, and, of course, thus the source of the name of the Blackfoot Indians.

Such a keen observer as Johnston could hardly fail to note indications of metals everywhere.

"It is to be remarked that the metallic rocks of the peninsula [Presque Isle] are the only ones in the whole circuit of the lake which have neither trees, shrubs or vegetation of any kind growing on them, though many others, not near so high and equally devoid of soil, are almost covered with stunted pines. This, the mineralists may account for as they please, but I found on them what was more acceptable than any vegetable: a quantity of sea gulls eggs which were as large as those of turkeys and which, when fried in the pan with some pork, made an excellent supper, with a dish of aromatic tea."

When the traveler rounds a certain headland near by, Johnston continues, he finds a fine sandy bay and a small river of clear water. This is Potter's Bay, he says.

"In the bed of the river, I found a part of one of the earthern pots used by the Indians before they had the use of copper and tin kettles. It is the only specimen of the kind that I ever saw, and a ruder attempt at pottery, I believe, was never seen."

No wonder modern archaeologists struggle largely in vain to find shards of early pottery about Lake Superior, if Johnston as early as 1792 could find but one specimen!

Something of the spirit of the narrator, which explains, too, why he was content in his wilderness home, is shown by his next description:

"Off Potter's head, about four leagues out, in a northerly direction, lies a small island, apparently round and pretty high, which, when looked at from the shore in a calm clear evening fills the mind with a pleasing melancholy and a desire for a quiet sequestration, where every worldly care and every mean passion should be lulled to rest, and the heart left at full liberty to examine itself, develop each complicated fold, wash out each stain with a repentant tear, and finally become worthy of holding converse with nature, approach the Celestial Portals and, though at an infinite distance, be permitted a glimpse of its Almighty Sovereign, but our Father and God. When I made my first voyage in the lake, which is now fifteen years ago, I tarried opposite Contemplation Island, as I called it, for four days, and I recollect having filled ten or twelve pages of my journal with reflections, remarks and some poetical effusions, the result of so much spare time."

How we wish we had today this first poetry inspired by the grandeur and otherworldliness of the Great Upper Lake!

Johnston continues west along the coast in his recollections:

"On doubling this point [Point Abbaye], you enter the Bay of Keeywaynan, which is four leagues broad at the entrance, and continues of nearly the same breadth for three leagues, and then narrows gradually to the end, which is a circular bassin of about a league. The mountains from behind Huron River bend back towards the south as if to make way for the two bays, and then wheeling around to the north form the tongue of land called by the French *L'Anse* and the Indians 'Keeywaynan,' or 'the way made straight by means of a portage.' . . . here the Indians have a summer village and cultivate some maize."

Like all who have had experience with Lake Superior, Johnston learned to know her mirages well.

"One fine evening, in the month of May, 1803, I was doubling a long and rocky point which leads to Huron River, where I intended encamping for the night; the sun was nearly settled and just gilded the skirts of the Keeywaynan Mountains with its horizontal rays, ripping the tops of the trees in the lower part of the ridge with burnished gold. I made my men rest for a few minutes on their oars, that I might indulge in the brilliant spectacle. As the rays of the sun became fainter, I saw trees on the skirts of the mountains . . . all in apparent motion and manoeuvring like an army attempting to gain a position. Soon after, the mountains began to rise, each retaining its proper form, the valleys, though high in the air, still kept their humble distance from the hills; among the real trees a few scattered rays of the immerging sun were still perceptible. At length, the majestic edifice gradually descended, and to the air built fabric succeeded a general blush which tinged the whole horizon. When the vapours rise suddenly from the hills and are dissipated in the air, a storm is shortly expected, but when they descend, warm and calm weather is generally the result."

Poor Johnston could not understand what happened to his watch in this area, soon to be recognized as one of the finest copper-bearing regions in the world, flanked by some of the best iron-bearing rocks.

"I have some reluctance in relating an accident which twice happened to my watch nearly in the middle of this *traverse* [across Keweenaw Bay], as it appears to have some thing of the marvellous in it. However, so it is that, in June 1792, I took it from my pocket to see the time, and it became instantly deranged, running down the whole chain in less than a minute. I sent it down to Montreal and got it up the ensuing year, and it again played me the same prank in the same place. Now, whether this was merely an accident, or was owing to some powerful magnetic influence I cannot say."

He describes Keweenaw Point, the river and portage. "Near this portage, the Indians have often found pieces of virgin copper of the purest kind." Between the point and Ontonagon River there are no rivers of note until "you arrive at the Notonagan. . . . This is the only river on the south shore, for one hundred and forty leagues, which does not flow black waters. A short distance from its entrance, the river has a branch coming from the south, but the main river descends from the south east, and about five leagues up this branch, there is a mass of copper ore in its bed where the Indians go and cut off pieces with their axes, when they want it." This boulder of copper aroused such national interest that finally, in the middle of the nineteenth century, it was taken to Washington, D. C., where it may still be seen.

The Porcupine, or Kakewishing Mountains, next took Johnston's attention. Though he refers to them as only one mountain "surrounded by steep perpendicular rocks, it is perfectly inaccessible, and inhabited by a Spirit to whom the Indians pay great respect." They are "upwards of three leagues in length and much higher than any other on the south shore." Between the mountains and La Pointe there are two rivers, he writes, that connect with important areas to the south, Montreal River and Bad River. Both of these were important canoe routes from French regime days till railroads changed the picture completely.

Johnston calls Chequamegon Bay the Bay St. Charles.

"Opposite *La Pointe,* to the north-east, is the island of Montreal [Madeline Island], one of the largest of those called Twelve Apostles. On the main land, the Indians had once a village amounting to two hundred huts, but since the traders have multiplied they no longer assemble at *Netoungan,* or the Sand Beach, but remain in small bands near their hunting grounds. When you double the point of Netoungan, the coast tends nearly west, and is composed of high rocky points of basalt with some freestone; there is one place in particular which is an humble resemblance of the Portals, but not near so high; it is about a league from *La Pointe,* and is a projection from the highest mountain from Porcupine Bay to *Fond-du-Lac,* a distance of more than forty-five leagues. From the summit of the mountain, you can count twenty-six islands extending to the north and north-east, islands which have never been visited by the boldest Indians, and have a chance of never being better known, as they lie out of the way of the North-West Company's vessels. Of the islands opposite *La Pointe,* ten or twelve have been visited by the Indians, some of which have a rich soil covered with maple and beech, with deep water and fine trout fishing. The trout in this part of the lake are equal in size and richness to those of Mackinac; I myself saw one taken off the north-east end of Montreal Island which weighed fifty-two pounds."

Fond du Lac, the French term for the farther end of any lake, was the terminus of Johnston's wanderings on Lake Superior. He describes the river entering the lake at that place as "deep, wide and serpentine, but is navigable only for four or five leagues from its entrance. The portages are many and difficult until you arrive at the Sand Lake [Sandy Lake, Minnesota], where the tribe of the Chippeways, called 'Pillagers,' reside. The furs of this country are the best assorted of any of this continent, and the quantity would much increase were it possible to repress the mutual incursions of the Sioux and Chippeways who carry on perpetual war. The tract of country lying between the two nations for near one hundred and fifty leagues in length and from thirty to fourty in breadth, is now visited by stealth, and if peaceably hunted would be more productive than the richest mine of Peru." One of Johnston's own sons ran the dividing line in this area between the Sioux and Chippewa some thirty years later; and another son dwelt among the Pillagers, but in their later home on Leech Lake, rather than on Big Sandy, as it is known today.

We have no such early description of the north shore of the lake between the Fond du Lac and Grand Portage as Johnston's for the south shore. Carver's is the first, but it has never been printed before. His log is brief and terse:

	July 14	ENE	9	End of Lake Superiour
Wed	15	NE	6	
		ENE	3	
		NE	2	Pass^d a Small River
		E	2	
Wedns^y July 15		NNE	2	
		ENE	2	here is a small Island Near shore.
		N	2	here Pass^d a small River
		NE	4	
		E	2	at the End of this is Bloody Point Call^d so by the Natives
		NE	1	
		E	1	here is a Small Island

		NE	12	to a Great Point
		NE	2	Very indented shore many Bluff Points.
Thursd[y]	16	NE	18	
		NNE	3	indent[d] Shore all the way high Bluff Point
		NE	22	
		NNE	1	to a small River and a small Island against the mouth
Fryd[y]	17	NE	10	all the way indent[d] Shore high Bluff Point
		ENE	5	to a Small River
Saturd[y]	18	ENE	7	Very indented Shore.
		NNE	3	begins some high mountains of in Lands indented Shore.
		E 10°N	8	
		ENE	34	all the way some small Bays & p[ts] at the End of this a few Island near Shore
Sund[y]	19	ENE	4	to the Bay at the Great Carry[g] Place

One who knows the north shore today can follow Carver's course without difficulty, but a stranger would get no idea of its grandeur from these typical Yankee entries. One looks in vain throughout extant printed accounts for a narrative written by someone who perceived the beauty of this remarkable shore line. Unfortunately, Agassiz did not complete the arc of the north shore, but turned back at Thunder Bay in his trip of 1849. His account of that trip gives an adequate idea of the rest of the north shore.

Other than Carver's the only early account that is at all detailed for the stretch between Duluth of today and Fort William is David Thompson's. Like Carver's it is unpublished. In 1822 David Thompson, the incomparable map maker and explorer, first of the Hudson's Bay Company and then of the North West Company, was a member of the British part of the international commission set up under the Convention of 1818 to settle the boundary dispute between Great Britain and the United States. He traveled along the south shore and to Grand Portage by canoe with other members of the commission party. His account, though frugal like himself, nevertheless reveals the deep piety and recognition of Nature's beauties that were so characteristic of the man throughout his long and varied career in the West. Thus on July 16, 1822, his diary records:

"Held on to the end of the Lake [Fond du Lac], and camped about 2 miles short of the River [St. Louis]. . . . Thank God, for our good passage hereto; and pray his care of us on our return. . . .

"July 17 . . . set off and went 2 M to the mouth of the River . . . held on and crossed the Bay to the north Shore . . . Rocks of Hornblende . . . Samuel picked up several small pieces of Carnelian. . . . When the upper part of the Rock sinks in its irregularities; there is a good bed of strong reddish Earth bearing small growth of W Birch, Aspin & Fir &c. . . . At 9.47 A M set off to try if we could proceed, went ab^r 1/2 M to a Point, and finding almost all before us perpend[icular] Cliffs of Rock &c with head sea wind and high Waves, we returned and camped. . . .

"July 18 . . . we now held on passing high Promontories of Rocks and in their Chasms & Ravines fine red Pebble Beaches on the Lake forming many snug Coves; passed several Rivulets. . . . the Sand Banks of the South Side appear at their full height. . . . They are no doubt so elevated by the common, and perhaps constant cause of great refraction, as Mirage: low dense Banks of white Fog, or vapour. . . . In the evening . . . we rounded a bold high Promontery of perpend[icular] Rock, and turned into a snug but spacious Cove of red Pebble at 7 PM. camped and set the net. . . .

"July 19th held on and came to the Barn Promontory, the . . . Gable ends of which are high perpend Rocks, reddish with vertical like Strata of 160 to 180 ft high at least, passed several Brooks & Rivulets. . . .

"July 20 . . . almost everywhere, an Iron bound Shore of Rock with very few places to camp. passed a . . . Rivulet of 30 y^{ds} wide; deep water, having a Fall of 40 ft perpend. shortly after another Rivulet of 8 ft—4 ft fall . . . At 7.20 turned into a fine Bay. . . . At 8.20 A M set off held on passed Isl^{ds} one had an Arch at its SW end a fine Campment opposite, and a deep River & low Fall. . . . held on along a rocky Shore, could find no place to land—until 3.20 P M when a small

Beach presented, and we dined.... fine evening Killed 3 Pigeons see none along this side except this small flock and they are poor....

"July 21 ... held on along a rocky shore, sometimes a vertical Strata, passed a bold River; counted the Hills 12 Ranges of Trees.... held on along low Lands and mostly very fine Beaches of red Pebbles with swampy like Ground directly behind ... passed a fine Ship Harbor ... many Midges & a few Musketoes. 2 Indians came to us from their Lodges in the Bay They and their looks pleaded Hunger....

"July 22nd rowed along a low Shore of Rocks and good Beach ... to 9 1/2 A M when Thank God we put ashore at the old Great Carry^g Place."

The following year Thompson was again on Lake Superior. This time a physician of considerable literary ability, Dr. John J. Bigsby, accompanied him and the rest of the boundary survey party. Bigsby kept a journal and made sketches, some of which are probably the earliest graphic representations still extant for the north shore of Lake Superior. Years later Bigsby wrote up his trip from his diaries and illustrated it with his sketches. The two volumes appeared as one under the caption, *Shoe and Canoe*. It contains one of the best accounts available of the north shore before the advent of settlement, though like all other printed accounts of that shore, it omits the section between Grand Portage and the Fond du Lac. One fact alone he mentions for that area, and it is a significant one, now that all trace of the former appearance of that section has vanished: At Michipicoten Bay he records "we distinctly saw a ridge of sugar-maples many miles long.... There is another, which stretches from the Perdrix [Pigeon] Falls, near the Grand Portage, to the Fond du Lac. Those extensive groves of sugar-maple are highly prized by the Indians."

Let us follow Dr. Bigsby in the year 1823 as he travels from the Sault along the north shore to Grand Portage.

"Having had our boat carted by oxen across the British Portage, we commenced on the 10th of June, 1823, our coasting voyage, so rarely made now, along the north shores of Lake Superior as far as the Grand Portage, a distance of 445 miles."

He does not explain the meaning of his phrase "so rarely made now." As already explained in this book, with the year 1821 practically all traffic of the amalgamated Hudson's Bay and North West companies began to go over the economically cheaper route by way of Hudson Bay.

"Lake Superior differs widely from Lake Huron, in having a more regular outline, in having but few islands, in the grander features of its coasts, and in its geological structure, which, as far as I know, have no parallel in America. We have here the advantage of plenty of named localities."

Fur traders had seen to the naming of every slightest point and bay along Lake Superior. Dr. Bigsby continues:

"The general course of the east coast of the lake from Gros Cap to the River Michipicotou [*sic*] (125 miles by canoe route) is about a point to the west of north. The most conspicuous promontories in this interval are Marmoaze [*sic*], forty-one miles from St. Mary's River, and Gargantua, ninety-three miles from St. Mary's. These are the outer points of great curvatures, which contain subordinate bays of considerable size. [On June 12] we crossed the mouth of the bay [Goulais Bay], and made for the lesser Maple Islands, leaving behind us the greater island of this name, sometimes called 'Parisien,' loaded with timber. Everything looked innocent and pretty.... Any thought of danger seemed absurd; and yet it was here that two well-manned canoes of the Northwest Company were cast ashore about the year 1815, and nine persons drowned. Among the saved were Mr. W. M'Gilvray [William McGillivray] ... and Dr. M'Loghlin [Dr. John McLoughlin], many years Governor of Fort Vancouver [the so-called 'Father of Oregon'].

"We next come to the Batchewine [*sic*] Bay, deep and large, with a flat island, called Green Island, on its north side, and lofty hills overhanging it; but the interior on the south and west is low and woody.... I observed on the sides of the nearer hills three patches of winter-snow not yet melted....

"Point Marmoaze, and its vicinity for seven miles northerly, consists of trap, vesicular amygdaloidal and compact in parts; all interleaved with pudding-stone, of rounded masses of granite, trap, amygdaloid, and sand-stone, from a size invisible to the naked eye, to that of some square feet. The shore, therefore, assumes a peculiar aspect. It is iron-bound, from ten to one hundred feet high, and scooped into windowlike holes, arches, and shallow caves. A considerable way into the lake are rugged islets, with short jagged needles of rock here and there. . . . The effect upon the eye, with its dark tawny colour, and large differently-coloured bowlders, is new and grotesque."

He passed Mica Bay, Huggewong Bay, the Island of Montreal and Montreal River—all a mining district in 1850, according to his friend, Sir John Richardson, the Arctic traveler, who had just returned from traversing the north shore when Bigsby was writing up his account.

"At the south and inner end of the bay [Huggewong] there is a cliff, 500 feet high, overlooking a terrace of white sand, thirty feet high, and half a mile long. . . . There are four rocky islets with high, sloping sides, off this point, besides several smaller ones around an indentation, an excellent harbour half-a-mile from the extreme point at the entrance of the bay. We here saw on a little cape an Indian signal or guide-post—a stick fastened to the rock, and holding a bunch of grass in its cleft end. It pointed in the direction which the Indian's friends had taken. From this conspicuous point to Gargantua, the next remarkable headland, the distance is twenty-seven miles. . . . The interior is high. . . . The streams are numerous here. . . . Point Gargantua is a prominent feature on the east side of Lake Superior. It has a very indented front, being composed of parallel ridges of black amygdaloid, rising one above another in retreating succession to the height of from thirty to eighty feet, from time to time much dilapidated; and with little coves of black sand. The granite region, a mile inland, is nearly destitute of any vegetation but burnt pines, looking most desolate; but the point itself, and the parts adjacent, being of amygdaloid, a fertilising rock, is clothed with fir, birch, poplar, &c., and a profusion of mosses."

He mentions the islets roundabout, and small pointed rocks rising out of the water.

JOHN TANNER   FREDERICK ULRICH GRAHAM

DR. CHARLES W. W. BORUP   RAMSAY CROOKS

PAUL KANE'S OIL PAINTING OF MOUNTAIN PORTAGE NEAR
KAKABEKA FALLS, ONTARIO, ABOUT 1846

"One of these, a few hundred yards from the point, is a rude pyramid from fifty to sixty feet high. Its strange shape, dark colour, and the surrounding gloom, have induced the Indians to worship it as an idol."

The doctor continues:

"A lofty style of country prevails in this part of Lake Superior; the hills rising in steps or ledges, or in slopes covered with foliage, or again in vertically-fissured precipices. The immediate shores are rocky, and often high.... All this region is very picturesque, but especially the bay south of Cape Maurepas [Michipicoten]. Its shores are a confused and steep assemblage of high rocks. A beautiful cascade near the bottom pours a ribbon-like stream from height to height, and so into the lake. This spot reminded me of some scenes in the Cape de Verd Islands, where we have the same bare red crumbling rocks."

Bigsby devotes not a little space to Michipicoten Bay and the trading post of the Hudson's Bay Company that he found there, and he speculates upon the ancient beaches of earlier lakes that his trained eye could not fail to notice all along the north shore. "These ranges or stairs of shingle are met with all over Lake Superior. We were never able to make accurate observations on this subject."

The next fourteen miles were "shore faced by deep and extensive sand-banks." Then Dog River was passed. "It undergoes a descent of twenty-five feet" close to the lake, "by two ledges in a chine or gorge of greenstone slate, whose dark colour, and some recent conflagrations, invest this scene with peculiar wildness and gloom." He adds a footnote at this point to the effect that "the Indians burn large tracts of pine barrens in order to favour the growth of very useful autumnal fruits.... I must not forget to say that, a few miles outside of this great bay, and twelve miles from the nearest main (on the north), lies the large island of Michipicotou."

"The interval of seventy-five miles between the crags and the River Peek [Pic] presents but two localities known by name, viz. the

Otter's Head, thirty-four miles; and the Smaller Written Rocks, sixty-one miles. . . .

"The Otter's Head we passed on the 17th of June. It is an upright slab, from thirty to thirty-five feet high, placed on some scantily-clad rocks, 120 feet above the lake.

"The coast between Otter's Head and the River Peek (forty-one miles) is more deeply indented than that between the former place and the crags. Its hills are higher, more massive, and often dip precipitously into woody dells. The water-margin is lined with low, jagged rocks, while the interior is very barren, the whole vegetation being a few small Canada pines, apparently dead, save a little pencil of leaves at the top. . . . The Smaller Written Rocks are, in a sandy cove, defended by islets fourteen miles south-east from the Peek River. They here are smooth and coated with tripe de roche and other lichens. Various names and figures of animals have been traced on them, both long ago and recently. The basalt dykes, which form such a peculiar feature in the geology of the north shore of Lake Superior, are particularly abundant in this region. They are from one to sixty feet broad, and they cut through all the primitive rocks indifferently, proceeding without the slightest change of size, texture, or direction, from one to another. In a district of white granite their appearance is very striking, and resembles a ruined staircase, cleaving and mounting acclivities of all heights. . . . The River Peek takes its name from an Indian word, signifying mud, as it pours out an ash-coloured, and, when swollen, a reddish-yellow water, ting[e]ing the lake for a mile or two round its mouth, and derived from beds of yellow and white clay some distance up the river."

Next he describes the Hudson's Bay Company post at the Pic and continues:

"The country here is of a softer aspect than has been the case lately. The hills swell in gentle, egg-shaped slopes, and are freely wooded with spruce and birch. . . . Seventeen miles and a half by canoe route, north-west from the River Peek, is Peek Island, opposite a lofty and broad promontory of fissured, dull-red rock. It is several miles round, and has three naked summits. One of these, 760 feet high, I ascended. . . . The view from that elevation was beautiful and wide."

Near this island Bigsby met Captain Bayfield of the Royal Navy, then and for a few years thereafter making his famous survey of Lake Superior.

He barely mentions the Slate Islands, today famous for their caribou. They were so named, he says, "from their being of green-stone slate," and "are rather large and high." Black River is mentioned and its area described. Here in particular he noticed the old beaches of former lakes. "I mention these particulars to point out that, in these regions, the same land-lift has taken place as in Europe, &c." Of Black River "the first fall is sixty feet high . . . pitching into a deep funnel-shaped chasm, 250 yards long, at the lower end of which several other jets of great beauty take place. The river then escapes into Lake Superior from a pretty basin, amid islets tufted with cedar, spruce, and alder. I found many traces of copper pyrites about the mouth of this river."

The Slate Islands brought him to the height of the arc in the lake and started him southwest, whereas he had been going northwest heretofore. He mentions another place where Indians had carved their hieroglyphics in the lichens of the rocks and thus given the name of Written Rocks (generally called *Les Ecrits* and today located near Schreiber) to the spot.

"They are seven miles west of the Black River. They occur in a cluster of islets close to a large headland of glaring red colour, like all in this vicinity. . . . The drawings . . . are made by simply detaching the dark lichens from the flat surface of the rock. At their west end there is a good representation of an Indian firing at two animals. . . . Here we saw snow again. From the west angle of a picturesque, but small bay, close to the Written Rocks, commences a line of iron-bound coast a mile long, a dangerous pass for canoes in particular winds. It ends abruptly at Cape Verd, to form the picturesque bay of Nipigon. Cape Verd is so called from the fine woods with which it is crowned. Its rocks are basalt. Wherever this rock or any of its congeners prevail, such as amygdaloid, porphyry, &c., there vegetation becomes luxuriant, and the trees numerous, but not large. Both here and at Marmoaze I found the woods completely impassable. For several hundred yards inland the ground is buried in blocks of stone, carpeted with moss a foot thick. Fallen trees are rotting in every direction, matted with briers and wild roses. Every step hazards the breaking of a limb in some unsuspected crevice.... From Cape Verd westward to Fort William (ninety to ninety-five miles by canoe) the north shore of Lake Superior is divided into three very large bays—Nipigon, Black, and Thunder Bays."

He found the area of coast near Lake Nipigon, called then as now the "Pays Plat," or Flat Country, a "translation from the Chippewa language, and refers only to the shallow black and red floor of the lake hereabouts.... generally speaking, it is an elevated region...."

"The islands are numerous. I made the circuit of the whole by going outside in June, and inside in the ruder month of September. St. Ignatius, the most westerly save one, is much the largest.... is twenty-six miles long by twelve broad ... Its centre is table land, sometimes 1300 feet high, and dipping on all sides in rough declivities and precipices, whose features change with the component rock. If this be porphyry (common here), we have long pilasters.... This we see on the south side of the island, in Fluor Island, at the west end of Ignatius.... If the cliffs be of red sandstone (often as hard as jasper, and fissured horizontally), they are only in patches at the very summits of lofty flanks buried in the woods. The islands east of St. Ignatius are often very high ... and ... they are worn by watercourses into singular shapes, such as pillars, arches, recesses ... and window-like apertures, which not a little resemble a street of ruined chapels and chantries shrouded by mosses, vines, and forest trees. We have this fissured state of the rock both in the inner and outer route.... On one of the islets at the west end of the Pays Plat we have a beautiful display of true basaltic columns.... The trappose and amygdaloidal districts are here thickly wooded, but the trees—mountain ash (very common), spruce, pitch pine, birch, &c.—are hide-bound and small, sheathed in the trailing moss called goat's-beard. The region around Nipigon Bay is full of enchanting scenery. As we journey up this great water we have the ever-changing pictures presented by the belt of islands on our left; while on our right we have the Nipigon mainland, an assemblage of bold mountains from 900 to 1200 feet high, tabular, rounded, or in hummocks, or sugar loaf, and only separated by very narrow clefts or gorges. . . . The bay is a beautiful lake of itself, so transparent that we can, for miles together, see its red pavement, and living and dead things there inhabiting. . . . The Nipigon . . . River, enters the bay at its west end. It is from 80 to 100 yards broad at its mouth, and discharges a muddy grey water. Its length is ninety miles, and on it are seven cascades and three rapids. It comes from Lake Nipigon (or St. Anne), which is sixty miles round, and in a barren country."

He next notices the Mammelles Hills.

"There are several, but the two most conspicuous are cones of soft and beautiful outlines, at least 800 feet high, and close together at the southwest corner of the great promontory between Black and Nipigon Bays, being the southern extremity of a long ridge coming from the north. The Mammelles district consists of this headland and the multitudinous islands which are in front of it. . . . next morning [we] plunged into a charming labyrinth of . . . islands, sheltered even from a hurricane. From time to time we saw the free lake at the bottom of a long vista of pine-clad islands; and we were glad, for the sake of change, to come suddenly . . . into open water, opposite Thunder Mountain . . . seven miles from us. . . . This magnificent headland is a principal feature in Lake Superior, and forms the north-west end of Black Bay. This bay, I am informed by Captain Bayfield, is forty-six miles deep, and extremely woody. It receives a large river. The mouth of the bay is partially guarded by a great assemblage of woody, and for the most part low islands. . . . Thunder Mountain is several miles long and of considerable breadth, except at the point, where it descends into the lake in three shelves. . . . About the middle of its south side an immense crater-like cavity, with steep woody acclivities, is scooped out of the body of the mountain. The precipices are largest and finest on the north-northwest, and extend in rude colonnades over two-fifths of the whole height, terminating in naked taluses, 300 to 400 feet high. On the side of Thunder Bay I saw no precipices. At and about the water-level, under Thunder Mountain, I saw a good deal of fixed limestone (without fossils), the only place where it is known to exist on the north shore of this lake. Thunder Bay, to which we have now arrived, under the shadow of its great promontory, is round, and from ten to twelve miles across. Grand Point is its western angle; its margin is swampy on the west, but its bottom is here and there bold and precipitous. The only islands in Thunder Bay are Welcome, Hare, and Sheep Islands, opposite the mouths of the River Kaministigua, or Dog River, where Fort William is placed."

He proceeds to describe Fort William as it was just after the height of its glory. Then:

"We left Fort William for the Grand Portage on one of the last days of June. We found the shore of Lake Superior swampy as far as Grand Point, but there the hills, which in lofty slopes and scarps for some way inland skirt the Kaministigua (and are perhaps the highest —1000 feet—at Mackay's Mountain, near the south fork), join the lake, and line it in precipices from 300 to 800 feet high, south-west-wards, to near Pigeon Bay. They are flat-topped, cut up by ravines, and clad with pines. A slope of ruins, clothed with birch and aspen, creeps up their sides. Pigeon Bay is three miles across its mouth and four in depth. In one of its coves, sheltered by an islet, a schooner belonging to the North-west Company usually winters. Its worthy commander bears the singular name of Maccargo. Pigeon River enters at the south corner of the Bay. It has a beautiful cascade, 120 feet high, a mile and a half from the lake. From Pigeon Point, a rocky coast for a few miles brings us to the bay of the Grand Portage. Anxiously we looked into it as a celebrated spot. . . . The North-west Company formerly had an important post here, of warehouses, stables, gardens, &c., which occupied a grassy flat, backed by high hills. . . . The whole voyage from Fort William to this place has been full of scenic beauty. The very lofty and broken interior is nearly naked; but where there are woods, we have the tender green of the aspen and birch down below, while sombre pines crown the black precipices."

Here Bigsby and his party turned inland and made a famous and well-reported trip along the waterways of lakes and streams that now form the boundary line between Minnesota, Ontario and Manitoba, as far as Lake of the Woods. Two of his sketches are included in the section of the book already quoted: Fluor Island near Nipigon Bay, and Thunder Mountain. Captain McCargo, incidentally, spent a long lifetime as a well-known navigator of boats on Lake Superior.

So much for the traders of the North West Company and the descriptions of Lake Superior as they must have seen it in the course of the company's heyday. The Canadian shore line between the Sault and Port Arthur has hardly altered in the intervening years, but the great forests of the south shore, and especially of the stretch of the north shore between Duluth and Grand Portage, have vanished, leaving quite a different aspect for the modern lake traveler. Travelers from Europe, however, used to find the "interminable pine forests" oppressive on the canoe route between Montreal and Rainy Lake; perhaps they would think the modern scenery about the south and west shores of Lake Superior vastly preferable to what they saw. At all events, it is still grand. The great cliffs and rocky headlands are not altered. The gorges and cataracts are as impressive as ever. Fringes of islets in all shapes and forms still add piquancy to the scene. Arches, caves, grottoes and magnificent colonnades may still be seen. No one has spoiled the crystal purity of Lake Superior's waters, so transparent that small objects may be seen scores of feet below the surface, nor made them any warmer. From Duluth north and east to the Sault the wilderness still prevails; only a few villages and three cities have sprung up.

Chapter 3

Yankee Notions

I see the swarthy trappers come

I see the swarthy trappers come
From Mississippi's springs;
And war-chiefs with their painted brows,
And crests of eagle wings.
　　　　—JOHN GREENLEAF WHITTIER

AMERICANS began to enter the Lake Superior country in effective fashion after John Jacob Astor started to win his struggle for monopoly of the fur trade in the United States in 1816. Mackinac became the central depot of his inland empire for some years, with subdepots at the Sault, La Pointe and Fond du Lac. His operations in Ohio, Illinois and Michigan Territory (embracing modern Wisconsin and Minnesota as well as Michigan) brought together a supply of fine furs that were sold at the great Leipzig fairs, in London, and especially in Canton. Teas and silks were bought with the proceeds of the China ventures, and were sold in Europe for industrial wares; these in turn were brought across the Atlantic and sold in America. The proceeds of the European investments were then put into Manhattan real estate, and thus the great Astor fortune, begun about Lake Superior and carried clear around the world, was made.

When Astor's charter of 1808 expired in 1833, he withdrew, and the old Lake Superior part of the business (known as the Northern Department) remained as the American Fur Company, with Ramsay Crooks as president. The western part of Astor's concern, centering at St. Louis, now formed another company. The American Fur Company operated with a great show of activity from 1834 to 1842, when it failed and was gradually liquidated. The outstanding men of the Lake Superior region in this period were Ramsay Crooks, Robert Stuart and Gabriel Franchere—all former Astorians—and their sub-

70

ordinates, William Aitken, William Morrison, Dr. Charles Borup, the two Warren brothers (Lyman and Truman), Samuel Ashmun, Samuel Abbott, William Brewster, John R. Livingston and a number of others. Several of these men are known for other reasons. Robert Stuart was probably the discoverer of the South Pass in the Rocky Mountains, through which the Oregon, Mormon and California trails passed. Gabriel Franchere's book of reminiscences of his adventures as an Astorian has long been a classic, both in the original French and in English translation. William Aitken was a Scotsman active about the headwaters of the Mississippi, where he ruled the Chippewa in semidespotic fashion. A county and a town in Minnesota are named for him, though spelled incorrectly on modern maps. William Morrison claimed to have discovered the true source of the Mississippi many years before Henry R. Schoolcraft made the officially recognized discovery of Lake Itasca. Lyman Warren was long associated closely with La Pointe and Madeline Island. His half-breed son wrote a famous book on the history, traditions and customs of the Chippewa Indians, centering at La Pointe. Dr. Charles Borup was a well-educated physician from Copenhagen, who spent his young manhood among the Chippewa Indians about Rainy Lake and Lake Superior. His post was La Pointe for many years. Later he became a pioneer banker and insurance man in St. Paul. Practically all of these men had Indian families and some of their children were able men and women in the West of their day. Many of them became associated with the missionaries. Crooks's daughter became the wife of a well-known missionary to the Chippewa, William T. Boutwell, who in conjunction with Schoolcraft gave Lake Itasca its name.

The fur trade of the American Fur Company was carried on by divisions called outfits. Thus the Fond du Lac Outfit controlled most of the trade north and east of the Little Falls in the Mississippi River, about a hundred miles above the Twin Cities of today. The post at the mouth of the St. Louis River had been important during the British period, as we have seen. During the American period it was moved upriver to a place within present-day Fond du Lac. Here began a long-established canoe route to the Mississippi by way of the St. Louis River and Sandy Lake. Fond du Lac was also a terminus of one of the many routes between Lake Superior, Lake Vermilion and Rainy Lake. There were Indian villages near the fort, and in the thirties of the nineteenth century missions of at least three denominations carried on their work there. In the middle fifties Duluth was established near by and soon overshadowed its parent, Fond du Lac.

La Pointe on Madeline Island seems to have maintained a continuous existence as a trading post from the French period till the fur trade ceased in the middle of the last century. Before it became the inland headquarters of the American Fur Company in 1834, it served an immediate hinterland in what is now northern Wisconsin and part of Michigan, as well as Isle Royale and much of the north shore between the Fond du Lac and Grand Portage. In 1835 it became the headquarters of the American Fur Company's fishing industry on Lake Superior.* For a time it maintained an Indian subagency, the main agency being at Sault Ste. Marie or Mackinac.

Sault Ste. Marie was an important post of the American Fur Company for several reasons. A portage there rendered warehouses necessary until the locks were opened in 1855. The spot was famous for its whitefish, which were caught both above and in the rapids. Here also were built the company's several vessels that operated on the lake after 1835. Indians had villages at the place and near by; missions were established fairly early; and the Hudson's Bay Company maintained a post across the narrow rapids. Like La Pointe, the Sault kept a continuous existence as a trading post from early French days until the fur trade waned.

At these posts and others maintained by the American Fur Company, the explorers of the American period stopped on their travels. The first important expedition was that of Lewis Cass in 1820. By legislation of 1818, when Illinois became a state, Michigan Territory was extended to include the land lying north of Illinois between Lake Michigan and the Mississippi River. Cass became governor of this great area and naturally desired to know something of it. When he applied to the Secretary of War for permission to make an expedition, he stated that his purposes would be to get better acquainted with the

* See Chapter 9.

Indian tribes of the region, to wean them from their British affilia-
ions, to extinguish the Indian title to land in the vicinity of the Sault
and other places, to investigate reported mineral deposits in the
vicinity of Lake Superior, and to prepare a correct map of the region.

With Cass went several men who later became famous: Captain
David B. Douglass to conduct the geodetic and topographical work,
Henry R. Schoolcraft as mineralogist, and Charles C. Trowbridge.
Several of the party kept diaries, the last of which to be published,
Trowbridge's, came out in 1942. About forty persons made up the
expeditionary force, which left Detroit on May 24, 1820, and reached
Mackinac two weeks later. The entire trip was made in birch-bark
canoes.

At the Sault an incident of importance occurred. The Chippewa
were still being drawn to the British side by annual distributions of
presents at Drummond Island in Lake Huron. Cass determined to
bring these Indians effectually under American influence. So, when
one of the chiefs ended a stormy debate by kicking out of his way the
presents that had been laid before him and stalking out of the conference, and when a British flag appeared in the camp a few minutes
later, Cass instantly ordered his guard under arms and pulled down
the British flag, indicating that no other banner than the American
flag was to fly thereafter above those regions. As a result of this bold
and firm attitude, the Chippewa ceded a tract of land at the Sault on
which Fort Brady was erected two years later. It is reported that the
Indian wife of John Johnston materially aided the American cause
by pleading with her relatives and acquaintance to yield to the inevitable. When the treaty was finally signed, it contained a clause,
insisted upon by the Indians, that they should forever have the right
to fish in the rapids.

Trowbridge was delighted with the Pictured Rocks on his way with
the expedition along the south shore:

"It is only 12 miles from LaGrand Sable to the Pictured Rocks, one
of natures works of grandeur and sublimity. These rocks extend 13
miles, are perpendicular, and generally about the height of 150 feet.
They are of that kind of Rock called by Geological men 'Grawacke',

which resembles sand stone, and is of a dusky white colour, it is easily worn and the action of the waves has caused as far as their influence extend, a succession of caverns, in many of which a boat of considerable size might be safely moored. They are called the pictured rocks from the circumstances of their being variegated with the veins of different kinds of ore running through, and colouring the surface."

He was enthusiastic about the scenery in the region of Grand Island:

"It contributes, with the shape of the opposite shore, to form one of the safest and most commodious harbors on the waters of the west. Vessells of any sise may ride here without least apprehension from wind or waves, and the beauty of the scenery renders it an enchanting place."

The city of Munising now occupies the shore of that safe haven. The party camped at Train Bay the following night, ate lunch at Chocolay River, and camped the next night on the site of Marquette. Of the scenery of this spot he remarks, "The country near presque Isle is very mountainous and presents a handsome prospect."

Making the "grand traverse" from the east side of Keweenaw Bay to the entrance of Portage River was as difficult as tradition had reported it: "We succeeded however after buffetting the waves for 5 hours, during a part of which time we gained hardly an inch, in making the mouth of the River, where we arrived in safety." The voyageurs were too much influenced by the tradition, apparently, for the diarist reports of them, "We were obliged to use our utmost exertions to enliven the spirits of the Voyageurs, who tho't of nothing but crossing themselves and going to the bottom."

Schoolcraft found virgin copper on the portage route, one piece weighing a half-pound. At the mouth of the Ontonagon the party found an Indian village: "At the mouth of this river are five permanent lodges of indians, who seldom leave this place, but subsist chiefly on sturgeon which they take in great quantities." There were few permanent Indian encampments on Lake Superior. A party from the expedition visited the famous copper boulder on the river, but were disappointed in it.

Trowbridge describes the sturgeon weirs of the Indians in some detail, notes the quiet beauty of the Porcupine Mountains, and describes the Indian dances that were presented while the party lay in camp at Ontonagon:

"They have the War Dance, which is, as we would say, the most fashionable, the pipe dance which is used only in peace, the Bear Dance & the Buffalo Dance, descriptive of their respective achievements in the chase. In one of these dances our attention was attracted and our affections excited towards a young chief, whose conduct clearly demonstrated to us, that greatness of mind, suavity of manner and filial affection are not altogether confined to the civilized world."

Of Chequamegon Bay the diary has much to say.

"We landed at Mon' Cadottes trading house or fort, (all trading houses in the indian country are enclosed by pickets) but we had not the pleasure of seeing Monsieur, he having sailed for Mackinac. The indians however were very well pleased to see us, particularly our old pilot Monsieur Roi, whom they knew: they fell on his neck and wept for joy."

Though the diarist reports the post as being on Oak Island, it was undoubtedly on Madeline Island, which has had a succession of names. Oak Island today is nearer to Bayfield than to the long sandy point which reaches out from beyond Ashland, and which the diarist particularly mentions as being "directly opposite" the post.

The next main stop made by the party was at the American Fur Company's post at Fond du Lac. Here Pierre Coté was in charge.

"This is the principal establishment of the Am. Fur-Company. They have some houses built, and a few acres of land cleared, on which they raise potatoes. We saw a number of cows, Bulls, & horses, which had been brought from Mackinac in batteaux."

The author has struck out the last clause in his diary, but it nevertheless represents the fact in all likelihood. There was no other way to get animals to Fond du Lac than by canoe or bateau.

The Cass party started inland from Fond du Lac, and their itinerary is of no further interest in the story of Lake Superior. After reaching the headwaters of the Mississippi, they returned down that stream to Prairie du Chien, where they took the Wisconsin-Fox route back to Lake Michigan and thence to Detroit, their starting point. As the expedition's sequel reveals, the way was being prepared for the erection of army posts, the arrival of missionaries and the beginning of the mining frontier. It was not long after the official report of Cass's trip was made before Fort Brady was established at Sault Ste. Marie, and before missionaries arrived on the scene. The miners did not appear for about twenty years; then Lake Superior was overrun with them.

Meantime other official expeditions found their way along the south shore of Lake Superior. Strange to relate, there was, in addition, an authorized American army expedition which skirted the north shore of the lake. In 1823 Major Stephen H. Long was sent by the War Department to determine, among other things, the exact location of the recently established boundary line between the United States and British possessions to the north. This had been arranged by the Convention of 1818 and related to the area west of the Lake of the Woods and as far as the crest of the Rocky Mountains. East of that lake the boundary line was still unsettled, and along the *supposed* line, as indicated by the Treaty of 1783, Long's party made its way, after fulfilling the other objects of the expedition. Thus they reached Rainy Lake and Lac la Croix. At that point they took the Kaministikwia canoe route instead of the Grand Portage way, and arrived eventually at Fort William. From that place they proceeded by boat along the north shore to the Sault.

The same summer David Thompson and Dr. Bigsby, representing the British boundary commission, were passing over the canoe routes between Lake Superior and Lake of the Woods. Both the Grand Portage and the Kaministikwia routes were followed, and reports of most of the separate groups of the expeditions are now available. We have already read portions of Thompson's and Bigsby's. The American expedition's report had never been printed in any detail until the diaries and other papers of the American representative,

Major Joseph Delafield, appeared in 1943. Delafield was largely responsible for the American insistence that the customary water route between Lake Superior and Lake of the Woods (stated by the Treaty of 1783 to be the line of the boundary) was the Kaministikwia River. His recently printed papers show that he proposed this claim because the British made the much less tenable claim that the treaty meant the St. Louis River was the customary canoe way. Had the Americans yielded, the great iron ore beds of the Arrowhead Country of Minnesota would have become Canadian, and the vast ore commerce of Lake Superior would doubtless have yielded its profits to Canadians rather than to Americans. The sober historical fact was, that when the treaty was signed by both British and American governments, the usual canoe route ran from the mouth of Pigeon River westward along the present boundary waters of Minnesota's northern edge. Earlier, it is true, and still later, the customary route *was* the Kaministikwia River and certain connecting rivers and lakes, but the St. Louis River was never a *customary* canoe route for the trade canoes. It was sometimes used, but that is not to say that it filled the condition of the terms of the treaty.

Delafield's papers are highly interesting for Lake Superior references. In May 1823 he left New York to join James Ferguson and George Washington Whistler of the American survey party, who had spent the preceding winter at Fort William. Whistler, incidentally, was the father of the noted artist. He was the expedition's draftsman, and Ferguson was the principal surveyor.

Delafield visited Governor Cass on his way to Lake Superior, reached Sault Ste. Marie on June 18, hired voyageurs and a guide, dined with John Johnston and also with the commanding officer of Fort Brady, and probably saw Lieutenant Henry Wolsey Bayfield, who sailed from the Sault on June 22 in the *Recovery,* carrying out his British Admiralty orders to survey Lake Superior.* His charts from that survey were for years the only guide that mariners had in navigating the lake. They are fascinating reading today, for they are full of details about the appearance of the shores and islands of the lake as they were in the middle of the 1820's.

Delafield himself left the Sault in a canoe on June 23, 1823, with a

---

* See page 262.

crew of six voyageurs. The trip was a lonely one, for Delafield was obviously a sociable person, who missed conversation with his kind. The voyageurs did not speak much English, and though Delafield understood French, he longed for others of his own class. Yet his is one of the most understanding reports on Lake Superior's voyageurs that has been printed. In one passage he says of them:

"In short, the more I see of the Canadian French, their mode of life, and connection with the Indians, the more I feel assured that without this very race of men, the fur trade of the North could not be carried on. They are more hardy than the Indian, are far more capable in the canoe, and in Winter will soon break down the Indian if travelling on snow shoes or with trains. Trains are little sleighs made up of a single piece of thin flat wood, bent up at one end in a curl."

He goes on to describe these dog sleds of the fur trade.

At the Pic trading post, the factor, McTavish, told Delafield that he was going to James Bay by way of the Michipicoten River and expected to get there in six days. Delafield doubted that such a trip, of many portages, could be accomplished in that time. He records in a later entry that McTavish went and returned in twenty-seven days, which is surprising enough.

The *Recovery** was at the mouth of the Kaministikwia near Fort William when Delafield arrived. "Fort William is a very large establishment in decay," he writes. "Since the coalition of the Hudson's Bay and North West Companies, this post has become very insignificant & fast going to ruin."

After a summer in the interior, Delafield returned to Lake Superior, where on August 24 he saw "a grand embarkation from Fort William for Montreal. Four Montreal Canoes, as called, which are of immense size, laden with packs, and four North Canoes, filled with free-men from the interior (just discharged) with their women and children, depart." Next day Thompson left for the Sault, two North canoes left for Montreal, and "the large establishment of Fort William is now deserted by all except the clerks in command, a few

* See page 119.

artificers and a few half-breeds (women), who have become dependents on the establishment, their husbands having left them & their children, when ordered to a different post, as heirlooms to the company."

Delafield himself left, with Whistler, on the twenty-sixth. He seems to have enjoyed the return trip on the lake, for he now had a companion with whom he could talk. After a rather stormy passage, they reached the Sault once more on September 14, where both men found quarters in the fort until their final departure for the eastern seaboard.

The next American expedition of consequence was Thomas McKenney's *Tour to the Lakes,* as he entitled his report of it. Governor Cass went along, but McKenney of the Indian Department was in charge. On July 3, 1826, the party reached the Sault. In his report McKenney has much to say about the place, the Johnston family, and the Schoolcrafts. On July 11 the expedition left for Fond du Lac, sixty-seven persons in three barges and a bark canoe. It included Schoolcraft, as well as an army captain, a second lieutenant, an army surgeon, three other commissioned officers, eight noncommissioned officers, four musicians and forty-eight privates.

McKenney reported the coastline of the lake in some detail as he traveled. He was struck with the beauty of bay and crag, was lulled to sleep by "the requiem of the waves," experienced cold, heat, mosquitoes and fog; and was present when one of the barges was wrecked. Of the great dunes, Grand Sablé as he calls them, he writes:

"This mountain of sand is a great curiosity. It fronts the lake so as to receive its billows, and the blasts from the northeast, which doubtless lash and sweep over its swelling sides, in those seasons when this wind prevails, but which have served only to unite the particles of which it is composed, until it shows a front like a rock. Its colour is in general yellow, and scarcely a sprig of verdure is to be seen, save here and there, in some of its chasms, made by the running over of the water from the world above, where may be seen a few shrubs of evergreen, and some long grass."

He tried to climb this mountain of sand, but had to return without reaching the top.

Unlike most expeditions on Lake Superior, this one passed around Keweenaw Point rather than across the portage route. McKenney was greatly impressed with the scenery of Lake Superior's "thumb."

"The lands rise in rocky and broken precipices, displaying a grandeur, and a barrenness equal to any thing of the kind I have seen. It is nearly all rock—the shores are cut out into little bays of from one hundred feet to a quarter of a mile, into many of which we entered, whilst the rocky projections of the mountain hung over us as if to threaten us with destruction. Huge masses of rocks, that had parted from the mountain, were lying out in the lake, some fifty and a hundred yards from the shore, between which, and others, that formed a kind of passage way, and with perpendicular walls, our little bark was passed on the smooth surface of the waters. It was like a mite in comparison to these ruptured and stupendous fragments."

McKenney was more aware of the presence of wild life than were most of the travelers who have left accounts of the lake in early days. He mentions birds in particular—the gulls, the loons and the many broods of mergansers, or sawbills. He quotes lines of poetry that his experiences on the lake call to mind, such as the following bit of *Childe Harold,* with McKenney's modification of "sea" to "lake" in the last line:

> There is a pleasure in the pathless woods,
> There is a rapture on the lonely shore,
> There is society, where none intrudes,
> By the deep lake, and music in its roar.

He perceived that the Indians were human, enjoyed their company and studied them with great appreciation. He was delighted with La Pointe and recalled what John Johnston had told him about seeing Count Paolo Andreani there in 1791 taking scientific observations. The Count seems to have been one of the few white men who have ever circumnavigated the lake. He has left some interesting records

of his visit at Grand Portage in the same year. These are to be found
in the Duke de la Rochefoucauld Liancourt's *Travels through the
United States of North America,* which was published in 1799. Even
those acquainted with the Italian nobleman's career probably do not
realize that he ventured so far into the wilderness, and doubtless
recall him chiefly for his interest in aviation. Perhaps at some future
date his diaries, which the Duke saw and used, will come to light
and open a new chapter in the lake's story.

At the Fond du Lac McKenney's expedition arrived with as much
pomp and splendor as possible, to the strains of "Yankee Doodle"!
The Indians were awaiting the newcomers and a grand council was
held, after several preliminary meetings:

"Never before had I witnessed such a display, nor such an exhibi-
tion of nakedness and wretchedness, nor such varieties of both.—
From the infant tied to its cradle, and to the back of its mother, to the
big Buffaloe [a chief]; from the little fellow with a dress made of
raccoon skins, himself not much above the size of that animal, and
looking, except his face, for all the world like one of them on its
hind feet, to *Wa-em-boesh-kaa,* one of the Sandy lake chiefs, dressed
like a king Saul. I have got his likeness in a sitting posture, with
his calumet, and a pouch, and smoking. His head dress is made of
the feathers of the duck's breast, and the wood-peckers' bills, and the
red feathers from the head of that bird, between. His wrists are orna-
mented in like manner; and around his neck he wears an ornament
of horse hair."

Bands of Indians came from all the hinterland, as far away as
Leech Lake and Lac du Flambeau. They finally signed the treaty,
and the presents were distributed—clothes, jewelry, medals, flags,
knives, tobacco and food. For the Lake Superior bands the treaty
ratified the treaty of Prairie du Chien of the preceding year, at which
many of these bands could not be represented. Among other provisions, the treaty of Prairie du Chien made peace between the Sioux
and the Chippewa and arranged for a boundary line between them
to be run through parts of Wisconsin and Minnesota of today. The
Fond du Lac agreement contained one highly significant clause:

"The Chippewa tribe grant to the government of the United States the right to search for, and carry away, any metals or minerals from any part of their country."

The next and last American official expedition of consequence on Lake Superior was Schoolcraft's of 1832. He was about Lake Superior's south shore in the summer of 1831, in an effort to make peace between the Sioux and Chippewa, who were warring again. This trip evidently gave him the idea of advocating another expedition, which should proceed beyond the head of the lake and locate the true source of the Mississippi, still unknown at that time. Such an expedition was authorized by the War Department in 1832, and plans went forward at once for the trip. It left Sault Ste. Marie on June 7, 1832, and reached Fond du Lac on June 23. This time Schoolcraft struck inland to the Mississippi, found and named Lake Itasca as the source of the Father of Waters, and returned by way of Fort Snelling, up the St. Croix, and back along the south shore of Lake Superior. With him on this trip went William Thurston Boutwell, who became an Indian missionary at Fond du Lac a few years later; Dr. Douglass Houghton, who was the surgeon, botanist and geologist of the party, and whose later career in the Copper Country will be discussed in another chapter; and Lieutenant James Allen, commander of the military escort. Both Schoolcraft's and Allen's published accounts of the trip discuss the Lake Superior part of the journey; and Houghton's diary, though unpublished, is available. It gives a most worthwhile narrative of the great scientist's first trip on the lake which he brought to the attention of the industrial world and which, many years later, caused his death by drowning, thus depriving the world of much erudition.

Chapter 4

Pro Pelle Cutem *

If studious youth no longer crave,
  Their ancient appetites forgot,
Kingston and Ballantyne the brave,
  And Cooper of the wood and wave,
So be it also! And may I
  And all my pirates share the grave
Where these, and their creations lie.
    —Robert Louis Stevenson

After the amalgamation of the North West Company and the Hudson's Bay Company in 1821, the latter organization became a power on Lake Superior. In 1821 its deputy governor, Nicholas Garry, traveled from London to Hudson Bay via Lake Superior. His diary has been published, and reveals a very observant traveler, who has put down many minutiae of the life led by voyageurs and traders, and of the scenery through which he passed. He tells of his herculean voyageur, who because of six feet of stature was nicknamed "La petite Vierge" (the little maiden) by his comrades; of the tomb of Nanabazhoo on the north shore, before which his canoemen laid their offering of tobacco, just as the Indians were wont to do; of traveling a hundred miles a day in his canoe on the lake; and of the great joy with which he reached and later left Fort William.

Just a year earlier the Hudson's Bay Company's agent, George Simpson, who in all likelihood knew Lake Superior through more frequent travels on it than any other person, made his first trip along the north shore. He was to repeat that trip a score of times in the years from 1826 to 1850, and he touched at the Sault each year from 1853 to 1859. The first detailed biography of this extraordinary man

---

* This is the Hudson's Bay Company's motto, meaning "A skin for a skin."

is about to be published from his voluminous diaries and other papers in the archives of the Hudson's Bay Company in London.

Simpson did nothing halfheartedly. When he traveled over Lake Superior or elsewhere in the fur country, his canoes were the best, his voyageurs the finest, his trips the fastest, his food the most delicate. His energy was boundless, his capacity for judging men very keen, his willingness to endure the hardships of canoe travel seemingly unbounded. Many are the stories of this little man as he sped over portage path and across Lake Superior. One relates how a giant voyageur, goaded beyond human endurance by the imperious Little Emperor's urgings for more speed, seized him and "dunked" him in the lake. Other yarns strive to excel even Solomon's record for his offspring, born of alliances with dusky maidens at the many forts at which the Governor stopped on his trips.

Here is Sir George (he was knighted after his dramatic journey around the world in 1841) arriving at Fort William in the year 1854, as described by an eyewitness of the event, Henry John Moberly:

"As we drew near the mouth of the Kaministiquia River the old flag of the Hudson's Bay Company broke out, guns were fired and a crowd—gentlemen, Indians and halfbreeds—gathered on the wharf outside the pickets to welcome the Governor and the officers from Moose Factory, Albany and posts between that place and Sault Ste. Marie, who had joined us on our way up Lake Superior. As Sir George stepped ashore he turned to the head Iroquois guide and announced: 'At ten minutes past six o'clock we start'; adding to the chief factor in charge: 'Council meets at one o'clock. Just two and a half hours for feasting and talking; then to business.'

"Before the council began, however, we sat down to dinner. Rather, a banquet—one such as, I think, could scarcely be provided today at any price; smoked and salted buffalo tongues and bosses, moose noses and tongues, beaver tails from the wooded country, the choicest venison, wild ducks and geese, fresh trout and whitefish, and a lavish spread of delicacies from the old world, brought by the Governor himself. Sherry and old port wine, with champagne, were all the beverages allowed, discipline being very strict in those days. Each person knew his place at table. The Governor sat at the head;

next, ranging on each side, came the chief factors, then the clerks in order of their standing, the apprentice clerks from above and below the Sault, the post managers and the interpreters. . . . At one o'clock all the officers belonging to the district rose and entered the council room, but I remained in company with the men on their way east, one of whom had been in charge of the Peace River for a number of years and was retiring. The other two were going out on furlough. One had been in British Columbia, the other at Athakasca. I gathered much information from these men, besides hearing many racy yarns. At five o'clock the council rose. General conversation followed until five minutes after six, when Sir George shouted: 'All aboard!' At the wharf we found the Iroquois ready with the loaded canoes. Each man took his place and at exactly ten minutes past six we pushed out."

The Canadian artist, Paul Kane, accompanied Simpson on his trip of 1846 and has left not only an interesting account of what he saw and heard, but also graphic illustrations of the scenes and persons that appealed to him. Some of the pictures, done in oils, are preserved in the Royal Ontario Museum of Archaeology in Toronto, and some in oils, crayons and other media are in Ottawa.

The next year another young diarist passed up the lake with the Governor. This was Frederick Ulric Graham, scion of the family in Scotland that had sent Lord Preston as British minister extraordinary to the court of Louis XIV. Probably Frederick did not know that in the 1680's, when Radisson, the first recorded traveler on Lake Superior, was changing his allegiance from France to England for a second time, it was his forebear, Lord Preston, who effected the change. Young Graham passed up Lake Superior with Sir George Simpson, though not in his canoe. His diary, privately printed, tells of the trip:

"Sunday, May 23rd.—Roused by the call of 'Lève! Lève!' at three in the morning, after a comfortless night enough. Very calm morning. Arrived at Gros Cap to breakfast. Found Sir George Simpson's canoe awaiting him there. The canoes are wonderfully good sea boats. . . . Crossed two fine bays, and ran into Mishomeocoton

[Michipicoten] River, in a thunder plump; the banks very pretty—all forest, of course—but less of the eternal pine, and more hard wood. Arrived at the fort to breakfast with Mr. Swanston. Lots of trout, lake herrings, eggs, and bread; but no milk or fresh butter. ... Thursday, May 27th.—Windbound. Started about 11, wind still contrary. Governor ran into Pic Fort about four; and after crossing the bay we dined on a rock. ... Saturday, May 29th.—Off at 4 a m., hoping to reach Fort William late in the evening. A lovely day, and a very bonnie journey among thousands of wooded islands, through the channels of which we twisted about throughout the day. Screwed the men up with the 'filet,' and reached the long travers off Cap de Tonnerre [Thunder Cape] about sunset. ... However, we passed over very merrily, the crews of the three canoes (thanks to the filet) being very musically inclined, and singing 'Belle Rose' and 'La Noisette' in chorus, the whole way—

'Eh, qui est la belle Rose,
C'est le fils de l'héritant*
Belle Rose—Rose et Blanc'

to Fort William, where we camped outside the stockade at one in the morning."

Another visitor to the Fort William area in the late forties was the great scientist, Louis Agassiz, the account of whose trip in 1849 along the north shore from the Sault to Fort William was written by J. Elliot Cabot. He describes the fort itself thus:

"The name of Fort, applied to this post of the Hudson's Bay Company, dates from the old days of the Northwest Company, (to whom it formerly belonged,) and their quarrels with the Hudson's Bay. At that time the place was strong enough to induce Lord Selkirk, who came up with hostile intent, to take the trouble to bring with him a field-piece, which he planted on the opposite bank of the river, to make them open their doors. In those days a grand annual council of the company was held here, and we hear traditions of banquets, and crowds of clerks, and armies of hangers-on of all kinds. But all

---

* Graham's French leaves something to be desired.

this has now disappeared. The trade has fallen off, the gross receipts being now, they say, only about £600 per annum; and moreover the Northwest is merged in its old rival, and all those troubles at an end, so that although the court-yard is surrounded with a palisade, and there is a barbican gate-way, as at the Pic, yet these fortifications are not very formidable at present; the old blockhouse behind is falling to pieces, and the banqueting hall has probably been burnt up for firewood, at least, we saw nothing there that looked like it. Even the little flower-garden opening out of the stone-paved courtyard was overgrown with weeds. . . . The post is still an important one, as being the portal to the Red River country, Lake Winnipeg, and the northwest, and furnishes various supplies to other posts, among other things, of canoes, of which some seventy or eighty were lying here in store. It stands on the left bank of the northern mouth of the river Kaministiquia, about half a mile from the lake. Outside, close to the water, are the log-cabins of the canadians attached to the post, and on the plain across the river the birch-bark lodges of the Indian hunters. Mr. Mackenzie, the gentleman in charge, received us very kindly, and handed to us a number of letters and newspapers that had been forwarded hither from the Sault."

In the minutes of council of the Southern Department of the Hudson's Bay Company in London are the lists of appointments of the Lake Superior District and two posts, as well as the Sault Ste. Marie District and its posts, all for the period 1822-1863. Under the Lake Superior District were Michipicoten, Pic and Fort William; under the Sault Ste. Marie District were the Sault Ste. Marie Depot and Batchawana. The chief factor's post of the former district was usually Michipicoten; in 1833 it was at Fort William. The chief factor often had a chief trader or two, and sometimes a clerk, and even an interpreter is listed for 1837. Sault Ste. Marie District had headquarters at the Sault Ste. Marie post till 1851; thereafter it is called the Depot. The chief officer was usually a factor. The Batchawana post was a small establishment, as can be seen from the fact that a mere clerk, or even a man of lesser rank, a postmaster, was in charge. The Pic post was usually in the charge of a chief trader or clerk, but after 1851 it descended in rank, so that a postmaster directed its affairs thereafter until 1863, when a clerk took over once more.*

As Stevenson's verse at the beginning of this chapter hints, a favorite writer for boys during the last century was Robert Michael Ballantyne, a former Hudson's Bay Company apprentice. His *Hudson's Bay: or Everyday Life in the Wilds of North America* was published in 1848 after he had finished seven years with the company and had returned to his home in Edinburgh. It is an account of his own experiences and observations at several posts and on an extensive canoe trip from Fort William to the Sault. Its literary merits were perceived by a well-known publisher of the day, who suggested that Ballantyne take up literature as a profession. *The Young Fur Traders,* his first novel, came out in 1855, and was followed by *Ungava,* also a story based on life in a company post. His later novels, some eighty in all, were based on other topics than the fur trade, but it is unlikely that he would ever have suspected his own genius except for the writing of the first three books.

---

* This information based on a list of the names of incumbents at the several posts has been kindly supplied by the Hudson's Bay Company and is cited by permission of the Governor and Committee.

Chapter 5

Carriers of the Cross

Fulfilled is now what David told
In true prophetic song of old,
How God the heathen's King should be;
For God is reigning from the Tree.
—Vexilla Regis

MEN of iron nerve and love of adventure were required for life on the great upper lake even as late as the twentieth century. How much more, then, in the seventeenth, eighteenth and early nineteenth centuries, when missionaries played a leading role! The men who carried the Gospel and civilization to the natives were of those mental and moral proportions that one associates with hazardous frontiers. Several of them would have made their mark in whatever calling they might have taken up: Allouez, Marquette, Bishop Frederic Baraga, Franz Pierz, Sherman Hall, William Thurston Boutwell, James Evans and many others.

The story of Fathers Allouez and Marquette has already been told so far as it touches Lake Superior. Little is known of the experiences of two or three other priests of the French period, who passed through and beyond Lake Superior on their way to the West. Then followed nearly three-quarters of a century when no missionaries reached Lake Superior, as far as available records show. The broken threads were taken up again in 1816, when Father Pierre Antoine Tabeau was sent by the Catholic bishop of Quebec to lay the foundations of missions on Lake Superior and beyond in the Red River settlements, where Winnipeg and St. Boniface now stand.

Unfortunately Tabeau sided with the North West Company in the bitter feud then raging between that company and the Hudson's Bay Company for the control of the Red River country. Consequently his mission was a failure, though apparently he did get as far as Rainy Lake. Whatever he accomplished at Fort William or elsewhere on Lake Superior was of little consequence, however, and the work had to be done over again two years later. Then he and Father Joseph Crevier journeyed to Fort William by birch-bark canoe, Tabeau starting from Quebec and Crevier from Detroit. In the same flotilla of canoes, which left Montreal in May 1818, went Father Joseph Norbert Provencher—soon to be Bishop Provencher of the Red River Valley—with his chief assistant in the Indian missions, Sévère Joseph N. Dumoulin. At the Sault, Tabeau and Crevier carried on a mission for several days before leaving for Fort William in the North West Company's schooner. The rest of the mission party traveled by canoe along the north shore to Fort William, where they arrived before the schooner. Thus they were the first to say Mass at Fort William.

Provencher and his party went on almost at once to the Red River country, where he was to remain for the rest of a long and useful life. He made the trip to Quebec and back a few years later, reaching Fort William on the return trip in July 1822. From that place he wrote to his superior that he had "baptized seventy-seven children en route . . . twenty-three at Drummond Island, forty-one at the Sault, twelve at Fort William, and one at the Pic." Dumoulin remained at the Red River colony until 1823, accomplishing much with the Indians. Then he returned to Canada, stopping en route at the Sault, where he reported spiritual affairs at low ebb. He never returned to the West.

Tabeau and Crevier continued their ministrations about Lake Superior for two more years, Tabeau making the trip in 1819, Crevier in 1820. Wood was cut for chapels at both Fort William and the Sault, but no building seems to have resulted. The promising beginning ended once more in failure, when the two companies united in 1821 to form the new Hudson's Bay Company. Tabeau's zeal had been wholly for the North West Company's missions, and apparently he took no further interest after the company passed out of existence. There were no more missions on Lake Superior for several years.

In 1830 a Protestant board of missions with headquarters in Boston, the American Board of Commissioners for Foreign Missions, turned its attention to the Chippewa Indians on Lake Superior and established a mission station at La Pointe. Its head from 1831 to 1853 was Sherman Hall of New Hampshire. He and his wife remained there until the Indians gave up their claim to the land of the region and many of them were moved to areas beyond Lake Superior. While Hall was at La Pointe he was in charge of an area containing several lesser stations on the lake or in the interior: Leech Lake, Fond du Lac, Pokegama, Yellow Lake and possibly others. To his mission therefore came many of his confreres from time to time: Boutwell from Leech Lake and Pokegama, Edmund F. Ely from Sandy Lake and Fond du Lac, Frederick Ayer and his wife, Elizabeth, from Yellow Lake and Pokegama, and several others. The diaries and letters of these individuals are replete with data about the Indians, fur trade and natural conditions of Lake Superior and its immediate hinterland. The La Pointe Mission was also a way station for travelers other than missionaries. Men like Henry R. Schoolcraft of the Federal Indian service, Dr. Charles Borup of the American Fur Company, his associate, Lyman Warren, and his chief, Ramsay Crooks, were constantly coming and going.

A school was kept for Indians and half-breeds. Translations were made for the Indians and printed—some of the first books to appear in the Chippewa language. Hall was a conscientious man, but his New England reserve probably prevented him from being completely effective as a civilizing agency with the natives. He was a good cabinetmaker and carpenter, and for the student of today some of his finest contributions are his letters and articles describing local architecture, particularly the voyageur type of domestic dwelling and chimney construction.

While Hall was at La Pointe, three Catholic missionaries came to work in his vicinity. These were Frederic Baraga, Franz Pierz and Otto Skolla. They were all Slovenians, from the Austrian province of Carniola. Baraga was a man of education and wealth from the lesser nobility. He was born in 1797, educated under private tutors at

Laibach and at the Royal Gymnasium, trained to speak German, French and other languages besides his native Slovenic, matriculated in the law department of the University of Vienna from which he graduated in 1821, and admitted to Holy Orders at the Seminary of Laibach in 1823. After pastoral duty in his native state he decided to go as a missionary to the North American Indians and in 1830 received permission to enter the diocese of Bishop Edward Fenwick of Cincinnati. He arrived in New York late that year, studied English and Indian during the winter at Cincinnati, and departed in the spring for his Indian mission among the Ottawa at L'Arbre Croche, near Harbor Springs, Michigan. There and at Grand River he spent the next five years among the natives, teaching, learning the language and converting such as would heed him. In the summer of 1835 he went to the field that was to be his for the next thirty years and more, Lake Superior.

For the first nine years he was stationed at La Pointe, already a settlement of respectable age as places go on the North American continent. As we have seen, it had been white men's abode as early as 1660 and had been "home" to Indians for unknown years before that time. Hall was already there—probably that was the reason Baraga also chose it as his residence. It was likewise by this time the center of the fur trade and fishing industry of the American Fur Company. From it Baraga traveled in all directions, but especially to Fond du Lac at the mouth of the St. Louis River at the extreme end of the lake, to Grand Portage to the northeast, and to L'Anse, or Keweenaw Point, to the east. He built the church of St. Joseph at La Pointe but found within a year that he must enlarge it. To get funds and assistants he traveled back to Austria late in 1836, secured the necessary funds, and returned to his post late in 1837. The church was enlarged the following year and embellished with eighteen oil paintings which he had brought from Europe. Over the altar hung a painting by Lange of Laibach representing the Holy Family in the carpenter shop of St. Joseph. "It is especially fitting for an Indian mission, because the Indians are naturally indolent. Missionaries are often compelled to animate them to work," wrote Baraga at the time. Later, in 1841, the church was again enlarged.

Baraga was a man of great physical vitality and enjoyed to the full his arduous missionary trips about Lake Superior. In summer they were made, when possible, on the American Fur Company's schooner, the *John Jacob Astor,* which had been launched in 1835; but often he could reach his destination only by birch-bark canoe paddled by Indians or half-breeds. Canoeing on Lake Superior is hazardous at best and not infrequently the missionary was in extreme danger. One such trip accounts for the naming of a picturesque stream on the north shore. Today the motorist pauses long on the arched concrete bridge midway between steep falls in Cross River to admire the fury of the coffee-colored water and white foam, or to peer down into the gorge of the river below the falls. Beyond the bridge he notices a sign pointing him to a short side road. If he enters and explores down to the shore, he finds the origin of the stream's name. At the mouth of the stream is a beautiful stone cross, the successor of many wooden ones that have stood there since Baraga erected the first one in 1846 in thankful recognition of his deliverance from the dangers of a great storm that had come up suddenly in making the long *traverse* from La Pointe.

In winter Baraga traveled by snowshoe or dog team. Naturally he was less active in his mission journeys when snow covered the land and ice filled in all the bays of the great lake. Then he turned to his letters to European friends and others, to his general writing, to his translating of the Bible and other religious works for his converts, and to the preparation of a Chippewa grammar and dictionary. He had a felicitous style and was widely read in Europe. He wrote equally well in French or German. Scores of his letters were printed in the reports of a missionary society in Austria, the Leopoldine Foundation; others appeared in the organ of a similar French organization, the Society for the Propagation of the Faith. Many more unprinted ones have been secured in recent years from monasteries, convents and homes of relatives and friends in his native land. His enthusiasm and unworldly interest in the Indians of Lake Superior brought funds again and again to support his work and to induce other priests to join him. Thus came Franz Pierz in 1838 to Grand Portage and Otto Skolla in 1845 to La Pointe to help him; and others came later.

In 1843 Baraga began building a log church at L'Anse, on Keweenaw Bay. The following year he transferred his residence from La Pointe to this new station, retaining general jurisdiction over the Lake Superior missions that he had established at La Pointe, Fond du Lac and Grand Portage, but entrusting the actual missionary labors of these three areas to the new missionary, Otto Skolla. Pierz, to his own and Baraga's sorrow, had been transferred from his beloved Grand Portage to the scene of his original work at L'Arbre Croche.

The south shore was suddenly the scene of great activity. Copper and then iron had been discovered near L'Anse, and white men and their families were arriving in numbers. Settlements sprang up overnight. Early in 1847 Baraga visited the mines. "I was dumbfounded at the fast spreading of civilization on these shores of Lake Superior. I found in many places neat houses with nice, carpeted rooms. In one house there was even a piano on which a young American woman played very skillfully." Many of the miners were Irish and German Catholics. There was nothing for Baraga to do but attend to their spiritual needs as well as to those of his red children. Increasingly as the years passed the whites encroached on the time formerly devoted by Baraga to the natives. His main interest was ever in the Indians and as one reads his prolific letters and diaries he cannot avoid the feeling that Baraga was torn between his duty to his white parishioners and his desire to work for his red children only. Perhaps this accounts for the stiffening of the lines about his mouth and the hardening of his bearing as he went into later life. Though he began his missionary career as a much more gracious and polished man than Sherman Hall, he reminds one of the New Englander when he ended it. Something of the sternness of Lake Superior in her rugged moods had entered his soul.

Yet his life at L'Anse was always a pleasure for him to recall in later years. He built a church there, traveled often to La Pointe, Fond du Lac and Grand Portage, continued his writing and publishing, entertained visiting bishops occasionally and prepared his famous Ojibwa dictionary for the press. In 1835 he was consecrated titular bishop of Amyzonia and Vicar Apostolic for Upper Michigan and prepared to change his abode to Sault Ste. Marie. He held his first

Pontifical High Mass at the Sault on September 12, 1854, upon his return from a trip to Europe that had consumed the better part of a year. Thereafter his diaries give us in detail the comings and goings of this extraordinarily active man. It makes one breathless to follow him—from the Sault by boat to Mackinac to establish a church, to Point St. Ignace with a new priest to see him settled, from writing the *Kagige Debwewinan* (Eternal Truths) at the Sault to translating the Catechism into English for the use of schools, by sleigh to Isle de Bois Blanc, to Detroit by steamboat, back to Mackinac, thence to Little Traverse, to L'Arbre Croche, to the Sault by propeller, on the steamer *Illinois* to Marquette, to L'Anse, Eagle Harbor and La Pointe by steamboat *North Star,* by dog sled to Bellanger, by small boat to Traverse City, to the mines, on the *Manhattan* to Eagle Harbor, and on and on, year after year. His diary reveals the growth of the settlements about the lake. Steamboats and propellers became common, and as one reads, one becomes attached to this and that vessel just as Baraga did—to the vessels already mentioned and the *Northern Light,* the *Superior* before it was wrecked, the *Iron City,* the *Lady Elgin,* which foundered with three hundred on board, the propeller *Montgomery,* the steamer *Princess,* the *Mineral Rock,* and many more.

In 1857 he was made a full bishop, the first bishop of Sault Ste. Marie. His beloved Indians were fading fast into the background; work must go on among the miners and fishermen and in the numerous little towns growing up so fast on the south shore: Superior, Maple Grove, Minnesota Mine, Rockland, Ontonagon, Bad River, La Pointe, Bayfield, Cliff, Eagle Harbor, Hancock, Portage Lake, Houghton and Marquette. Schools must be established, pastors and teachers must be found, convents must be established, disputes must be settled, and his own parish church must have himself as pastor when, as frequently happened, he lost some young priest who could not stand what he himself had to endure. It is hardly to be wondered that he became ill and finally succumbed. But first his see was transferred to Marquette in 1866. When he had first landed on Lake Superior's shores, the Sault seemed the important place because all transportation had to pass through it. Times changed. Mines were opened and railroads and highways were constructed. The Sault was isolated in winter when ice stopped lake transportation. But railroads and highways operated winter and summer at Marquette. Some urged him to change to Hancock. Characteristically he replied, joking about the name of his see as it would appear in official Latin, "I choose Marquette, first because of the name; *Marquettensis* is more proper than *Hancockensis*. Hancock was a heretic or perhaps an infidel; Père Marquette was a saintly missionary." He did not have long to work in his new home, for he died on January 19, 1868. For much of Europe he had made Lake Superior known through his writings, just as two centuries earlier Allouez and other Jesuits had made most of the civilized world aware of the Great Upper Lake.

The man who most resembled modern travelers in his reaction to Lake Superior was a Wesleyan missionary from Canada, James Evans by name. Late in 1838 he left the Sault to go by canoe to trading posts on the northeast side of the lake. His unpublished diary is good reading. The first night out "we encamped ... by moonlight on a small island. On awaking in the morning we had only to look under our blankets & eat whortleberries [blueberries] the ground being blue with them. Sun sinking in Sup[erior] fine moon mountains & limpid waters."

Fancy a missionary of the year 1838 who could give himself to the spirit of the lake sufficiently to write the following:

"Started early in order to breakfast with Nanaboozhoo, who sits here in the north, but unfortunately not being acquainted with his deityship we passed him by without the pleasure of a smoke with him, a custom existing with Indians from time immemorial & continued by the voyagers to the present day. I must say I felt great disappointment when I discovered that we had with a fine stiff breeze passed him by beyond the possibility of return, for I had been led to believe that Nanaboozhoo, was nothing more than a mere being of fancy painted on the canvas of the pagans imagination and although I had frequently been told that he sat in the north up Lake Superior, I must acknowledge I was so atheistic in my principles that I still denied his very existence. judge how great is my surprize & confusion when I find that he does actually exist in propria persona, that he is here, can be seen & felt that he has remained on his rocky throne seated in majesty until the cedars have rooted in & grown on his head, that the waters of the Superior obediently wash his feet, immovably fixed on the rock. Nanaboozhoo is a large fragment of rock, which bears some resemblance to the human form. whether divine honors were ever paid to Him as some have imagined is a matter of doubt as the indians beli[e]ve that Nanaboozhoo has existed as an indian & never speak of him otherwise than as such, and I believe that many of the pagans to the south & east when they speak of Nanaboozhoo sitting in the north have no knowledge that the tradition which they have learned is founded in truth as far only as regards this huge rock but believe that the great ancient Indian deity does really make the North of Lake Sup[erior] the place of his residence."

Longfellow had not yet written his great poem on Nanabazhoo when Evans penned these lines. What a pity the poet substituted another name for the one he first chose! Nanabazhoo is known east, north, south and west of Lake Superior; Hiawatha is a minor Iroquois substitute.

After reaching the post at Michipicoten Bay and staying there a short time, Evans decided that he must go to the Sault to get permission from the Indian chief to establish his mission on the north shore. So, late in October, when Lake Superior is always in her most tempestuous moods, he started back in a fifteen-foot canoe with two Indian lads. Ice was already forming on the lake and clogged their canoe constantly. Even the discomforts of tenting in the open in such weather could not dim Evans' appreciation of the sublime in Nature. His diary records for that night:

"Camped last night in a little bay, into which we entered among loose rocks, and shot two ducks. We made a good fire spread down some branches eat our suppers & camped without any cover save the sky which was beautifully clear & a full moon shining in all her northern lustre, while the Aurora Borealis threw up brilliant corruscation from the Northern horizon forming a beautiful combination at the Zenith. slept well after commending ourselves to God."

All was not beauty on that great expanse of water, however, as Evans found the next day.

"We have had a fearful day. . . . About an hour 1/2 after the wind came directly off the lake and as we had rounded a point where we could not weather by turning back we down sail & plied our oars, making but very slow progress against a tremendous swell & a strong south west wind. several times we neared the shore to attempt a landing but the fearful surf gave us full assurance that the shore was unapproachable, and we were obliged to pull on. . . . The sun set in a clear sky, and sunk beautifully as he appeared to us who rode on the heaving billows to dip in every wave. In a few minutes after his disappearance, the wind rose with redoubled fury the heavens were covered with flying scud and the darkness closed finding us in spite of every effort four miles from our intended landing, we again approached the shore but rugged rocks & a tremendous roar dared us to approach & we pulled out and onward. Our oars & paddles were now coated with ice . . . but he who said 'peace be still' watched over our lives & about ten oclock the moon which was nearly full peeped out and showed us the channel between the island & the main shore. We pul[l]ed in and found an excellent harbour erected our tent where with a good fire at my feet after a tin of hot tea & some corn soup, I am in gratitude to God accounting his mercies, & almost forgetting past afflictions."

After reaching the Sault and accomplishing his business he again headed for Michipicoten, much too late in the season for any reasonable person to be on Lake Superior in a bark canoe. Again and again they nearly perished. One evening he records in his diary:

"The day has been severly cold—our paddles & oars & canoe coated with ice, and when we landed our clothes & our loading were nearly an inch thick with ice, nor could we erect our tent until it had lain nearly an hour before the fire, but its all over, thanks to God we are now warm on the fire side, and by changing sides can keep comfortable."

He had a "good night rest in wet & icy blankets, which I found stiff enough to stand alone," and then tried to push on, only to be obliged to stay windbound in camp.

"We are baricaded with our canoe & evergreen tops, and upon the whole tolerably comfortable. it has snowed all night and there is about 8 inches. . . . the roar of the lake, Soaring eagle howling wind & . . . crackling fire & Indian language with many accompanyments tell me I am far from home."

The next day was the worst yet. They started out, only to meet such seas as even their navigating skills could not master. Again and again great waves broke over the canoe, necessitating constant bailing by both Indians, who, naturally, were terrified.

"At last I turned to run for shore & risk all in running through the breakers before the wind, but providentially at this moment the wind favoured us a little & we weathered a point & with the wind right aft run for a little bay which afforded shelter from the swell & wind. . . . but as we wanted to square our sail we found it impossible being frozen stiff, and fast to the canoe, nor could I change my stearing paddle over as my right hand near the water was so fast frozen in my mitten & my mitten to the paddle in one solid ball of ice that I could not remove it, & we had to cut the halliards of the sail as the knot could never be loosed being enshrined in ice. twice the wind took us aback & threw our stiff blanket up against the mast before we could secure it. And in rounding the point we had to run over a reef of rocks where the heavy swells broke in angry surf but the wind being right aft we ran along the foaming tops without any danger, which would have swallowed us up in a moment had we not been before a gale of wind. . . . God be thanked I am here yet to labour on Lake Sup. but my future sailing will I think be earlier in the season or not at all."

Even the diary suffered in the last days' miseries and some of it is illegible. However, enough can be read to learn that they were reduced to almost no food at all. "I have now but one biscuit & the ham bone well picked remaining, & my boys have shaken the flour bag this morning & have only two small fish & six or seven small potatoes frozen as hard as stones. We are now embarking. May the Lord preserve us!" Suddenly the boy in the bow cried out in fear, "Oh, the wind is coming. Oh too much. Alas. We shall be lost. Its all in vain. alls over now." Evans says that he "endeavored to quiet the poor boy's fears."

"Looking back, I saw the lake at a little distance foaming on every wave and the blackend surface contrasted with the white surge truly looked frightful. for a moment I felt my knees tremble, but instantly looked up to God, and felt my mind calm, and a confidence in his protection. The Indian boy urged hard to let down the sail, but I still kept the halliards fast, knowing that under Divine defence our lives depended on keeping the canoe under strong headway. and surely in a few minutes she has headway enough particularly when on the top of the sea. . . . the boy in the centre kept bailing, & the other poor fellow laid his face in his hands in the bow of the canoe, as he has since told me, that he might not see himself drowned. . . . our little bark trembling on the surf ran as if partaking in our fears & our anxiety to reach the bay about half a mile ahead."

They finally reached shore and started on foot to cover the remainder of the way "in two feet of snow, having no snow shoes & being very wet . . . occasionally . . . with the handle of the tomahawk knocking off the ice, which fast accumulated on our feet & ancles. This day I ate nothing from an hour before day until I sat down in the evening at the hospitable board of my kind friend Mr. Cameron"— the Hudson's Bay Company officer at the post at Michipicoten.

Evans' missionary life was just beginning. Soon he passed beyond Lake Superior to the northeastern end of Lake Winnipeg. There he worked for a number of years among the Cree Indians; and many are the stories still current in that region about the man who reduced the Cree language to writing. He also had the hardihood and vision to go out, seemingly the first missionary ever to venture so far, into the Athabaska country. He had the misfortune, however, to kill his beloved native assistant by the accidental discharge of his gun. Indians did not allow for accidents in their elemental system of justice, and so Evans had to leave his field. He died shortly afterward in London.

The roll of missionaries on Lake Superior is a long one and cannot be called here. Among their many services rendered to their own generation, but more especially to posterity, is the recording of what they saw and heard on the great lake. Fur traders were usually men of action, whose hands stiffened when they took up the unaccustomed pen in place of the familiar pack. Accordingly, only rarely does one of them make Lake Superior's scenery, natives and general life real to us after the lapse of generations. Not so the missionary's (and his wife's!) accounts in letters, diaries and religious publications. Fortunately, the literary remains of these devoted explorers are enormous. In London, Boston, New York and Chicago alone there are literally thousands of them. The diary of Jeremiah Porter at the Sault and his letters to the American Home Missionary Society have been preserved. To a greater or less extent the same may be said of Hall at La Pointe; James Peet at Superior, Bayfield and Oneota (now a part of Duluth); John H. Pitezel and his assistants all along the south shore; Pierz at Grand Portage, Michipicoten and Okwanokisinong on the north shore; Skolla at La Pointe, Duluth and Grand Portage; Evans along the Canadian shore, and his associates, William Mason at Rainy Lake and Thomas Hurlburt at Fort William; Abel Bingham and William MacMurray at the Sault; the native missionaries, Peter Marksman, George Copway, Peter Jacobs and others at various places on the lake; the Jesuits Pierre Choné (Chonné), August Kohler, M. S. V. Hanipaux, Nicholas M. J. Fremiot and Dominic Duranquet, at the Fort William mission; Edmund F. Ely and Samuel Spates at Fond du Lac; and many more. Of all these much could be written because most of them were articulate. Because the records of two of them, Peet and Pitezel, are especially good for telling the story of Lake Superior, let us examine them briefly.

One of the first home missionaries on Lake Superior was James Peet, a Methodist missionary from western New York state. In 1856 he was ordered by his conference from Stillwater on the St. Croix River to the brand-new town of Superior at the head of Lake Superior. He and his wife went by trail, in a sleigh, through the vast pine forests of western Wisconsin, already beginning to resound to the cries of "Timber!" as the great red and white pines toppled and crashed. A few years later this trail was cut out as a military road by the United States Government, but it was barely passable in 1856, and then only in winter. Indeed, Mrs. Peet just escaped serious injury when her sleigh stuck between two trees, one of which had to be chopped down to release her.

As the reader goes on and on through Peet's diaries, kept meticulously day after day in little pocket journals, or through his letters printed in the *Western Christian Advocate,* the *Christian Advocate* and elsewhere, he becomes a part of a movement at once typical and unique. The frontier of settlement reached lower Lake Superior in the forties, and the end of the lake in the fifties. (It was to be many years before Minnesota's north shore would be settled, except at Two Harbors, Beaver Bay and Grand Marais.) Like other American and Canadian frontiers, this one of Peet's, Pitezel's, Baraga's, and Ely's witnessed the arrival first of a few hardy souls and then the arrival and mixing of many nationalities; the development of many kinds of transportation; the dispersion of the red men; the quick growth of towns; the rawness of many phases of life while others were curiously conventional and even sophisticated; and the awareness, on the pioneers' part, of the role that they themselves were playing in the great drama of the conquest of a continent.

The uniqueness of Lake Superior's frontier in the years just before the Civil War may be ascribed primarily to the great lake itself. It was the easy means of getting to a place, of communicating with the rest of the world, of getting a large part of one's sustenance and of providing one's employment. The shores of the other Great Lakes had been settled—along the fringes—in the days before steamboats, or even sailboats, were common. These craft appeared on Lake Superior in considerable numbers just as the first settlements were made. From the start, therefore, there were ample means of transportation between April and December; but for the five winter months these settlements were as completely isolated from the rest of the world as Boonesborough in the 1780's or Ablavik in 1930. Food must be stored in the autumn for a long and cold winter, when the snow would stand several feet deep on the level. Whatever traveling occurred was performed by sleigh, snowshoes, dog team, or horse *travois.* Any communication with the outside world came by messenger by one of these modes of travel. The community had to be completely self-reliant. It had to supply its own teachers, doctors, midwives, nurses, undertakers and pastors. Whatever amusement the inhabitants had, they had to furnish for themselves.

Then, when the April sun opened the Straits of Mackinac, cleared St. Marys River, unblocked the bays and approaches to the Sault—then came a happy day when the first schooner or steamboat or propeller was sighted. Prices for food and necessities, which had been fantastic the preceding day, dropped to normal by nightfall. Everyone knew which vessel had arrived, who was her captain, what news she bore from below, who had arrived, who was departing and what one could buy.

All of these facets of life on Lake Superior are turned to the reader in succession as he pores over James Peet's diaries. Thus he reads of the arrival and departure of every vessel and usually of her class: the *Iron City,* the *North Star,* the *Lady Elgin,* the *Illinois,* the *Manhattan,* the *Ocean,* the *City of Superior,* the *Michigan*—all arrivals in 1857 at Superior. Most of them appear again and again in Peet's daily entries. Early in the navigation period of 1858 the *Northern Light* appears on her maiden trip. In 1859 the United States revenue cutter arrives. The *Coaster* is wrecked that year, as was the *City of Superior* in 1858 and the *Lady Elgin* in 1860. A vessel of the Federal coast survey, the *Search,* came also that year. The steamer *Seneca* is also mentioned for the first time. The large schooner, *E. C. Roberts,* of "over 450 Tons burthen" has a special reference in the diary. The schooner *J. W. Sargent* is a new arrival. In 1860, when Peet left the lake, he mentions the schooners *Ford* and *J. Fretter,* the scow schooner, *Neptune,* and the propellers *Ogontz* and *Ontonagon.*

Other modes of transportation are also touched upon by Peet in his diary. He himself, of course, had his own boat, in which he delighted to travel as far upriver as Fond du Lac, and, during his stay in Bayfield, to the Odanah mission of the Indian reservation on Bad River. Then there was a small steamer designed for use only in the magnificent harbor at the mouth of the St. Louis River. There were the sleighs on the bay, as well as the skating, which occurred on Sunday and on other days and so disturbed the peace of the good dominie's mind. On January 23, 1858, he mentions in his diary that the mail from St. Paul had just arrived by dog team at Bayfield. On February 20, 1859, he records that he came back from his lecture at the Odanah lyceum on "a one horse 'Traino.'" On April 15, 1859, he worries about the nonarrival of the mail carrier [from St. Paul via the Bayfield trail]: "He is some 5 days behind time." In June 1943 the last of the mail carriers on that trail, Antoine Gordon, or Gaudin, died, a year after having given the author a graphic account of his duties and experiences while tramping the lonesome way from Gordon to Bayfield during the years from 1864 till the end of the trail's existence. That came when the first railroad entered the region in the middle eighties. An entry in Peet's diary describing a winter jaunt up the St. Louis River mentions still another method of transportation:

"A little before noon I started with Mr. Ely for the Chipewa Indian agency on the St. Louis river Indian Reservation. Only one Settler living the whole distance we 'Camped out' of course on the ground. . . . slow travelling with our 3 ox teem through the unbeaten snow . . . 15 or 16 inches deep."

As for frontier customs, joys, tragedies and commonplaces—the diary is full of them. A few quotations will serve to give a thumbnail sketch of life between Bad River and Duluth about 1860. On December 5, 1857, Peet mentions in his diary at Bayfield: "I counted 17 fishing boats on the Bay this morning." Next day he counted twenty-three. "They are getting very good hauls I understand." On December 14 the number had increased to twenty-nine and the explanation is given in a subsequent remark, namely, that the weather was very warm. In 1860, at the mouth of the St. Louis River, he tells how "They are catching vast quantities of the 'wall eyed Pike' with a sein." The next day, April 19, he helps "haul in sein with 523 good fishes." A few days later he makes the following entry: "Mr. Harringtons party have caught over 15000 fish Br Barlow's party abt 30 barrells—he says 90 fish make a barrel."

Other entries that tell of that all-important part of human existence, eating, are the one in 1857 that reads, "Bears are very numerous in the woods on this part of Lake Superior now," and the one at

Oneota of November 7, 1859: "Brother Merritt butchered a hog this morning which I suppose is the first Pork that has ever been fatted and killed in this town & perhaps on the North Shore." Still other entries mention that geese and wild ducks are plentiful and that his neighbor shot two moose.

Items of housekeeping interest are these: (June 15, 1859) "We got 6 bundles of Straw to fill two beds for $.20 the first Straw we have slept on since coming on Lake Superior, having used pine shavings as a substitute"; (November 7, 1858) "Making a trundle bed"; (July 2, 1859) "Lent br. Merritt 25 3/4 lbs Flour"; (January 4, 1860) "A Swede came to saw my wood for me for 50 cts per day & board."

As for the natives, who were omnipresent, here are a few references to those who assembled, some two thousand strong, at the payment at Bad River: "22 Bands of Inds are paid at Bad River this year"; "Mr. Drew the Indian agent informs me that there are about 12,000 Chipewas Indians in·the vicinity of Lake Superior 5,000 of whom are under his jurisdiction—about 1,200 are supposed to be living on Bad River Reservation." He records the hieroglyphics "carved" at Bad River on a "high sandy rock." New Year's day found the Indians arriving at all homes for their accustomed New Year's gifts. Long association with Canadian voyageurs had taught them the French emphasis on *le jour de l'an* till it, like the customary Indian greeting throughout North America, even to this day, a corruption of *bon jour,* seemed actually a native custom. Learned from early explorers and voyageurs, the terms became part of the Chippewa vocabulary. Early in the spring of 1858 Peet records that the half-breeds of his congregation are going thirty to forty miles to Bad River to make maple sugar. On February 27, 1859, the entry in his diary reads, "Nearly all the La-Point people of my Congregation leave this week for the woods to make Sugar."

The diary is replete with entries about social usages and customs. From the very start the people of Bayfield held annual celebrations of the founding of their community. Thus in 1858 the entry is, that as this is the second anniversary of the first settlement of Bayfield, a celebration is being held in the shape of a picnic dinner and dance. The next year on March 23 he writes, "The larger scholars staid home to cook for the morrow, which is the 3rd Anniversary of the settlement of this Town." He points up that remark with the following one on March 26: "There are in the Town site of Bayfield 42 adult males—28 adult females 19 male children—26 female children—115 total population, & 45 more persons living on farms just out of town." A large part of the population, according to him, was of German origin. Later, in Oneota, to which he went in 1859, he has much to tell of the Scandinavians in the community. Thus on August 3, 1859, he distributes *Missionary Advocates* and Swedish and Danish tracts and catechisms. "I sold an Eng. & Sweed Testament to Mr. Swanstrom" is the entry for January 4, 1860. On March 18 of the same year he is in distress over the reaction of "Bro Larson a Sweed" of his congregation to Peet's text, "Be not conformed to this world." "He took it as a personal rebuke publicly given for his having taken counsel with the wicked which I knew nothing about till he acknowledged it to me." He also mentions quite a number of German families in Oneota. Perhaps the most interesting reference to the Scandinavian part of the community is found in the entry for June 4, 1860: "Br Larson came in from his work on the Military road for a day or two. Whenever I call to see his Mother (a Swede woman) she always kisses the back of my hand & bows very low." Old-country respect for the cloth was a matter of astonishment to Peet.

Peet's published articles in 1856 tell of Superior as a town of three years' growth, with the primeval forest still standing in some of the streets, mentions its fine harbor, and recounts the plan for the immediate construction of a railroad to St. Paul. He also tells of La Pointe as an establishment of great age, where the American Fur Company's former buildings could still be seen, curious in their architecture and with door and window casings still trimmed with purple or slate color in contrast to the whitewashing of the buildings themselves. He describes Bayfield, where "a great effort is being made to found a large city, which is to be the terminus of a projected railroad from the Upper Mississippi country," to which "a wagon road has been cut, some fifty or eighty miles through the woods, to the St. Croix river, this season, and will be passable for teams in the winter through to St. Paul in Minnesota"; and he mentions Ashland, where "we ... found a few houses and a few tents on the shore, which, as we soon learned, belonged to Rev. Mr. Wheeler, the Indian Missionary, and a party who had accompanied him some fifteen miles from the mission, to celebrate the *Fourth* with the few citizens of the new town."

Nor does he neglect the story of what was happening on the north shore of Lake Superior. On August 20, 1856, he wrote an article to the "Editors of the 'Chronicle'" entitled "North Shore of Lake Superior." It shows in an admirable way how the frontier was extended into that area by settlers.

Pitezel was another home missionary, though his activities on Lake Superior began in 1843 among the Indians. His post at first was at Sault Ste. Marie, but in 1844 he was sent to the Methodist mission at the bottom of Keweenaw Bay, opposite Baraga's new post. Here he remained for some time. His accounts of trips along the south shore and inland along a famous canoe trail to the Sandy Lake mission on the upper Mississippi are fascinating to those who would see Lake Superior and the adjacent country in all their pristine glory. Yet Pitezel never understood Indians, except converted ones, and so his writings on that head are not reliable. For example, he attended a notable Indian payment at La Pointe in 1844 and describes the natives as "ignorant, morally polluted, and debased to the level of the brute. Their insolent pride gave the finishing stroke to their morally depraved condition. They were much addicted to gambling—some of them would part with all they had, in their strife to win the game. All that was wanting to complete their wretchedness was, to let them have whisky, which fortunately, at this payment, by untiring vigilance, was kept from them. In looking at our Christian Indians, by the side of those, I wanted no further proof of the power of the Gospel to elevate the red man."

With such an outlook, it is not strange that Pitezel soon found himself working with white men. Copper was discovered at the Cliff mine on Keweenaw Point in the middle forties and heralded the influx of many miners, operators, speculators, prospectors and the usual hangers-on. Pitezel made his first mission trip among the miners in 1847. He traveled over Keweenaw Point to nearly all the locations, making, as he wrote of this trip, "about one hundred and ninety miles—fifty-five by water, and the rest by land." Very soon the Conference ordered Pitezel to leave the Indian mission at the bottom of the bay and take up his work among the miners at Eagle River. His description of them, their work and the depths of the mines in which they labored is worth reading.

He also gives some idea of the bustle and hum of life on Lake Superior during the navigating season. On one occasion he describes what he saw on board one of the many vessels that he took to carry him on his circuit:

"Among the passengers was Mr. Richmond, the Indian Agent, and his brother, on their way to La Pointe to make the Indian payment. Here was Mr. Ramsay Crooks, a noble-looking man, who figures largely in Irving's 'Astoria.' After all his perils in and beyond the Rocky Mountains, he appeared to possess the vigor and sprightliness of youth. On board were the editor of the Lake Superior News and lady, and numerous others bound for La Pointe; also brother K. and wife on their way to the Ontonagon, with Mr. S., pale and blanched with the ague. It had given him a cruel shaking on the lakes. Here was also Mrs. L. Hanna, wife of the Agent of the Cliff Mine, with her three little children, going to meet her husband after a long separation."

Pitezel may or may not have known that Ramsay Crooks was much at home on Lake Superior, having been John Jacob Astor's agent in that region for many years before becoming the head of the American Fur Company in 1834. Thereafter he frequently visited his company's chief depot, La Pointe; and sometimes passed on to Fond du Lac, where his half-breed daughter, the wife of the missionary, William Thurston Boutwell, lived and taught in the Indian school. The great figure in Wall Street was simply "Grandpa" in the log mission buildings at the mouth of the St. Louis River, to which he frequently sent letters and dolls for the little granddaughter. He was one man who understood the Indian pretty thoroughly, and the half-breed even more so. Hours and hours of his and his wife's time in

New York went to hunting up worsted for the embroidery frames of little half-breed girls in the fur country, or books for their brothers, or magazines and periodicals and odd orders of one sort and another for their elders on Lake Superior. Nothing seemed too trivial for them to attend to. Perhaps Crooks remembered the tedium of winters he himself had spent in the same area. His letters, too, contain many an understanding paragraph tucked away in the welter of orders and criticism relating to the minutiae of business.

Thus the missionaries reveal to us the original, untainted wilderness about Lake Superior, the gradual progress from savagery to civilization, the arrival of white settlers, and the sudden alteration that the forties and fifties produced all along the south shore. By the time of the Civil War the south shore was much changed, and with the effective opening of the iron mines, and after the building of the ship canal at the Sault in 1855, the south shore was set for that stupendous activity that has characterized it ever since. In many ways the building of the canal may be considered as a major event in American history, comparable to the opening of two other canals, the Erie and the Panama, and probably of more effect in changing the habits and customs of the American people. For years the copper of the south shore was the major contribution to world production of that ore; and a great part of the world's iron today comes from the mines on the rim of Lake Superior. The cheap and plentiful iron ore mined there since 1885 has made possible the network of railroads, the concentrations of mass-production machinery, the skyscrapers—in short, the steel that forms the frame and foundation of the modern industrial United States.

Part II

VULCAN'S SHOP AND NEPTUNE'S REALM

Chapter 6

From Birch Bark to Steel

Thus the Birch Canoe was builded
· · · · · · · · · · ·
And the forest's life was in it,
All its mystery and its magic,
All the lightness of the birch-tree,
All the toughness of the cedar,
All the larch's supple sinews;
And it floated on the river
Like a yellow leaf in Autumn,
Like a yellow water-lily.
　　　　—HENRY WADSWORTH LONGFELLOW

THE birch-bark canoe had its most severe test on Lake Superior—and demonstrated its complete seaworthiness. For ages it was the only craft on the lake. To discover how to make such a basket of wood splints and bark covering, that could take the buffeting of Lake Superior and yet be carried over portages on men's shoulders, was no mean feat. It was almost certainly the invention of Algonquian Indians, for the birch tree grows only in northern regions where that subdivision of the Indian race has lived in recent centuries. It was perfectly adapted to the needs of that tribe, since it enabled them to go where they would, over the small creeks or the great lakes of their country. It was light, strong and graceful. Moreover, it could be constructed of materials that grew in that country, and could be repaired en route without difficulty. What more could one ask?

Thomas McKenney describes the making of a canoe, which he watched with much interest on Lake Superior in 1826:

"I have attended the progress of the work in building this canoe. It is curious enough. Stakes are driven in the ground at certain dis-

113

tances, along each side of where the canoe is to be built, and for the entire length of it. Pieces of bark are sewn together with wattap [small rootlets of a coniferous tree], and placed between, from one end to the other, and made fast to them. When the bark is thus in, it hangs loose, and in folds, and looks, without its regularity, like the covers of a book with its back downwards, its edges up, and the leaves out. Next, the cross pieces are put in, pressing out the rim, and giving to the upper edges the form which the canoe is to bear—then the ribs are pressed in, the thin sheathing, in strips, being laid between them and the bark, and these (the ribs,) press out the bark, and give form and figure to the bottom and sides of the canoe. Weights (large stones,) are put on the bottom of these ribs, which had been previously soaked, and kept there till they dry. The next process is to remove the stakes, gum the seams, and the fabric is complete. There remains no more to do but to put it in the water, where it floats like a feather. This canoe is thirty-six feet long, and five wide across the middle."

The Indian canoe was much smaller than this Montreal, or *maître* canoe. There was also the intermediate size, the North canoe, and still a third size, called the bastard canoe, which was larger than the Indian, but not so large as a North canoe. McKenney does not mention the type of wood used in the construction of the canoe. It was nearly always made of white cedar. The oars were made of red cedar as a rule, and varied from the short kind used in the center of the canoe, to the very long ones which the end paddlers employed. Oars as well as paddles were used on Lake Superior. Probably that was the only variation in method of canoe transportation caused by the size of that great body of water. How early oars were used is not certain, but probably only in the later stages of the fur trade.

Louis Agassiz tells how they were used on his trip of 1849 along the north shore:

"While on the lake the canoes are not usually paddled, but rowed, the same number of men exerting greater force with oars than with paddles. By doubling the number of men, putting two on a seat, more of course can be accomplished with paddles. The gunnel of a canoe is too slight to allow of the cutting of rowlocks, or the insertion of thole-pins: so a flat strip from a tree, with a branch projecting at right angles, is nailed to the gunnel, and a loop of raw hide attached, through which the oar is passed."

Agassiz also describes the loading of his canoes:

"On the bottom were laid setting-poles and a spare paddle or two, (to prevent the inexperienced from putting their boot-heels through the birch-bark,) and over these, in the after part, a tent was folded. This formed the quarter-deck for the *bourgeois,* (as they called us,) and across it was laid the bedding, which had previously been made up into bolster-like packages, covered with buffalo-robes, or with the matting of the country, a very neat fabric of some fine reed which the Indians call *paquah.* These bolsters served for our seats, and around them were disposed other articles of a soft nature, to form backs or even pillows to our sitting couches. The rest of the luggage was skilfully distributed in other parts of the canoe, leaving room for the oarsmen to sit, on boards suspended by cords from the gunnel, and a place in the stern for the steersman. The cooking utensils were usually disposed in the bow, with a box of gum for mending the canoe and a roll or two of bark by way of ship-timber. Our canoe was distinguished by a frying-pan rising erect over the prow as figure-head, an importance very justly conferred on the culinary art in this wilderness, where nature provides nothing that can be eaten raw except blueberries."

Agassiz and members of his party were surprised to note the blue eyes and light hair of his Canadian-French voyageurs. The good professor seems to have forgotten the Viking origin of the inhabitants of Normandy, from which a large percentage of French Canadians came. It was not by mere chance that the voyageurs found themselves at home on great bodies of water.

The bateau and Mackinac boat were the intermediate craft used on Lake Superior in the era when canoes were becoming too small, and the sailboats had not yet appeared except for the fur companies' schooners. The bateau was a wooden boat of red cedar wood pointed at both ends, flat-bottomed, long in proportion to its width, and high-ended. It had no keel and was merely the white man's version of the canoe—made of sturdier design, because it was for use only in deep water and did not have to be portaged. It was thus capable of carrying a heavier load. Moreover, it could sail in many winds. Canoes also sailed, but in a makeshift fashion. The Mackinac boat was a barge of red or white oak boards with a flat bottom and rather blunt ends over a stiff heavy frame. It was designed to take advantage of wind whenever possible, and had a rudder that could be used at will, a mast that could be keyed into position quickly and easily, and a sail. As one old voyageur wrote in his reminiscences, "With a mild breeze these boats will sail from 60 to 70 miles per day, while they cannot be propelled with oars more than one-half that distance."

By 1825 the Mackinac boat had largely supplanted the canoe on the south shore, as far as the fur trade was concerned. It could carry more men and more freight than a canoe, and with the proper-sized crew could make as good time, if not better. Martin McLeod, a trader and later a prominent man of affairs in Minnesota, made a trip from the Sault to the Fond du Lac in 1836 in such a craft. There were twenty persons in the boat, besides their baggage and provisions. Of these, ten were crewsmen. They made the trip in the period of autumn storms and were from September 15 to October 23 in traveling the distance of some five hundred miles. McKenney, in the period of fine weather, required from June 11 to July 27 by canoe. It may be added that the "barges" of McKenney's party were probably Mackinac boats. Travelers of the period often referred to them under the name of barges.

No one has ever written an authoritative account of the decked vessels that have plied on Lake Superior since the days when the ensign of Louis XV floated proudly from the mast of the first one. Yet it is a story of high adventure. Navigation is at least as dangerous as that on the North Atlantic. Submerged rocks and reefs are always a menace, and the water in case of shipwreck is numbing in either summer or winter. Storms rise with almost unbelievable speed. There are few good harbors, especially on the north shore. Everywhere about and on the lake one has the feeling that he is looking upon the waters of an ocean, so mighty is this great lake. There are few places along its circuit from which a view of an opposite shore is possible. Its surf comes pounding in on basaltic rocks and a few shingle beaches, breaking in showers of spray.

The earliest known decked vessel to sail the great lake was La Ronde's,* built about 1735 at Pointe aux Pins. It was of twenty-five tons burden and carried at least two sails. It was used mainly in the copper-mining ventures of La Ronde and his associates on the south shore and to take his supplies from Sault Ste. Marie to his post at La Pointe. What happened to this little craft when mining ceased to be profitable is unknown. There is, however, a record of the loss of a French vessel on Lake Superior about 1763. Perhaps it was La Ronde's.

With the British conquest of Canada an accomplished fact in 1763, shipping advanced promptly on the upper lakes. Alexander Henry built first a barge and then a sloop at Pointe aux Pins for his copper ventures. The sloop was of forty tons burden and we know from a license taken out by the "Proprietors of Mines on Lake Superior," as the adventurers termed themselves, that three anchors, three cables, some dead eyes, block and rigging, and four swivel guns were sent up the lakes to Pointe aux Pins during the season of 1770-1771, presumably for this little vessel. She was launched in August 1772. This sloop also operated on the northeast side of Lake Superior, where Henry was prospecting in 1772 and 1773.

Decked vessels were traversing the lake in the 1770's. By 1778 John Askin of Mackinac had at least two vessels, the *Mackinac* and the *De Peyster,* sailing between Grand Portage and the Sault, and sometimes even getting past the rapids as far as Mackinac. Just how this difficult feat was accomplished is a mystery. It seems to have been done in a rather easy and certainly in an expeditious manner. Askin's letters leave no doubt on that point.

An Indian, "Big Charlie," managed one of the vessels on at least one trip, the one of the Revolutionary War period when a British officer and several soldiers went up to guard Grand Portage from any

---

* See page 161.

possible "rebel" attack. Ordinarily the vessels were used to carry the North West Company's goods and supplies, which Askin forwarded to Grand Portage from Mackinac. The difficulties under which he got and forwarded trade goods and, especially, corn, hominy and other provisions would daunt modern merchants, but they did not seem insuperable to him.

The next decked vessel seems to have been the *Athabaska,* or *Athabasca.* She, too, was built at Pointe aux Pins—she was launched August 15, 1786—and had a burden of forty tons. She proved inadequate for the purposes of the company, and so was sent down the Sault rapids to join the same company's *Beaver* on the lower lakes.

In his diary of 1793 John Macdonell, a trader on the Assiniboine River, refers to the building and first trip of the *Athabaska's* successor, the *Otter.* He writes under date of July 2:

"Stopped at pointe au Pins where two leagues above the Sault we found M[r] Nelson building a vessel for the North West Company to navigate the Lake Superior and to be called the Otter. She is to be launched shortly."

Later, at Grand Portage, he records under date of August 2 that the *Otter* had just arrived and was now anchored at the company's wharf. She was a sloop of seventy-five tons burden and made four or five trips a season between Grand Portage and the Sault. As late as 1802 she was still making that run.

The next vessel was doubtless the *Invincible,* which is mentioned as being at Kaministikwia on July 3, 1802. She was still sailing during the war of 1812, but was wrecked sometime before 1823 off Whitefish Point. She, too, was owned by the North West Company, which in 1797 had built a three-thousand-foot canal on the Canadian side of the Sault, with a lock that would raise the water nine feet, thus enabling canoes to avoid the tedious portage on the American side of the water. The canal seems to have been too small for sailing vessels, however, for those that reached the upper lake from the lower ones were all portaged at this time; and those which reached the lower lakes from Lake Superior ran the rapids, disastrously as a rule. Records of the War of 1812 tell of such disasters.

The *Mink,* one of two schooners built on Lake Superior by the North West Company at the time of the War of 1812, was run down the rapids to Lake Huron, where she was captured by the Americans, along with a valuable cargo of furs. She was a vessel of fifty tons. Her sister schooner, the *Perseverance,* of eighty-five tons, was also captured by the Americans, as she was attempting to run the rapids. The Americans destroyed her there and wrecked the canal and lock. Another vessel of this period, the North West Company's *Fur Trader,* of some forty tons, was wrecked in the Sault in 1812. The *Discovery* is also reported running down to her doom.

In 1817, according to James C. Mills in *Our Inland Seas,* the brig *Wellington* towed a vessel of some thirty tons, the *Axmouth,* from Lake Erie to the Sault. She was hauled over the Canadian portage and launched on Lake Superior. She was in the employ of the American Fur Company, which had just commenced operations on Lake Superior.

Two vessels of the same name appear on the records at the time of the War of 1812 and shortly thereafter. The *Recovery,* of ninety tons, owned by the North West Company and commanded by Captain McCargo, was hidden in McCargo Cove on Isle Royale during the war. After that struggle she was brought out, used by Lieutenant Bayfield and others until the middle twenties, and then broken up at Fort William. The other vessel of the same name was begun by the North West Company before its union with the Hudson's Bay Company in 1821, launched by the new company in 1823 at Fort William, and used by Lieutenant Bayfield for his survey of Lake Superior for the British admiralty during the years 1824 and 1825. She was a schooner of 133 tons, under the command of Thomas Lamphier, whose temper was so short that he was usually called "L'Enfer" (Hell) by the Canadian voyageurs, who were famous for their puns on the names and characteristics of the *bourgeois.* The new *Recovery* was dismantled in 1825 and laid up in Michipicoten River until the spring of 1828, when she was run down the rapids and sold to Messrs.

Merwin Gidings and Company in Ohio, for £500.* Again the records are confused, however, for Dr. John Bigsby recounts meeting Bayfield near the Pic in 1823 in "the trim schooner, the Julia . . . in which . . . he was surveying Lake Superior." He goes on to say that during that summer Bayfield did not have "a sick man among his crew."

There appears to have been a lull in shipbuilding after the union of the two competing companies and until the American Fur Company began its fishing industry on the lake in 1834. That activity, which will be described in the chapter on fishing operations on the lake, necessitated greater expedition in marketing fish than was possible in canoes and Mackinac boats. So, on July 30, 1835, the schooner *John Jacob Astor,* 112 tons burden, was launched, with considerable difficulty, on the American side of the Sault and served admirably till she was wrecked at Copper Harbor in September 1844, despite frantic efforts of soldiers from the recently established Fort Wilkins to aid her gallant captain, Benjamin Stanard. Her launching and success in the trade spurred the Hudson's Bay Company to build a vessel to serve the purposes of that company. This was the *Whitefish,* mention of which occurs in the annals of the period. Gabriel Franchere, the American Fur Company's representative at the Sault, speaks disparagingly of her in a letter of February 1837, saying that she is being built at Pointe aux Pins and that her principal timbers are of pine, so that he predicts she "will prove a coffin for some of their people." She was a schooner of about forty tons, according to her owners. Another of their vessels on the lake was the *Isobel,* or *Isabel.* According to company records she was built between 1851 and 1853 to replace the *Whitefish,* and she continued on the lake until 1863.

In September 1837 Franchere wrote that the American Fur Company had decided to build three slip-keel boats for the fisheries, two of them for Lake Superior and the other for use between the Sault and Detroit. They were to be forty feet keel and twelve feet beam. One of those designed for Lake Superior, probably the *Madeline,*

---

* These data and those for the *Whitefish* and *Isobel* (see *post*) have been supplied by the Hudson's Bay Company and are here cited by kind permission of the Governor and Committee of that company.

was of twenty tons and was wrecked on Minnesota Point. On account of faulty construction the other seems never to have been launched. Early in 1837 the company built a scow capable of carrying 300 barrels of fish; in 1838 the schooner *William Brewster* was launched; and sometime after 1838 the *Siskawit* was put on the lake.

In the last months of 1839 a Cleveland company, desiring to compete with the American Fur Company in the fishing business, brought its vessel to the Sault, where, during the ensuing winter, it was drawn over the portage, inch by inch, and launched on Lake Superior. This was the schooner *Algonquin,* which was abandoned some years later outside Superior, Wisconsin. It lay there for many years. Another vessel, this time a propeller, the *Independence,* was taken over the portage during the winter of 1845-1846. In 1846 the steamer *Julia Palmer* was hauled over the portage and introduced to the great upper lake. Her captain was John J. Stanard. By this time it is recorded that there were on the lake, besides the three above-mentioned vessels, some nine schooners: the *Chippewa, Florence, Swallow, Uncle Tom, Fur Trader, Napoleon, Siskawit, Ocean* and *Merchant.* The American Fur Company's ledger, "Bills of Lading," at the Sault, for 1846, 1847 and 1848, shows these vessels plying between ports all over the lake, carrying prospectors and miners with their supplies, taking Indian missionaries to their posts, carrying supplies and soldiers to the recently established Fort Wilkins on Keweenaw Point, and, in short, reveals the names of vessels, captains, mates, prospectors, mining companies, missionaries, villages, settlements and mining locations from the Sault along both shores for the entire circuit of the lake. Transportation was such a paying business that the American Fur Company's agent at the Sault preferred to keep the *Siskawit* "about here at freights of 6/ & 7/ p^r bbl bulk all along shore" rather than carrying the company's own freight. "She has made 2 trips and her gross proceeds are about $450 for the 2 trips."

In 1853 ground was broken for the ship canal at the Sault. It was completed two years later. The first ship to pass through was the steamer *Illinois,* 927 tons, Captain Jack Wilson master, on June 18, 1855. The same month the *Baltimore,* the *Sam Ward* and the *North Star* passed through the new canal. They were the forerunners of the immense fleet that shortly was cutting the waters of Lake Superior. In 1855 there were 193 passages through the locks; in 1870, 1,828; in 1885, 5,380; in 1895, 17,956. By 1910 the number had risen to 20,899 and the peak before 1935 was reached in 1916, when the total was 25,407. After that year the number decreased, though tonnage increased.

In the fifties all vessels with engines used wood for fuel. There were regular "wooding" stops and stations on the lake, just as on the Mississippi and other rivers. These wood docks were established along rivers and islands. Necessarily the stops for fuel delayed the vessels many hours and otherwise reduced profits. At the stations men were kept to cut trees and store the wood, cut generally to four-foot lengths, in yards ready for immediate transfer to the vessel when she arrived. Many crewmen were required for this sort of arrangement. It has been estimated that about 150 cords of wood were required by a steamboat for a trip through the Great Lakes. The average cost was about $1.75 per cord.

This period was one of the most interesting in the history of Lake Superior navigation. Masters sailed without charts. The lake was still largely unexplored and unsounded. Companies were in their infancy and transactions were made on faith and on the reputation of the master. Perhaps the best way to see it is to follow the career of one of the men who navigated the lake year after year.

Captain Alexander McDougall, like so many of the early captains, was born in Scotland. He migrated young to Canada and grew up at Collingwood, a very busy lake port at that time, and the terminus of a Lake Superior line of boats. In 1864 he became second mate on the *Ironsides,* carrying iron ore from the Menominee mines to Cleveland, and copper from Lake Superior to Detroit. McDougall writes:

"Exploration was rampant. Everyone was excited by wonderful prospects or great discoveries, and people were spending money as they do in flush times. . . . We had to land passengers at all sorts of out-of-the-way places. It would be my duty as second mate to go ahead in a small boat when we were making a landing in strange waters and take the soundings. I learned the pilotage of lakes and rivers and became expert very early in heaving the sounding lead. . . . The only reliable map was one made by Lieut. Bayfield, which had very few soundings, and even so it was hard to get copies of it. All the time I sailed the Lakes I never had a chart in my hands."

In 1865 McDougall was first mate on the steamer *Iron City*. There was no canal across Keweenaw Point and at Eagle River he found the steamer *Lac La Belle* aground on a shoal, loaded with Indian supplies for a payment at Grand Portage. He spent two days and nights there without sleep supervising the transfer of the cargo to his own ship.

"After we got started for Grand Portage, it was my watch on deck. While the Captain, Indian Agents, and others were having a good time, I was walking about the deck half asleep. In approaching the Apostle Islands, it was smoky and, my eyes dim, I made a mistake in the island we were about to pass and up she slid on the rocky, gravel bottom of Gull Island Shoal among thousands of gulls."

He got her off by working the double screws ahead and back, and finally reached Grand Portage, where they "made this last payment to a tribe of Indians from the interior, north of Lake Superior. I think there were about 1400 Indians there for two days and they had a good time of it, our cargo of supplies being divided among them."

The next winter he cut cordwood for forty cents a cord and hunted deer. In 1866 he was back as mate on the *Iron City,* being now twenty-one years of age. But the war had ended, prices for copper and iron had fallen, the ship had to be laid up, and he was transferred to the side-wheeler *Illinois.* He could get no pay, however, and late in the season he took the side-wheeler *Clement* to Marquette with a cargo of hay. The following winter he made barrel hoops at two dollars a day, and was back on the deck in the spring, this time as mate on the steamer *Meteor,* running between Cleveland and Lake Superior. "We handled masses of copper from mines at Ontonagon and Eagle Harbor, Michigan, to Detroit and all classes of freight up and back." He carried one piece of mass copper weighing 1,111 pounds.

In 1868 he was again mate and pilot on the *Meteor,* which this year extended its late-season run to include Minnesota Point in present-day Duluth. "Near the Portland land office building . . . our few passengers were landed on the gravel beach to begin to build a town later called Duluth." In 1869 he was back on the same run, and the winter of 1869-1870 he and another lake captain went to a night school in Detroit.

"I had two or three months of school in the winters from 1856 to 1859, inclusive. That and the two years in Glasgow was all the schooling I ever had in regular course. Later, when I worked on the Lakes, I spent two winters in a night school in Detroit. What was needed for navigation, such as mathematics, in my later life I picked up mostly from the captains under whom I sailed."

That, it may be said, was the way most of the lake captains learned their navigation.

In 1870 he got his first assignment as captain. This was on the *Thomas A. Scott,* the first boat of the Lake Erie & Western Transportation Company, which in time became the Anchor Line, and more recently the Great Lakes Transit Corporation. The *Scott* plied between Buffalo and Chicago, with an occasional trip to Lake Superior. In September of that year he became captain of the *Japan,* one of three new iron ships of his company, the first iron fleet on the lakes. The other two were the *China* and the *India*—according to McDougall, "the most popular boats on the Lakes then and for thirty years afterward." Later the *Alaska* was added. One writer says of them: "It is doubtful if any four steamers contributed more to the popularizing of lake travel to about 1890, than these liners." It was with this line that McDougall had his first introduction to shipbuilding, in which he became famous some years later. "Until then, I should say," he continues, "there had been only two iron steamers on the Lakes, the *Merchant* in 1868 and the *Philadelphia* in 1869." The triplets cost $180,000 each, had accommodations for 150 passengers, and carried 1,200 tons of cargo. McDougall helped build these ships.

In 1871 he built a home in Duluth, and here the twenty-six-year-old captain brought his mother and three sisters.

"There was no landing at Duluth, and for that matter not very much of a landing at Superior. Whenever we called there, I used to go ahead in a small boat to find the channel. . . . The next few years I was constantly in the Duluth trade. The Lake Superior & Mississippi railroad was building, the first elevators were put up near the foot of Third Avenue East, the Northern Pacific was reaching out for the West. Flush times returned to Lake Superior and Duluth enjoyed its first boom."

Coal was gradually becoming the regular fuel on lake vessels, and iron ships were taking the place of wooden ones. It was proved that iron vessels were not only as seaworthy but also better able to withstand the vibration of the engines, which was strong in the old side-wheelers. In 1841, a vessel driven by a screw propeller had appeared on the Great Lakes. This was the steamer *Vandalia,* of 138 tons, whose length was 91 feet. Propellers became popular at once, and today most vessels on Lake Superior are driven by one or more propellers. They are great spacesavers. Their machinery requires little room, and is all compactly stored away in the stern end.

Wooden sailing vessels remained on the lakes, of course, for many years after steamers and propellers became common. From 1864 to 1868 was the golden age of sailing schooners. In 1868 there were 1,875 officially listed. Thereafter there was a slow but steady decline, and by 1890 sailing ships were definitely passing in favor of the new steel vessels. In the meantime, after 1870, some iron vessels had been built, but the freight charges on iron ore were still too high to make iron ships cheap. In 1867 the ore rate from Lake Superior to lower lake ports was over four dollars. However, relief was in sight. In the early sixties, the steam barge began to operate on the lakes, and soon there was a new era in the transportation of heavy, coarse freight.

The steam barge inaugurated the era of "tows." The steam barges themselves were much larger than most sailing vessels on the lakes, and soon proved that the larger the coarse-freight carrier, the cheaper the freight rates. The older and less efficient sailing craft were thus eliminated from immediate competition, but to save investment the owners took off all sails except the fore, main and aft sails, cleared the decks, and with stout hawsers over bow and stern towed several former sailing vessels tandem style behind a steam barge. The sails could help in fair weather and protect the tows by their buoyancy and height in storms. These tows became a common sight all through the last years of the last century and even in the opening years of this one. They were especially useful in transporting lumber. As those years were also the period of lumbering on Lake Superior's shores, it is easy to see why this novel, unique and cheap form of transportation was so common. Lumber "hookers," as they were termed, were the cheapest method of transportation ever devised for carrying forest products.

Steel vessels were made possible by the discovery of new ways of making steel and the opening of the great Lake Superior iron mines, the largest bodies of ore in commercial operation in the world. For a period beginning with 1889 there was a special type of vessel on the Great Lakes. The steel whaleback was perhaps the most notable achievement in the varied career of Captain McDougall. It was designed and built by him for the most part at the American Steel Barge Company's shipyard in West Superior. It was like a huge metal cigar floating in the water. Though one or two of these craft have survived, the making of them has been discontinued because their hatches cannot match the dimensions of loading and unloading devices. Nevertheless, they were an important step toward the modern steel vessels on the lakes.

McDougall in his autobiography tells of the events leading up to the idea of the whaleback.

"The Anchor Line struck it rich the first season. Wheat was beginning to come to the new port of Duluth from the Red River Valley of Minnesota by rail and there was not enough cargo capacity to handle it. . . . That golden time was not to last long. When Jay

Courtesy of the Royal Ontario Museum of Archaeology

PAUL KANE'S OIL PAINTING OF A CHIPPEWA ENCAMPMENT AT SAULT STE. MARIE, ABOUT 1846

PAUL KANE'S OIL PAINTING OF THE KAKABEKA FALLS NEAR FORT WILLIAM, ABOUT 1845

Cooke failed in 1873 and Northern Pacific collapsed, the traffic of the upper lakes dwindled to almost nothing. The next two years there was not enough to keep the Anchor Line going on the lakes."

In 1874 he went to Russia to study their grain trade. In 1875 he was back on Lake Superior, this time with his own commercial fishing company operating out of Marquette. It was a failure—more fish than he could market.

In 1877, he writes:

"I accepted the position of captain and kind of manager of the new passenger and cargo steamer *City of Duluth,* which ran between Chicago and Lake Superior ports in company with two other boats of different owners, all of these boats going to the same dock in Chicago and elsewhere, each boat independent of the other. We made fourteen-day trips from Chicago to all Lake Superior ports on both shores, and I worked very hard with good success for my boat, the largest of its kind on the Lakes. We picked up all kinds of building material, freight such as cobble stones for street car lines, brown sandstone, and lumber. At one time the port of Duluth held ten thousand tons of skins. All warehouses and cars available were used for storage. Part of the lot were 150,000 buffalo skins. The invasion of the white man drove the Indians and wild animal life further westward and in a short space of time the tonnage of skins and furs was replaced by wheat."

During the winters he was still carrying on fishing enterprises on Lake Superior, mostly at Bayfield and Ashland. The winter of 1879-1880, he writes:

"I agreed to go with Thomas Wilson to look after the building of the largest wooden boats on the lakes, the *Hiawatha* and the *Minnehaha,* at Gibraltar, Michigan. . . . I later sailed the *Hiawatha* and towed the large vessel *Minnehaha.* We carried a great deal of railroad iron to Lake Superior where so many railroads were being built."

It was difficult to get stevedores. He became the leading supervisor of such men on the lake, making a good profit from the special way he worked out for handling railroad steel. "Owners of other boats wanted me to look after big contracts they had. The Northern Pacific engineering department wanted me on shore to look after their rails." In 1881 he returned to Duluth to live.

"I went to work on the docks to handle rails for the Wilson fleet and Smith-Davis & Company, Buffalo; also for the Northern Pacific railroad company at Superior, Ashland, and Washburn, in Wisconsin, Two Harbors, Minnesota, and later at Port Arthur, known then as Prince Arthur's Landing, and Fort William, Ontario."

He used Swedish immigrants in the main for his stevedores.

"This brought a lot of good men to me. I finally had about a thousand steady men and some good leaders among them that I could send to Ashland, Washburn, Two Harbors or Port Arthur with a crew of men, together with cash to look after the rapid unloading of vessels. Thus I controlled the trade of chartering grain and insuring the cargoes, having the confidence of all the lake fleet owners at Detroit, Cleveland and Buffalo. . . . While captain of the *Hiawatha,* towing the *Minnehaha* and *Goshawk* through the difficult and dangerous channels of our rivers, I thought out a plan to build an iron boat cheaper than wooden vessels. I first made plans and models for a boat with a flat bottom designed to carry the greatest cargo on the least water, with rounded top so that water could not stay on board; with a spoon-shaped bow to best follow the line of strain with the least use of the rudder and with turrets on deck for passage into the interior of the hull."

Of course his idea was derided by shipowners and makers. Late in the eighties, however, he made one model, No. 101, on his own land in Duluth, chiefly with stevedore labor. She was loaded with ore at Two Harbors and towed to Cleveland. Then in 1889 he designed a new one, No. 102, for which he finally got financial backing through an associate of John D. Rockefeller. A company was formed, the American Steel Barge Company. He made No. 103 at once, then the steamer *Colgate Hoyt,* naming her in honor of his financial sponsor.

She had compound engines and "proved to have cost so little, with such good results in operation, that the lake fraternity feared competition more than ever." He needed a bigger shipyard now than his property in Duluth allowed, and so, in 1889, after lack of success in getting a proper building site in Duluth, he established his shipyard in West Superior, just then starting on its way to success. He also built a dry dock there. By 1890 he was employing two thousand men.

"In 1893 we built ten steel ships at once. . . . That year we launched a ship every Saturday for eight Saturdays and on the ninth Saturday launched two ships and a tug. We also built the World's Fair steamer *Christopher Columbus,* probably the most wonderful ship contracted for and constructed up to that time."

Between 1888 and 1898 he constructed forty-six whaleback-type boats. Meantime he became interested in carrying iron ore from the newly opened Mesabi mines back of Duluth.

McDougall's life on Lake Superior typifies, in many ways, the entire development of the lake transportation—from shipping before the mast to building radical steel ore carriers with which to make the nation the greatest producer of steel products.

It should be remembered, however, that all the while a transition was being made from wood to steel (via iron), there was a continuing interest in wooden vessels. The idea that white oak was the only proper material for a vessel died hard. Famous wooden steamers, propellers, schooners and other types continued to cut the limpid water of Lake Superior until there was so little white oak left that no more wooden vessels could be built. One of the largest and most popular lines of wooden vessels was Ward's Central and Pacific Lake Company, which had a fleet of ten steamers making five departures every week from both ends of the route between Buffalo and Duluth. Thus there was the steamer *Keweenaw,* Captain Albert Stewart, 300 feet long and very swift. There were the *Northwest,* the *Iron Sides,* the *Sea Bird,* the *St. Paul* and the *St. Louis.*

Then there was the competing line—the Union Steamboat and

Atlantic, Duluth, and Pacific Lake Company—with the *Winslow,* the *Arctic No. 2,* the *Pacific* and the *Atlantic.* There was the local line, the Duluth Lake Transportation Company, which had the steamers *Metropolis* and *Manistee* running between Duluth and Marquette. There was the side-wheeler *Ivanhoe,* running between Houghton, Hancock and L'Anse. The books kept at the Sault locks and the ledgers of shipping companies at the Sault for this period, still preserved in the public library there, tell the story of the great wooden and iron steamers and propellers, as well as of the sailing vessels, that passed back and forth around Lake Superior and between the upper and lower lakes. It is instructive to run through the columns, noting the names of the vessels, their types, destinations, cargoes, and names of their masters. It is to be remarked how many of the captains were of Scotch origin.

In most of this period Canadian vessels passed through the American locks and so are recorded in American books. The first Canadian vessel through the locks was the small schooner *Isabel,* Captain Tozen, in 1856. The first steamer was the side-wheeler *Collingwood,* Captain McLean, bound for Fort William, July 27, 1857. This vessel carried the Dominion government's geological expedition under Professor William Y. Hind. In 1858 the *Rescue* was added as a mail carrier between Collingwood and Fort William. This was the beginning of regular Canadian service. The twin-screw propeller stopped at Pointe aux Pins, Batchawana, Mamainse Mine, Michipicoten Harbor, the Pic, Red Rock (Nipigon), Fort William, and later at Prince Arthur's Landing, now Port Arthur. In 1859 an opposition line put the *Ploughboy* on this run. In 1864 the *Algoma* passed through the locks on her first trip on Lake Superior. She had passengers, mail and freight. Her last Superior trip was in 1874. The former blockade-runner, the *Chicora,* entered the Lake Superior trade from Collingwood in 1869. She was later taken back to the lower lakes, and as late as 1934 she was being used as a tow barge around Toronto. In 1870 she carried Lord Wolseley's expedition to the Red River Valley to assist in putting down the first Riel Rebellion.

In 1867 the *Waubuno,* a side-wheeler, with the S. J. Dawson party of explorers aboard, passed through the locks on her first Lake Superior trip. The Dawson portage and canoe trail beyond Port Arthur are named for this man, who was trying to find a transportation route between eastern and western Canada for the government of that country. The *Waubuno* continued to ply on Lake Superior under Captain P. M. Campbell, until she foundered near Collingwood in 1879 with all on board. In 1870 the *Frances Smith* appeared on the Collingwood-Fort William run. She ran frequently thereafter between Duluth and Fort William. The diaries of American mining prospectors out of Duluth often mention her and several of the other Canadian vessels as the means of transportation of these men and their supplies from Duluth to Spar Island, Silver Islet, and other mining locations of the seventies. In 1877 the *City of Owen Sound* appeared on the run between Georgian Bay and Fort William.

In 1878 the *City of Winnipeg* was added to the *Frances Smith* and the *Owen Sound* to make the fleet of the Lake Superior Royal Mail Line. The *Winnipeg* burned at Duluth in 1881. To replace her the *Campana* appeared in 1882. The Canadian Pacific line of boats appeared on the lake in 1884 and the doom of the Collingwood line was practically sealed.

Operating simultaneously with the Collingwood line was the Beatty Line after 1871. Its terminals were Sarnia and Thunder Bay. The first vessel was the *Manitoba*. The *Acadia,* a propeller, also operated between 1871 and 1873. In 1874 the *Ontario* and the *Quebec* were added, and later the *United Empire* and the *Monarch*.

Many other companies brought vessels into Lake Superior: the Windsor-Lake Superior Line in 1875; the Jacques Line from Montreal in 1882; Marks North Shore Line in 1883; Graham's North Shore Line also in 1883; the Owen Sound Steamship Company in 1884; and the Canadian Pacific in the same year. Vessels of the Duluth and North Shore Line carried mail after other vessels stopped running in the fall. Between 1875 and 1882 passenger steamers of the Lake Michigan and Lake Superior Transit Company touched at Prince Arthur's Landing. During the building of the Canadian Pacific Railway the meat firm of Smith and Mitchell used two vessels to transport supplies and men to the ten vessels employed by the railroad. In the seventies at least four small steamers were on more or less regular short runs which included stops at Prince Arthur's Landing.

In 1899 the Great Northern Transit Company and the North Shore Navigation Company of Collingwood combined as the Northern Navigation Company (today a division of the Canada Steamship Lines) and sent the *Majestic* and the *City of Collingwood* onto Lake Superior. The following year the Beatty Line joined with them and the new company's head office was moved from Collingwood to Sarnia. The company in 1902 built the *Huronic,* the *Hamonic* in 1907, and the *Noronic* in 1914. The last two are the only regular passenger boats still plying on Lake Superior.

With the advent of competing railroad service to Chicago from the seaboard, it was fairly certain that large rail companies would put their own fleets on the Great Lakes. We have seen the Anchor Line, representing the Pennsylvania system, and the Canadian Pacific fleet. There was also the Michigan Central fleet; the Western Transit Line; the Mutual Transit Company, controlling the Union Steamboat line for the lake fleets of the Great Northern and Northern Pacific railways; the Lehigh Valley Transit Company, whose vessels plied between Duluth, Chicago and Buffalo in connection with the Lehigh Valley Railway; and others.

The most famous of all the vessels of these railroad lines were certainly James J. Hill's Great Northern boats, the *North West* and *North Land.* They were exclusively passenger boats and appeared more like ocean liners than lake steamers. The purpose of these floating palaces was to secure eastern passengers for Hill's railway at Duluth, so that they would proceed thence to the West on his cars. A pamphlet printed by the company in 1896, *A Summer Cruise on Inland Seas Via the Great Lakes to the West,* slips in this enticing idea to spinster schoolteachers:

"Duluth is a city of men. It has a population of 60,000, a large percentage of which is made up of rich, eligible bachelors. And yet young ladies crowd to Eastern summer resorts, season after season, where there are not enough to make up a set of lanciers. In these days, when emancipated womanhood goes everywhere, why does she pass Duluth, the lair of the lonely but decidedly eligible bachelor?"

The pamphlet goes on to describe the other vessels of the fleet:

"The freight fleet of the Northern Steamship Company loads here; we saw two ships in port, the *Northern Wave* and the *Northern Star,* and learned an interesting feature of the nomenclature of all vessels of our line. Each one has the title North or Northern, thus; the *North Land,* the *Northern King,* the *Northern Queen,* the *Northern Wind,* etc."

The modern cargo vessel that one sees on all the shipping lanes of Lake Superior, as well as on the lower lakes, is unique and endowed with the qualities of all true works of art, a high degree of utility and efficiency, consummate grace and lines that satisfy the eye. As in the old *Vandalia* of 1841, the engines are aft instead of in the center, as in most ocean-going vessels. The living quarters are in the forward end. Between these two raised ends lies uninterrupted space, topped by a flat deck efficiently divided by standardized hatches. These correspond to similar divisions at the great ore, grain, and other docks on all the Great Lakes, but particularly on Lake Erie and Lake Superior. It is between ports on these two lakes that most of the tremendous bulk cargoes of Great Lakes commerce are carried. The hatches can be opened so completely that all the space between the two ends appears almost as one great yawning hold. As the profile of an ore or grain vessel appears on the lake, one has the impression of two high ends and a long, low bridge connecting them. These ore boats and other lake vessels have long lives unless disaster overtakes them, for there is no corroding salt water to eat away their hulls. The first iron vessel on the lakes, the United States Ship *Michigan,* was launched at Erie, Pennsylvania, in 1844, and she is still in existence, though her active career was ended in 1923 by the breaking of a connecting rod on her port engine. Since then she has lain idle in the bay at Erie, the victim of decay and vandalism.

The first modern bulk freighter was the iron steamer *Onoko,* launched at Cleveland in 1882. The first ship on the lakes with hatches spaced on twelve-foot centers, as all ore boats and bulk freighters are today, was the steamer *James H. Hoyt,* launched in 1903. In 1906 two 600-footers were built, and in 1908 the first self-unloading bulk carrier appeared.

The average bulk carrier is 600 feet long, 60 feet wide and 32 feet deep. It has a triple-expansion engine which permits an average speed of 12 miles an hour. Its gross registered tonnage is about 8,000, and its carrying capacity about 11,000 tons. The largest Canadian steamer, the *Lemoyne,* was built at Midland, Ontario, in 1926 and is 633 feet long over-all, 621.1 feet along the keel, and has a 70-foot beam. Her gross tonnage is 10,480 and she is in the grain trade out of Port Arthur. The American stone carrier, *Carl D. Bradley,* is slightly longer than the *Lemoyne,* but her tonnage is only 10,028 tons. As of November 1943 the largest ore carriers are five new ships of the Pittsburgh Steamship fleet. They came into the trade in 1943, and are 640 feet by 67, carrying between 17,454 and 18,161 gross tons.

A remarkable feature of these carriers is the speed of their loading and unloading, many of them carrying their own machinery for these purposes. As of 1937 the ore-loading record was held by the steamer *D. G. Kerr.* On September 7, 1921, she loaded 12,508 gross tons of iron ore in 16½ minutes at the Duluth & Iron Range Railroad ore dock at Two Harbors, Minnesota. The speed record for loading grain was held by the steamer *G. A. Tomlinson,* which loaded 157,565 bushels of wheat in one hour at the Pool Terminal Elevator No. 7, Fort William, Ontario, on July 7, 1932. In 1928 the steamer *Elbert H. Gary* established a record for unloading bituminous coal by discharging 9,366 net tons at the Duluth, Mesabi & Northern Dock at Duluth, Minnesota, in 6 hours and 5 minutes.

Automatic handling of cargo reduces the time in port and enables lake vessels to crowd more voyages into the short navigating season. By 1936 it had cut the average time in the lower (Lake Erie) port to 11 hours and 18 minutes, less than half a day, and reduced the stay in the upper (Lake Superior) port to the astonishingly short time of 7 hours and 38 minutes. The time saved in port by automatic cargo handling goes into hundreds of miles of added sailing.

A typical bulk carrier, *William K. Field,* made the following record in 1924: she carried twenty-four cargoes of coal westbound, mostly between Ashtabula and Duluth, and twenty-two cargoes of ore eastbound from Allouez (Superior), Wisconsin, to Ashtabula. Only two trips were made deviating from this route, one between Ashtabula

FIRST ORE BOAT OF THE SEASON ENTERING THE SHIP CANAL
AT DULUTH

THE BRIG "COLUMBIA"
The first vessel to carry a cargo of iron ore through the Sault locks, 1855.

Gallagher Photo

SPOUTING GRAIN INTO A GRAIN BOAT AT SUPERIOR, WISCONSIN

Gallagher Photo

LOADING IRON ORE AT THE ALLOUEZ DOCKS,
SUPERIOR, WISCONSIN

and Sheboygan, Wisconsin, and one between Lorain, Ohio, and Green Bay, Wisconsin. Her navigation season that year was 7 months and 17 days.

In 1928 there were forty-three self-unloading vessels on the Great Lakes. By 1936 that number had been increased to sixty-five. Of these, fifty-four are under American registry and ten under Canadian. Vessels of this type handle such commodities as coal, coke, broken stone, gypsum, sand and gravel. These vessels were of the usual iron-ore and coal-handling types, but changes in their holds and the addition of special unloading machinery have converted them into efficient and inexpensive carriers of much of the commerce on the Great Lakes. The cargo holds of vessels so converted have compartments with W-shaped bottoms. Hand or electrically operated gates at the two points of the bottom allow the materials to drop upon two parallel, endless rubber-belt or linked-metal conveyors underneath, which carry their loads forward to cross conveyors in the bow of the ship. The materials are then carried ashore by means of a conveyor boom supported by an A-frame with a swinging radius of up to 226 degrees.

Prior to the improvement of communications between Lake Superior and the lower lakes, the chief obstruction was the Falls of St. Marys River, which had a drop of about twenty feet. The river is about sixty-three miles in length and has a total fall of about twenty-one and a half feet. In addition, there were a number of shoals, which might be only five to seventeen feet in depth at mean low water. As already stated, the North West Company built a small canal on the Canadian side in 1797-1798, which provided a depth of about two feet. This was sufficient for canoes but impracticable for larger craft. Moreover, the Americans destroyed it in 1814 during the War of 1812. Though it was rebuilt, from that time until 1855 most goods and crafts were portaged over the mile-long carry on the American side. To be sure, after Fort Brady was established by the United States Government at Sault Ste. Marie in 1822, there was a partial canal on the American side, dug by soldiers, by means of which canoes avoided some of the obstruction.

In 1855 the State of Michigan completed a canal with a double lift lock, which allowed for vessels having a draft of 11.5 feet at mean stage of water. This canal was turned over to the United States in 1881.* In 1888 the original locks were destroyed while excavation for the Poe lock was going on. Prior to 1943, on the American side, the modern canal had two branches: the South with the Weitzel and Poe locks; and the North with the Davis and Fourth locks. The Weitzel lock, built in the years 1870 to 1881, was 515 feet long, 80 feet wide in the chamber, narrowing to 60 feet at the gates. It had a depth of 11.4 feet of water on the sills at low-water datum. It had been out of commission since 1918 when it was destroyed by the construction of the MacArthur lock in 1942-1943. The Poe lock, completed in 1896, was 800 feet long, 100 feet wide, and had a depth on the sills of 16.8 feet at low-water datum. The Davis (third) lock, opened in 1914, and the Fourth lock, opened in 1919, are 1,300 feet long, 80 feet wide, and have 23.3 feet at low-water datum on the sills.

The existing improvement of the St. Marys River provides depths at low-water datum of 20 feet in upbound channels and 24 feet in downbound channels, over a minimum of 300 feet for one-way traffic and of 600 feet for two-way traffic throughout the river. The present dredged areas afford a least width of 300 feet, increasing at angles and other critical places up to 1,500 feet. The Dominion of Canada between the years 1888 and 1895 constructed a canal 1.4 miles in length, 150 feet wide, with a lock 900 feet long and 60 wide, having a depth of 17 feet on the sills at low-water datum. In July 1943 a fifth American lock, the MacArthur, named for the hero of Bataan, was opened seven months ahead of schedule. This is doubtless much larger than the other locks, but wartime restrictions prevent the disclosure of its dimensions. It was built to speed the shipment of iron ore, so vital to the war effort.

During the first eighty-one years of their existence, that is, till 1935, the canals were the passageway for 2,394,472,474 tons of freight, or an annual average of 29,561,389 tons. Of this, 1,500,263,300 tons or 62.6 per cent of the total, were iron ore. Other commodities, in the order of tonnage, were as follows: coal, 475,479,059 tons; wheat, 6,870,-

---

* See page 235 for a discussion of the building of the several locks at Sault Ste. Marie.

958,194 bushels or 206,128,745 tons; other grains than wheat, 2,508,401,789 bushels or approximately 53,685,486 tons; wood products, 24,245,472,000 board feet, or about 44,000,000 tons; general merchandise, 40,520,072 tons; and some other listed items.

These figures tell very tersely the story of what is happening on and about the shores of Lake Superior. Ore is being mined at a great rate; returning ore vessels, and other craft, carry coal to the Midwest; wood is still being cut, primarily pulpwood for paper, and especially on the Canadian side; and the grain from the northern tier of American states, and especially from the Canadian prairie provinces, passes over the lake en route to eastern mills.

One would expect different types of vessels to carry these several kinds of cargo, and he is not disappointed. Official figures for 1935 show that there were 550 American vessels with a gross tonnage of 2,575,455; and 364 Canadian vessels with a total gross tonnage of 751,094, available for use in the transport of freight or passengers or both on the Great Lakes. The total number of American and Canadian vessels in the Great Lakes fleet in the same year was 2,749, with a gross tonnage of 3,671,544 tons. Of the 550 American freight and passenger carriers, 441 were classed as bulk-freight carriers, exclusive of tankers; they represented 87 per cent of the total tonnage of American vessels of 1,000 gross tons and over. There were 119 vessels, both Canadian and American, in 1935 in the passenger and package-freight business. Then there were automobile carriers, tankers, and sand and gravel boats.

For the decade 1926-1935 inclusive, the average annual tonnage of the combined Great Lakes ports was 114,837,300 short tons. Nearly 50 per cent of this was handled at six ports: Duluth-Superior with an average of 38,001,551 tons consisting largely of iron-ore shipments; Toledo, with an average of 17,150,713 tons, also largely iron ore; Buffalo, which includes the New York Barge Canal traffic, 17,096,517; Chicago, 12,010,926 tons; Cleveland, 10,783,089 tons, also largely iron ore; and Ashtabula, 8,774,902, likewise largely iron ore. Thus it will be seen how far the great Lake Superior port outdistances all the others. Indeed, it is second only to New York, and very close to it.

As for total tonnages by the individual Great Lakes: for the ten-year period already mentioned, Lake Erie led with 40 per cent of the gross total; Lake Superior followed with 25.5 per cent; Lake Michigan was third with a little over 22 per cent; Lake Huron had only 5 per cent; and Lake Ontario was last with a little less than 1 per cent.

The ports officially listed by the United States Government for Lake Superior are as follows: Grand Portage, Grand Marais (Minnesota), Agate Bay, Duluth-Superior, Port Wing, Cornucopia, Bayfield, Washburn, Ashland, Ontonagon, Keweenaw Waterway, Baraga, L'Anse, Pequaming, Marquette Bay, Marquette, Munising, Grand Marais (Michigan), and Sault Ste. Marie.

In the period from 1919 to 1935 the United States and Canada produced a little more than one-third of the world's grain, excluding Russia's and China's, for which figures are not completely available. The territory tributary to the Great Lakes includes the very parts of the United States and Canada which produce the grain. Thus the importance of the lakes for the world's grain trade is obvious. The four ports of Fort William-Port Arthur, Duluth-Superior, Milwaukee and Chicago ship most of the grain which moves from the upper lakes. Buffalo receives most of this grain destined for North Atlantic ports in the United States; while certain Canadian ports receive most of the Canadian grain. During the sixteen-year period between 1920 and 1935 inclusive, Fort William-Port Arthur shipped 49.6 per cent of the grain from the four upper lake ports; Chicago shipped 25.1 per cent; Duluth-Superior 19.4 per cent; and Milwaukee 5.9 per cent. These figures show that nearly 70 per cent of the grain traffic on the lakes passes through Lake Superior ports.

The opening of navigation normally finds the elevators at Fort William and Port Arthur filled to capacity and there is usually a large amount of grain in storage at Duluth and Superior. With the opening of navigation there is a rush of grain by way of the lake route. This creates a spring peak, usually within the month following the opening of navigation. When this winter storage has been disposed of, the grain traffic subsides until July. Then the first movements of winter wheat reach Chicago and Milwaukee. Chicago does not ship as much grain by water as by rail, however, and this first movement of the new crop by way of the lakes is not very heavy as a rule. It is joined in August, however, by the spring wheat from Minnesota and the Dakotas, which moves through Duluth and Superior. About the first of September, the tremendous flow of wheat from the Canadian prairie provinces, focusing directly upon Fort William and Port Arthur, joins the flow of winter and spring American wheat, and from that time until the close of navigation, the facilities of the transfer elevators and of the Welland and St. Lawrence canals are taxed to the limit. The heaviest flow is usually during November, but not all the grain seeking the water route can be accommodated at the lower lake ports and Montreal, and there is therefore usually a large amount left over in vessels and in elevators at upper lake ports and intermediate transfer ports, such as those on Georgian Bay. Grain at the Georgian Bay elevators moves throughout the winter season to the seaboard and to interior consuming points, and this is true to some extent of the grain left in elevators at upper lake ports, but the larger share of the latter is held over for shipment during the following season.

The Duluth-Superior port draws its grain from a hinterland extending through Minnesota, the Dakotas, and as far west as Columbia Falls, Montana. Duluth-Superior and Chicago have competed for the grain trade of this region and engaged in frequent rate wars, but the advantage is in favor of the more northerly port, except for parts of southern Minnesota, parts of southern South Dakota, and regions to the south and west. These areas ship to Chicago as well as to Duluth-Superior.

The port at the head of Lake Superior—called for the twin cities that have grown up there, Duluth in Minnesota and Superior in contiguous Wisconsin—is one of the best in the United States, as well as next to the largest in point of commerce. There are twenty-four grain elevators having an aggregate storage capacity of 49,890,000 bushels. Sixteen of these have facilities for unloading from cars and fifteen for loading to cars. Nine are equipped for unloading vessels and fourteen for loading vessels. At the largest of these elevators, that of the Great Northern's S elevator, 100,000 bushels of grain can be loaded per hour to vessels. This building is steel throughout except the flooring on three floors and the cleaning machines. Its storage capacity, along with that of its annexes, is 11,000,000 bushels.

The entire plant is operated by electricity. Movable power-shovel or scraper rigs are used. The bin hoppers underneath the cars in this plant are nearly as long as an ordinary car. When the car door has been opened, the power shovel or scraper rig is moved into position in front of the door and the grain scraped from the car. Two men and two scrapers are used, one working in each end of the car. The track facilities provide for unloading eighteen cars of grain in one setting, and the plant has a record of unloading 350 cars in ten hours. From the bins under the track, the grain is elevated to the scales and then conveyed to storage bins. When it is shipped, it is again weighed, conveyed to the eight shipping bins, and delivered to the boats by gravity through spouts. There are two spouts to each bin, making sixteen spouts through which grain is delivered. Twenty thousand bushels an hour are delivered through a single spout. This elevator has a record of loading 1,400,000 bushels into boats in one day of ten hours.

Fort William-Port Arthur is likewise the joint port of twin cities, this time just north of the international boundary, on Thunder Bay. Fort William is at the mouth of the Kaministikwia River, and Port Arthur has an artificial harbor protected by an extensive breakwater system. Both harbors are concerned primarily with the exporting of wheat and other grain from the prairie provinces of Canada. Through both ports passes the Canadian Pacific Railway, which brings the grain at low freight rates, thus insuring against competition from American railways in adjacent territory. Practically all of the western Canadian grain reaches this port and is shipped therefrom by boats on the lake. Thus have arisen the modern elevator facilities of the port, the most extensive at any grain-shipping port in the world. In 1935 there were thirty elevators, with a total capacity of 92,615,000 bushels. Since that time even more storage facilities have been erected —some temporary—because of the stagnation in the world's wheat markets consequent on the great depression of the thirties of this century. In May 1935 over 87,000,000 bushels of grain were stored in the port's elevators at one time. This record has been improved upon since that time. Up to 1935 the greatest number of cars unloaded at these elevators in one day was the record of October 2, 1928, when 2,748½ cars, or 3,794,208 bushels, were unloaded. The greatest number of bushels shipped from the port in one day was that of November 29, 1928, when 6,395,814 bushels went out, nearly the entire amount by boat.

What do the bulk carriers bring back on their return trips? As far as Duluth-Superior and Fort William-Port Arthur are concerned, the answer is: largely coal. In the strange and equitable economy of Nature, the very ports that receive the iron ore from the Lake Superior mines are the chief shipping points for coal, which is almost entirely lacking in the Lake Superior basin. Most of these ore-receiving ports are on Lake Erie. The total movement of bituminous coal from Lake Erie ports in 1935 was 34,777,299 tons. Of this amount Lake Superior ports received 8,225,056. The twin ports of Duluth and Superior led all ports on the Great Lakes, with a total of 6,667,167 tons; Fort William and Port Arthur were second in the westward flow to the upper lakes, with a combined total of 598,832 tons; Ashland was third with 351,762 tons; and lesser amounts went to other upper lakes ports, both Canadian and American. Thus the importance of at least two Lake Superior ports in the coal business of the continent is easily perceived.

From the upper lakes ports coal is distributed throughout Minnesota, Wisconsin, parts of Michigan, North and South Dakota, Montana, Iowa and Nebraska, as well as to parts of western Canada. The coal is stored at the ports and distributed as needed, thus constituting a fine steadying influence in a region where storms often paralyze rail traffic for days. In 1871 the first cargo of commercial coal was unloaded at the Duluth-Superior harbor by means of wheelbarrows. At that time there was no provision for stocking coal at the port. In 1878 a special type of derrick utilizing a small steam hoisting engine marked a development in the discharge of coal cargoes. The year 1901 saw the construction of the first electric coal-handling plant ever installed. Meantime both the shovel bucket and the clamshell bucket had begun to supersede the old-style tubs for unloading. Most of the Lake Superior ports are equipped with modern and efficient mechanical means for handling coal. In the most modern types of electrically operated traveling coal bridge, the unloading, stocking, repreparing, reclaiming and car-loading operations are accomplished with one single unit. Most of the installations are also equipped with boxcar loaders, thus enabling the grain cars to be used on the return trip. The total storage area available for coal at Duluth-Superior has a capacity in excess of 11,000,000 tons.

Another return cargo for the ore and grain vessels in normal times is new automobiles. It is a great sight to see not only the hold, but every available inch of deck space, filled with shining new cars. When they reach Duluth and Superior, or other ports, they are run off and taken by transport truck or in tow to central distributing points like the Twin Cities. The motorist between Duluth and those cities knows the caravans of new cars to his sorrow, since they stretch for miles just after a boat has docked.

In the piping times of peace, one may take a trip on a bulk carrier on Lake Superior and beyond, if one wishes. It is a novel journey. The long white-topped ships are unusual in construction, each with the distinctive letter or insignia of its fleet painted on the funnel at its stern. The Canada Steamship Lines' is a black and white banding at the top of a red funnel. The Bethlehem Fleet has a yellow funnel topped with black. The Interlake Steamship Company (Pickands, Mather and Company) has a red band toward the top of the black funnel. The Pittsburgh Steamship Company's funnel is silver, banded at the top with black. The Midland Steamship Line has a black M on a red band toward the top of the black funnel. Many other lines use distinctive letters in much the same way. The Hanna fleet's is a rather small red H in a white star; the Cleveland Cliffs' is a red C on a black funnel. There are many others. Anyone familiar with Lake Superior's commerce takes a look at a high-riding ore vessel coming into Duluth-Superior harbor and says almost without thinking, "One of the Cleveland Cliffs coming in empty." Of course, it is not empty. The ore vessel is so constructed, a shell within a shell, that bilge water can be added as the cargo leaves, and can be let out as the boat fills with ore. Nonetheless, a vessel ballasted only with water rides with noticeable difference from a boat heavily loaded with ore or coal. The latter's deck is practically parallel with the water, from bow to stern; an "empty" boat rides with a high bow.

Before your boat leaves the dock—supposing that you are taking a trip down the lakes after loading at Duluth or Superior—she will have been thoroughly swept and then scrubbed down with the aid of a steam hose, if her new cargo is grain. The quarters for guests are palatial and the food is excellent. The trip to Cleveland or some other Lake Erie port takes only a few days, four or five, sometimes fewer.

In fair weather there is not much to do but plenty to see. As you go down the lake, you will ship a number of birds, particularly in fall and spring—warblers, sparrows, swallows, etc.—which weary of flying across the lake and conclude they may as well ride. Some will stay with you for the journey. Others will leave when they recover from their fatigue, or when they are frightened away. Many young birds perish every year in making their first great flight over the lake. This was particularly true of the young passenger pigeons, before the species became extinct. They nested in great numbers about the lake, and those that were born late in the season suffered for their lack of strength and experience when they tried to follow the older birds across.

Your boat will take a lane well toward the center going down the lake; and very much closer to the south shore coming back. The lanes are regulated by the Federal Government. All international channels are also maintained by the United States; the Canadians take care only of their own harbors. There are no charges in locking through at the Sault, because of the provisions of the Rush-Bagot agreement of 1817 between the United States and Great Britain. That instrument likewise accounts for the fact that there is an unfortified boundary running through the Great Lakes, with no armament allowed.

If there is a storm, your vessel may put into the Keweenaw Waterway for protection. In mid-October 1943 the author was at Houghton during very stormy weather. Dawn one morning revealed the waterway bright with great ships passing through. They had come in during the night to escape the bad weather around the point. In fair weather it is shorter to keep to the open lake rather than to cut through the canal.

If you are so unfortunate as to run into a bad storm, do not be alarmed if your long vessel writhes and twists under your feet as you stand at the stern looking forward. She is accommodating herself to waves and wind, and if she did not act in this serpentine fashion, in all likelihood she would break up.

Your skipper very likely will be a Scandinavian. In the early years Scotch captains were usual, but since the great Scandinavian migration began, Swedish and Norwegian captains, especially Norwegian, have become more and more the rule. Many of your crew may also be of the same origin. These men were accustomed to sea life and vessels in their homeland, and it was very natural for them to go into the same kind of work in America, particularly as they tended to settle near the Great Lakes. Wages and salaries for sailors and officers were much higher than on European vessels and offered great attractions. Once members of the family entered the Great Lakes shipping life, it was customary for later generations to follow their example. These men are remarkable mariners, judged by any standard, but particularly by salt-water standards. They have learned their profession the hard way, by experience; they know the lakes through personal contact; they bring their own vessels up to the docks as a rule, without the aid of pilots; and they know that in a storm they must maneuver in relatively short spaces, not in a boundless Atlantic or Pacific ocean. There is little possibility of riding before a storm for long on the Great Lakes. In the customary late fall storms, gales may last for days, with accompanying snow. So these mariners must perforce be better navigators than their salt-water brethren.

Fog is another curse of the lakes. It is often bad in June and July, just at the height of the navigation period. Then the foghorns and whistles may be heard all about the lake, morning, noon and night. Navigation is treacherous at such times, but infinitely better than in the days before lighthouses, fog warnings, and other aids to navigation were installed by the Federal Government and by Canada. In the old days there were many wrecks; today there are comparatively few. A whole chapter could be written on the installation of safety aids and of the gallant men who tend the lighthouses and operate the coast-guard stations.

Chapter 7

Ironclad and Copper-Bottomed

*Yet am I saved from midnight ills
That warp the soul of man.
They do not make me walk the floor
Nor hammer at the doctor's door,
They deal in wheat and iron ore,
My sons in Michigan.*
—RUDYARD KIPLING

OWHERE in the world, probably, has geology more of an
appeal to the casual traveler than around Lake Superior.
At a glance this lake is seen to have been formed in a different way from the other Great Lakes. Almost from the moment of
approaching it the traveler realizes that here is a great rock basin
not filled to the top with water. If it were filled to the brim, no one
but a geologist would perceive the problem of the origin of the basin.
As it is, the great headlands, the peculiar color and quality of the
rocks, and the continuation on one shore of the formations on the
other shore, hundreds of miles away in some instances, all pique
the traveler's curiosity.

Obviously something unusual happened in earth's development
and is here recorded in durable material for all to see. Early in the
dawn of past geological ages this was the southern edge of the first
great land mass, the border of the initial North American continent.
Convulsion followed convulsion till mountains of Alpine heights rose
in the regions now known as northern Wisconsin and Minnesota,
and the Laurentian heights were formed in Canada. As these mountains were eroded in long ages of geologic time, with volcanic seas
entering now and again, upheavals produced the older and younger
granites of the region, and the iron ores were laid down—first the

145

Vermilion and some of the Ontario ranges, and then the great Mesabi bodies and the Michigan and Wisconsin ores.

Then came more sedimentation from the old rocks to form slates and conglomerates; and finally another period of volcanic activity from beneath the highland where Lake Superior's basin would eventually be. Under that height was a great chamber of magma, or molten rock material. Some of it spewed out as lava flows that covered the surface of the earth and cooled quickly, forming the special texture of the dark basaltic and the reddish rhyolite rocks that are seen so frequently about the edge of the lake. Some of the magma, however, was pushed here and there wherever it could be forced into chambers and cracks below the surface. There it cooled slowly as gabbro and diabase. One of the largest chambers of gabbro known throughout the world is now at the surface back of Duluth and running generally parallel to Lake Superior just back of the north shore as far as Reservation River. One can only imagine the time and earth changes necessary to bring this great laccolith to the surface today. The diabase sills and dikes are also numerous along the north shore.

When all this magma had been ejected from below the highland, that highland began to sink, and finally it dropped so far that its surface was below the level of surrounding rocks. A trough or basin was thus formed. Glaciation came, and as the ice retreated, water stayed in the basin to form a succession of lakes, the present one being Lake Superior.

The glaciation period is only less interesting than the creative age in the Lake Superior basin. Great ice sheets gathered in three centers of northern North America, from which they worked outward. After a period of advancement the ice would melt back. Later a lobe might advance from another direction. The Superior, Chippewa and Keweenaw lobes occupied the lake Superior basin. As the ice melted, lakes formed at the retreating edge of the glacier. One of these early lakes was the so-called Lake Nemadji of the geologists. It drained southwest of Carlton, Minnesota, into the Mississippi River. Next came the Lake Duluth stage, when the outlet was directly southward through the St. Croix River into the Mississippi. At this stage the beaches were formed that are now so noticeable, especially on the highlands back of Duluth. One is utilized to form much of the Skyline Drive of that city's scenic highway. Next the waters escaped first through Green Bay and the Wisconsin River, and then past the site of Chicago through the Illinois River into the Mississippi. These periods lasted for a long time, as is shown by the broad beaches, lower than those of Lake Duluth, near Houghton, Swedetown and Marquette.

The episode of the Chicago outlet was followed by a retreat of the glacial barrier to the northeast, and the glacial lake which came gradually into existence occupied all of the basin of the present Lake Superior, overflowing above part of the northern peninsula of Michigan and joining the waters of the present Lake Michigan and Lake Huron. This stage is called Lake Algonquin. The ice barrier now stood east of North Bay in the Ottawa valley. It had also retreated northward from Lake Superior beyond the height of land. During the Lake Algonquin stage the waters ceased to use the Chicago and Illinois river outlets and began to flow through two lower outlets to the east. One led past Port Huron and through the present Lake St. Clair and Lake Erie into Glacial Lake Iroquois, which covered somewhat more than the basin of the present Lake Ontario. The second outlet also led into Lake Iroquois, but through the Trent River valley out of Georgian Bay. The Lake Iroquois waters flowed eastward through the Mohawk River into the Hudson and entered the ocean at New York. All around the Lake Superior basin one may see Lake Algonquin beaches elevated high above the waters of the present lake. At this stage glacial lakes probably occupied the Kaministikwia and Nipigon valleys, including all the basin of present Lake Nipigon.

Next came the Nipissing Great Lakes, when the Ottawa River drained the basins now occupied by Lakes Superior, Michigan and Huron. This reduced the glacial waters to a much lower level. The largest area to be uncovered at this time was the lowland east of Marquette in the upper peninsula of Michigan. Now Lake Nipigon began to assume its present form and to be independent of Lake Superior. Isle Royale, where small islets had existed during the

Algonquin stage, now likewise assumed practically its present size and form. The beaches of the Nipissing stage were the largest in the history of the Lake Superior basin, cut so broad and with such high, wave-cut cliffs that we can only infer that this stage of the lake lasted for a very long time. In fact, it lasted longer than the present level of Lake Superior has.

Next occurred a slight tilting of the land about and probably in the Lake Superior basin, as well as in the whole Great Lakes area to a greater or less extent. It is not known whether the warping that now occurred lifted the region to the north of the lake, or made the area south of it sink. What is known is that the Ottawa River outlet was no longer the lowest drainage channel, and the St. Lawrence River became, as it still is, the outlet of the Great Lakes. Moreover, the tilting is still going on. Beaches that once were horizontal are now tipped from north to south at a slight angle. On the south side of the lake the water is being canted into bays and river mouths, so that what were formerly valleys are now becoming bays and estuaries. River navigation is thus made possible for some distance from the great lake, as, for example, between Duluth and Fond du Lac on the St. Louis River. On the other hand, all except the largest rivers of the north shore cascade in falls and rapids almost directly into the basin of the lake itself. Hence the fewer good harbors on that side.

The canting of the lake waters has had a very important effect in promoting man's occupation of the south shore and the development of extensive shipping there. The best of the harbors thus made is the great Duluth-Superior harbor, which, in addition, was also given its protective sand bars by this canting operation. A still further result of the canting is the present form of the Apostle Islands, which were produced by the submerging of old stream valleys.

By this tilting, moreover, the old beaches of the high-water mark of Glacial Lake Nipissing have been submerged on the south side of the lake and lifted very much higher on the north shore. At Duluth the old shore line is now estimated to be twenty-five feet below the surface of Lake Superior; it appears above the present water surface at Beaver Bay; and beyond that, the beach rises with an average slope of about seven inches to the mile. A beach of noticeable strength may be seen high on Mt. McKay just outside Fort William. The highest beach seems to be the one at Michipicoten, where it is now 843 feet above Lake Superior, which, in turn, is 602 feet above sea level. Here it may be added parenthetically that the deepest known part of Lake Superior is 1,290 feet below the surface.

At present tilting is going on throughout the Lake Superior basin and as far east as Green Bay, at the rate of about 0.42 feet per century. The amount is small, but if continued indefinitely it would result eventually in changing the outlet of the Great Lakes once more, this time from the St. Lawrence River to Chicago and the Missisippi.

Lake Superior's immense basin of rocks is one of the great mining centers of the world. Iron ore, copper, silver and gold, but primarily iron ore, are found close around the rim of the lake. It is fortunate for mankind that such is the case, for some of the best iron-ore deposits in the world, notably the great Minas Geraes of Brazil, are miles away from easy transportation routes and thus practically useless. Water transportation is nearly always much cheaper than any other kind; hence iron and steel products are much cheaper in America than could be possible if the ore had to be transported by rail. The current lake rate is about eighty cents per ton from the head of Lake Superior to the ports on Lake Erie and Lake Michigan, which receive practically all the ore. The same amount of money would transport a ton of ore by railroad for only about a hundred miles.

The chief deposits of iron are along the south shore of Lake Superior, just to the west and north of the lake in Minnesota, and at various places in Ontario. Their range names are: the Marquette, Menominee, Gogebic, Vermilion, Mesabi and Cuyuna in the United States; and the Atikokan, Kaministikwia-Matawin, and Michipicoten in Canada. By far the most productive district is the Mesabi, which in 1937 supplied about sixty-two per cent of all the ore mined in the United States. Today the percentage is much greater because of wartime conditions. The Mesabi region's ports are Duluth, Two Harbors and Superior.

Most of the iron ore now being mined was laid down in what geologists term the Upper Huronian or Animikie series of rock formations, that is, in next to the oldest geologic period, millions of years ago. The Vermilion is even older, having been laid down in the so-called Archean period. All of these were pre-Cambrian, or before the period of land-animal life, so that the few fossils that exist are of crustaceans, brachiopods, seaweeds and other early life.

It is still a moot question just how the iron was formed, but one theory quite generally accepted is as follows. After the Archean series had produced Ely greenstone and granite, with lesser exposures of slate, quartzite and limestone, volcanism occurred which resulted in the precipitation near by of chemical sediments, consisting of iron carbonate, the very finely crystalline silica (quartz) known as chert, and subordinate amounts of iron silicates, aluminum silicates, manganese oxide and carbonate, lime and magnesium carbonates, lime phosphate and iron sulphide. This volcanism occurred in all likelihood beneath the ocean or beneath waters that ran to the ocean, for the precipitation occurred in water, and fairly near the seat of volcanic action. Above some of the iron formations occur granites and other intrusives, with a thick layer of mud, altered into slates, capping the whole geologic column up to that point. These slates are known today on the Mesabi Range as the Virginia slates, and farther to the north as the Rove slates.

Then two more conditions necessary for the making of iron ores prevailed: mountain-building and weathering. In their original form, the precipitates were gelatinous accumulations, which later hardened into black or dark-gray slaty-looking rocks, hard as flint and decidedly "lean" as to ore content. When concentration has not occurred and they have remained unaltered, we call them taconite. Mountain-building forces worked on the taconite, tilting and folding the rocks so that they became jointed, faulted and pierced with intrusions of masses of molten rock. Then came erosion, with percolating waters. Water is a solvent of silica, and silica must be removed from the taconite before the iron ore is of much use commercially. These meteoric waters percolated through the cracks and fissures already described, and leached out the silica, leaving concentrated "soft" ores in practically horizontal troughs on the Mesabi Range, and "hard" ores in veins on the Marquette, Ontario, and Vermilion ranges. The latter ranges were also the product of a baking process caused by the intrusion of molten rock at a certain stage of concentration.

The iron-forming era ended in the eruption of the great copper and silver-bearing series of flows, which was followed by the sinking of the ceiling of the great magma chamber already described, and the resulting formation of the Lake Superior basin.

Iron ore was discovered at Negaunee on the Marquette Range in 1844. Dr. Douglass Houghton was largely responsible for the discovery. Soon Marquette was founded and it was shipping ore by 1846. Ishpeming and other towns came rapidly into existence and the busy industrial life of the south shore, soon to be described in these pages, began.

The Gogebic Range was discovered in 1848, but exploration did not follow until 1860, and the first shipment occurred through the range's port, Ashland, only in 1884. This was also the date of the first shipment from the Vermilion Range, which had been discovered in 1848 and explored in 1875.

The really dramatic story is that of the Mesabi Range. It was discovered in 1866, when it was crossed by the hurrying feet of eager gold-seekers of the Lake Vermilion area, who were mostly so obsessed with the thought of gold as to be unwilling to pay heed to anything else. So they missed the really valuable material that lay before them and spent their energy on a worthless boom that came to nothing. One or two men, however, were not too blinded by other thoughts to see indications of iron, and a few men, chiefly the so-called Seven Iron Men of the Merritt family of Duluth, began to search patiently for iron. As they plodded over the pine-covered area, they finally discovered indisputable proof of the presence of ore, though in a state unlike anything they had been acquainted with. This was the famous "red dirt" of the Mesabi. In 1892 the first shipment of ore was sent down the hillside to Two Harbors, and a new era had begun in American industrial life.

How much of Lake Superior's story is represented by the iron industry is obvious from the number of vessels that constitute her ore fleet. In 1938 there were 308 vessels, owned by 21 companies, totaling 2,640,000 tons capacity, and making an average of nearly twenty-five trips a season. Those figures mean that if all this tonnage had entered one port, say New York, there would have been 7,700 vessels entering every year with cargoes of ore, grain, or coal or other heavy substances. The normal tonnage of ore from Lake Superior is about 63,186,000 gross tons. In 1942 the tonnage became 92,076,781 tons; and in 1943, because of adverse weather conditions, 84,404,852 tons. The heavy tonnage of the last two years was, of course, due to war production and cannot be regarded as normal.

The ports to which all these cargoes of ore are taken are, in order of amount of receipts: Cleveland, Conneaut, Chicago, Ashtabula, Gary, Buffalo, Lorain, Erie and Huron. Thus the busy life of Duluth, Superior and Two Harbors on Lake Superior has its counterpart in ports of two other Great Lakes—Michigan and Erie—where unloading of the cargoes makes for as much activity as the loading. It should be added that the chief port for the Gogebic Range is Ashland; and that the Marquette Range sends most of its ore through the port of Marquette. The Menominee Range's port is not on Lake Superior, but at Escanaba on Green Bay.

Back from the ports run railroads. Serving the Minnesota ranges are four such roads: the Duluth, Missabe and Iron Range; the Great Northern; the Northern Pacific; and the Minneapolis, St. Paul, and Sault Ste. Marie (the "Soo" line). The Michigan and Wisconsin iron ranges are served by the Chicago and Northwestern; the Chicago Milwaukee, St. Paul, and Pacific; the Soo line; the Duluth, South Shore and Atlantic; and the Lake Superior and Ishpeming. The last two serve only the Marquette Range, which also has the benefit of the Chicago and Northwestern.

These railroads are only less spectacular than the fleet of ore boats, for they operate the docks where the boats are loaded. In addition, the railroads have a huge task to perform in seeing that the ores are properly graded. Every vessel must carry its proper kind of cargo, properly mixed and containing the specified kind and quality of ore.

The docks are great trestles of steel and concrete, some eighty feet above the water. Each dock is flanked with pockets, usually to the number of three hundred or more. Into the pockets the ore is dumped by the cars that bring it from the mines. On many of the docks four trains can be stationed abreast while the dumping proceeds. The cars are built of steel with hopper bottoms which contain hinged doors. As soon as a car is in place on the trestle, the doors are opened and the ore falls into the pockets. Each pocket holds approximately the contents of six cars. Thus a chance is given to make the proper mixture in each pocket according to the specifications sent ahead for every incoming ore vessel. Specifications have been sent to the ore-dock office, which, in turn, is informed by telephone about the contents of every car in a train leaving the mines. Sampling of every car has gone on before it started on its journey to the docks and the analysis has been determined at a chemical laboratory maintained for that purpose. Before entering the ore dockyards the train passes over automatic scales at the rate of about two miles per hour. The gross weight is automatically registered and placed on a card waybill, which accompanies the car. Thus before either the ship or the car reaches its destination the office is supplied with all data necessary to assign every car to its proper place on the dock. The sorting engines then begin their work of assembling the cars in accordance with the analytical requirement of the particular blast furnace in Ohio, Pennsylvania or Illinois to which the cargo is going.

When the vessel actually reaches the dock to which it has been assigned, its cargo is already awaiting it in pockets reserved for it. These pockets are spaced to align perfectly with the hatches of the vessel. Whether it be day or night, the loading begins at once. The electrically operated and hinged chutes at the bottom of the pockets, some forty feet from the water, are lowered and the pockets discharge the ore into the hold of the vessel. Care must be taken to load the vessel evenly so that it will not list. This can be accomplished by raising and lowering the chutes. The cargo assigned to any one vessel is determined largely by its draft at the Sault Canal and river, through which it must take its load on its journey to the lower lakes. Into the calculation, which is extremely close, is reckoned the amount of coal that the vessel will burn before it reaches the Sault! An equivalent weight of ore can be added to the cargo. The average cargo weighs about 12,500 gross tons and can, if necessary, be loaded in less than twenty minutes. The average time required is three hours and forty-two minutes from the time the vessel docks until it is on its way again.

The speed and efficiency of ore transportation are due in no small degree to the quality of the men who operate the railroads, docks and vessels. Skilled navigators and pilots are necessary, for the great lake is treacherous and there is less room to navigate than on oceans. The United States Government maintains a fine service in its Board of Engineers for Rivers and Harbors, in its Corps of Engineers of the Army, which operates on and about Lake Superior, and in local coast-guard stations, hydrographic offices of the United State Navy, Bureau of Navigation and Steamboat Inspection offices of the Department of Commerce, and other services. The Canadian government maintains similar navigation aids for its harbors and channels.

As already mentioned, eight railroads carry ore to the docks and all have their own docks except the Soo Line at Superior, which utilizes the Northern Pacific dock. The equipment for the ore movement on these roads is very special. The types of cars and docks have already been described. In 1937 there were 40,042 cars in operation by the ore-carrying railroads. These served both the open-pit and the underground mines. As it is inexpedient to handle ore twice, unless necessary, and the open-pit mines do not operate during the winter as a rule, the cars load from stock piles only at the underground mines. At the open-pit mines the cars are loaded as the ore is removed from the earth, either by steam or electric shovels, or by small, quick-moving tractor shovels. Sometimes railroads run directly into the mines; more recently the loading is being accomplished by trucks and trailers and by inclined conveyor-belt systems. These last extend from beneath the ore body to a railroad loading-hopper near the edge of the pit. The belts are loaded through hoppers in the pit floor to which the ore is conveyed by trucks or drags.

The pits themselves have become the subject of the novelist's tale and the artist's canvas. No one who has not seen the great Hull-Rust mine at Hibbing, Minnesota, can completely understand the genius of the United States and of Americans. Here is combined the overawing evidence of geologic forces reaching back into the earliest years of this planet—for this is a part of the earliest land mass on the globe—and the result of man's genius in utilizing the product of those forces. Here is a great hole dug in the earth by man, leaving scars that for beauty of color and color combination are unsurpassed, and that for volume of excavation far exceed the cuts of the Panama Canal. The ore body is composed of layers of black, brown, red and yellow iron ores, which together make an impression on the eye that is hard to describe. Against such a backdrop of color and line, pigmy men and railroad locomotives occupy a stage on which is played the first act in the drama of making railroads, bridges, locomotives, yes, and, unhappily, the arms and ammunition for a large part of the world. If the work in this hole should stop for one day, disastrous effects would be felt around the globe.

As if to be helpful to mankind, Nature placed the ore bodies on heights back of Lake Superior's shore line, so that loaded cars go down to the docks *with* the force of gravity; and when they return *against* it, they are empty. A whole volume could be devoted to the "Life on the Range," which is so unique and interesting that every American should be aware of it and its compelling power in the life of the nation. Here are gathered from the far corners of the world a motley army of mineworkers and executives, who *together* have fused a civilization that has utilized much of earlier ways of life in America and then added just that bit of progress, just that disregard for established regimes, just that love of European civilizations and loyalty to American, just that tinge of imagination and poetry, which have made sensitive observers write ecstatically of it. It augurs well for a country that such vision and contentment can be produced within its borders.

It is too early to predict the eventual effect of the iron-ore resources that lie along the rim of Lake Superior on the Canadian side. The Michipicoten district has had many prospects but only two mines: the Helen and the Magpie. The former was discovered in 1897, began shipment in 1900, and ceased operations in 1918. The Magpie mine began shipping in 1913 and stopped in 1922. In very recent years the Steep Rock mine west of Port Arthur in the Atikokan district has been revealing its possibilities and may conceivably develop into something of note. In December 1942 plans to work this mine were announced. Julian Cross, director of the Steep Rock Iron Mines,

Ltd., said at that time: "The ore bodies have been uncovered to date and there is sufficient ore in sight to last approximately thirty years." At Port Arthur a new ore dock is to be built for the shipment of this ore as soon as Steep Rock Lake has been drained and mining begun.

The demands of the war and the obvious end in no great number of years of the commercially valuable beds on the south shore and, especially, on the Mesabi Range, have stimulated beneficiation efforts in those areas. The war has shortened appreciably the estimated period before the high-grade ores in the Lake Superior districts will have run out. Frantic efforts are being made—somewhat belatedly, in the estimation of many persons—to discover successful ways for beneficiation of the leaner ores. These are so overwhelming in their mass that should cheap and easy methods be discovered, the problem of where to get ore in the United States would be solved for many years. For a long time scientists have been studying the problem; and many mines already use one or more of the common processes of beneficiation—sintering, washing, crushing, jigging, screening and magnetic concentration.

The earliest mining of copper on Lake Superior was done so far back in prehistory that little is known about it. Remains of copper utensils and weapons have been found so eaten by acids in the soil that only the passage of many centuries could account for their appearance. These articles were produced from the native or mass copper that occurs here and there about almost the entire circuit of the lake, but mostly along the south shore and on Isle Royale. Nowhere else in the world is metallic copper to be found in this fashion and it is related that officials of the British Museum as late as 1844 scoffed at first at the notion that a great rock of pure copper had been found in Michigan. At that time an early American miner, John Hays, took specimens to England, where seeing was believing.

In later ages in prehistory, miners of the so-called Hopewellian phase of culture took out pieces of native copper from the Lake Superior mines and worked them into artifacts. Many of them were found in the Hopewell mounds in southern Ohio, when the mounds were explored in the last century. Still later, in the Woodland phase of Indian culture about the head of the Great Lakes, copper artifacts were also made from the pure copper of the Lake Superior mines. Remains of these have been found in Minnesota, Michigan and Wisconsin.

Geologically the copper deposits fall into three classes: the veins of metallic ore; the amygdaloidal deposits; and the ore associated with conglomerates. Of these, the amygdaloidal deposits have produced by far the greatest proportion of ore in the Michigan mines, where most of Lake Superior's copper is found. These, as the name signifies, are found in the amygdules, or gas-bubble holes, in lava flows, where they with other substances fill in the interstices in the older rock.

The origin of the copper deposits are thus described by the chief geological authorities on the Lake Superior basin:

"It is an interesting and significant fact that rocks of probable Keweenawan age are closely associated with a considerable variety of ores on the north and east sides of Lake Superior. On Silver Islet, on the northwest side of the lake, and thence westward on the main shore are igneous dikes of probable Keweenawan age cutting the slates of the Animikie group and carrying native silver and other minerals. On the north shore of Lake Huron basic igneous bosses and dikes of probable Keweenawan age are associated with quartz veins carrying chalcopyrite, which is the source of the copper ores of the Bruce mines and many small prospects in this district. In the Sudbury district, to the northeast, basic igneous rocks of probable Keweenawan age are closely associated with the nickel deposits; and still farther to the northeast basic igneous rocks, probably of Keweenawan age, are associated with cobalt-silver deposits. The main structural lines in all these districts trend north of east and south of west, corresponding to the axial line of the Lake Superior syncline. All these districts have certain ore-bearing minerals in common. The difference is primarily a difference in proportion. For instance, the Lake Superior copper deposits are associated with metallic silver and a minute amount of cobalt and nickel. The silver deposits of Silver Islet carry small amounts of copper, cobalt, and nickel. The Sudbury nickel deposits carry considerable copper and a small amount of cobalt and native silver. In the Cobalt district the native silver and cobalt ores carry considerable amounts of nickel and copper. In the discussions of general geology ... it will be shown that this general region was probably a geosyncline of deposition during pre-Cambrian time, affected by repeated foldings along axes parallel to the shore, and a locus for igneous activity. The distribution and character of the ores through the general zone further suggest the generalization that here is a metallographic province along which igneous rocks have brought up quite different but still related ores, these ores taking a considerable variety of structural, mineralogical, and chemical characteristics, partly because of original differences in the composition of the ore-bearing solutions in these different districts and partly because of the different conditions under which they approached the surface, those in Canada remaining as intrusive beneath the surface and those at Keweenaw Point coming largely to the surface. Still further, in pre-Keweenawan time this same general region was a shore line of deposition with repeated outbursts of volcanism. The attempt has been made [earlier in the volume] to connect the iron-ore deposits of the Lake Superior region with this volcanism. Thus along this great geosyncline earlier volcanism was associated with extrusion of iron salts and later volcanism with a variety of cobalt and silver, copper, and nickel salts."*

Within a decade of the first Frenchmen's visit to Lake Superior the main deposits of copper were known fairly accurately. The group of traders who went to Lake Superior in 1660 and returned in 1663 reported finding copper and probably carried away some specimens. In 1664 Pierre Boucher published his *History of Canada,* in which he reports:

"In Lake Superior there is a large island, about fifty leagues around, in which there is a fine mine of red copper; there are also found in several places large pieces of this metal in a pure state. ... They [the traders] have told me that they saw an ingot of pure Copper, weighing according to their estimate more than eight hundred pounds, which lay along the shore; they say that the savages when passing by,

---

* Charles R. Van Hise and Charles K. Leith, *The Geology of the Lake Superior Region* (Washington, 1911), pp. 591, 592.

OPEN PIT MINING AT CHISHOLM, MINNESOTA

Gallagher Photo

UNDERGROUND MINING AT VIRGINIA, MINNESOTA

Gallagher Photo

LOADING ORE BY STEAM SHOVEL AT HIBBING, MINNESOTA

make a fire above this, after which they cut off pieces with their axes; one of the traders tried to do the same, and broke his hatchet in pieces."

These ancient Indian workings are still visible. One of the favorite jaunts of tourists on Isle Royale is to investigate one or more of them, particularly those in McCargo Cove. Some of the stone axes lie as they were left by their former owners, or did so lie when first noted by modern explorers. Charles Moore, in his pamphlet *The Ontonagan Copper Boulder in the United States National Museum,* reports the discovery of some of these implements during the winter of 1847-1848. Samuel O. Knapp, the agent of the Minnesota mine, observed on the present location of that mine a curious depression in the soil, caused, as he conjectured, by the disintegration of a vein. Following up these indications he came upon a cavern, the home of several porcupines. On clearing out the rubbish he found many stone hammers; and, at a depth of eighteen feet he came upon a mass of native copper ten feet long, three feet wide and nearly two feet thick. Its weight was more than six tons. This mass was found resting upon billets of oak supported by sleepers of the same wood. The marks of fire used to detach the copper from the rock showed that the early miners were acquainted with a process used with effect by their successors. This fragment had been pounded until every projection was broken off, and then had been left. From similar pits on the same location came ten carloads of ancient hammers, one of which weighed thirty-nine and a half pounds and was fitted with two grooves for a double handle. There was also a copper god, a copper chisel with a socket, in which were the remains of a copper handle, and fragments of wooden boiling bowls.

Father Allouez was given instructions, when he went to Lake Superior in 1665, to search for copper mines. He reported that he found the natives very unwilling to talk about them. Such, incidentally, was the experience of all later white men who attempted to get information on copper from the natives. The latter held the copper in reverence and did not wish to talk about it or any other "sacred" article or creature. Father Allouez did succeed, however, in obtaining several large samples of copper ore and some information on the places from which they had been procured. These were: the mines of Isle Royale, where the McCargo Cove mines were located with precision; the deposits west of Chequamegon Bay on the south shore; the large deposit on the Ontonagon River; and the appearance of mines on the Keweenaw peninsula.

His report incited further exploration. In 1667 Jean Baptiste Péré was sent by the Intendant of New France, Talon, to discover more mines. He was chosen, no doubt, because he had already been to Lake Superior and had noted copper. This venture ended in nothing. Twenty years later Duluth's young brother, La Tourette, brought to New France in the summer of 1687 a large ingot of copper, but preparations for following up his discoveries had to be abandoned soon after they were started because of Iroquois wars.

Another explorer, Baron Lahontan, then at Mackinac, wrote: "Upon that lake [Superior] we find copper mines, the metal of which is so fine and plentiful that there is not a seventh part lost from the ore."

The Intendant of New France wrote in 1710:

"It is almost certain that there are copper mines on the borders of this lake [Superior] and in the islands within its extent. There are found in the sands pieces of this metal, which the savages make into daggers for their own use. Verdigris rolls from the crevices and clefts of the rocks along the shores, and into the rivers which fall into the lake. They claim that the island Minong [Isle Royale] and small islets in the lake are entirely of copper. Among the pebbles of this lake are pieces of a lovely green color which crush easily."

Again, however, preparations to go on with exploration and mining had to be abandoned because of another Indian war, this time with the Fox Indians of the interior.

In 1722 another effort was made to find and work these mines, and for that purpose Governor Vaudreuil of New France obtained permission from his superiors in France to send three canoes to explore for copper mines on Lake Superior, particularly at Ontonagon River.

But once more Fate intervened, and it was only in 1727 that the man who was to be the first to exploit the deposits actually arrived on Lake Superior.

He was Louis Denis, Sieur de la Ronde. He was given the post of Chequamegon in 1727. He found it decidedly interesting and appealing. Indians brought him stories of a floating island of copper in the lake, which no mortal might approach, for it was guarded by spirits who would strike all intruders dead. La Ronde got some specimens which, when assayed in France, proved to be of good value. Meantime La Ronde and the son of an earlier commandant of the same post formed a partnership for the mining of copper. One of their ideas was to build boats to carry the ores, for it was realized that the only craft on Lake Superior to this time, birch-bark canoes, could not be used in mining operations. A shipyard was established near Sault Ste. Marie, at Pointe aux Pins, and there a little vessel of twenty-five tons, the first to cut the waters of the great lake, was constructed. Specimens from the Ontonagon River region were chosen and taken by La Ronde in person to Quebec. Only one person in New France had any skill in assaying minerals. So La Ronde sent to the colonial minister in Paris asking for some miners of established reputation to be sent out. In 1737 John Adam Forster and his son were dispatched. They went up to Mackinac by the first canoes in the spring of 1738. At the Sault they expected to find La Ronde, but he was at that moment beating his way down the lake against head winds. So the two experts went off with a trader named Guillory in an attempt to locate mines and there was nothing for La Ronde to do when he got to the Sault but await them with such patience as he could muster. When they did return, he found they had not been to the proper places and, now that their contracted time was spent, were on their way back to Europe. La Ronde, as one can imagine, was almost in despair, but by dint of much persuasion, as well as other inducements of a more tangible sort, he got them to return along the shore of the lake to inspect the sites already investigated by him and the men he had set to work in some places. They went as far as La Pointe, where they found young La Ronde. He took them to the Ontonagon River. Here they pronounced that there were four mines that looked very promising. One was on the Ontonagon, a second at the mouth of Black River, and the other two on the cliffs that faced each other at the mouth of a stream called the Ste. Anne River—now, in all likelihood, the Iron River. They wrote of one of these mines: "One could never see a finer mine, apparently, and it is certain that if one wished to start in the business and invest money there, a great return of copper might be hoped for."

"La Ronde was jubilant; he saw in perspective all his plans justified, he himself on the road to wealth, and hailed as a benefactor of the entire colony. He determined to conduct the Forsters in person to Quebec, receive the governor's congratulations, and then to arrange for working the mines. At the Sault he engaged twelve *voyageurs* to begin an establishment on the Ste. Anne River, there to build a fort, a forge, and a smelting furnace. He planned to transport his ore by the Toronto Portage, and to have for that purpose a vessel of eighty tons built on Lake Huron; he also expected to transport cattle and horses to Lake Superior from Detroit, and to begin an agricultural settlement at the mines. Most of these well-laid plans were never carried out; so far as we know the vessel for Lake Huron was never built, nor were cattle transported from Detroit, nor was a permanent settlement made. He did, however, begin mining operations and take out considerable ore, and La Ronde may well be known, not only as the first practical miner on Lake Superior, but as the first to open that region to civilization. He had at La Pointe a fort with a garrison, horses and probably a mill, also a dock, and some beginnings of agriculture—all this on the present Madeline Island, then called St. Michel. It was during this period also that the name 'Apostle Islands' was first given to the group at the mouth of Chequamegon Bay."*

The Sioux-Chippewa feud prevented the further exploitation of Lake Superior's copper during the remainder of the French regime, but French officers and traders told Englishmen at the time of the conquest of Canada what they knew about the mineral resources of the great upper lake. Therefore it was not long before miners were again at work on the south shore. Robert Rogers, of Northwest Pas-

---

* Louise P. Kellogg, *The French Regime in Wisconsin and the Northwest* (Madison, Wisconsin, 1935), pp. 354-355.

sage fame, reported the existence of copper there when he was in England preparatory to leaving for his new command at Mackinac in the middle sixties. He was instructed to carry on. So, when he arrived at Mackinac, he engaged an English trader, Henry Bostwick, for the purpose. At the Sault, in the spring of 1767, he secured the services of Jean Baptiste Cadotte, and these two men skirted the south shore and proceeded up the Ontonagon River. When they reached the great copper rock, they broke off specimens with their hammers and hatchets, while Cadotte, well versed in Indian psychology through long experience and residence among the savages, allayed the natives' fears with presents.

In the summer of 1767 Alexander Baxter, Jr., son of the Russian consul at London, arrived at Mackinac. He had been sent out as a mining expert by the British noblemen whom Rogers had interested in the project. Having satisfied himself that the prospects were pleasing, he returned to London, taking Bostwick with him. The favorable report of the two men aroused much enthusiasm in England. Many prominent persons became associated with the venture, among them Sir Edward Walpole, brother of the famous Horace Walpole; the brother of the king, the Duke of Gloucester; and other influential persons. In Canada and the other colonies the interest and money of men like George Croghan, Sir William Johnson, Edward Chinn, Alexander Henry, and Jean Baptiste Cadotte were enlisted. A petition was drawn up and presented to the king asking a grant of all the mineral rights on Lake Superior.

Bostwick returned to Montreal in 1768, spent the winter there, and started for the mines in the spring of 1769. Baxter arrived in Canada with some practical miners that summer and on July 19 started for the West with them and merchandise valued at £2,000. At Sault Ste. Marie he looked about for a shipyard, found the same pine-covered point that La Ronde had used and that later was to be the shipbuilding region of the American Fur, North West, and Hudson's Bay companies, and began the building of a good-sized barge. He also laid the keel of a forty-ton sloop. In 1770 the "Proprietors of Mines on Lake Superior," along with the fur traders going into the fur country, took out a license. It states that the following articles are to be transported up the St. Lawrence and thence by one of Captain Grant's vessels as far as the Sault: three anchors, three cables, deadeyes, blocks, rigging and four swivel guns.

At the Sault, Baxter built a fort, which he named Gloucester in honor of the royal duke interested in the mining venture. An assaying furnace was also begun and men were sent out to find and secure ore. All these activities alarmed the fur traders, who began to make complaints, fearing that they might be shut out from Lake Superior. The complaints eventually reached General Gage, who replied that the mining operators must obtain the free consent of the Indians to the operation of mines and associated activities; and that they must not disturb the fur traders.

John Nordbergh, a Russian-born officer of the Royal Americans, arrived about this time. He was something of a mining expert and he found a mass of silver that assayed seventy-five per cent when investigated in London. Enthusiasm mounted to new heights in that city's social circles. Meantime Nordbergh, Baxter and Henry coasted the south shore to the Ontonagon River. Here they built a house and left a few men to mine during the winter of 1771-1772. When the provisions barge reached them in the spring it was found that the mine had caved in and that the men were unwilling to continue their work. Alexander Henry and John Johnston intimate in their reminiscences that the workmen were poorly maintained and did not get adequate food, and that they retaliated by concealing the veins of metal they actually found.

At all events, that summer Baxter and Henry changed the scene of operations to the northeast coast, after the sloop was launched. Between Point Mamainse and the Montreal River on the Canadian shore they blasted rock and dug a shaft of thirty feet into a vein, only to find that it diminished constantly and finally vanished for all practical purposes. Discouragement replaced enthusiasm among the patrons of the enterprise, and although quite a body of ore was sent to England, the company closed down. The charter, which had passed the great seal, was never taken from the office. Henry says that Baxter sold the sloop and paid off the debts in America.

So ended copper and silver mining on Lake Superior for a long time. The copper ores were noted by Henry R. Schoolcraft in 1820 and by Major Stephen Long in 1823, when he returned through Lake Superior after making a government survey in the Minnesota country. It was the eminent young naturalist and scientist, Dr. Douglass Houghton, however, who brought the ores effectively to public notice once more. He visited the copper country in the early 1830's and began combined geologic and topographic surveying there a few years later under commission from the legislature of the state of Michigan. His first report appeared in 1841. In it he told the world that vast stores of copper existed on the southern shore of Lake Superior. Pressure was brought to bear upon the Federal Government, and in 1843 an arrangement was concluded with Houghton whereby he was to combine a linear survey for the United States with a topographical and geographical survey he was then making for the state of Michigan. It was necessary that the linear survey be made before mining locations could be granted by the Federal authorities, since there were no boundaries other than those of nature before that time. His work was begun in 1844, and during that year and the following one rapid progress was made. Houghton's career was brought to an untimely end by his accidental drowning near Eagle River in the late fall of 1845, but his work was then so far advanced that it was taken up and pushed to early completion by competent successors. The first modern copper mining about Lake Superior was done in 1844, and the first product secured was a few tons of oxide ore—not native copper—taken from a fissure vein near Copper Harbor by the Pittsburgh and Lake Superior Mining Company, which later developed the Cliff mine, nearly twenty miles to the southwest. The Minnesota mine, in Ontonagon County, was opened shortly after.

For many years the Michigan copper mines were the important ones in the United States. From 1850 to 1877 the Michigan mines produced three-quarters, four-fifths or an even higher proportion of the nation's copper. After 1877 their relative output fell off gradually till, in 1887, the Butte district of Montana began to surpass it; in 1904 it was also surpassed by the Arizona copper districts. By 1910 it had dropped to twenty per cent of the nation's output.

The deposits first to be worked were the transverse fissure veins rich in mass copper. These were located in the Eagle Harbor region and the Ontonagon County area. The amygdaloid deposits of the central part of the ore-bearing district were next. They stretch down the Keweenaw Peninsula. By 1907 they were producing 73.1 per cent of the total copper ore of the district. Finally the third of the principal types of deposits was found, the conglomerates. These were interspersed with the amygdaloid deposits along the backbone of the narrow peninsula, whose structure has given the name to a whole series in geological history, the Keweenawan. At one time ores from one of these mines, the famous Calumet and Hecla, reached a total of 66 per cent of the total Michigan production. Up to January 1910 the dividends of this mine had aggregated $110,550,000 on a capital of $2,500,000. No other mining company in the world has paid an equal amount, it is said. Up to 1925 world production of copper showed a constantly expanding ratio for 130 years. For the last hundred years of the period it was equivalent to an increase of 100 per cent every 18 years. Nearly half the tonnage was contributed by the United States, and until 1887 the Lake Superior district in Michigan was the most important source of production.*

The first modern mining on Isle Royale was begun soon after the opening of the Keweenaw Point mines in 1844, reached its height in 1847 and 1848, and waned until 1855, when the island was again without permanent inhabitants. In 1871 and until 1883 operations went on once more, but the mines produced *in toto* less than 10,000 tons of copper. In 1874 a mass of the metal weighing 5,720 pounds was found on Isle Royale and exhibited in the centennial exposition of 1876 at Philadelphia. Larger pieces were found later. There was a brief reopening of mining activity between 1889 and 1896. The ores are essentially the same as those of Keweenaw Point. They occur chiefly in fissure veins in the traprocks. They are of low grade as mined, probably less than one per cent.

---

* The several mines and their history are discussed later in this volume, in the section devoted to the Copper Country.

Copper mining on the Canadian shore has never been very successful. In 1846 William Logan spent the summer voyaging around the Canadian shore of the lake under instructions from the Canadian government. He made a report and soon twenty-seven grants of land were made to prospective mining operators. Work was begun on St. Ignace Island that year, but had been abandoned by the next summer when Graham's party passed. Graham's and Agassiz' accounts both refer to these mining activities, as already mentioned earlier in this book. In 1853 operations were commenced on the east end of Michipicoten Island by the Quebec and Lake Superior Mining Association; and on the north side of the island at a place known as the Bonner Mine. There some interesting nickel and silver minerals were associated with the copper. At this same time the Montreal Mining Company began work on the Meredith location at Mamainse Point. The Begley, Palmer, and Point aux Mines properties had all been discovered by 1856. In 1863 another attempt was made on Michipicoten Island for about a year; in 1881 an English company revived activity there and continued work for several years. That same year the Quebec and Lake Superior Mining Association acquired the old McDonnell location at Mamainse Point; and the Silver Islet Company also began to work there. Nothing of importance resulted.

Silver occurs with copper and other minerals about Lake Superior. Except as a by-product, however, the chief deposits are veins in the slates of the Animikie group on the northwest side of Lake Superior and on Silver Islet at the end of Thunder Cape. The mainland mines are chiefly the Shuniah, Rabbit Mountain and Silver Mountain groups. Up to 1903 they had produced to the value of $1,885,681 as compared with Silver Islet's total of $3,250,000. They are in the so-called Rove slate formation, which is characteristic of the area of the international boundary between Minnesota and Ontario, from Gunflint Lake to Thunder Cape and Pigeon Point, and is also seen in the islands near by. Besides silver this formation contains other important minerals. The region is noted by the casual observer to be characterized by a "sawtooth" topography, *i.e.,* hills that have a steep slope on the north, with a much gentler slope to the south. The sawtooth profile is due to the weathering of the Rove slates between sills of hard diabase. The hard rock has preserved the softer formation below it. There is a slight dip to the south throughout this area.

"The Logan sills stand out as the most prominent topographic features of the region. The high ridges and especially the northward-facing bluffs are for the most part made of intrusive diabase. . . . Nearly all the boundary lakes have a bluff of diabase on the south side of the lakes. Many bluffs contain several sills that alternate with slate and for the most part have a thick sill at the crest. Near Grand Portage and from that locality north and east . . . dikes seem to be more common than sills, but both dikes and sills traverse the Rove from end to end. . . . The dikes form ridges that are just as conspicuous as the sawtooth mountains formed by sills, but the dike ridges are different in that they commonly have a bluff on both sides."*

Silver Islet is a small island of nearly flat-lying Animikie slates about a mile out in Lake Superior off Thunder Cape. It is so tiny that it is hard to believe that for fifteen years it was the world's greatest silver mine. It resembles a human skull, about ninety feet each way, and at its highest point it is only eight feet above Lake Superior. It was discovered in 1868 by a small party of prospectors headed by Thomas MacFarlane, a mining engineer of the Montreal Mining Company, who were looking for copper at the base of Thunder Cape. They chanced to land on the island to plant observation stakes, and discovered a vein of galena. A few strokes of the pick and a blast revealed the presence of pure nuggets of silver. A vein was immediately uncovered, twenty feet wide, extending out into the lake, where large nuggets of pure silver were visible. These were dislodged with crowbars while the men nearly froze in the cold water of Lake Superior. They could work only about a half-hour at a time. In a short time nearly a thousand pounds of ore were dug out. This sold for $6,751.67 and caused great excitement in mining circles. The Montreal Mining Company owned the island, but it was

* Frank F. Grout and George M. Schwartz, *The Geology of the Rove Formation* (Minneapolis, 1933), p. 36.

estimated that $50,000 would be required to exploit the mine. So the company sold out to an American syndicate headed by Major A. H. Sibley of New York, the brother of General Henry H. Sibley of St. Paul, the first governor of Minnesota. The island was now given its present name and in September 1870 the propeller *City of Detroit* arrived with the mining engineer, Captain W. B. Frue of Detroit, on board, along with thirty miners, two horses, machinery and supplies. The steamer had in tow a large scow and a great raft of timber. Work began immediately. Captain Frue knew the islet was so small that waves occasionally swept over it. He decided to sink a shaft in the middle and to encircle it with a crib of timber filled with rock to break the force of the waves, while a stone and cement cofferdam was to furnish protection for the mouth of the shaft. This work was pushed to completion in ninety days, with the men working eighteen hours a day. The cribwork was washed away twice. Undaunted, however, Captain Frue tried again and was successful, this time building a breakwater seventy-five feet broad and twenty feet above the water halfway round the islet on the most exposed sides. Stone and cement were sunk as a casing all around the shaft, making a solid watertight wall many feet thick. The cribbing, when completed, was ten times the size of the original rock. On this cribwork were built the shaft house, four large boardinghouses, machine shops, blacksmith and carpenter shops, a search house, offices and clubrooms, comfortable quarters for certain employees of the mine, a lighthouse and a system of range lights, storehouses, heavy buildings filled with costly machinery, huge engines and massive docks for shipping ore.

A village was established on the mainland, where officers of the company and their families lived. It was famous for the lavish hospitality it dispensed and the tone of its society. A steam yacht, the *Silver Spray,* was at the residents' disposal for pleasure excursions. Many vessels docked at the company's pier. The stock of the company went up from fifty dollars to twenty-five thousand dollars in some instances. Men made their fortune quickly there. It is said that it was Silver Islet's ore which won a titled husband for the daughter of one of the largest shareholders, a man of Detroit, Michigan. The amount of silver ore taken out between 1872 and 1875 amounted to 996,432.04 ounces. In 1877 the works were stopped for three months on account of unfavorable changes in the mine when the eighth and ninth levels were opened. In 1878 a rich vein was struck beneath the fourth level, which in a few months yielded 721,632 ounces of silver. This enabled the company to recoup its fortunes and to lay by a working capital of $300,000, but the boom was short. Mining activities went on spasmodically until 1884 when the mine shut down for good. Various reasons have been assigned, the flooding of the shafts, the failure of the coal barges from the lower lakes to reach their destination in time to keep the pumps working constantly, and so forth. The real reason seems to be that the mine became unprofitable. It was necessary to go deeper and deeper under Lake Superior to find the ore. This necessitated terrific expense and danger. Attempts were made about 1920 to revive the old mine, but little seems to have come from them. Today the ruins of former glory may be seen on the little islet, and on the narrow strip of beach on the mainland where the village formerly stood, and where a picturesque summer colony now exists in the old houses.

Chapter 8

Fins and Finns

If the fish won't bite, you've saved the worms anyhow.
Big fish eat little fish.
There are always wise men on land when there's an
  accident at sea.
He who sleeps in a calm must row during a gale.
—Marjorie Edgar, "Finnish Proverbs
in Minnesota"

Many persons who know practically nothing else about Lake Superior can mention two of its assets—its trout and whitefish. From earliest days of exploration it has been famous among gourmets for these two choice articles of food, especially for its whitefish. Let a traveler north of Mason and Dixon's line order a meal on a Pullman diner anywhere west of Buffalo and east of the Dakotas and the chances are good that he will find one or other of these two fish featured on the menu.

McKenney arrived at the Sault in 1826 very hungry and tired, and at two o'clock in the morning was feasted on Lake Superior whitefish. His description is worth repeating:

"Meanwhile preparations were going on to get us some refreshments, and among these was a *white fish*. On hearing that we were to have one of these fish, the Governor [Cass], who had retired, got up, and prepared to join us. This fish being, in the universal estimation, the finest that swims, I have procured a perfect drawing of one, and inclose it herewith. It resembles our shad, except its head, which is smaller and more pointed. The one from which this likeness was taken, weighed four pounds. Their weight varies from this to ten, and sometimes fourteen pounds. The meat is as white as the breast of a partridge; and the bones are less numerous and larger than in

171

our shad. I never tasted any thing of the fish kind, not even except-
ing my Oneida trout, to equal it."

A decade or so later Mrs. Anna Jameson, an Englishwoman,
visited the Sault and reported in her *Winter Studies and Summer
Rambles:*

"Here, at the foot of the rapids, the celebrated whitefish of the
lakes is caught in its highest perfection. The people down below
(that is, in the neighborhood of Lake Ontario and Lake Erie) who
boast of the excellence of the whitefish, really know nothing of the
matter. There is no more comparison between the whitefish of the
lower lakes and the whitefish of St. Marys, than between plaice and
turbot, or between a clam and a Sandwich oyster. I ought to be a
judge, who have eaten them fresh out of the river four times a day,
and I declare to you that I have never tasted anything of the fish
kind half so exquisite. If the Roman Apicius had lived in these
latter days, he would certainly have made a voyage up Lake Huron
to breakfast on the whitefish of St. Marys River. Really it is the
most luxurious delicacy that swims the waters. It is said by Alexander
Henry that people never tire of them. Mr. McMurray, missionary at
the Canadian Sault, tells me that he has eaten them every day of his
life for seven years."

Everyone who visited the Sault in the early days made a point of
going to watch the Indians and half-breeds catching whitefish in the
rapids. With nets in their hands they stood upright in their swaying,
careening bark canoes, which were not famous for stability even on
quiet waters. Mrs. Jameson was ecstatic over the skill of these fishermen:

"I used to admire the fishermen on the Arno and those on the
Laguna, and above all the Neapolitan fishermen, hauling in their
nets, or diving like ducks, but I never saw anything like these Indians.
The manner in which they keep their position upon a footing of a
few inches, is to me as incomprehensible as the beauty of their forms
and attitudes, swayed by every movement and turn of their dancing,
fragile barks, is admirable."

Fish was indispensable to the Indians and fur traders. The main reason for Indian villages at the Sault and at certain other places on Lake Superior was the fact that the fisheries were good at those places. The extra fish were either dried over racks and thus preserved for a time; or else, when taken late in the autumn, they were hung, heads down, from racks of poles and allowed to freeze quickly. We moderns boast of our frozen foods, but the Indians anticipated us here in several instances, notably in their frozen fish and frozen cranberries.

Few persons realize that the great fishing industry on Lake Superior was at its height over a hundred years ago. In 1833 the charter of the American Fur Company expired. The following year John Jacob Astor withdrew from the company and a reorganization took place. The name was kept by the Northern Department of that company, the part of the concern that had traded about Lake Superior. The new president was Ramsay Crooks, who will be mentioned many times in this volume.

Crooks's life at the outlet of Lake Superior seems to have bred in him a great desire to exploit the whitefish, trout and other fish of Lake Superior. He was hardly ensconced in his new position when he announced his intention. There is some evidence, however, that he got the idea from a fellow Astorian and agent of the original American Fur Company, Robert Stuart of Detroit. In 1823 Stuart wrote to Crooks recommending that a plan be evolved for exchanging Lake Superior whitefish for the corn, cheese, lard and other provisions which the company bought in large quantities in Ohio. Even he may not have been the originator of the idea, for in the letter already mentioned, Stuart refers to an unprofitable venture, "Duncan Stuart's White Fish speculation." Crooks was not ready for the trial in 1823, but eleven years later he wrote in a letter of December 1834 to General Charles Gratiot in Washington: "We have great hopes of adding to the usual returns of our trade, a new and important item, in the Fisheries of Lake Superior." He then requested Gratiot to "enquire of the Secretary of the Treasury whether Fish *taken* and *cured* within the jurisdiction of Canada on Lake *Huron* by American Citizens, cured with American Salt, and transported wholly in American Vessels, the entire capital employed being exclusively American, are, or are not, subject to duty." He explains his use of Lake Huron instead of Lake Superior in the inquiry by stating, "We do not at present wish it known that we have it in contemplation to establish any fishery."

When the fisheries were begun, little knowledge of the good fishing grounds was available. It was still eight years before the international boundary question would be settled in 1842 by the Webster-Ashburton Treaty, and no one knew definitely where the boundary line lay. Hence Crooks's wish to know what would happen if he took fish on what was claimed to be Canadian territory. Even an accurate map of Lake Superior was difficult to obtain. It was true that one had been made, but Crooks had been unable to get a copy as late as February 28, 1835, for he wrote at that time to an English correspondent:

"Lake Superior has however been fully & scientifically explored by the British Government, and a chart has been published though I understand its circulation has hitherto been confined pretty much to the public Bureaus, and the Officers of Government.... If I remember correctly these surveys were executed by Lieut. Bayfield."

As a matter of fact, Bayfield's map was the only one of any value for Lake Superior until the period just prior to the Civil War, when George H. Meade, of Gettysburg fame, made another survey.

The years 1835, 1836 and 1837 saw the exploration of the lake by the American Fur Company, and the establishment of the chief fishing stations. Crooks, who had been at Fort William when the change of the great inland rendezvous of the British traders to that post from Grand Portage about 1804 was still a recent event, probably remembered that great quantities of fish had been taken in the vicinity of those places. Indeed, he wrote to Gabriel Franchere early in 1835 that the place at which the North West Company used to get its fish was "a large Island not far from and directly opposite Point Quiwinan." This, of course, was Isle Royale, close to both Grand

Portage and Fort William. In April 1836 he wrote to William Aitken, the trader in charge of the Fond du Lac area:

"Explore the north shore to the old Grand Portage, and even if you went all the way to the River Kaministiquia (where Fort William stands) it will no doubt furnish us with useful information. A visit to Isle Royale if practicable for you to go entirely round it, and examine it well, will also still better enable us to determine where we ought to place permanent Posts for the fisheries."

The necessary qualifications for a station, he added, were a safe harbor for the schooner *John Jacob Astor,* just launched, and good fishing grounds.

Aitken's explorations resulted in the establishment of a post at Grand Portage in the fall of 1836. Crooks wrote enthusiastically that it "being on the *north* shore the Lake is rarely agitated by the prevailing winds, and the operations of the fishermen are seldom interrupted there, while the whole southern coast is constantly exposed to the heavy Winds from West to North, and the sea too rough to allow the people to visit their nets sometimes for several days at a time. This happens most frequently in the very best of the fall fishery."

This post was placed under the direction of a half-breed Pierre Coté, who made an agreement with the company to fish for it from 1836 to 1840 inclusive, on a five-per-cent commission basis. He had the assistance of two coopers, who made the barrels in which the fish were shipped to market, and of three other men in 1838 and of nine in 1839. The coopers received $200 per year, the fishermen and boatmen from $100 to $150. He also employed about twenty Indians, whom he furnished with salt, nets and barrels, and to whom he gave $3 per barrel for fish.

In the summer of 1839 Franchere and another American Fur Company agent, James P. Scott, made a tour of inspection of the posts at the end of Lake Superior. Their report, in beautiful script, is still in existence. Of the Grand Portage fishing station the report has to say:

"This fishing station extends in a Westerwardly direction 45 Miles to Grand Marais, having along the coast several fit places for setting nets and lines—and to the Eastward as far as Pigeon River 5 or 6 Miles. Fishermen are also sometimes sent to the Western extremity of Isle Royal distant 18 or 20 Miles. . . . The Establishment at this place consists of One dwelling House for Coté, situated on a gentle rising ground, overlooking the Bay, a dwelling occupied by his son on the West side, and a new Store fronting this last building on the East Side, forming a hollow square; two mens houses, 1 Coopers Shop, 1 Fish Store, Stable Barn, Root house &c below or near the beach, placed here and there without order or symetry. . . . The dwelling houses and Store on the hill are finished in a Substantial manner and all new. There is on Sheep Island at the entrance of the Bay, an appology for a Store house to receive Salt &c from on board vessels, or to deposit Fish from the Establishment, ready for Shipment. The soil around this station is good. There is at present about three acres of it under cultivation, and laid in potatoes, the crop estimated to produce about 200 to 250 Bushels. The fisheries being extended along a barren and rocky bound coast, the collecting of the fish to Grand Portage is necessarily attended with expense and risk, besides taking away the hands from the fishing, and if the fish can not be all brought in, they of necessity must remain exposed all winter on the beach. At Grand Marais, however, there is a building of sufficient capacity to Store all the fish which could not be brought away."

Three hundred to five hundred barrels of fish were the usual result of a year's activities at Grand Portage. Whitefish and trout formed the bulk of a season's catch. Wood for staves and hook poles was cut out during the winter, but a dozen men could hardly be kept busy for eight months getting materials for five hundred barrels. Trout did not begin to run in toward shore to their spawning grounds until August 20 or thereabout. For two months all hands were busy setting nets, taking them up, cleaning and packing the fish in salt, and transporting the barrels to the storehouses. Then the whitefish appeared and stayed into November. The remainder of the year the company supported men who had little to do except to make nets or to cut and haul a small amount of wood. After Franchere's visit to the post in 1839, he recommended that all but four men should be transported to La Pointe at the close of the fall fishing, to be available for other fishing grounds in the late fall and in the spring, and to help with the winter's work at La Pointe. This recommendation was adopted in 1840.

Franchere made the same recommendation for Isle Royale, one of the most extensive of the fisheries. The stations there were established in July 1837, and placed under the direction of Charles Chaboillez, another half-breed. His stipend in 1838 was $350. He employed about twenty-five men as coopers, fishermen and boatmen, and also contracted with nine "freemen" who fished on their own account and received $4 for 200 pounds of fish, the company transporting their salt, barrels and fish.

There were five stations on Isle Royale: Siskiwit Bay, the chain of small islands southeast of that bay, Rock Harbor, the northeast end of the island and apparently also Belle Island and Washington Harbor. The main depot seems to have been Siskiwit Bay.

"The buildings at this place are very good, and comprise, one dwelling House for the resident clerk, one Men's house, one coopers Shop, one store house for Fish Barrels, One large Store house, with Store attached to it, and an additional building at the West Gable, a long Shed South and contiguous to the warehouse, for the Storing of Salt, and lastly, one Fish Store House."

Trout, siscowet and whitefish were caught in the waters about Isle Royale. The fishing season began about the middle of June and lasted until the second week in November. Whereas 300 to 500 barrels were caught at the Grand Portage station, about 2,000 barrels were the normal complement for Isle Royale.

La Pointe was the center of the Lake Superior fishing industry of the American Fur Company. Here, after the new company was organized, a whole new settlement was built, including storehouses for furs and for fish, a pier for the vessel and a cluster of dwelling houses for clerks and *engagés*. From time to time new fishing grounds were found among the numerous islands that make up the

Apostle group, as well as along the shore in both directions. Lyman Warren, a veteran clerk in the company's service, was in charge. An inspector was established there shortly after the fishing business got into full swing and thereafter all the fish from upper Lake Superior were inspected and shipped to the Sault at that place.

Many minor fisheries were established: at Encampment Island near present-day Two Harbors; at L'Anse on Keweenaw Bay; at Montreal River; at Whitefish Point; at Grand Island; and probably at other places. At the Sault many whitefish were taken in the rapids, and pickerel were also secured. Franchere was in charge of this post, receiving also all the Lake Superior fish and shipping it to Detroit. William Brewster was in charge at Detroit. In 1839 he wrote of his new warehouse, which he had been obliged to build because of the great success of the fisheries: "All of our Fish on hand at this time are stored in our new ware House, which is quite a sight, as the first floor is entirely filled, three Bbls deep."

On August 3, 1835, as already mentioned, the *John Jacob Astor,* a schooner of 112 tons, was launched on the waters of Lake Superior. By the fall of 1836 the need for additional craft was felt, especially for a small vessel that could run close to some of the rocky islets from which fish must be gathered. The schooner was busy from the opening of navigation till the close in early November. Five to seven trips from the Sault were made during that period. When only furs were to be carried, the vessel plied between La Pointe and the Sault. As soon as some fish had been packed, the vessel extended its course to Grand Portage, Isle Royale and other points. A scow, capable of carrying 300 barrels, was built early in 1837 as an auxiliary to the *Astor.* Still the men in charge of the fisheries kept urging Crooks to build another schooner, saying that the fishing business was being greatly curtailed by lack of proper transportation facilities. Therefore, in November 1837, the company let the contract for a new vessel and the next year saw the schooner *William Brewster* on the lake. Later the company also built the *Siskiwit.* These craft established decked vessels on the lake once more and began the modern fleet. Since 1835 there has always been at least one decked vessel on Lake Superior.

The fisheries were *too* successful. In 1836 Crooks made a tour of the lake and felt so well pleased with the state of the fisheries that he wrote to his associates in New York: "There is therefore much more encouragement than ever to prosecute the fisheries with vigour. . . . Next year should give us 2000 Barrels, & 1838 2500 to 3000."

The yield for 1837 was almost exactly what Crooks had anticipated, despite untoward circumstances and lack of proper facilities. The season was unusually late, and the spring fisheries were almost total losses. As late as September 7 the season appeared to be an entire failure. The fall fishing retrieved the situation, but Brewster was very indignant over the carelessness in packing and inspecting the fish he received at Detroit. The inefficient inspector at the Sault was nearly removed from office, and fear of the company finally induced him to do a satisfactory job there. Then, in addition, the company got the appointment of an inspector at La Pointe. This action meant the saving of time at the Sault, where the fish were removed from the *Astor* to the *Ramsay Crooks* bound for Detroit.

With 1837 came one of the most disastrous panics in the annals of the western world. Markets for the company's fish were not to be had in sufficient size and number to realize a profit. In July trout was selling at $11 a barrel. By October it had dropped to $10.50 with a long credit. Still later in the year it had dropped to $10.

The yield for 1838 was 4,000 barrels and for 1839 nearly 5,000. Crooks made another tour to Lake Superior in 1838 and found so much carelessness, maladministration and extravagance that he discharged Aitken at Fond du Lac and Warren at La Pointe, and put Dr. Charles W. W. Borup in the latter's place. At the same time John Livingston succeeded Franchere at the Sault. Results were seen immediately in the quality and numbers of fish taken. By November 1839, Brewster was taking out $30,000 worth of insurance on the fish stored in his warehouse in Detroit, and quite a lot had already been sold.

Indeed, so much fish had been taken that it became necessary to try to create a market for them. Franchere was sent through Ohio, Indiana and Illinois, drumming up trade; Captain Stanard was sent down the Ohio and Mississippi; the South was experimented with, and even New York City—all to little avail. Money was not to be had, and farmers with a superabundance of farm produce could hardly be expected to turn to a new article of food for which money had to be paid. On October 24, 1840, Borup wrote paradoxically, "At present we are engaged in fishing, and I try to get as few as possible." Contracts with fishermen were still valid and they must be paid their wages whether or not fish sold in New Orleans or New York.

On February 5, 1841, Crooks wrote to a western New York salt dealer from whom came much of the coarse salt in which the fish were packed:

"As the usual time has arrived for speaking about our supply of Salt for the current year we deem it proper to inform you that Fish has sold so poorly the past season that we are not inclined to prosecute the business with our former energy until prospects brighten."

Prospects did not brighten in 1842. Indeed, the American Fur Company failed in that year. Thus ended a too-successful fishing industry on Lake Superior. Fish were caught every season during the liquidation of the company throughout the forties, but only in sufficient numbers to support its *engagés*. It is interesting to speculate as to the probable outcome of the American Fur Company's venture, had the years from 1837 to 1842 not been the trough of a serious depression. Perhaps in the interest of conservation of our natural resources it was fortunate that such extensive operations did not last longer.

The American Fur Company's records show exactly how the fish were obtained and with which kinds of equipment. Nets were made at the stations, of gilling, Holland and sturgeon twines. The different species of fish required different numbers and kinds of strands. Mesh sizes for the various fish are discussed in detail in the letters to and from the fishing stations. In his report of 1838 Franchere mentions that the mesh size for whitefish was larger than that for the siscowet and trout. For the trout five and a half inches was the regular size, whereas six inches was the usual one for the whitefish.

This seems strange to modern Lake Superior fishermen accustomed to the remnants of the once great whitefish schools. Then as now the mesh size was such as to hold the fish by the gills and prevent him from swimming back out of the net. The modern whitefish is apparently a dwarf in comparison to his ancestors. Floats, headlines, leads and so forth for setting the nets were much the same then as now, except that war emergencies have substituted plastics for earlier cedar and aluminum floats. Today gill nets are set down to a depth of twenty to one hundred fathoms—shallow for herring—very deep for ciscoes. Lead sinkers on the bottom of the net and wooden or plastic floats on the top side hold the nets vertical. A net is about six feet wide and six hundred feet long. Besides the three kinds of fish already mentioned—whitefish, trout and siscowet—the American Fur Company caught herring.

After 1841 there was little commercial fishing on the lake for over a decade. The first settlers on the south shore began fishing as soon as they arrived. Generalizing, one might call this date the year 1850. Everyone who lives on Lake Superior today becomes familiar with fishing methods, usually does at least a little fishing and develops a great fondness for fish as an item of food. We have already noted Peet's diary references to fisheries at Bayfield and in the St. Louis River between 1856 and 1860. By 1879 in Bayfield 130 men were employed in the fisheries and nearly twice that number in 1880. Ashland, on the other hand, had only twenty-five to thirty men in the fisheries. Both sets of men were still largely French-Canadian or half-breed by origin. Gill nets, pounds, seines and lines were in use, but then as now, the favorite apparatus was the gill net. About 1,680 of these were owned at Bayfield; about one-fourth or less at Ashland. Their average length was about sixty-five fathoms. There were twenty-seven pound nets in operation at Bayfield; and only three or four at Ashland. They were of various sizes and depths, but all formed after the usual model still in use, a maze through which the unwary trout or other fish is lured into a mesh prison from which he is incapable of finding his way out. These nets are strung between poles set in relatively shallow water, and have to be let down again into the water after every catch. Seventeen or eighteen seines were employed, of an average length of about sixty rods. In winter hook fishing was carried on among the islands near Bayfield. The Mackinac boat was the ordinary one in use then as in earlier days. The fishermen found their prey alongshore for ninety or one hundred miles to the east. The pound nets were set among the Apostle Islands and in Chequamegon Bay.

The catch at this part of the lake in 1880 consisted chiefly of whitefish, trout, herring and pike. About 300,000 pounds of fresh fish and 9,000 half-barrels of salt fish were secured in 1879. Altogether the value of the fisheries at this part of the lake was about $45,000. Three firms cared for the shipping. A schooner for the trade was owned at Bayfield. At least seven-ninths of the salt fish went to other lake distributing points—Buffalo, Toledo, Chicago and Port Clinton. The rest went to St. Paul and Minneapolis. The fresh fish was shared about equally by Chicago and St. Paul. The fishermen fished on shares, the outfitters furnishing boats, nets and other apparatus, and paying a set sum for the fish when salted. Provisions were advanced on credit to fishermen's families during the fishing season. Already it was being noted that fishing grounds were being depleted.*

In the section between Ontonagon and L'Anse in 1879 and 1880 there were about one hundred and thirty-four fishermen, eighty-eight of whom were engaged in gill-netting, thirty in the pound-net fishery, and the rest in seining and other minor fisheries. Though the owners of fisheries were principally Americans, the actual fishermen were still, as in bygone days, Canadian-French and half-breeds, in about equal proportions.

About 1,100 gill nets were in use, each 60 fathoms or a little less in length and with 4¾ or 5-inch mesh. The catch consisted of whitefish, trout, siscowet and a few suckers. A small steam tug of about twelve tons burden was employed in the fisheries and in transporting the catch to shipping points; and a little schooner was also in use. The boats did not need to be as seaworthy as the boats used farther to the west on Lake Superior, principally because the coast was not so exposed as the Bayfield region. The gill-net fishermen

---

* For a discussion of present-day fishing near Bayfield, see page 265.

operated as far west as Ontonagon and almost as far east as Marquette.

The yield for 1879 was nearly 405,000 pounds of fresh fish and about 4,200 half-barrels of salt fish. Much of the entire harvest went to the copper and iron mines in the vicinity; and most of the remainder was shipped to Detroit, Cleveland, Buffalo, Chicago and Milwaukee. The fishermen on this shore agreed that whitefish had decreased noticeably the preceding ten years, and mentioned as causes the sawdust from the lumber mills dumped in the lake, increased navigation and overfishing.

Marquette by 1880 was engaged principally in mining and lumbering but there were thirty-three fishermen there in 1879, twelve of whom were engaged in gill-netting and the remainder in the pound fishery. They were of various nationalities, not entirely French-Canadian and half-breed men as at the south shore fisheries already described. About a third were native Americans. One fisherman lived at the south end of Grand Island, just east of Marquette, a famous fishing ground for the Indians at much earlier periods. The gill-netters fished at points as far east as fifty miles from Marquette, but the pound nets were set in sheltered positions in the shallow bays and at the mouths of rivers between Marquette and Grand Island. Seining was still being prosecuted in Marquette Harbor. The famous trout bank known as Stanard's Rock, which was named for the American Fur Company's captain who discovered it, on the maiden trip of the *John Jacob Astor,* was the scene of some trout fishing. We have already noted McDougall's fishing ventures there.

The gill-net fishermen employed several steam tugs, and larger and better boats than formerly were employed in this stretch of coast. The catch consisted of whitefish, trout, siscowet, herring and lawyers (*lota maculosa*). The harvest in 1879 was about 450,000 pounds, of which enough to make 200 half-barrels was salted. The fresh fish was shipped to Milwaukee to the amount of 25,000 pounds. Part of the remainder was sold to the steamboat companies and to miners living in the vicinity, and a part went to inland towns in Wisconsin and Illinois.

Three firms handled the entire shipment of fish. Again, as farther to the west, the fish were caught on shares. The dealers furnished outfits, including boats, and took one-half the fish caught as compensation. The remainder they bought from the fishermen, paying a uniform price of seven cents apiece.

Whitefish Point had long been a fishing ground among Indians and voyageurs, but in 1870 a New York firm purchased the fishing rights and set up business on a commercial basis with a pier and several buildings. During the winter the place was deserted, but in the fishing season twenty or thirty persons were located there. By 1880 it was generally conceded that fishing in that region was not very profitable. Pound nets were introduced about 1870, but by 1880 neither they nor seines were profitable, though the gill-net industry seemed to be improving. The establishments could be reached only by steamers, which picked up the fish in calm weather.

At Sault Ste. Marie in 1880 the Indians and half-breeds were still the chief fishermen, and their age-old practice of netting the whitefish from canoes in the rapids was still in full swing. Several hundred pounds were frequently taken in this way by a single canoe in one day. During 1879 about 2,500 half-barrels of fish were shipped from the Sault, all but about 50 half-barrels of which were whitefish. They were all salted and shipped to Chicago, Detroit and Cleveland.

On the American north shore the fisheries were still unimportant in 1880. This was the period of the beginning of extensive lumbering operations in that region and the fisheries were decidedly a minor activity. However, some fishermen from Duluth and towns on the south shore fished along this rocky and heavily wooded shore, and Norwegians were already settling here and there on isolated coves accessible only by water. They subsisted largely by fishing. In 1879 Duluth's fisheries were carried on by thirty-five men. Although seines and pound nets were used, gill nets were preferred by the majority of fishermen.

The Duluth fishermen operated both on the south and the north shore and about Isle Royale. The spring operations were on the south shore, the autumn ones at the other two places. The pound nets were set in the entrance to Superior Bay near Superior City, about eight miles from Duluth. Seining was prosecuted in the vicinity of Fond du Lac at the head of St. Louis Bay. Whitefish, trout and herring were taken in the pound and gill nets; the seines produced only pike. Until 1880 one firm handled all the shipping, and all the fish were shipped fresh—as far west as Deadwood, Dakota Territory, and as far south as Omaha. The bulk went to St. Paul and Minneapolis. At the head of the lake it was felt in 1880 that the fisheries were just beginning instead of being on the decline as at other places to the east. In 1879 the yield of whitefish, trout and herring amounted to about 280,000 pounds; and about 16,000 pounds of pike were secured.

Although fishing in the lake never stopped, by 1920 some changes had taken place. The following tendencies are the most noticeable. From a commercial point of view the whitefish had become virtually extinct along the American shore and was present in appreciable numbers only around the Apostle Islands and in the vicinity of Whitefish Bay. The catch of 1922 was only 380,000 pounds, whereas in 1885, the peak year of nine censuses (1880-1922), it had been 4,571,000 pounds. Trout had increased from 1,464,000 in 1880 to 4,954,000 in 1903, and then had declined to 2,833,000 pounds in 1922. About 1899 a bluefin fishery of considerable scope sprang up to meet the growing demand for smoked fish. It was prosecuted with exceptional vigor, chiefly out of Grand Marais (Michigan), Marquette, Ontonagon and Bayfield. After about six years the supply declined sharply. Fishing continued until about 1915 but the bluefins became rarer and rarer and practically disappeared. By 1922 chub fishing had been carried on, for short periods only, at several ports, chiefly American, but they had found no favor in Chicago markets and so local trade had to take care of the small yield. This fish and the bluefin are not recorded prior to 1893. Herring, from being insignificant as a commercial fish in 1880, had risen to first place by 1908. In 1917, because of war conditions, a harvest of 12,258,000 pounds was recorded. By 1922 that figure had dropped to the more normal 7,394,000 pounds, still far in the lead of all Lake Superior fish. In 1943 there was an exceptional run of these fish.

The same trend is to be seen on the Canadian side. In 1880 whitefish and trout were nearly equal in pounds caught. By 1895 trout was in the lead and herring was being recorded. In 1910 trout was far in the lead: 3,987,000 pounds as against 281,000 for whitefish and 801,000 for herring. This was the peak year for trout. By 1922 the figure had dropped to 1,495,000 pounds, but it was still well above whitefish (300,000 pounds) and herring (604,000 pounds). The catching of herring in November became an increasingly important industry after 1900 in both countries, especially around the Apostle Islands and in Thunder Bay. It was during this period that fishing grounds east of Port Arthur became important, where many islands give shelter to the fishermen and stimulate trout spawning. Canada had no closed season for trout, and there were evidences that even here the species was becoming less abundant. However, artificial propagation was becoming extensive in both countries. Whitefish was being caught in only a few spots along the Canadian shore. It had dwindled to an alarming extent. Laws regulating the mesh size of gill nets and establishing closed seasons were chaotic and missed their purposes because adjoining areas varied so completely.

In 1940 herring was still in the lead, with 17,116,902 pounds recorded for the United States part of Lake Superior, and 1,441,515 for the Canadian. Trout had increased slightly in both countries and stood at 2,677,176 in American waters and 1,261,211 in Canadian. Whitefish had more than held its own in both countries, with 692,174 pounds in American waters and 385,024 in Canadian. No sturgeon is recorded from American waters in 1938 and very little from Canadian. Menominees, a kind of whitefish, are listed at 14,940 pounds, all caught in American waters. Canadian figures include this fish in the "Miscellaneous" grouping.

As for fishermen and gear—in 1938 there were a total of 1,360 men for the entire American side of the lake. In 1939 the total was 1,837. There were 72 vessels in use in 1939, 689 motorboats, and 478 non-motor boats, all of small tonnage. Gill nets were listed by mesh and totaled 11,939 (3,147,600 square yards). There were 75 troll lines with 525 hooks; and 5,202 trotlines with 1,049,575 hooks. These reflect the sudden development of deep-sea trolling which had just come about, chiefly because of tourists' interest in that kind of sport.

To tell the story of Lake Superior's fisheries only in terms of statistics would be to devitalize a story throbbing with life and appeal.
The only way to understand them is to loiter along the north and
south shores, season after season, talking to individual fishermen; to
take that quaint craft, the *Winyah,* Andrew Carnegie's once palatial
yacht, now converted into a strange-appearing vessel, and make the
tour of Isle Royale; to stop at La Pointe and Bayfield, set so pictur-
esquely in the fold of hills; or to go out in one of the tugs or fishing
boats from Rossport, far beyond Port Arthur on the Canadian side, or
even in an individual fisherman's boat from Jackfish, still farther to
the east. Thereby one catches the real spirit of the Lake Superior
fisheries. If one has witnessed fishing operations in Norway, or even
seen the little hamlets in Norwegian fjords, one can appreciate still
better the Lake Superior fisheries, especially those on the American
north shore, for most of the fishermen there hail from Norway.

It was perfectly natural for Norwegians to settle on that stretch of
rocky headlands separated by tiny coves and a few shingle and sand
beaches. It was the kind of shore they knew from their old-country
life. It takes an experienced man to keep his footing in an open
boat, tossing precariously on Lake Superior in an October sea. One
lurch into waters not much above the freezing point and there is a
fisherman the fewer on that stretch of coast.

Two old brothers, now the Nestors of the industry on the shore,
still fish occasionally near Two Harbors. They came from Norway
in 1882 and have been engaged in the trade almost continuously
ever since. Now they go out infrequently, and they can be found
sitting in their fish shed among gear and tackle, mending nets or
gazing out over the water they know so well. They tell of their life
before there was a road on that part of the coast. All communication
was by water, summer or winter. Fish were salted instead of being
iced as at present. One of their neighbors, who drops in occasionally
to chat, tells of fishing three years in the eighties at Cross River, one
year at Cascade River, one year at Two Island River, and one at Split
Rock River. At each place his father, with whom he went for company, erected his shanty and lived during fishing season. In those
days life was pretty well self-sustaining, with great pines at the back

of a settlement for fuel; deer and moose to be had for the shooting; little plots of garden for a few green things; strawberries and raspberries growing wild here and there; occasional ducks and other game birds available; and fish in quantities, to eat or to sell for the things one could not make, raise or secure with one's own prowess.

In the 1880's and 1890's a fisherman, such as a certain well-known resort owner at Lutzen, would come as a young man from Norway; choose a spot where water and landing, and perhaps water power, were proper; clear the spruce and other trees back of his rocky landing; erect a log cabin, boathouses and fishhouses, dock and stable; clear a spot for a garden; put up his great wooden reels for drying his nets; buy his boats; bring his wife and settle down. His nearest neighbor might be miles away, to be visited only by boat in summer and by snowshoe or dog team in winter. Or he might be one of a group that settled fairly close together, as at Larsmont. This was a Swede-Finn group, that is, men and women from Finland, whose ancestors had been Swedes and who had maintained themselves as Swedes rather than as Finns.

The vessels plying between Duluth and Fort William in summer would stop, when signaled, to pick up passengers and perhaps fish; and would deliver provisions. He would put out in his skiff to the vessel, anchored offshore; but frequently these great vessels ignored his signal, or passed in the night when they could not see it. Therefore, as time went on and gasoline launches were built, they began to supersede the big steamers and propellers. One man of a famous boat-building family of Knife River told the author in 1943 of having served in the so-called Mosquito Fleet of seventeen or eighteen gasoline launches, thirty to sixty-five feet long and owned and run by fishermen, which operated out from Two Harbors from about 1907 till 1924. Then the building of a highway close to the water along the north shore made truck service preferable, especially in winter.

There were also tugs and vessels like the *Grace J.*, the *Hazel,* the *Argo,* the *Winyah,* the *Easton* and the *America.* Some of these made stated trips alongshore, perhaps including Isle Royale, serving the fishermen and their families. Other names of vessels that belong to the period of the last years of last century and the first quarter of this one are: the *Thor, City of Two Harbors, Goldish, Alvina, The Islander, Esther A., Amethyst, Evanston, Camp, Charley, Siskiwit* and *Brower.* Doubtless there were others. Late in the last century the Booth Fisheries Company took over the *Easton* from a man named Singer, who owned several vessels running along both the north and the south shores. These included the *Moore, Mabel Bradshaw* and *Bon Ami.* The Booth company also had the *Dixon* and the *Barker,* which, like Singer's boats, ran along the north shore in the fall, after general navigation had ended, serving lumber camps.

The *Grace J.* was put on the fishermen's run early in the century by Hans Christiansen and Son, of Duluth. After the *American* foundered at Isle Royale in 1928 and Booth Fisheries Company ended operations in Duluth, the Christiansens took over the marketing of fish there. The firm is still in operation, running the *Winyah* to serve the fishermen on Isle Royale and along the shore as far as Grand Marais. They handle some six million pounds of fish a season, which they ship to twenty-six states. They serve some four hundred fishermen, operating about three hundred skiffs and ninety powerboats. The *Hazel* was the Christiansens' boat in their early operations.

Life changed completely for the north shore fishermen when the highway was built, close to the shore, in the middle 1920's, though for some of them the earlier conditions already described had altered even before that time, when the railroad was built between Duluth and Two Harbors in the middle 1880's. If one wishes today to get a taste of the earlier primitiveness, he must take the *Winyah* to Isle Royale. There communication is still entirely by water. Between early spring and late fall all mail and provisions, as well as most passengers, arrive on the semiweekly trip of the *Winyah.* Few if any persons now remain at the island over the winter. The fishermen whom one encounters there have their residences at Two Harbors, Castle Danger, Schroeder, Grand Marais, or some other place on the north shore, and merely spend a part of the year on the island, where they formerly owned cabins and ground. Since the island became a national park, there is no individual ownership of real estate there, but former owners may retain a life interest in their erstwhile property.

As the *Winyah,* carrying thirty tons of ice, makes its semiweekly tour of the island and notes a signal flag raised at some dock, she stops and fishermen put out in powerboats from hidden coves and lonesome bays to place their iced fish aboard the vessel and receive mail, more ice, the weekly newspaper and the provisions that the captain has secured in Duluth from a list handed him on the previous trip.

It is a unique experience to watch the procedure, from the pausing of the vessel at the entrance of some bay after its warning blast has advised the fisherman of its near approach, till the little dory has maneuvered alongside and the fisherman has balanced himself with agility on the gunwale of his swaying craft, and the exchange of fish for other things has been accomplished.

This is the sole contact of many of these fishermen with the outside world for months at a stretch. Their bronzed faces and hands and their agility in handling a boat tell of long experience on deep waters. There is an alertness and resourcefulness about them that is refreshing. Here are men who meet Nature on her own terms and survive. As they look scrutinizingly at baby's shoes (oh, yes, their families are with them in their island retreat) which Captain Ole has procured in a Duluth store, they know at once whether they are of the right size and shape and whether the good skipper has obtained full value for the hard-earned dollars of the fisherfolk, or whether the footwear is to be handed up over the vessel's side to be returned to Duluth. The newspaper there has published now and again some of the unusual orders that the captain has been asked to fill for the islanders. Being the skipper of the *Winyah* obviously requires more than a knowledge of navigation and fish.

Along the American north shore or about Isle Royale, the full sweep of Lake Superior is felt by the fishermen, but at Rossport on the Canadian side there is protection among the countless islands that shield that coast line. In October, when the trout are running well, take a trip out with a tug or an open boat. The former will require two or three days and the novice may prefer the shorter pe-

FISHING BOAT AND BOXES, NORTH SHORE

FISH HOUSE AND REELS NEAR GRAND MARAIS, MINNESOTA

FISHERMAN'S BOATHOUSE AND NET REELS, NORTH SHORE

riod of the open boat. The clothing of midwinter sports such as skiing is recommended, for though the sky is deep blue and the sunshine is pure gold on the reds and yellows of the magnificent autumn foliage, the blasts from the lake are icy. Yet the fisherman in his open, slow-speed motorboat must have his hands in the water most of the time taking up and setting his nets. Most of them will be gill nets, but occasionally one visits a pound net. With what anticipation he comes to each net and lifts it! On the number of fish entangled in its meshes depend his very food and clothing. These are the great red, black or yellow trout that are spawning among the islands, and the females are heavy with roe. As the fisherman pulls in his net, he can tell long before he can actually see a fish that one is caught in the net. So he reaches for his gaff hook and as the struggling trout emerges from the water, it is caught with one sure stroke of the hook and lifted into the boat. Pans are handy for receiving the roe, which is stripped from the fish with a deft stroking motion and left in the pans like big golden globules. When a male is also caught, he is stripped of sperm and the eggs are fertilized. They are taken later to the fish hatchery, and a season or two later the fingerlings or mature fish are returned to the section of the coast from which the roe came originally. Thus is Lake Superior restocked. In 1939 the planting of fish in the lake was as follows: herring, including cisco, 3,332,000; yellow pike perch, 1,500,000; lake trout, 9,959,000; and whitefish, 7,365,000. The grand total for both Canada and the United States was 22,675,000 fish of all kinds.

Occasionally a net will reveal a marauder. On the Rossport sector otters are great nuisances, but they are protected by law, much to the fishermen's disgust. The animal is clever enough to realize that he is saved endless prowling if he is able to find a gill net stocked with trout. Again and again he dives and grabs off a chunk of fish. He may be caught in the very act, or the fish may be still alive when the fisherman pulls it up, showing how recently the theft occurred.

Much farther to the east and beyond all road communication lies Jackfish, a coaling station on the Canadian Pacific Railway. Jackfish Bay is a deep inlet into an otherwise wind-swept coast line. The most unprotected part of the entire shore of Lake Superior lies along this stretch and on the east shore. Not far from Jackfish, however, lie the Slate Islands, among which are good and fairly protected fishing grounds. Every Canadian fisherman pays $50 for a license, which entitles him to be the sole fisherman for a certain defined area off the shore or among islands. A Swede from a south-central province of Sweden has a permit for at least a part of these islands. He sees caribou quite often as he visits his nets. Frequently he is windbound for several days there and cannot reach his home in Jackfish. His boat is a metal lifeboat formerly belonging to an ocean liner. To go out with him is an adventure, especially if the sea is choppy. Lake Superior's waves, it should be noted, are much shorter than an ocean wave. To a less experienced hand the waves that come driven before a wind straight from Duluth, 250 miles away, would spell disaster, for one must turn the bow just in time, in order to avoid swamping, and then return to one's course again. Up one goes on the crest of the wave and then down, down into the trough, from which one can see nothing but craggy headland and scudding clouds. It is a dangerous business, this moving about over the surface of Lake Superior, but it appeals to the sturdy sons of Scandinavia and Finland who now form the majority of Lake Superior fishermen.

They bring with them the sterling qualities that have advanced their homelands—reliability, honesty, industry, careful craftsmanship and ability to wring a living from rocky shores and turbulent waters. It is worth a tourist's while to inspect the cabins that he sleeps in as he visits the north shore in July and August. Since the highway was built in the 1920's, the Scandinavian fishermen have turned with vigor to the tourist business, often maintaining it along with fishing. Practically every home has three to ten tourist cabins adjacent to it. Most of them have been built by the owner himself and reveal many an Old World detail. Note the cabin whose logs are upright instead of horizontal. Centuries ago the French on these shores built their log houses in the same manner. It seems to have been the Americans many years later who introduced the horizontal log cabin with logs locked at the corners. The voyageurs used horizontal, but *squared* logs, held in place by a unique device described earlier in this volume.

Scandinavians and Finns use both the upright and the horizontal log cabin. One cabin on the north shore, put up by two Norwegian brothers about thirty years ago, has upright logs in the original portion, and horizontal in the modern section.

Many of the cabins have fine woodworking details in the interiors: beds of hand construction, made of diamond willow; cabinets constructed especially for the cabin, cupboards made to order, and so forth. One cabin put up by Swede-Finns (the distinction is made carefully on the north shore) reminds one of nautical architecture in the ribbing and vaulting of the roof as seen from the inside. Something suspiciously like ship knees has been utilized.

The homes also show the same careful workmanship and the Scandinavian influence, especially in the gay colors used. Blue roofs are a common sight. Many home-constructed martin and wren houses are to be noted. Few *saunas,* or Finnish steam bathhouses, occur on the immediate shore, but a little back in the interior they are common.

These Finnish settlements supply a characteristic part of north-shore life and scenery. Every farm has its grouping of log structures: a dwelling, a barn—no Finnish farmer who has even begun to establish himself is without a cow or two—a stable, a *sauna,* a corncrib with sides that slope inward toward the ground, "gumdrop" piles of hay, and a few other excrescences on the meager soil of the recently cleared plantation in the woods.

As a group, the Finns are neat, thrifty and intelligent. The housewives are noted for their immaculate housekeeping. The men and women prize education and work hard to provide educational opportunities for their children. Finnish youngsters are usually in the top ranks of their high-school and college classes.

With time a new dialect is developing, a mixture of English and Finnish which is now commonly called "Finglish." But the *Kalevala* is still known and recited. Old-country songs are so well remembered and so frequently sung that a whole book of them has been collected for Minnesota alone by Miss Marjorie Edgar and is awaiting publication. Charms and magic are still recited. These, too, have been collected and some have been published, along with scores of homely sayings, axioms and proverbs. One that is often heard is indicative of the unexpected humor of these solemn-faced Northerners: "Who should hoist the cat's tail but the cat itself?" Another is "Frost brings the pigs home."

Besides the social steambath in the *sauna* (I wonder if anyone ever occupied a *sauna* alone during his bath!), there are the gay *laskiainen,* or Shrovetide sliding parties of whole communities. Customs, clothing, songs and foods of these annual winter parties are traditional.

True to their homeland rearing, these Finns and Scandinavians are partial to co-operatives. Almost from the beginning they had such an organization, called the Duluth Fishermen's Union. They met once in a while to organize opposition to some pending legislation or to make contracts. Theodore Thompson of Larsmont was chairman and D. W. Tomlinson was secretary. About fifty per cent of the fishermen of the American north shore belong today to the North Shore Fishermen's Trucking Association, whose trucks gather up the fish taken along the shore. It has been in operation about ten years. The truckman hauls with his own truck at a commission of twenty per cent of the value of the fish sold. The fishermen feel that they get better prices by thus combining in their own sales agency.

Chapter 9

Drives, Hookers and Rafts

Come all ye true born shanty-boys, whoever that ye be,
I would have you pay attention and listen unto me.
(The beginning of most of the shanty songs.)

FROM 1880 to 1925 was the period of great lumbering activities on Lake Superior. The south shore was logged mainly between 1880 and 1900. The north shore began large-scale operations during the nineties; and the last big shipment of lumber was in 1924. The chief centers of operations on the south shore were Marquette, Ontonagon, Baraga, Houghton and Bayfield counties. Superior and Duluth were in a place by themselves, at the head of the list. On the north shore there were few real centers, for most of the activity radiated from Duluth, but Knife River, Beaver Bay, Schroeder and Grand Marais were secondary centers. Fort William and Port Arthur are still ports for lumber.

In all these areas there were sporadic lumbering operations and sawmills from early days, usually from the fifties, but conditions in other parts of the country would determine when large-scale lumbering should begin. Thus, as long as there was timber standing in other parts of Michigan, there was small incentive for big companies to go beyond the reach of railroads in the Northern Peninsula. By the end of the seventies, however, it was necessary for these companies to find new stands or else go out of business. The result was the opening of operations on the north side of the peninsula.

In Ontonagon County original estimates of standing white and red pine amounted to 4,000,000,000 feet. There were early logging operations and sawmills, but in 1881 the Ontonagon Lumber Company began large-scale logging and milling. It was capitalized at $250,000 and immediately bought 13,000 acres of excellent pine land, and put up a mill with a daily capacity for 200,000 feet of lumber and 300,000 shingles. It had circular and gang saws and a shingle mill. In 1882 George D. Sisson and Francis Lilly of Grand Haven erected an even larger mill. But the heaviest operators for many years were the Diamond Match Company. Their annual output was 75,000,000 feet, as well as 30,000,000 shingles. Their plant burned in 1896.

In Houghton County the great demand for lumber came from the mining companies. The Calumet and Hecla Mine in one year required 2,600,000 feet of pine and hemlock, as well as 13,000 railroad ties. There were many operators. In 1895 Matt M. Moralee was an important one located at Hancock; the Joseph Gregory estate had a big mill at Lake Linden, but it was already declining in production, having an output of only 2,600,000 feet of lumber that year and 4,000,-000 shingles; at Chassell the Sturgeon River Lumber Company ran a mill with an output of 15,000,000 board feet and 6,000,000 shingles.

In Baraga County two of the great lumbering concerns of the country operated for many years. These were Hebard and Thurber Lumber Company at Pequaming, and Thomas Nestor (later the Estate of Thomas Nestor) at Baraga.

The former was organized in 1878 as a stock company with a capital of $200,000. Charles Hebard was president, Edward Hebard was vice-president, and H. C. Thurber was secretary and treasurer. It held over 100,000 acres of pine land as early as 1880. Its average annual output was 25,000,000 feet of lumber and 25,000,000 shingles.

Thomas Nestor was an Irishman who had been in other lumber centers of Michigan before entering the northern district in 1881. That year and the next he put up a very modern mill at Baraga, which had an annual capacity of 40,000,000 feet of lumber and 6,000,000 shingles. He had his own transportation system on the lake: the steam barges *Schoolcraft* and *J. E. Potts,* and the tow barges that he built at Baraga, the *Marion Burke* and the *George Nestor.* These were the first craft of any considerable size ever built on Lake Superior. Each could carry 1,000,000 feet of lumber. The large barge *Keweenaw* also belonged in his fleet. It was towed by the steam barges. Nestor died in 1890 at Baraga and the work was carried on thereafter in three states by his sons and a brother, under the name of the Estate of Thomas Nestor. By 1895 the annual cut was 50,000,-000 feet of lumber. The business office was in Detroit. Nestor's estate at the time of his death was valued at $3,000,000.

In 1896, when pine was becoming scarce in the Michigan part of the south shore, it was estimated that the amount thus far produced by that section was 6,000,000,000 board feet of lumber. At that time, besides the companies already mentioned in Baraga County, there were John Finck's mill at Baraga with an output of 9,000,000 feet; J. B. Smith's at L'Anse, with 10,000,000 feet and 4,000,000 shingles yearly; De Hass, Powell and Company's at Huron Bay, averaging 4,500,000 feet; and some others.

In Wisconsin's short strip of Lake Superior coast Ashland and Superior were the centers of lumbering and milling operations. In 1872 the Ashland Lumber Company organized a mill on Chequamegon Bay with a capacity of 50,000 feet daily. In 1878 the Union Mill Company erected a mill capable of cutting 55,000 feet a day. In 1881 Mueller and Ritchie of Chicago put up a mill whose capacity was 60,000 feet. As there were no railroads yet, all the lumber was shipped to Chicago by way of the lake. In 1895 the cut of Ashland amounted to 154,000,000 feet of lumber and 6,000,000 shingles. The Keystone Lumber Company was operating day and night in the last years of the century. It was capitalized at $1,000,000 and had very modern equipment: gang, band and circular saws, etc. Its white pine was secured mostly in Bayfield and Douglas counties by a crew of 300 men, who together with the men of the Ashland Lumber Company used the thirty-nine miles of narrow gauge railroad that brought in the lumber. J. H. Cochran, of an old Maine lumbering family, was president of the company, of an Ashland bank, and of the railroad already mentioned.

Bayfield's milling operations began early. Julius Austrian of the American Fur Company started them, probably before 1842, for at that time the fur company went bankrupt. In 1856 he sold out to Elisha Pike, who continued to cut and saw for many years. In 1881 the Superior Lumber Company was organized. By 1892 the R. D. Pike Lumber Company had reached a capacity of 18,000,000 feet of lumber and 2,000,000 shingles. In 1895 Hall and Munson at Bay

Mills was getting out 31,500,000 feet. Washburn's chief mill was that of Bigelow Brothers of Chicago, formerly of New England. They purchased a tract of land in Bayfield County and erected their mill at Washburn. In 1892 it cut 46,917,449 feet of lumber and 3,500,000 shingles. Another large Chicago company made Washburn its milling center early in the twentieth century. Other local companies were the South Shore Lumber Company, reporting a cut of 36,912,428 feet and 10,000,000 shingles in 1892; C. C. Thompson of Chicago, whose company of the same name cut 25,000,000 feet in 1888, along with 8,000,000 shingles; Rood and Maxwell, cutting 10,000,000 feet in 1887; and the North Pine Lumber Company doing a business of 6,000,000 feet in the same year.

In 1897 the Ashland district, comprising Ashland and Bayfield counties, had a total manufacture of 265,350,000 feet of lumber and 30,764,000 shingles. It had fine timber resources, not only of pine, but also of hemlock, spruce, maple, red oak, and white and yellow birch. A. A. Bigelow and Company had dockage for 12,000,000 feet and did their own shipping to Chicago in the steamer *Madagascar* and the barges *Fannie Neil, Parana* and *S. M. Stephenson*. In camp and mill this company employed 450 men. Most of the logging was done in the summer months and moved to Ashland by a narrow-gauge railroad thirty-five miles long, radiating in various directions. It operated five engines, 110 cars, and had its own shops for repairs.

Superior had a sawmill in operation as early as 1853, but large-scale activity did not become prevalent until 1880, when the Peyton, Kimball and Barber Company was formed. It grew out of an earlier Peyton mill on Connor's Point. Its capacity in 1880 was 100,000 feet daily. Another company of 1880 was the Paige-Sexsmith Lumber Company, which produced 150,000 feet per day. It was bought in 1888 by Charles S. Murray and Company. In 1889 the West Superior Lumber Company erected a large saw and planing mill near the base of Connor's Point. It likewise produced 150,000 feet of lumber daily. In the same year Frederick Weyerhaeuser and his associates secured an option on a large tract of land on Allouez Bay near the mouth of the Nemadji River. Later they obtained vast areas of pine lands in the general area of northwestern Wisconsin, justifying the name that

Weyerhaeuser had already earned of "Pine Land King of the North-west."

By the last years of the century Superior was deriving its pine from the Nemadji, the St. Louis and other north and south shore rivers. It was towed from the mouths of those rivers in great rafts. This timber was not of the quality of earlier Michigan and Wisconsin pine, but found a ready market in the Dakotas and in northern Minnesota. Later, when all the fine pine was gone, it was acceptable even in the eastern and Chicago markets.

Duluth began its lumbering history at the same time as Superior. The two cities can hardly be distinguished in this part of their history any more than in so many other phases. Mills were erected and cutting began in the middle fifties, but the panic of 1857 left prostration for many years. With the boom of the late sixties, when the first railroad to the Far West was commencing near Duluth, another spurt in lumbering began. Again a panic, this time the disastrous one of 1873, quickly ended the boom, and revival did not occur until 1880. Between 1880 and 1883 no less than eleven sawmills were erected on the harbor. The market for the lumber was in the area being opened to settlement by the Northern Pacific Railroad. The Dakota boom ended in 1884 and the lumber business was quiet until 1889.

In 1892 the great period in Duluth's lumbering history began. In 1894, 3,700 men were employed there in the industry, making a product valued at close to $4,500,000. In Superior in the same year only 300 men were employed. There were fifteen mills in Duluth against two in Superior, with capacities ranging from 5,000,000 to 40,000,000 feet of lumber annually. Duluth was drawing its logs from both the south and the north shore, and from inland in both Wisconsin and Minnesota. The logs scaled on the Minnesota side in 1894 came from the following sources: Duluth and vicinity, 123,-000,000 feet; Cloquet, 43,985,828; Carlton, 12,000,000; Rainy River and its tributaries, 12,000,000; Tower, 15,000,000; Duluth, Mesaba & Northern Railway, 8,500,000; and the Duluth and Iron Range Railway, 8,000,000. The total was 222,485,828 feet. It will be noted that the north shore is not specifically mentioned. As a matter of fact, that region was just beginning to contribute in any large fashion. The next two decades were to be its heyday.

A detailed report of the Duluth district was made in 1895 by Mr. D. A. Woodbridge, then and still a resident of Duluth. A paragraph of his report reads:

"It has been the aim of those locating waterfront mills on the Duluth side to put them near together in the upper bay. . . . Between the ends of Rice's and Grassy points, which bound the bay, and are less than three miles apart, stand seven mills, with an aggregate annual capacity of 210,000,000 feet, and they are all new, having been built or completely overhauled within three years. All ship by water to eastern points, through the canal at Sault Ste. Marie, no less than 722,788,000 feet passing through that canal from various ports on Lake Superior during the year 1894, of which 174,418,000 was reported from Duluth and Superior."*

It would be idle even to attempt to name all the big companies that operated in Duluth during the boom period. Mitchell and McClure turned out 43,500,000 feet in 1894; Merrill and Ring, 40,-000,000 feet; C. N. Nelson Lumber Company, 37,500,000 feet; and Duncan, Brewer and Company, 26,400,00 feet. There were twelve others listed for the two cities, yielding between two and twenty million feet each.

By 1908 the names of the big companies had altered. The Alger-Smith, Scott-Graff, John C. Mullery, Red Cliff Lumber, and Virginia and Rainy Lake companies were sending most of the lumber out of Duluth. They contributed 141,428,000 feet out of a total of 218,886,633 feet shipped from Duluth, both by rail and by boat. Most of the yield, or 182,886,663 feet, was shipped by boat; the remainder by rail. Rail shipments of lumber into Duluth amounted to 57,004,633 feet, coming largely from Cloquet, Scanlon and Virginia. The year 1899 was the peak of shipments. In that year 462,000,000 feet were shipped. In 1906 the figure stood at 446,950,000 feet. Thereafter there was a pretty steady decline. In 1915 the figure went below 200,000,000 feet

---

* *The Mississippi Valley Lumberman*, February, 1895.

for the first time. In 1919 it went below 100,000,000. By 1923 it had fallen to 12,500,000 feet; and the following year, the last of any consequence, only 11,600,000 feet of lumber were shipped from Duluth and Superior. Meantime the value per thousand board feet had risen from $10 in the early and middle nineties, to $17 by 1904, $20 by 1910, $23.26 in 1917, $44.38 in 1920 and $28.17 in 1924. The estimated total number of board feet shipped from Duluth between 1891 and 1924 inclusive was 7,722,452,000; the value, $129,285,842. The estimated cost of logging, freight, sawing, etc., of this lumber was $80,542,600.

In 1925 there was one mill operating in Duluth. That tells the story of lumbering in the early part of this century. The cut had been completed. After the south shore stands had been depleted, the attack began on the less productive watershed on the north shore. Drives had been usual on the south shore. The streams of that area make them possible and even normal. Inland, over the north shore watershed, drives were common, even in the areas fairly close to the lake—for example, on the Stony and Kawishiwi rivers. It was almost impossible to do any driving on the north shore. There were too many gorges and waterfalls on the Knife, Beaver, Baptism, Gooseberry, and other north shore streams of scenic beauty. Hence, the great cuts of timber awaited some other system of transportation. Railroads had been in use on the south shore, as we have seen, to supplement the drives. Now the railroad became the regular way of getting the logs out of the woods, though not necessarily all the way to the mills.

Years ago the north shore stretch was heavily wooded with pine, spruce, balsam, white cedar, birch and poplar. Some cutting began as early as the 1850's, for instance, at Flood Bay and Beaver Bay; but nothing of any importance was done until the eighties. Then Miller and Gould logged the region near Castle Danger. Other Duluth companies logged the north shore as far as Knife River, notably Peyton, Kimball and Barber, Scott and Holston, and the Taylor mill. By 1890 big rafts of logs were a common sight between Castle Danger and Duluth-Superior, for they were still the only way of getting the logs to market. The trees were cut and hauled in winter to landings close to the lake. There they were marked and dumped into the water, made up into rafts, and towed by steam tugs to Duluth and Superior mills.

In the nineties the first logging railroads were built on the north shore, which was to see a complete gridiron of them before 1925. Until railroads were built, the cost of rafting and the availability of south shore lumber kept the logging companies from extending their operations much farther east than Castle Danger. In the nineties the Alger-Smith Lumbering Company, which became the largest north shore operator, put in a railroad with headquarters at Knife River. It tapped the stands of pine along the Knife and Sucker rivers. Knife River lumberjacks, their associates and their vehement mode of life are still the subject of lurid tales on the shore. The company continued to operate until 1918. The Lesure Lumbering Company also built a railroad, the end of which was near the mouth of French River. It reached back up French River and along its watershed. The logs were taken to the mouth of the river and rafted to Duluth.

Other companies that logged the north shore at this time were Mitchell-MacClure, operating near Castle Danger and rafting 5,000,-000 board feet of logs to Duluth in the year 1890; Scott-Graff, operating along the lower Knife River and near Two Harbors; Barney Toppurn at Castle Danger; and Wheelihan and Potter at the same place. The last two outfits rafted their logs to Duluth.

In the period between 1900 and 1910, which saw the heaviest logging on the north shore, railroads became the important method of getting logs to the mills. Many spurs were added to the main lines to bring the logs from far and near in the interior. The so-called Arrowhead Country, *i.e.*, the area north and east of Duluth and as far west as Bemidji, was crisscrossed with rails, all abandoned now these many years. The Alger-Smith concern extended its railroad to Cramer and built many branch lines; the Brooks-Scanlon Lumbering Company was a big operator, with its own railroad of forty-four miles of main line and many spurs; the Split Rock Lumbering Company had a railroad extending from the mouth of the Split Rock River along the watershed, as well as rafting operations to Duluth; the Estate of Thomas Nestor, which we have met on the south shore, and which cut mainly along the Gooseberry River watershed, had railroads reaching far back into the interior; the Red Cliff Lumbering Company used the Alger-Smith and the Duluth and Iron Range railroads; and the Schroeder Lumbering Company operated along Cross River, near modern Schroeder, where their logs were made up into rafts and towed to Ashland. By the end of this period pulpwood was becoming important, and large numbers of spruce were being cut. In this era, too, began the use of balsam, cedar, white spruce, tamarack, and even black ash and poplar for crating, box lumber, telephone poles, ties, posts, piling and other purposes.

The area beyond Schroeder was, in general, the last to be logged on the north shore, though there was some activity there even in the nineties. The Schroeder Lumber Company between 1895 and 1905 logged off approximately thirty sections of pine on the watershed of the Cross and Temperance rivers. A dozen other companies followed it and logged over wide areas. In 1929 and 1936 disastrous fires raged in this general area north and northeast of Schroeder.

White and Norway pine ended on the lake shore almost precisely with the international boundary. Though there has been milling and marketing of lumber at Fort William and Port Arthur, there has been little logging on the Canadian shore to compare with American lumbering. Wood for pulp mills is still being cut in quantity on the Canadian side and one may still see rafts of the small spruce and other logs being towed across the lake. There are also big pulp mills on the Canadian shore.

The years from 1911 to 1925 saw the decline of the lumber industry on the north shore. The Scott-Graff, the Alger-Smith and a few other companies continued operations, and a number of new concerns even entered the field, but ceased in the 1920's. Portable sawmills began to take the place of the big stationary mill, especially after the highway along the shore was constructed. It is obvious why a highway was not built in the region until after 1920, and why most of the settlement of the north shore has occurred since 1924, after the logging companies began to sell the land there. The pine was gone and other trees were cut or burned. Trucks began to take the place of railroad spurs. Rafting disappeared almost completely. The land was the only asset after the timber had been cut, and that could now be sold at a low figure by the companies.

In addition, fires had swept what was left of the smaller stands of timber—unprofitable to big lumbering companies—and the slashings. There were fires on the north shore in 1850, 1878 and 1910. The last year was probably the most disastrous of all the fires. From 1913 to 1918 there were fires every year, culminating in the memorable blazes of 1918, which swept as far east as Palmers, and which snuffed out many lives just south of Duluth. The years 1920, 1922, 1923 and 1925 saw bad fires at Cramer and Cross River, Manitou River, Gooseberry River and Sucker River. In 1926 occurred the last bad conflagration west of Schroeder. In 1926, some 40,000 acres were burned over on the watersheds of the French, Knife, Beaver, Baptism, Manitou and Cross rivers.

Roads, better conservation methods, more vigilance, and better fire-fighting equipment have contributed to an improved record since 1926, but mostly the reason lies in the fact that lumbering has ceased on any large scale. As late as the middle 1930's the land beside the scenic coast drive was practically a continuous forest of blackened stumps. When camps of CCC men entered the area at that time, they began an excellent work of removing the unsightly charred stumps. Today there is hardly a trace of them to be seen. Moreover, the second growth of trees has sprung up so quickly that old wounds are hidden, and the land side of the highway is once more a fitting complement to the grandeur of the lake side.

Before taking up the picturesque way of life of the lumberjacks of Lake Superior, it may be well to consider briefly the part that the lake played in getting the finished product of the sawmills to market; and something of the equipment used throughout the logging and manufacturing process.

Probably the place of the lumber shipper on Lake Superior is best exemplified by one man, who handled 42½ per cent of the entire 7,750,000,000 board feet of lumber shipped out by water from Duluth in its lifetime. This man's name is Percy M. Shaw, and he has considerately supplied records of his operations since the early nineties, when he began his work there.

From 1891 to 1899 inclusive, the rate of freight on the lakes from Duluth, Two Harbors and Ashland to Lake Erie and Lake Michigan ports ranged between a low of $1.40 and a high of $3.25 on cargo lumber per thousand feet of board measure. In 1900 the rate was $2.24 and it continued on that general level, between $2.24 and $2.39, until 1911. Then it began to go up gradually until the war, when it took a mighty leap in 1917 to $5.37 and continued to be over $5.00 for the rest of the period.

Mr. Shaw and a few of the other large concerns in the business had their own boats, but the large majority of buyers were dependent upon outside tonnage. Sizes of cargoes varied greatly, some being as small as 250,000 feet and others amounting to 1,500,000 feet. The average might be said to have been in the neighborhood of 800,000 feet. That was the average of Mr. Shaw's own fleet, as a little red notebook of his, covering shipments from 1895 to 1911, reveals. In alphabetical order the boats carrying his lumber cargoes are all listed by date of shipment, with the amount carried in every vessel. He used nearly two hundred different vessels, some of which formed his own fleet.

Lumber was shipped at Duluth. Mr. Shaw gives an interesting description of how it was handled in loading:

"If we had but one pile to work on, we would have from twelve to sixteen men, according to the kind of lumber. A lot of lumber 8-10-12″ wide could be loaded much quicker and cheaper than a lot of 4 or 6″ wide. Where we could work four, five, or six piles front we would have as high as fifty or sixty men. The sailors on the boats were expected to work at loading. These laborers were longshoremen, or sometimes called stevedores, also dock wollopers. Practically all lumber was loaded by hand labor. Occasionally extra heavy timbers would necessitate the use of a steam hoist from the boat. Practically all cargo shipments were sold through firms of shippers, same as my own. We did not call ourselves brokers. None of the manufacturers employed travelling salesmen, unless they were also doing a car trade. It cost about half of the rail rate to move lumber by boat to Chicago up to the time of the World War, if lumber was green. If lumber was dry there was but little saving. . . . As far as the rates to Buffalo, there was never any competition as the rail [rate] was prohibitory."

Some of the boats used were regular steamers; others were barges and were towed by steamboats or tugs.

In an article published by Mr. Shaw in the *Christian Science Monitor* for July 2, 1925, he makes the following summary of the shipping business from Duluth:

"About 1891 the large sawmill companies, operating on the Saginaw River in Michigan and on the western shore of Lake Huron, saw the end of their timber resources. Some of them came here, building in 1891 and 1892. Two of these mills were the largest in this part of the country. With the advent of these new concerns, which had been used to selling their lumber to the large distributing yards in Chicago and cities located on Lake Erie, the method of marketing lumber manufactured here changed. Up to this time the lumber as it came from the mills was sorted and piled with widths, lengths and grades separated. A buyer could purchase just the sizes and grades needed. This method of handling was quite expensive. Up to about 1892 the large bulk of lumber manufactured here was, outside of that used locally, marketed along the lines of railroads leading out of the city, largely in western Minnesota and North Dakota. At one time Winnipeg yards bought heavily in this city. In a general way the market extended from Kansas City, on the southwest, north to Winnipeg. In 1892 and 1893 large sales were made to the eastern trade, and from then on the large fleet of lumber carriers arriving light and departing loaded with lumber was a common sight to one watching the lake commerce of Duluth."

After 1895 lumber manufactured elsewhere than on the lake proper was shipped into Duluth for transshipment down the lakes. Most of the lumber cut by Iron Range mills was shipped to the eastern markets. From 1910 to 1917 large shipments from the Pacific Coast came to Duluth to be shipped east. After the war the Pacific and Idaho mills no longer sent by way of Duluth.

Thus it is obvious that the lumbering business meant much to the life of Superior and Duluth. Besides the men employed in the mills, the business employed hundreds of men as stevedores. Both the sawmill men and the longshoremen went into the woods in the winter to cut logs. (Toward the end of the era, hot ponds made winter layoffs of sawmill men unnecessary, for the frozen logs could now be thawed out.) In addition, Duluth became the great outfitting place for logging companies, and that fact is still visible in the displays of merchandise in some of the shop windows in Duluth. Food, equipment and clothing were all bought there and contributed to the city's prosperity.

Logging operations were much the same along the entire American shore of Lake Superior. In the whole area there was never much of the so-called "State of Maine" method of building camps and logging. More modern methods had arrived before large-scale operation began in the eighties. The earlier way was crude as regards both equipment and methods. Oxen were employed for hauling logs to the skidways; there was little if any mechanical equipment; drives took the logs to the lake; and the camps were made of horizontal logs laid only a few feet high topped with a very steep-pitched roof, making them inconvenient and unsanitary. All this had changed in most places before the eighties, except that drives were still employed where feasible.

In the tar-paper camp buildings there were now bunks, stoves for heating and cooking, a much more varied diet, and many more of the comforts of life. Horses had replaced oxen in most places, and during the period the horse gave way to mechanical devices for hauling the logs. Railroads were substituted for the drives almost completely after 1900, or else were a supplement to other mechanical vehicles like the "steam-hauler." Finally trucks displaced all other forms of hauling; and portable mills replaced the large stationary ones that had been the rule from the beginning. Even the nationalities of the loggers changed. Whereas the early lumberjacks had been Bluenoses or down-East Yankees, or at worst French-Canadians, "foreigners" were the rule throughout this era and increasingly so as time went on. Scandinavians were very numerous in all the camps; so were Finns; and even South Europeans became noticeable before its end.

The essential methods of getting into the woods and cutting and getting the logs to the skidways, however, did not alter much. It was still necessary to have timber cruisers size up the best places to log and report on them; to have an advance crew put up the bunk-house and stables before the crew of loggers arrived; to have roads cut from the camps into the area of logging and to have the trees marked that were to be cut; to divide the crew of loggers into swamp-ers, undercutters, sawyers and teamsters; to ice the road so that the great loads could be hauled by the fewest number of horses; to throw hay on the hill roads, on the downward slope, so that the load would slow up and not come crashing onto the horses' heels with the force of gravity; to have the logs cut into convenient sec-tions and hauled to the skidways, there to be loaded by loaders and jammers on the great bobsleds of the business; and to haul the logs to the landing, either for rail or lake transportation, as the case might be.

The bunkhouses were built of logs, fifty to seventy-five feet long, and either roofed, or perhaps entirely covered, with tar paper. On either side were long rows of bunks, two high—the origin, it is said, of the idea of the Pullman car. In front of the lower bunks ran the deacon seat, just as in the old days when the State-of-Maine type of house prevailed. On this seat under the glow of kerosene lamps the crew gathered between supper and bedtime, while dozens of socks and mitts were drying on lines high above the stove and filling the room with an indescribable odor. At one end stood the heating stove, a big, long, barrel stove which would take four four-foot sticks and kept the place more than warm even in very cold weather.

At the other end was the "dingle," or passageway into the kitchen. Here the cook was sovereign. The dining table was close to the cook-ing range so he could serve hot food quickly to his crew, direct from the stove. His assistants, often young boys, were cookees. They helped with the serving, washing of dishes, and so forth; and the one with the loudest, most stentorian voice was chosen to waken the men at dawn with "Roll out!" or "Daylight in the swamp!"

Food was ample, if not too varied. Ordinarily there was little fresh fruit, few green vegetables and little fresh meat, but there was plenty of potatoes, baked beans, pie, cake, cookies, pancakes, doughnuts, bread, some canned fruits and vegetables, dried fruits, etc. Fresh meat, when obtained, was often the product of the countryside, usually deer or, in northern Minnesota, moose. Hundreds of moose were killed, and even some elk and caribou, in the Arrowhead country. All three meals of the day had the same menu. Silence was enjoined on all diners at the long, high tables of lumber camps, partly to expedite the process of eating, partly to prevent rows and heated arguments. No liquor was allowed.

The men were up at dawn and in the woods ready for work by daylight. At noon a cookee brought a hot lunch to them in the woods by means of the "swing-dingle," a rude kitchen, or perhaps buffet service, on runners. The men seated themselves on stumps or logs and ate picnic fashion. Work continued till dusk in the early winter evenings; then came a blast on the long tin horn of the cook, and it was home to a hot supper, an hour or so on the deacon seat with one's fellows, and finally a literal "hitting the hay," before the Great Dipper was high above the horizon.

Sundays were free days, when one might write a letter, wash one's clothes, take a stroll in the everlasting woods, or even listen to the itinerant sky pilot. One was a Duluth man, who later published a little book of his experiences. He tells of many adventures on the north shore, particularly about the Split Rock camps; and of the Bethel he served in Duluth, which welcomed the derelict or unfortunate lumberjack when he came to town, out of luck and with nothing to eat and nowhere to sleep.

The sky pilot, the nuns, and others who furnished religious services to the camps were always respectfully heard and well treated. Hand organs were sometimes brought in on hand sleds by the sky pilots, so that the singing might be better and more enjoyable.

One night, in a camp that tolerated a broken-down Scotch bull cook, much too fond of his whisky, the service was getting well under way. The singing became more and more spirited. Suddenly a magnificent voice joined in. Everyone turned in amazement. It was the despised bull cook. After the service the men tried to coax him into explanations, but he refused to talk. Only some time later, in his cups, he confided to a persistent inquisitor that in his boyhood he had sung in the choir of one of the largest cathedrals in his native isle.

The camps had "inspectors," too. This was the lumberjack's name for hoboes. One would appear with his turkey (luggage sack), apply for work, get a good supper and a bed, and after breakfast next morning go out with the crews to begin chopping. When no one was watching, he would slip away, return to the camp, secure his turkey surreptitiously, and pass on to "fresh woods and pastures new."

As for the lumberjack's dress—the most conspicuous item in it was the Mackinaw coat. It might be red, green, blue, or some other bright color, but it was always checkered in pattern. Any kind of cap was worn, provided it could be pulled over the ears. Fifty degrees below zero was not uncommon in the North Country. Shoes varied, too; but a style often seen had a rubber sole with leather legging running well up toward the knee. Inside these shoes woolen socks were worn, not one pair, but many. Underclothes were also woolen. Trousers— sustained by what were variously known as braces, suspenders or galluses—and a woolen shirt completed the costume, except for mit-tens. Two pairs of these were customary, woolen ones next the skin and leather ones outside. A man on the drive wore special spiked, or calked, boots, and the adjective soon degenerated into "corked" boots. Nothing would have been so abhorrent to a river hog as true cork on his boots.

The drives began in the spring when the ice went out of the rivers. The logs had been hauled to the landings, after swampers had lopped off the branches and a tender had attached a chain, by means of which it was dragged by horses to the skidways and there placed by the cant hook men on a pile of logs awaiting the teams. A cant hook differed from a peavey in having no steel-shod point. Peaveys were the pikes used on river drives, especially in jams, where sharp points were necessary. Four to six horses drew the low, broad bob-sleds of logs to the landings. The teamster was the highest paid man in camp. He was on a salary basis, whereas the others were paid daily wages. It is no easy task to drive six horses on a road of sheer ice, the load being many logs high and very heavy. A top and a bottom loader rolled the logs onto the sled. This was dangerous work, and reliable, skilled men were required.

Now the journey to the landing began. Road monkeys had already put the roads into good condition, filling up low spots and removing branches and debris, and a water tank had been over the route, icing the ruts. The road monkey's sled had a blade set in the runners so that as he passed along, he cut ruts just as wide as the sleds. This process aided in keeping the heavy sleds from getting out of bounds.

At the landing the logs were rolled out in perfect order by the landing men, who knew just how they should lie to be in proper position when the ice should melt in the spring and the water journey to the mill should begin. If it were a stream on which the landing was located, it was necessary frequently to build dams to raise the height of the water. At the proper moment, dam after dam was opened in the spring and the logs went through on the momentum of the first surge. Finally they reached the main stream or lake. If it was a river, they would be turned over to professional "drivers," who did nothing but guide logs to market down the swollen streams of spring. Small camps often did their own "driving," however.

Along the main stream a well-worn path was beaten by the feet of the river pigs, or river hogs, as the drivers were termed. As long as the logs rushed on, the drivers could walk along the shore, but when some impediment halted the drive, it was necessary to go out on the logs, find the key log, release it, and start the logs onward once more. It is hardly necessary to remark that the river pig's life was full of danger and discomfort. But he was paid high wages, and for them he endured sleepless nights, or, at best, nights in wet clothes which could not be doffed. If the men slept, it was in the wanigans, or houseboats that accompanied the drive, carrying food and a cook as well as sleeping arrangements.

There were landings all along the north shore of Lake Superior between Duluth and Grand Portage. Today it is fairly easy to distinguish them, and if one cannot detect them unaided, there are many persons still living who will point out all the landings in a given locality. A full list of them is being prepared for the state conservation department in St. Paul, along with a map showing them, all the mills, and not only all the railroads, but all the railroad spurs as well.

Early in the century, especially in Minnesota, logging transportation began to change, as already noted. Railroads were poked into every nook and cranny of the forest where pine trees were to be found in any numbers; Russell cars, a special make for logging operations, shipped the logs straight from the skidways to the mills without reloading; McGiffert loaders did mechanically the work of former jammers at the skidways; and the steam hauler began to act in place even of the locomotive and railroads. These odd contraptions, half tractor and half skis, could haul the loaded cars without the aid of rails. They were the progenitors of all modern tractors and "cats." When locomotives were used, they were usually the Shay variety of wood-burning, screw-drive engine that could be heard miles away as it proceeded on its course, a very uneven one without benefit of much grading, around corners, uphill and downdale, at a very slow rate of speed. Many of the wealthy fishermen and hunters who in princely regalia and with magnificent equipment came to the north shore for its speckled trout and deer, found these engines and their odd little passenger cars unique and most attractive; and as they were the only way to get into the deep wilderness of that day, the Nimrods enjoyed them to the full and can now tell you romantic stories about their experiences on them.

In the spring, on the lake, the logs melted into the water or were rolled over the brink into it, made up into rafts of many compartments, each log having been duly branded with the owner's mark, and towed downshore to Duluth. This was a slow and tedious process even in good weather. If a storm arose, matters could get much worse. The logs would wash over the boom logs and their chains, and the raft would disintegrate. The logs would spill hither and yon, taking their final refuge along the shore, perhaps many miles away or in the numberless coves of Isle Royale. After a bad storm not many years ago the writer found every inlet along the island yellow with pulp logs. Later a tug must go the rounds, picking up the lost logs—a costly procedure.

Part III

THE CORD OF THE BOW

Chapter 10

Saintly Cities

Indians were quick to see resemblances in natural objects. It was they who first noticed that Lake Superior's outline resembles a bow and arrow, of which the cord is the south shore and the arrow is Keweenaw Point. The north shore is the bow drawn back for action. Worth a comment, too, is the fact that the dreaded God of the Waters in Chippewa mythology appears in their picture writing with a distinct resemblance to the shape of the lake.

Although the south shore of Lake Superior lacks the unity of the north shore, its several parts still have sufficient similarity to be discussed under one heading. Both the Canadian and the American cities at the Sault consider themselves a part of the south shore in a practical sense; and the city of Superior classes herself with the south shore cities. Between these extremes lie Munising; Marquette; the Huron Mountains; the Copper Country, including Keweenaw Point, Houghton, Hancock and Calumet; the Porcupine Mountains; Ashland and its adjacent country, including La Pointe and Madeline Island; and several other points that deserve at least a mention.

This is an area which is sinking geologically and so has better harbors than the rising north shore. Ashland has a remarkably fine harbor. Marquette's is good naturally and has been improved by man. Grand Marais is a fine harbor of refuge. There is less magnetic

215

variation of the compass on most parts of the south shore than on the north, where ships in days gone by were often lured unsuspectingly to their doom. The contours of the shore are less bold on the south rim, though even there one finds plenty of grand scenery and rugged shore line. The snow is deeper in winter, there is a greater rainfall, and the vegetation is slightly different. The original forest in Michigan and Wisconsin contained more hardwoods than the region across the lake, as well as all the hemlock that grew along the shore. Like the forests of the north shore, however, the stands of white and red pine were much scattered, interspersed between the hardwoods and tracts of spruce, white cedar, tamarack and balsam. About twenty-five per cent of the original acreage of pine, forty-five per cent of the spruce and fir, and about seventy-two per cent of the hardwoods are still occupied by the same kinds of trees. About three-fourths of the virgin forest area, however, has been cut over at least once.

Some of the story of the south shore has already been told—the early mining history, the missionaries, fur trade and exploration, lumbering and the fisheries. It remains to tell of present-day conditions and more of the personalities and histories of certain of the cities, towns and areas.

Sault Ste. Marie, on both sides of the falls or rapids, may justifiably be considered the focus of the entire life of the lake. Here the great body of water was first discovered; here passed all the great explorers, almost without exception; here were some of the earliest settlements, missions and fur-trading posts; and to it came all the commerce of the lake, at least until very modern days.

The greatest body of fresh water in the world discharges itself through a narrow outlet which descends some twenty feet over a ledge of sandstone studded with granite boulders, creating the famous rapids, the "sault" in French parlance. Today these rapids have been so altered by canals, locks and other man-made devices that they are only about a fourth of their former size. Even so, they are a dazzling sight, especially from below. The true voyageur cannot gaze upon them and not feel the pull of the waters, the mad desire to be swept down the boiling, dancing stream. Throughout the decades before the first lock was constructed. it was considered *de rigueur* for every traveler to the Sault to descend the rapids in a canoe. Many are the tales of those trips. Occasionally a life was lost, but usually the story ended with thrills and an adventure to report.

The earliest part of the Sault's story has been told earlier in this volume. With 1750 the intermediate portion begins. In that year a seigniory six leagues square was granted to Ensign Louis Le Gardeur, Sieur de Repentigny, whose family had long been connected with the development of the western parts of New France. The other recipient of the grant was a Captain Louis de Bonne, Sieur de Miselle, a nephew of Governor de la Jonquière, of whom less is known. The purpose of the establishment was to intercept commerce going to the English traders and colonies and to preserve the West for France. Accordingly De Repentigny and a garrison of soldiers arrived shortly and put up a stockaded fort 110 feet square, enclosing four houses. Agriculture was begun, stock was imported, and all boded well for the little establishment until the Seven Years' War began half a decade later. That contest between two imperialistic nations ended the French regime about the Sault and brought a garrison of British soldiers under Ensign John Jamet in 1762.

Late that year fire broke out in the post, injured the ensign and destroyed part of the stockade and all the houses except that of the interpreter, Jean Baptiste Cadotte. The garrison was withdrawn to Michilimackinac, where Jamet was the first to fall in the savage massacre that inaugurated Pontiac's conspiracy there. Only the Indian village and the Cadotte family remained. Probably the post was never rebuilt as a garrisoned fort, though Jonathan Carver's manuscript diary, under date of August 7, 1767, speaks of the "fort," which he says "consists only of some old stockades round a house, the whole much decay'd and gone to ruin." Alexander Henry, in his mining operations late in the 1760's or early in the 1770's, established Fort Gloucester there. This was never a garrisoned post, it would seem, but a mining and possibly fur-trading establishment. In the fur-trading era any stockaded establishment was a "fort." The voyageurs' name for the palisades collectively was, indeed, *le fort.*

Fur-trading began in earnest with a change of policy on the part of the British government late in the 1760's, which allowed trading

outside the garrisoned posts. In 1777 John Long found a small pick-
eted fort and about ten log houses of traders, both French and English, at the Sault. These were on the American side of the rapids, for
as yet there was little if any settlement on the British side. The
portage was easier on the southern side of the St. Marys River, as the
strait between Lake Superior and Lake Huron was known by that
time. Late in the century, however, it became apparent to Canadians
and the British government that it would be advisable to have British
trading posts and a portage route, or other means of avoiding the
rapids, on the north side.

Accordingly, late in the 1790's, after Great Britain and the United
States had composed their difficulties, at least temporarily, by means
of Jay's Treaty, and while the British garrisons were being withdrawn from American soil, the Canadian fur traders, including the
North West Company and its recent offshoot, the X Y Company,
"moved to the British Side of the St. Mary's and there erected store-
houses, and improved and converted a part of the straight or channel
on that side between the Lakes Huron and Superior into a species of
canal or dam, on the lower end of which they have erected a saw
mill, and which canal or dam facilitates the conveyance of merchandise and furs between the said lakes." This quotation is taken from
a petition of Forsyth, Richardson and Company, Parker, Gerard,
Ogilvy and Company, and John Muir of Quebec, April 17, 1802.
These firms were heavily involved in Lake Superior's fur trade.

This lock of timbers, thirty-eight feet long, eight feet nine inches
wide, and with a lift of nine feet, was partly destroyed by American
troops during the War of 1812, but its timber floor and sills remained.
When restoration occurred subsequently, it was constructed in stone,
and may still be seen just north of the Abitibi Power and Paper Company offices on Huron Street in Sault Ste. Marie, Ontario. Along it
lay a towpath for oxen that towed the canoes and bateaux from one
lake to the other. No other canal was built on the Canadian side till
the latter part of the nineteenth century. Then an event occurred
which determined the Canadian government to build a ship canal
with a lock on the north side of the rapids. In 1870 when British
troops were being sent to the Red River Country at the time of the

first Riel Rebellion, one of the outstanding events of Canadian history, which also involved the United States, the American government quite properly refused the passage of foreign soldiers through the American lock. As there was practically no other way to get troops and matériel to the interior part of Canada, the British predicament was acute. The empty ships were allowed to pass through the lock, but the men and their supplies had to make a very difficult portage on British soil. This event determined the government to construct its own canal. Work was begun in 1889 and completed in 1895. The canal is 1⅛ miles long and 150 feet wide. It is 23 feet deep. The lock chamber is 900 feet long and 60 feet wide, having 22 feet of water on the miter sills.

There was a North West Company post on the Canadian side of the rapids until the union of the great rival companies occurred in 1821. Thereafter it was a Hudson's Bay Company post, a "blockhouse" of which is still shown to tourists on the paper-mill grounds. Actually this is the remodeled powder magazine, made into a luxurious home for an industrialist of the first part of this century. For the North West Company this was a very important post, since it controlled the long and difficult transportation route for its men and supplies from Montreal to Grand Portage and beyond to the Pacific. Only the keenest kind of business arrangements could make the fur trade profitable when conducted thus by canoes over immense distances, with long and numerous portages. Everything had to be transshipped at the Sault, either into canoes or sailing vessels. It is not strange, therefore, that the company was the first to maintain vessels on Lake Superior.

George Heriot in his *Travels through the Canadas* (London, 1807) has this to say about the post at the Sault:

"The factory of the company . . . is situated at the foot of the cascades of Saint Mary, on the north side, and consists of store-houses, a saw-mill, and a bateaux-yard. The saw-mill supplies with plank, boards, and spars, all the posts on Lake Superior, and particularly Pine point which is nine miles from thence, has a dock-yard for constructing vessels, and is the residence of a regular master-builder, with several artificers. At the factory there is a good canal, with a lock at its lower entrance, and a causeway for dragging up the bateaux and canoes. The vessels of Lake Superior approach close to the head of the canal, where there is a wharf; those of Lake Huron to the lower end of the cascades. . . . The company has lately caused a good road to be made, along which their merchandise is transported on wheeled carriages from the lower part of the cascades to the depôts."

At the Sault during the years after 1821, several Hudson's Bay Company factors had charge of the post. John Siveright, a Scotsman, who had served with the X Y and North West companies, was the clerk in charge of the depot when the new concern took over in 1821, having been there since 1815. He remained two more years. The Governor, George Simpson, has this to say of him:

"A poor well behaved little Man who is sickly Deaf & Worn out; was promoted to the rank of Clerk from being a Gentleman's body Servant and to his present situation on account of his Age and infirmity. . . . He shot a man in cold blood a good many years since and altho little is now said about it, he is still looked upon as a Murderer by many of his colleagues, but in that affair I believe he was more influenced by personal fear and want of Nerve than by any worse feeling."

Regardless of Siveright's character, he has left some interesting letters, written to James Hargrave, his friend and at one time his companion at the Sault. In September 1821 Siveright wrote to Hargrave giving the news, especially about the Johnston family on the American side, for one of the daughters of which Hargrave had apparently conceived quite a passion. Charles Oakes Ermatinger, the former agent of the North West Company at the Sault, had gone to Montreal, he wrote; the new sawmill was expected to be running by the end of October; and the Earl of Dalhousie and "Suite in two canoes" had been "up at Gros Cap to have a look at Lake Superior." Major Hinnute and a party from Drummond Island had also been at the Sault "taking the amusement of Trout Fishing, but not with the same success as formerly."

In a letter to Hargrave of May 10, 1823, Siveright has more to say of the physical appearance of the Sault: "The population of the place on this side has a good deal augmented since you left us.—No fewer than sixteen dwelling houses between this & Windmill Point & two or three times that number further down." He goes on to describe "Mr. Ermatinger's New Elegant Mansion," which was evidently the show place of the settlement, with its two stone towers, "all . . . on a grand scale." Across the river, on the American side, the change was even greater. His description of the new Fort Brady there is more detailed even than that of the new elegant mansion. He again gives news of the Johnston family, including plans for the wedding of Schoolcraft and "Miss Jane." Finally he winds up with, "Little or no alteration has taken place at the establishment since you left us, except getting a couple of new buildings up."

In the thirties of the last century a very observant Englishwoman visited the Sault. This was Mrs. Anna Jameson, who in 1839 published her account of her North American experiences, as already mentioned. After describing the American side, with its "unmilitary looking" garrison and a "fortress of cedar-posts," she tackles the Canadian side of the river:

"On the Canada side, we have not even these demonstrations of power or prosperity. Nearly opposite to the American fort there is a small factory belonging to the North-West Fur Company; below this, a few miserable log-huts, occupied by some French Canadians and voyageurs in the service of the company, a set of lawless *mauvais sujets,* from all I can learn. Lower down stands the house of Mr. and Mrs. MacMurray, with the Chippewa village under their care and tuition, but most of the wigwams and their inhabitants are now on their way down the lake, to join the congress at the Manitoulin Islands. A lofty eminence, partly cleared and partly clothed with forest, rises behind the house, on which stand the little missionary church and schoolhouse for the use of the Indian converts. From the summit of this hill you look over the traverse into Lake Superior, and the two giant capes which guard its entrance."

Mrs. Jameson was the guest of various members of the Johnston family during her stay at the Sault. She was very much impressed by Mrs. Johnston and her daughters, Mrs. Schoolcraft and Mrs. Mac-Murray. Mrs. Johnston was an Indian, the daughter of a celebrated chief from La Pointe, Waub-Ojeeg, according to Mrs. Jameson's spelling. Her grandfather was Mongazida, the Loon's Foot. She married the Irish fur trader John Johnston, who settled at Sault Ste. Marie about 1790 and had a large family of boys and girls. Henry R. Schoolcraft married Jane, and the Church of England missionary to the Indians of the Canadian locality, William MacMurray, in 1833 married Charlotte, whose Indian name means Wild Rose. MacMurray arrived at his Sault post in 1832 and, according to Mrs. Jameson, had had such good success that five years later there had been one hundred and forty-five baptisms, seven burials, and thirteen marriages according to the ritual of the Church; and the number of communicants in 1837 was sixty-six.

The chief of the Canadian settlement was Shinguaconse, The Little Pine, commonly known only as The Pine. He had taken part in the war of 1812, on the British side, and had fought in Ohio. Mrs. Jameson wrote at some length about him and his tribe, largely from what the Johnston family had told her. It is for him that the Indian school in modern Sault Ste. Marie is named.

Many others visited the Sault after Mrs. Jameson's book appeared. A steamboat through the Great Lakes from some Eastern port with a stop at Mackinac and the Sault became a sort of Grand Tour. In 1846 the Canadian artist, Paul Kane, stopped briefly at the Sault on his way to the far western prairie forts. Both he and a young Englishman who visited the same area in 1847, Frederick Ulrich Graham, agree in extraordinary fashion in their reports. Both are very brief. Kane writes:

"On the Canadian side, about half a mile direct across, the Hudson's Bay Company have a trading establishment, and the Customs House officer, Mr. Wilson, a tolerably handsome house. With these two exceptions, the British side presents to the traveller a collection of poor miserable hovels, occupied solely by half-breeds and Indians. In strolling among these hovels, I made a sketch of a good-looking half-breed girl, whose sudden appearance, emerging from such a wretched neighbourhood, took me by surprise."

INTERIOR OF A LUMBERING CAMP BUNKHOUSE, ABOUT 1890

Roleff Photo

LUMBERJACKS' LUNCH IN THE WOODS BY SWING DINGLE,
NORTH SHORE, ABOUT 1910

Roleff Photo

STEAM HAULER, NORTH SHORE, ABOUT 1913

Graham reports:

"We went over to the fort with Ballandane [John Ballenden, who was in charge from 1840 to 1848], the factor, having made the necessary purchases for our voyage. The fort is situated close to the falls, and is surrounded by an 'embarras' of burnt forest on three sides. Shot snipe in the afternoon, and exhausted the supply. . . . Dawdled about with Ballandane and Wilson, the Revenue officer. Went to visit the lodges of some Saulteux. Made the acquaintance of a very pretty young lady, the daughter of the lady of the lodge, in whose agreeable society I spent a good deal of my time during the following week, learning Chippewa, and other little Indian accomplishments."

With the discovery of the Bruce and other mines near by, the opening of the American ship canal and the establishment of Canadian steamship companies that plied regularly through Lake Superior, and finally the opening of the Canadian canal and lock, the Canadian Sault, as it is usually called, began to grow and become a modern city. Its modern development is so closely linked with that of its twin across the rapids that it will be described a little later in the chapter, when the industrial growth of both cities is taken up. Today the Canadian city rivals its sister city across the narrow stretch of water.

A transcontinental highway, completed to the east, but still under construction to the west, runs through the Canadian Sault. The day is not far off when you will be able to drive straight through to Port Arthur. Already the road extends from Port Arthur east to Jackfish Bay (a bridge was lacking between Schreiber and Jackfish in 1942, when the writer was last there); and west from the Sault to Montreal River. It is a scenic drive that will reward anyone who cares for wild country and rock mountains coming down with a bold sweep to transparent waters. The Batchawana Road, as the eastern sector is called, skirts the edge of an area that has been the paradise of huntsmen and fishermen for many years, but that hitherto has been accessible only from the lake or by means of the Algoma Central and Hudson Bay

Railway. In the early 1920's a man determined to visit this little known area and publish his account of it. The result is a charming travel narrative written by T. Morris Longstreth and entitled *The Lake Superior Country.* Except for the partially completed highway, the region is still very much as he reported it in 1924.

The division of the province of Ontario in which Sault Ste. Marie lies is called Algoma. This name is a strictly regional product, being the creation of a famous resident of the area, Henry R. Schoolcraft. He was addicted to making up words that sounded like good Indian names—witness, for example, his *Itasca,* as the source of the Mississippi River, which was created out of two Latin words, *veritas* and *caput,* supposed to mean "True Source." By omitting the first syllable of the first word and joining it to the first of the second word, he obtained something that could easily fool even a student of Chippewa. *Oneota* is another of his creations. As he made a thorough study of the local Indians and their language, and published many books about them, he could easily make up words that had a genuine ring to them.

Algoma is a rich hinterland on which Sault Ste. Marie draws to support her abundant industrial life. One of the largest steel plants in Canada is located at the Sault. The largest nickel mine in the world is situated two hundred miles away. A great hardwood forest lies back and north of the city. The power and paper company in the city produces groundwood, unbleached sulphite fiber, newsprint, wrapping paper, and wood-pulp board. There are a chromium mining and smelting corporation, a tar and chemical company, a foundry and machine company, a hydroelectric company, and several other important industrial organizations.

The modern city on the Michigan side of the straits still has the government garrison, Fort Brady, which was established there in 1822. John Siveright wrote his friend Hargrave on May 10, 1823:

"You have heard of the arrival of the Americans, two hundred & fifty troops exclusive of officers & other followers. It could scarcely be credited the work they have done, & well done too, all by themselves. Not an individual of the place was employed by them. They had selected workmen of every discription below, & were independent of casual assistance. Their Buildings are large well finished inside better than any we could boast of at the Sault. Each Officer's Quarters, (& there are seventeen) consist of three rooms, Hall, Bedroom & Kitchen, with elegant brick chimney in each, & they were all in quarters on the 15th Nov."

He goes on to praise the quality of the officers and to tell how they allowed him to use the regimental library, "which being contrary to the rules I considered the greatest favor."

Shortly afterward, in 1828, the first modern mission of any duration was established at the Sault. This was a Baptist station and was headed by the Reverend Abel Bingham of that faith. He established a chapel, a school for Indians and half-breeds, and served the region from points on St. Marys River to others up the south shore of Lake Superior. He labored in this field for some twenty-five years and is commemorated in the modern city by an avenue and a tablet to his memory.

When he arrived at the Sault, he found another Indian missionary already there, Alvin (Alvan) Coe, who is well known on the early missionary frontier, both domestic and Indian, from Connecticut to Fort Snelling in Minnesota. In 1829 Coe had progressed to Fort Snelling, having been earlier in Ohio and Michigan. It would seem that recently established military posts had a decided attraction for him. Just how long he was at Fort Brady and what he accomplished there is not known, but he seems to have made as little impression there as later at the mouth of the Minnesota River. Even Coe cannot be termed the first modern missionary at the Sault, however, for Tabeau, Crevier, Provencher and Dumoulin, as already recounted, stopped at the Sault for missionary services on their several trips through Lake Superior. For example, the records of St. Marys parish, Sault Ste. Marie, show three baptisms by Dumoulin. Other itinerant work was done, but Coe seems to have been the first resident clergyman.

Almost as short, but of more consequence, was the mission of the

Presbyterian clergyman, the Reverend Jeremiah Porter, who is known better for having established the first Presbyterian church in Chicago than for his earlier services at the Sault. He was a graduate of Princeton Theological Seminary in 1831 and was deputed at once, under the aegis of the American Home Missionary Society, to the Sault. He remained until 1833, having aided Bingham, meantime, in bringing about a great revival among the soldiers and officers at the fort. Among his white parishioners were Schoolcraft, Schoolcraft's brother-in-law, the sutler of the fort; Bela Chapman, a well-known trader; William Thurston Boutwell, later a well-known Indian missionary in Minnesota; the commandant of the post; and several officers and their wives.

The Methodists, who in the long run had more missionaries among the Indians of the Sault and the south shore than any other denomination, sent their first regular missionary to the Sault, the Reverend John Clark, in 1833, though an Indian convert, John Sunday, had come earlier from his native Canada in the interest of the Wesleyans. Clark is a very well-known figure in North American missions. Soon there were many more native preachers, such as Peter Marksman, John Kahbeege, John Johnson (Enmegahbowh), and Joseph Bushay. In 1837 D. M. Chandler came, and in 1838 William H. Brockway, for whom the beautiful scenic drive on Keweenaw Point is named. He was a blacksmith by trade and only reluctantly entered the holy field, feeling himself unworthy. However, his service was a long and effective one at the Sault, for he remained until 1848, not only as Indian missionary, but also as chaplain at Fort Brady most of the time. Pitezel, whose story has already been recounted in this volume, arrived in 1843. His diaries now lie in the Carnegie Public Library at the Sault.

The Methodist mission extended along the entire south shore, with stations on Keweenaw Point among the miners as well as the Indians, at L'Anse, Fond du Lac, and even inland at Sandy Lake and Mille Lacs in the region now known as Minnesota. Such men as Samuel Spates and John Johnson served there for many years, traveling to conference meetings at the Sault occasionally and receiving visits from the chief missionary at the Sault. From 1848 to 1852 Pitezel was superintendent of the Indian Mission District, which later became the Lake Superior District with James Shaw as superintendent.

Father Pierz arrived at the Sault in 1836, where he remained till 1838. This energetic Slovenian priest maintained a school for native children and built "one of the finest churches in the state," to quote the remarks of a visiting bishop. It was not the first Catholic house of worship at the Sault, for a Redemptorist, Father Francis Haetscher, who arrived in the summer of 1834, constructed a small log chapel. He remained only a short time. Many bishops and priests other than the resident missionaries visited the Sault in the 1830's and 1840's, some of whom have left records of their impressions of the place.

Finally in 1846 the Jesuits formally accepted the mission task at that place and appointed the first actual pastor, Jean Baptist Menet. He was still acting in that capacity when Frederic Baraga became the first bishop of the diocese and came to his see at Sault Ste. Marie in 1854. An Ursuline school had been established in 1853, but the nuns and the Jesuits left in 1860 and 1861 respectively and makeshift arrangements were pursued for a time. Finally, in 1864, the Jesuit Menet returned to his former charge. Since that time Jesuits have had charge of the parish. The see was moved to Marquette in 1866.

Though the Catholics clung long to the Sault, even they finally realized that the village was not fulfilling its early promise. This was due to the fact that after navigation closed in the fall, the place was practically isolated until the spring thaw came. The summer months are full of intense activity. With the filling of the locks in the spring, usually in April, and the arrival of the first boat to pass through them, there is new life, and this continues till December. As at Duluth, Fort William and Port Arthur, the arrival of the first "boat" (on the Great Lakes, vessels of all kinds, including ships, are almost invariably termed "boats") is made the occasion for a celebration. The captain is feted and usually presented with some trophy, and a parade sometimes takes place. Of recent years at the Sault the trophy has consisted of a desk set—consisting of a clock, set in a replica of a steering wheel, and a barometer. At the Twin Ports it is more likely to be a silk hat. At other places and times it has been a brass ship on a hardwood base with a metal plaque below giving information about the occasion and the ship. Not infrequently the captain is asked to return the actual trophy for use in another season, but he is given the equivalent in money.

The season is hastened as much as possible by ice crushers. These vessels come over from Mackinac. They have a propeller at the bow, which sucks water out from under the ice and leaves it high and dry. When the bow strikes the ice shelf, it shatters it into millions of pieces.

The old marine district of Sault Ste. Marie had great charm, if one may judge from pictures and descriptions of it. It lay along the water's edge from the present MacArthur Lock, where the American Fur Company buildings and old Fort Brady began, down past the rapids with their original little islands of exquisite beauty—now dredged out, alas! to make the passageway clear for great steamers—and as far down as the Little Rapids and the beginning of the large and beautiful Sugar Island. At this lower end of town was the Methodist mission, no trace of which seems to survive today. The visitor to the Country Club, however, can realize how fair the setting of the mission was, as he sits on the porch and watches the proud white bridges of the ore boats moving majestically behind the tree-tops. It was here, too, that an Indian village began, being close to the rapids from which the famous whitefish was obtained. It is a well-wooded area even today, and full of birds and flowers. High above the rapids, silhouetted against the horizon of the Canadian hills, ospreys wheel, watching for fish in the gleaming waters of the rapids and river. Gulls are ever in view, too, the descendants of Radisson's "goilants" without a doubt. A little ferry connects with near-by Sugar Island. All is peace and beauty despite the continual movement of ore boats up and down St. Marys River. Their almost soundless passage and the grace of their long bodies merely swell the contentment of the observer.

Something of the beauty of the scene and the impression it made on a poet is preserved in the account of William Cullen Bryant's visit to the spot in 1846:

"In the afternoon we drove down the west bank of the river to attend religious service at an Indian village, called the Little Rapids, about two miles and a half from the Sault. . . . We walked through the village, which is prettily situated on a swift and deep channel of the St. Mary, where the green waters rush between the main-land and a wooded island. It stands on rich meadows of the river, with a path running before it, parallel with the bank, along the velvet sward, and backed at no great distance by the thick original forest, which not far below closes up on the river on both sides. The inhabitants at the doors and windows of their log-cabins had a demure and subdued aspect; they were dressed in their clean Sunday clothes, and the peace and quiet of the place formed a strong contrast to the debaucheries we had witnessed at the village by the Falls."

Up in the town there is bustle and movement where the Baptist mission stood, close to the site of the old French fort. But there, too, a peaceful and pleasant scene must have originally greeted the French soldiers and officers and the missionaries both of Bingham's establishment and the not-distant Catholic "palace" of Bishop Baraga, as they glanced from windows and doors at the dancing, foaming rapids before them. Closer to the water than any of these establishments was, and still is, the Johnston home, sole survivor of that idyllic past. As this is being written, however, there goes forth the edict that a new slip is to be made on the present water front, which will necessitate the removal of this, one of the oldest buildings in the Old Northwest.

The memories that cluster about this remnant of a once fine home, the center of civilization and culture in an otherwise unbroken wilderness, serve to summarize almost the entire history of that Northwest. Here John Johnston lived with his Indian bride and did business with her relatives and neighbors along the entire south shore to Fond du Lac. Here he or his family entertained famous traders, visitors and explorers. Hardly a traveler to the Sault or beyond in the years from 1792 to the mid-century but experienced hospitality from some resident in this house, or not far away at Jane Johnston Schoolcraft's home. That also is standing, protected by the great industrial company in whose grounds it is included.

Johnston saw the British post established on the other side of the rapids, witnessed the arrival of John Jacob Astor's agents of the American Fur Company after the tragic days of the War of 1812, experienced great personal loss in that war because of his adherence to the British cause despite his American residence and occupation as a government employee, knew through Lord Selkirk's sojourn at the Sault of the bitter struggle waging between the Earl and the North West Company, saw peace return with the coalescing of the two rival companies under the name of the Hudson's Bay Company in 1821, observed the boundary commissioners of England and the United States surveying the Sault and northwest through the great lake and beyond in the early 1820's, watched the arrival of the Fort Brady garrison and the construction of their post, and may even have seen the first missionary arrive.

Then he died and his widow carried on, going up into Lake Superior for the fall fisheries and returning with a great harvest; retiring to her "sugar bush"—Sugar Island—in the early spring to make hundreds of pounds of maple sugar; marrying her three daughters as well as any family of half-breed girls were ever wed; watching her sons do at least reasonably well as trader, government interpreter, and Indian subagent; and remaining throughout her long life the simple, dignified Indian woman. She is a credit to her race and to the history of Sault Ste. Marie.

It would take too much space to catalogue all the famous men and women who visited Sault Ste. Marie from 1790 to the opening of the canal. Alexander Mackenzie, Daniel Harmon, David Thompson, Gabriel Franchere and Ramsay Crooks were among the traders. All of them have written of their experiences, though Crooks's accounts have never been published. William Cullen Bryant and Eastman Johnson among the literary men and artists should be included. Governor Lewis Cass, Thomas L. McKenney of the Indian Department of the United States Government, and Major Stephen H. Long belong with the public officials who visited the place and have left accounts of what they saw there and on Lake Superior. The Sault was also visited by prelates like Bishops Provencher, Taché, Resé and the Bishop of Montreal; titled gentlemen like Lord Milton, the Earl

Ent Juner 0/81

STATEMENT OF ARTICLES

PASSING THROUGH

ST. MARY'S FALLS CANAL.

On _Str Penley_

May 1 1881.

From _Chicago_

To _Hancock_

BOUND UP.

Apples, bbls.	24	Lard Oil, bbls.	34
Butter, lbs.	27000	Lard, lbs.	
Bacon, lbs.	43000	Liquor, bbls.	
Beef, bbls.	60	Malt, lbs.	37500
Boilers.		Machinery, tons.	14
Beer, kegs.	65	Nails, kegs.	68
Bar Iron, tons.	3	Pork, bbls.	64
Barrel Hoops, M.		Powder, tons.	
Barrel Heads, M.		Potatoes, bushels.	214
Brick, M.		Railroad Iron, tons.	
Cattle.		Railroad Spikes, kegs.	
Coal Oil, bbls.		Mowers and Reapers.	
Coal, tons.		Salt, bbls.	15
Candles, boxes.	1874	Sugar, bbls.	84
Cheese, lbs.	26	Sheep.	19
Coffee, bags.		Soap, boxes.	125
Coarse Grain, bushels.	9000	Soda, lbs.	4200
Cement, bbls.	10	Syrup, bbls.	
Coke, tons.		Staves, M.	
Dried Fruit, lbs.		Tea, chests.	37
Engines.		Tobacco, lbs.	2800
Eggs, bbls.	60	Tallow, lbs.	19500
Fish, kegs.		Vinegar, bbls.	15
Flour, bbls.	25	Vegetable, bushels.	
Furniture, pieces.	1890	Window Glass, boxes.	60
Fire Brick, M.		Wagons.	
Fire Clay, tons.		Miscellaneous Mdse. tons.	250
Ground Feed, tons.	60		
Horses and Mules.			
Hogs.			
Hay, tons.		Total cargo tons.	500
Lime, bbls.		Passengers.	20

H D Haddock Clerk.

ENTERING THE SAULT LOCKS AT NIGHT

of Southesk and Count Andreani of balloon fame; scientists like Louis Agassiz, George Barnston and Dr. Douglass Houghton; and bizarre characters like that mysterious filibuster, "General" James Dickson, who passed with his officers and "troops" in 1836, bound for the Red River Settlements to get reinforcements, and for the Far West to wrest an empire from the Mexicans. His passage through the lakes brought an excited Detroit editor to the point of publishing "Pirates on the Lakes" in his newspaper. Dickson passed along the south shore to Fond du Lac and across the Minnesota country to Red River, where he met the opposition of the Hudson's Bay Company and saw his dreams of empire vanish into thin air.

One of the strangest characters was a resident of the Sault for some years. John Tanner as a lad had been stolen about 1790 from a Kentucky home by Indians and adopted first into one tribe and then into another. For about thirty years he lived along the present international boundary waters between Ontario and Minnesota. In 1823, when Major Long's party passed that way, Tanner was just attempting to take his half-breed children with him to the "States." He had become practically an Indian, probably in thought and certainly in language. His Indian wife, unwilling to see her children leave her, managed to have Tanner shot by another Indian near Rainy Lake on his way to Lake Superior. He was only wounded, and was cared for by the factor at the Rainy Lake Post and by others. He finally reached the Sault, where he took up his residence and became interpreter for the Indian agent there. Dr. Edwin James, the post surgeon, became interested in his story and wrote it down at Tanner's dictation. It was published in 1830. It is almost as genuinely Indian in psychology and spirit as though Chippewa blood flowed in Tanner's veins.

Finally in 1846 a murder was committed at the Sault. Suspicion pointed to Tanner, who had become morose and irascible in his later years. It was known that he had threatened the murdered man, Henry Schoolcraft's brother James. To add to the suspicion, Tanner disappeared at the very time of the murder and was never seen again. However, years later, a Lieutenant Tilden, who had been at the fort at the time, is said to have confessed to it on his deathbed. If this story is correct, the officer probably made away with poor old Tanner, too, whose reputation had been under a cloud all the intervening years. When William Cullen Bryant arrived on a visit soon after the murder, "Tanner must have done it" was the explanation for the forest fires burning and for everything else untoward that was happening. He had become the bogeyman of the Sault.

The dominating characters at the Sault in the years after John Johnston died were Gabriel Franchere and Henry R. Schoolcraft. The former was the agent of the American Fur Company in the 1830's. His first visit to this place occurred on his return trip from Astoria in 1814. His *Narrative* is as exciting as are all the records of that gallant band of young men who were trying to carry out John Jacob Astor's (and probably Thomas Jefferson's) imperialistic ideas by establishing an American post at the mouth of the Columbia River. On the return trip, having crossed the width of the continent to Fort William on Lake Superior, Franchere and his party took a canoe, manned by fourteen voyageurs and filled with six passengers, bound for the Sault by way of the north shore. They arrived in time to see the smoking ruins of Johnston's home on the American side, of Charles Ermatinger's and his North West Company fort on the Canadian shore, and of Captain McCargo's schooner, the *Perseverance,* in the rapids, left thus by the retiring American troops engaged in the pillage of the War of 1812.

Thus Franchere's introduction to the Sault was not a happy one, and he doubtless little thought at the time that he would be spending part of his later life there, and as a citizen of the very country whose actions he so decried in 1814! From at least 1835 to 1838 he was the chief agent of the American Fur Company at the Sault, as the extant letterpress book in his handwriting reveals. With 1834 and the retirement of John Jacob Astor from the company, Ramsay Crooks became president and changed the inland headquarters of his concern from Mackinac to La Pointe on Lake Superior. Naturally, therefore, the Sault became an important place in the estimation of the company, and an experienced man was needed as agent there, not only for the fur trade, but also for the extensive fisheries that the new firm began that same year. He also had nearly the entire oversight of the vessels that the company built for the Lake Superior trade. His letters afford our best insight into the life of the Sault during the years of his incumbency. He was followed by John Livingston, whose letter book and other volumes carry on the story of the Sault for another decade.

Henry R. Schoolcraft's story is so well known that only an outline need be given here. After the peace following the War of 1812 had ruined the glass industry in which he had invested his money and energies in New York and New England, he went to the western parts of the United States. His narrative of his adventures there, other books and articles, and some excellent good luck brought him recognition in Washington, so that when Governor Cass asked for a man with scientific experience and knowledge to accompany his expedition of 1820 to the sources of the Mississippi, young School-craft, then twenty-seven years of age, was given the assignment.

On that trip he first saw Sault Ste. Marie, and left an account of it in his printed narrative. The trip's purpose was in part to make preparations for a military post at the Sault. When it was organized, Schoolcraft was offered the post of Indian agent there in 1822 and arrived at his new residence in July of the same year. He was to remain there until 1833, when the agency was transferred to Mackinac.

In Washington are the official letter books that he kept as Indian agent from 1822 to 1841. They fill 1,822 pages and treat of an infinite number of topics and persons, from the Red River Valley on the west to Sault Ste. Marie, Mackinac, and even beyond on the east. He was one of the first to attempt to understand the Indian and to put on record as scientifically as he could the facts regarding the red man's manner of life, beliefs, traditions, vocabulary and legends. He was aided inestimably by the fact that his wife was a part-blood Chippewa woman, the granddaughter of a man of importance in his tribe.

With her aid and her family's, especially his father-in-law, John Johnston, and his brother-in-law, George Johnston, Schoolcraft gathered information about the Indians and their country which he published in many books and articles in the years between 1821 and 1860. Some tell of his trips of exploration with Cass and others in the years

1820, 1831 and 1832, through Lake Superior and to the southwest and west, in the regions known today as Wisconsin and Minnesota; one is entitled *Algic Researches, Comprising Inquiries Respecting the Mental Characteristics of the North American Indians* (New York, 1839); another is called *Oneóta, or The Red Race of America;* and the most ambitious and influential bears the title, *Historical and Statistical Information Respecting the History, Condition and Prospects of the Indian Tribes of the United States.* It consists of six enormous volumes, was collected and prepared under the direction of the Bureau of Indian Affairs as authorized by act of Congress, and was illustrated by an army officer of long experience in the Indian country, Captain Seth Eastman, grandfather of an Indian author of our own day, Dr. Charles Eastman. It was destined to exert an influence not dreamed of by its author, for from it Henry Wadsworth Longfellow got the idea and the material for his *Hiawatha.*

Sault Ste. Marie was also the local land office for a number of years. With the development of copper and iron mines to the west, the land office was moved to Marquette in 1857. In 1843 Chippewa County, whose seat was Sault Ste. Marie, was cut down from its original huge dimensions. It had extended since 1826* from Isle St. Vital on the north shore of Lake Huron west to the Mississippi River, up that stream and to the boundary line of the United States, and eastward along that line through Lake Superior to the mouth of the St. Marys River and to the place of beginning. Thus the entire south shore was included, as well as the Mesabi and Vermilion ranges of present-day Minnesota. A county that included much of the copper and almost all of the iron of the United States!

After Schoolcraft departed from the Sault, James Ord became the Indian agent. Many and strange are the tales of this man's birth. Because he and his aristocratic wife lived rather aloof in the agency building, where many influential visitors were entertained, and where they received letters with great seals from abroad, he became the topic of many a yarn about being the son of the King of England, of the King of France, or of a German nobleman. Thus the Sault vies with other midwestern towns in having its Dauphin.

---

* Of course, the western part was cut off when Wisconsin Territory was formed in 1836.

The story of the building of the locks at the Sault has been told so many times that one would suppose the residents would weary of the topic. To the contrary. It is a subject of perennial interest and discussion. The first attempt of the state of Michigan to build a canal around the rapids, in 1839, was prevented when the workmen were driven from the grounds by the soldiers of Fort Brady! The War Department objected on the ground that it would cut the United States millrace, which had served the sawmill at first and later had been enlarged for use as a transportation canal for the fort. The contractors, seeing themselves thwarted in making a canal, turned to commercial fishing, much to the concern of the American Fur Company!

Within the next few years the state of Michigan made no less than five appeals to the United States Government for assistance in building a ship canal at the Sault. Henry Clay opposed the project and said so in the Senate. No Federal aid was granted until a group of businessmen happened to be at the Sault in 1851 at a public land sale—the mines were in full boom by this time and Sault Ste. Marie was the local land office—and saw the jam of freight waiting there for transportation. They memorialized Congress, urging that aid be given Michigan for the construction of a canal. This resulted in a donation of public lands in 1852.

Work was begun in 1853. As many as 1,600 men were employed on the construction at one time. This increase of population in the little village of Sault Ste. Marie must have caused just such confusion and congestion as were witnessed there some ninety years later when another lock was being rushed to completion.

The earlier lock had to be finished in 1855 under terms of the contract. Great difficulties were encountered, but they were solved brilliantly by the engineering skill of the men in charge, including the contracting company's agent, the youthful Charles T. Harvey. The reader may not approve of Harvey's ethics in selecting fine copper beds as the land to be donated by the Federal Government to defray the expense of the company—among others the site of the famous Calumet and Hecla Mine—but in that day such sharp practices were merely thought of as good business. This was the beginning of Harvey's spectacular career. At the moment he was serving such men as August Belmont, Erastus Corning and John M. Forbes of Boston. They were capable of recognizing the measure of a man whose first act was to capitalize on the knowledge he had of the valuable mineral lands so recently discovered on the south shore. A whole book could be written about the investment of eastern capital in the mining lands of Lake Superior, but no one as yet has ever had the patience and energy to do so.

The canal was finished on time and great was the rejoicing. The response of shipping was immediate. Before 1870 the State canal and locks were definitely too small for a commerce that was now exceeding half a million tons. So the United States Government again came to the rescue. The Weitzel Lock was constructed and the canal deepened between the years 1870 and 1881. The new lock lay to the south of the State locks and was named in honor of one of the engineers in charge, General Godfrey Weitzel. Now it became apparent that one state could not go on taking charge of a public work like a great ship canal on an international boundary, which served the people of many states and countries. So, in 1881, just before the completion of the new lock, the state legislature passed a bill which authorized the transfer of the canal to the United States.

Traffic through the Sault continued to increase, making the old canal and locks more and more inadequate. Several new locks have been added to meet the increasing demand, culminating in the MacArthur Lock in 1943. All this development was described in connection with lake shipping in Chapter 6.

With the middle eighties a railroad reached Sault Ste. Marie and changed it to a modern city. In 1886 the flour millers of Minneapolis—aided by the Canadian Pacific, which now built its line from Sudbury—finished their road, the Minneapolis, St. Paul, and Sault Ste. Marie Railroad (the Soo in common parlance), to the Sault, to avoid Chicago and its exorbitant rates. In 1887 the Duluth, South Shore and Atlantic reached the Sault. This became the mining road of the district. The Canadian Pacific comes into the Canadian Sault, and the Duluth, South Shore and Atlantic passes through the Michigan Sault on its way to Mackinaw City. A great railroad bridge spans the canals and rapids between the two cities.

Thus a boom began in the two Saults about 1887. Fort Brady felt the pressure of the growing town and moved, between 1886 and 1893, to its present location farther back on the hill. Part of the old reservation was sold and part of it became the site of the present post office and other Federal buildings. Fire destroyed much of the business district in 1886 and again in 1896 and forced the larger part of it to move back from the water front to Portage and Ashmun streets. In 1887 Sault Ste. Marie, Michigan, organized as a city.

Meantime, the pressure for use of the local water power was being felt, but attempts to get sufficient financial backing were unsuccessful. In 1894 assistance came through the agency of Francis H. Clergue, a young Maine man looking for possible water-power investments for a group of eastern capitalists. He was favorably impressed with what he found at the two Saults and the result was an integrated program, magnificent in its conception, which shortly changed the entire aspect of the two cities.

What he saw first was water power from an eighteen-foot waterfall with an inexhaustible natural millpond behind it, Lake Superior. He revamped an existing water-power canal on the Canadian side and commenced offering water power for sale. The panic of 1893 was at its height and no one would or could buy his product. He decided to utilize the installation by making paper pulp.

Back of Sault Ste. Marie, Ontario, lay one of the finest spruce forests in the world. Clergue had had experience in paper mills in Maine. He constructed a pulp mill, the product of which he at first offered wet. There is considerable loss from additional water weight and decomposition in transportation of wet pulp. He equipped his plant to manufacture it dry. Soon he had as large a market as he could serve, including purchasers in the Orient and in Europe. He had everything that a pulp manufacturer could ask for—natural water power, a natural millpond, water of the purest kind, and a seemingly inexhaustible stand of forest close at hand. He added a mill for the manufacture of chemical instead of ground pulp. To obtain his sulphur he bought nickel mines in the Sudbury district to the east. Then he constructed the Manitoulin and North Shore Railway to bring the product to his mills, and got huge Canadian government grants of land to encourage the building of the railroad.

From the Canadian government Clergue also got for his company great grants of land to enable it to build the Algoma Central and Hudson Bay Railroad from the Sault to the Canadian Pacific, two hundred miles away, and eventually to Hudson Bay, five hundred miles distant. The grants included mineral and timber rights. Soon the wilderness of that beautiful region of forests and waterfalls was swarming with prospectors, geologists and woodsmen as well as railroad builders. In 1897 a prospector searching for gold in the Michipicoten country found an outcropping of hard hematite iron ore. He sold his rights to Clergue. Diamond drills were taken to the area and a body of ore was found under Lake Boyer, about twelve miles inland from Lake Superior. In 1900 the first cars of ore passed down newly laid track and dumped their contents into the pockets of a dock on Michipicoten Bay that had been constructed during the preceding winter. Ships were there to receive the ore, 50,000 tons of which were shipped the first season. The Helen mine, named after Clergue's sister, had begun its career. Later the Josephine mine was discovered ten miles beyond the Helen and was operated.

Having found ore, Clergue saw as his next step the building of a blast furnace. By 1902 he had not only the furnace, but also the Algoma Steel Company, making both Bessemer steel and rails, with a battery of by-product retorts for recovering the products of distillation. Thus the acetate of lime and wood alcohol recovered were made to pay the cost of obtaining charcoal. Beehive kilns were built along the Algoma Central in the heart of the immense hardwood forest, where charcoal was made. Veneer mills and sawmills were built to utilize the hardwoods to best advantage, only those parts not usable for furniture being sent to the kilns. An electric light plant was constructed for lighting Sault Ste. Marie; a street railway was established; and town waterworks were constructed.

On the American side he took up the plan for a water-power plant, which had been unsuccessful thus far. The result was the building of a great canal which diverts a tremendous quantity of water from Lake Superior and divides the city of Sault Ste. Marie into two distinct parts, the northernmost of which is now an island between the rapids and ship canals on the north and the water-power canal on the south. The canal's width is 224 feet and its depth 22 feet. It is two and a third miles long. An immense plant was constructed for the manufacture of power. In October 1902 after six years of construction of the entire canal and works, the water was let in and the power was turned on at the massive house at the eastern end of the canal. Thus began the Michigan Northern Power Company.

Today, under different ownership, its power is largely used in the manufacture of calcium carbide by the Union Carbide Company. Its blue and gray drums are familiar everywhere. Its products are used by practically every railroad in the country for one or more purposes, by oxyacetylene welders and foundrymen, and by miners, fire departments, physicians and lighthouse tenders. Union Carbide affords a favorite means of lighting rural and suburban homes, schools, churches and stores. It is uniquely used in Coast Guard lifesaving equipment.

The Sault is a mecca for tourists during the summer, for those who come by water, cars or trains. The great lakes on all sides, the forests, the fishing, the cool weather, all attract tourists. The Sault is a focal point. From it one can go easily to the lakes of Michigan, Wisconsin and Algoma. But the attractions of the immediate vicinity are many.

The Sault country is one of the major centers of secondary bird flyways for the continent. The main flyways proceed along the east and west coasts, through the Great Plains, and in the valley of the Mississippi. There are important secondary ones, and Sault Ste. Marie is one of them. In addition, Sault Ste. Marie seems to be the center of an east-west migration for certain birds, notably the evening grosbeaks and the purple finches. Incidentally, it should be of record that it was the versatile Schoolcraft who first recognized and announced as a new species the beautiful evening grosbeak. It is common about Lake Superior, especially on the north shore, but it was hardly known to students of birds before Schoolcraft's time. A Sault man, Mr. M. J. Magee, has made detailed studies of both these east-west-migrating birds through his extensive bandings.

Chapter 11

Peter White's Country

An' he's leevin wit' us now, Pierre Le Blanc, dit Peter White,
But he won't say not'in more about hees name.
Let heem try it if he can, makin out he's Yankee man,
But never min' for Pierre Le Blanc he's good man jus' de same.
So if you want to know de State of Michigan
Very easy to remember—in case you might forget.
Only two man make her go,'cos ma fader tole me so,
An' wan is M'sieu Pierre Le Blanc, de oder Pere Marquette.
                                    —WILLIAM HENRY DRUMMOND

As ONE proceeds westward from the Sault along the south shore, he sees much to interest and inspire. There are many who find the great sand hills more unusual and awesome than the Pictured Rocks near Munising, of which so much has been written since white men first saw them. The descriptions by some of the early travelers have already been given. The Grand Portal of the Pictured Rocks, which Radisson seems to have named—at least he mentions it by that name in his narrative of 1668-1669—is still so called, though it no longer has the same appearance. The arch collapsed in the present century. Other wave sculpturing in the sandstone rocks makes likenesses of chapels, pulpits, sailboats, Indian heads, and many other resemblances in the beautifully colored cliffs. Everywhere there are small waterfalls.

All this shore is still a relatively wild area, full of appeal to lovers of fine scenery. All the area back from the shore between Laughing Fish Point and Au Sable Point is Hiawatha National Forest. East of that, between Tahquamenon Bay and a point nearly to Grand Marais, lies Lake Superior National Forest. At Tahquamenon Bay begins Marquette National Forest, with an adjacent Mackinac State Forest on its west border. Marquette National Forest extends east to Waiska

Bay, not far from Sault Ste. Marie. Hiawatha-land this stretch of
shore is indeed. One can hardly turn without encountering something named from or in the poem.

West of the Sault, Munising is the first town of any size. It is
nestled between hills, water and the large island—still called Grand
Island as originally named by the voyageurs—which protects it from
the north. Around the town stand the hardwood and other forests
characteristic of the northern peninsula of Michigan, that make possible Munising's career as a modern industrial town. Thousands of
chopping bowls and salad bowls carry the Munising label. Besides
the hardwood factories that make it known, there are paper mills,
veneer works, a shingle and tie mill, and so forth. An early attempt to
make it develop as an iron manufacturing city failed, though the
redoubtable Peter White was one of its promoters. His career will be
described a little later. He built a large blast furnace at Munising in
1867 for the manufacture of charcoal iron, but it did not succeed,
and only the picturesque ruins are to be observed today in East
Munising.

Traveling west along the south shore, one comes next to Marquette. The shore turns north just before Marquette is reached, and
the traveler is likely to find the points of the compass all apparently
in the wrong directions. Marquette, with Houghton, Hancock and
Ashland, are the chief industrial towns on the south shore between
Sault Ste. Marie and Superior, and all of them are ports for mining
hinterlands. Here in the Marquette region the mines are of iron,
the first very large bodies of iron ore to be discovered and developed
commercially on the North American continent.

One can go to the very spot in Negaunee, just southwest of Marquette, where ore was discovered in the fall of 1844 by a surveying
party of Dr. Douglass Houghton's:

"On the morning of the 19th of September, 1844, we started to run
the line south between ranges 26 and 27. As soon as we reached the
hill to the south of the [Teal] lake, the compassman began to notice
the fluctuations in the variation of the magnetic needle. We were,
of course, using the solar compass, of which Mr. [William] Burt was

the inventor, and I shall never forget the excitement of the old gentleman when viewing the changes of the variation—the needle not actually traversing alike in any two places. He kept changing his position to take observations, all the time saying: 'How would they survey this country without my compass? What could be done here without my compass?' . . . Mr. Burt called out, 'Boys, look around and see what you can find.' We all left the line, some going to the east, some going to the west, and all of us returned with specimens of iron ore, mostly gathered from outcrops. This was along the first mile from Teal lake.'"*

This was the beginning of the Jackson mine. Negaunee was founded in 1846, a year after Marquette was established by the owner of the new mine. Ishpeming was founded in 1856. The following year saw the completion of the Iron Mountain Railroad, the first railroad in the Upper Peninsula. Its terminus was Marquette, which in 1856 had completed the construction of its first ore dock. The plan from the start was to send the ore down the lakes to the large furnaces situated near coal fields. To be sure, in 1847 the Jackson Mining Company had built a forge on Carp River, three miles east of Negaunee; and in 1849-1850 the Marquette Iron Company completed a forge near the lake shore in Marquette. Like all other forges in the area, these did not succeed. Indeed, it was on the site of the Marquette forge that the Cleveland Iron Mining Company, one of the Big Three in Marquette's early mining history, built a trestlework and pier for shipping ore. It is said that this was the first ore dock to use the side pockets now so characteristic of ore docks everywhere. The idea came from the coal fields.

Blast furnaces around Marquette and on the iron range back of it did rather better than the forges. There was ample hardwood for the making of charcoal. Today as you wander about the region, you may suddenly find yourself face to face with the remains of one of the charcoal kilns built in the early days of the iron-ore industry.

These mid-century years were the era of the first great railroad boom in the United States. This fact doubtless explains to no incon-

* Alvah L. Sawyer, *A History of the Northern Peninsula of Michigan and Its People* (Chicago, 1911), 1:408, quoting Jacob Houghton.

siderable extent why the Lake Superior ore mines prospered despite the panic of 1857. Then followed the Civil War, with its terrific demand for iron and steel—terrific for that day, at least. Probably it was fortunate for the Northern cause in the struggle that the great body of ore *had* been discovered. Fortunate, too, that the Sault locks and canal had been constructed and were sending the ore down to the Pittsburgh district in ever-increasing loads.

The first boats were very small, of course, and were loaded and unloaded by hand, usually by means of wheelbarrows. In 1869 the first steamer designed especially for ore-carrying purposes was built by Peck and Masters of Cleveland. She was built for the Jackson Mine ore, and was called the *R. J. Hackett*. She was 211 feet long and 33 feet in the beam. The next year her consort was built, the *Forest City*. Soon it became usual or at least common to see a propeller with her consort carrying ore from the Lake Superior mines to Lake Erie and other lower lake ports. Today "tows" or "barges" are a common sight on the lake. They have their own crews, smaller than those on the towing boat. Most of the barges are fitted with sails in order to permit them to ride out a gale in the event of the tow rope's breaking. They are equipped with deck winches, steam windlasses, and donkey boilers, but no engines for self-propulsion.

In 1864 Charles T. Harvey's Peninsula Railroad was completed from Negaunee to Escanaba, linking the Upper Peninsula with Green Bay, Milwaukee and Chicago. Still there was no direct winter connection tying the Upper Peninsula to Detroit and the rest of the Lower Peninsula. In an endeavor to get a grant of land with which to finance such a connection, Peter White got himself elected to the state legislature in 1874. He had already become a leading figure in the Upper Peninsula after arriving in Marquette as a mere boy in 1846 and being one of the founders in the mining boom. Since that time he had gone from success to success. Now he succeeded in getting the grant, and in 1881 Marquette had direct rail connection with Detroit. White continued to be one of the first citizens of Marquette, as banker, real-estate and mining man, candidate for mayor, state senator and so forth. The beautiful city park at Presque Isle is his gift to the city, as is the Peter White Memorial Library.

The Marquette iron range extends in a westerly direction from Negaunee to the western end of Lake Michigamme, a distance of about thirty miles. In the vicinity of Negaunee and Ishpeming the iron formation outcrops in an area about five miles wide. West of Ishpeming it divides into a north and a south limb, the north limb extending westward to Michigamme and the south limb to Champion. There it turns to the south and extends in a narrow section to Republic. To the southeast of the Negaunee area is located the Cascade district and about twenty miles farther in this direction is the Swanzy district, which is entirely separated from the Marquette range. However, from a mining and commercial point of view, these districts are regarded as part of the Marquette range. The range is served by four railroads, the Chicago and Northwestern, the Duluth, South Shore and Atlantic, the Chicago, Milwaukee, St. Paul and Pacific, and the Lake Superior and Ishpeming. By 1872 prospecting was practically completed, with the opening of the Republic, Michigamme and Spur mines.

The ores in this range are soft or hydrous hematites, hard hematites and magnetites. Many bodies are at great depth. The new Mather mine at Ishpeming is already nearly two thousand feet below the surface and has not yet begun producing. Its owners expect it to become the deepest iron mine in the world. The iron-bearing rocks are very beautiful, banded in iridescent blues, reds and grays. Both hard and soft ores are found, and both shaft and open pit methods of mining are practiced.

Between the sand dunes to the east of Marquette and the Huron Mountains to the west lies the countryside made famous by the wild-life photography of George Shiras, III. His wilderness lodge was established at Whitefish Lake between Marquette and Munising about 1880, and he spent practically every summer and many winters there until his death in 1942. His family had become associated with the region as early as 1849, when his grandfather, George Shiras, hearing marvelous tales of the speckled trout along the south shore of Lake Superior, visited Marquette. He continued to return until his eighty-ninth year. In 1859 his son, George Shiras, Jr., associate justice of the United States Supreme Court in his later life, came to fish. He returned yearly until his ninety-second year. His son, George Shiras, III, began his pilgrimages at eleven years of age, in 1870. Likewise the latter's son, George Shiras, IV, grandchild of Peter White as well as of George Shiras, Jr., visited the region until his untimely death in 1915.

About 1890 George Shiras, III, began hunting with a camera and flashlight instead of with a gun. His numerous articles and books not only tell the story of the Upper Peninsula's and Lake Superior's wild life, but illustrate it and the scenery of the area in striking fashion. His photographs were frequently taken at night by flashlight as a means for getting better results than can be secured by daylight photography of animals. Toward the end of his long life he collected his pictures and books and published them in two substantial volumes, *Hunting Wild Life With Camera and Flashlight, A Record of Sixty-five Years' Visits to the Woods and Waters of North America,* with 950 photographs by the author (National Geographic Society, 1936). Anyone who wishes to know Lake Superior will find some of his most graphic data in those books.

At the western end of Shiras' south shore precinct were the Huron Mountains, some forty miles northwest of Marquette. Here in 1889 articles of association were executed for the club that is now known as the Huron Mountain Club. Its real founder was Horatio Seymour, Jr., and with him were eleven other charter members, including Peter White and J. M. Longyear of Marquette, and five MacMillans of Detroit. T. H. Newberry of Detroit was an early member. George Shiras, III, was a member from 1892 to 1894, his father from 1892 to 1901. The club was established after the adjacent area had been cut over but while this oasis of wilderness remained in much of its virgin glory. The mountainous character of the region shows up better from the lake than from the shoreward side. Its highest elevation, Mt. Huron, is 932 feet above sea level. There are about a dozen interior lakes in the twelve thousand or so acres in the club's holding, besides two fairly considerable streams, Pine River and Salmon Trout River.

A famous Lake Superior geologist, Frank Leverett, says in a club publication:

"The granite knobs and ridges of northwestern Marquette County, Michigan, to which the name Huron Mountains has been applied, rise only a few hundred feet above Lake Superior, whose waters they overlook. They are much more prominent when viewed from the direction of the lake than from the interior of the Northern Peninsula, for parts of the interior are higher than the highest points in the Huron Mountains. Between the Huron Mountains and the shore of Lake Superior there is a narrow strip, two to five miles in width, of low country, underlain by beds of brown sandstone, which are exposed in cliffs 20 to 60 feet high, fronting the lake."

Though men from Marquette founded and sustained the club for years, eventually the ruling membership passed successively to Detroit and to Chicago, largely as a result of changes in transportation methods. Longyear's boat between Marquette and the club provided transportation, though at a substantial financial loss, until 1900. Then a hiatus came, with no good method of transportation until 1906, when a railroad reached Big Bay, and wagons could transport members and their families to the cabins and dormitories, as well as other buildings which had been built in the founding years along the two streams of the club's holdings. With the coming of automobiles and good roads, the railroad was no longer necessary, for members of the club could motor as quickly from Chicago as they had formerly moved by boat from Marquette or by rail from Detroit.

The club has been a great force for the conservation of wild life throughout the area and even beyond. To the natural big stand of hemlocks and smaller ones of pines and hardwoods, the membership has added many plantings, especially of pines. Fire prevention has been a major concern. Streams and lakes have been restocked with fish. Rules for the prevention of killing wild animals and birds have been adopted. Naturalists and scientists have been invited to spend summers at the club and study the geology and wild life of the area. The result of some of this study is seen in a book of exquisite format published by the club in 1929, *The Book of Huron Mountain, A*

Roleff Photo

CROSSCUT SAW AND SAWYERS, NORTH SHORE, ABOUT 1915

Roleff Photo

A LOG LANDING AT KNIFE RIVER, MINNESOTA, ABOUT 1915

SAULT STE. MARIE, MICHIGAN, ABOUT 1870

MUNISING, MICHIGAN, ABOUT 1870

Collection of Papers Concerning the History of the Huron Mountain Club and the Antiquities and the Natural History of the Region. It gives information that is pertinent not only to the Huron Mountain area, but also to much of the Upper Peninsula.

In the early 1900's President Theodore Roosevelt included the Huron Islands, at the mouth of the river of the same name, in his first northern bird refuges. Shiras had noted the islands white with gulls when he passed thirty-five years before. James Oliver Curwood wrote many of his Lake Superior books in the Huron Mountain area.

The Copper Country is next as the traveler continues along the south shore of Lake Superior toward the west. After leaving the wild beauties of the Huron Mountains, one comes to the quieter loveliness of Keweenaw Bay (L'Anse of the French voyageurs). Here historic memories come thick and fast. Radisson and Des Groseilliers passed through the bay in 1659. On this long arm of Lake Superior Father Jacques Ménard spent the winter of 1660-1661. Here a Methodist mission was established in the 1830's and a Catholic mission in the 1840's. There was a trading post here for many years. Later the American Fur Company established a fishing station at L'Anse. Now the towns of L'Anse and Baraga face each other across the protected waters of the bay; and their lights twinkle and wink at one another at night.

It is pleasant to think that both Pitezel, the Methodist missionary, and Baraga, the Catholic, likewise looked across these same waters with friendliness and with more of Christian brotherhood in their hearts than was often felt where Protestant and Catholic missionaries operated in the same area. These sturdy pioneers actually visited each other, did little favors for each other, and at least in their printed accounts recognized some good in each other. Today a mission still operates among the remnants of the Indians on the site of Baraga's former establishment. It is now called Assinins. There is likewise a Methodist establishment.

This is an interesting area because of the diversity of life and people here. There is good agricultural land as well as the great Ford forests, model village and lumber mills at Alberta, just south of

L'Anse, and at L'Anse and Pequaming. Deep-sea fishing is very popular. Besides Indians one encounters Finns and Swedes. Skanee on Huron Bay is Swedish in origin, presumably a corruption of Skane, the southernmost province of Sweden. It began as a lumber camp. Near Baraga is a Finnish bath or *sauna,* which is open to the public. How the shades of White Fisher and his tribe would smile! A steam bath, almost identical in operation with their own!

Cranberries grow abundantly at Lighthouse Point north of the village of Baraga. There are big and important cheese factories in the general area. At one time this was also a great logging center for the surrounding pineries. Pequaming began around the Hebard and Thurber saw and shingle mill in 1878.* At one time the mill had 500 persons in the place, besides 400 more out in the woods getting out logs. This was also a quarrying region, when the brownstone house was all the rage.

After leaving Baraga one comes soon to the eastern end of the Portage Lake Ship Canal, a waterway of twenty-two miles, which enables steamers and other vessels to pass through Keweenaw Point instead of going around it. Ordinarily it is shorter for the boats bound from Duluth to the Sault or vice versa to pass around the point, but in bad weather they usually make better time and everyone aboard is more comfortable if the waterway is used. For trips between certain intermediary points, however, it is shorter to go through the canal. This canal was built by the Lake Superior and Portage Ship Canal Company between 1868 and 1873.

Near the middle of the canal the twin cities of Houghton and Hancock stand on opposite sides of the water. They are the entrance to the Copper Country. The two cities are the centers and ports for the ore region.

The effective discovery of copper was made in the year 1840 by Douglass Houghton, the first state geologist of Michigan. He made known his discovery in his report of 1841. This report caused the immediate rush of prospectors to the area and began the great copper boom of succeeding years. Indian treaties were made, ending in the one of March 12, 1843, which enabled the United States eventually to

---

* See page 195, the chapter on lumbering activities on Lake Superior.

throw open the area to settlement and ownership of land by individuals. Meantime Houghton had taken upon himself not only the geological survey but also the land survey of the area and was proceeding with this difficult task when he was drowned near Eagle River, October 13, 1845.

Some way had to be devised to open the area to miners while the survey was continuing and before the land was sold at public auction according to usual procedure. In 1818 Congress had passed an act authorizing the Secretary of War to issue permits to individuals to explore for minerals and locate tracts of land in the lead districts of Illinois. A similar procedure was now followed in Michigan. At first the grantee was allowed to select a tract three miles square; later he was allowed only one square mile. He was required to make a selection within one year, to mark the corners of it, to have a person in charge to point out the bounds, and to file with the War Department a description of his claim. He was then entitled to a lease for a term of three years, on condition that he pay to the United States six per cent of all the metal produced. Extensions of the lease were to be permitted for six additional years.

About a thousand such permits were granted and some nine hundred and sixty selections were actually made. Copper was soon being "discovered" over an extensive part of the peninsula and in adjacent parts of the south—and even the north—shore, parts that today show no trace of the mineral. The boom was on.

The first actual miners were James K. Paul, or Paull, and Nicholas Miniclergue (Miniclear), who arrived in 1842 at the mouth of the Ontonagon River. Paul proceeded up that stream and found the great boulder of native copper about which stories had been rife since earliest exploration of Lake Superior. While he was in the midst of attempting to move it, Major Walter Cunningham arrived with a party. He had been instructed by the Secretary of War to secure the rock and take it to Washington. Paul defended his preemptive right, as he termed it, with force of arms. A compromise was finally effected and Cunningham got the rock to Washington, where it was found to weigh 3,708 pounds. A second copper rock was discovered by Paul and sold to a Yale professor who happened to see it and wanted it for his college. Paul then platted the present town of Ontonagon and as the town grew, he continued to live there by keeping the local hotel.

A mineral land agency for the United States was opened at Copper Harbor in 1843, with Cunningham in charge. It remained there until the spring of 1846. Then it was removed to Sault Ste. Marie, but assistant agents were established at Copper Harbor and Ontonagon. To insure the proper protection of government interests roundabout, it was deemed advisable to have troops available. So Fort Wilkins was constructed on a narrow strip of land between Copper Harbor and Lake Fanny Hoe. Two companies of the Fifth United States Infantry were stationed there until the outbreak of the Mexican War in 1846. After a brief period of abandonment, except for a custodian, the fort was maintained until 1855. During the Civil War it was occupied once more by troops. It was finally abandoned in 1870 and the buildings allowed to decay until a few years ago, when the establishment was restored by WPA labor. Today it is a state park, and in its exquisite setting is a fitting terminus to the highway which has been constructed recently along the craggy north shore of the peninsula. That road is practically, though not nominally, the northeastern extension of U. S. Highway No. 41, which begins at Tampa, Florida, and ends on this "thumb" of Lake Superior.

Today the entire peninsula is dotted with the remnants of old mining locations. Of all the numerous attempts to mine copper only a few were really successful and still fewer have maintained their success until today. The period from 1843 to 1848 was notable for the number of prospectors on the ground. It was, in fact, a preview of what was to occur a few years later in California, Colorado, Montana and Idaho. However, there was one notable difference. There was little lawlessness in the Copper Country, and the troops at Fort Wilkins were never called upon to suppress turbulence or rioting. Judge Lynch was conspicuous by his absence, and there were never any Vigilantes.

Copper Harbor, Eagle Harbor and Eagle River were settled soon after Ontonagon. The only easy route into the area was from Lake Superior, and so these shore villages grew up around the best available harbors. Today they are at best harbors of refuge for the great ore vessels that could hold the original ore schooners on a part of their decks. To these villages and to others came miners of all nationalities, but those who stamped their impress on the region more than others were the "Cousin Jacks," the Cornishmen. In their own native land they had been miners of copper or tin. They found the rugged shores of Keweenaw Point not unlike their own craggy country. Besides such common mining terms as "adit," "skip" (an elevator in a mine), "whim," and many others, they gave the Copper Country their delicious pasties or meat turnovers. Pasties are advertised widely throughout the Copper Country and are well worth sampling.

Much of the mining capital of the Copper Country came from Boston and its vicinity. Sea-borne commerce, Boston's chief means of subsistence for centuries, was at its peak, though it would soon decline. Capital made on the Seven Seas was clamoring to be invested, and Boston maritime interests, looking about for the best method of putting it to work, saw Lake Superior's possibilities. The Copper Country looked inviting to them. The Lake Superior Copper Company, backed chiefly by Boston financiers, was the first organized company in the district. It and its successors sank shafts, built stamping mills, and otherwise expended $1,000,000 between 1844 and 1877, but the only returns were one dividend of $1.00 a share—$20,000! The company exhausted its capital several times but invariably reorganized, once optimistically calling itself the Phoenix Copper Company. It passed out of existence in 1905. The old Phoenix Mine is one of the landmarks along the scenic Keweenaw Point highway today.

Another famous spot is the Cliff Mine. It was discovered in 1845 by a party of explorers working for the Pittsburgh and Boston Company. Unlike the first company, its immediate success was spectacular. It purchased 5,000 acres of land, which included the site of Eagle River. There it built a large dock and warehouses. It built warehouses also at the mine itself, to which a good road was constructed. A large stamp mill was erected on the river near the mine. The company owned its own smelting furnace at Pittsburgh and shipped its mineral there for refining. The stock was owned by men in Pittsburgh as well as in Boston, as the name of the company indicates. By 1853 enough copper had been taken out of the mine to net a sum of $1,328,406, or $77 a share, whereas the total assessments had amounted to only $18.50 per share. In June 1854 the stock was quoted at $175 per share on the Boston market. The mine exploited a fissure which cut across several amygdaloid beds. It was rich in mass copper, as it was called, lumps of which sometimes weighed from 100 to 150 tons. About three-quarters of the entire product was mass copper; the remainder was divided about equally between stamp and barrel work.

After 1860 the mine began to become unprofitable, and work was discontinued in 1870. Nevertheless, up to that time, the aggregate sum paid in dividends was $2,627,660, a little over 2,000 per cent of the paid-up capital. After many vicissitudes the mine became the property of the Calumet and Hecla Company. It has not been in operation for many years.

The success of the Cliff Mine stimulated other operations to a marked degree. The Central Mine, about seven miles east of the Cliff, was opened in 1854. It operated until 1898. The company went out of existence in 1908. In its productive period it has paid over 2,000 per cent on the paid-up stock. The buildings still stand around the deserted shaft, unpainted like most of the simple frame dwellings in the Copper Country. When I saw them in the dusk of a late October day in 1943 only one weak, solitary light gleamed from a window in this otherwise deserted village.

This was largely a settlement of Cornishmen. They were usually big men, of meager education, clannish, loyal to their local mine and company to an extraordinary degree, resistant to outside influences such as that of labor organizers, deeply religious, music-loving, and appreciative of education for their children. Many who were miners during the week were local preachers on Sunday. They led a hard life, ate frugal fare, lived in rented Company houses, went to a Company hospital when sick, and worked by the contract system, whereby all advancement and increase of pay depended on their own skill and ability to produce results quickly.

Such a system was hard on the average man but meant promotion to the richly endowed. Many of the sons rose to prominence as agents, mining captains, and shift bosses, because their fathers worked hard and sent them to the local mining college, which was established in Houghton in 1885 as the Michigan College of Mines. When general science courses were added to its curriculum about fifteen years ago, its name was changed to the Michigan College of Mining and Technology. It is the alma mater of many prominent mining men throughout the country and has a long and enviable reputation.

The survivors of the old Central Location hold a reunion every summer, usually on a Sunday, at the old church. Then it is nearly impossible to get a seat in order to listen to the fine singing of the old favorite hymns and to be present for the other parts of the program. People come from a wide area especially for this day, and those who formerly lived on the Location are now joined by many tourists and others who have heard abroad of the special quality of these reunions.

In the Ontonagon region a mine that was spectacular in its first profits was put into operation in 1848. This was the Minnesota Mine, which before 1876 had returned nearly thirty dollars on every dollar invested. It was famous for its mass copper. Here the largest complete mass of native copper ever found was discovered. It weighed in the vicinity of 500 tons and netted the operating company about $150,000 as well as much publicity. Pieces weighing many pounds were purchased and taken to Europe as curiosities. This mine had already been worked by prehistoric men. In one of their shafts a hemlock was growing, whose annular rings were counted in the year 1848 and numbered 395. This mine was also known for being the parent of many other mines, such as the Rockland, the Lake Superior, the Flint-Steel Peninsula and the West Minnesota. Hence its name of Mother of Mines. Workings in one mine led to the discovery of other ore bodies. In 1870 operations ceased, because of the low price of copper at the moment, a pinching of the vein where work was being carried on, and the need for costly equipment to continue. Attempts have been made to revive activity, but never with any success.

One of three major districts of the Copper Country centers about Portage Lake, now a section of the waterway passing through Keweenaw Peninsula. As the name indicates, it was part of an old portage route for Indians and voyageurs in the fur-trading era. As the area on either side of the lake and along connecting streams was more accessible to prospectors than much of the peninsula and adjacent country, a good deal of exploration occurred there in the middle 1840's. The prospectors had fissure veins in mind and passed by the indications of copper in other forms. So the rich Pewabic amygdaloid lode was not discovered until 1856, although two companies, the Quincy and the Pewabic, had organized before that time and were doing a great deal of exploring along the hillsides facing Portage Lake. In the process of their work they founded the towns of Hancock on the north side of the lake and Houghton on the south in the year 1852.

Today a gray, weather-beaten shaft house with numerous roofs and angles stands outlined against the sky above the unusual hill slope on which the city of Hancock reposes. It catches the eye of every visitor to the region—and holds it. It has been a favorite subject for artists and photographers, so that it has come to be a symbol for the Copper Country. The company owning the Quincy mine has operated continuously in this area for ninety-five years, having absorbed the Pewabic, the Franklin, the Mesnard, the Concord, the Arcadian and the St. Mary's companies. These were the first low-grade producers, and their success—the Pewabic paid a dividend of $60,000 in 1862— showed that mass copper was not necessary, and that a sustained yield over many years was more desirable than the investment of great amounts of capital in rich but limited ore bodies.

South of the lake the Isle Royale mine was started in 1852 and was followed by the Portage, the Huron, the Grand Portage, the Baltic, the Columbian, the Shelden and the Atlantic mines. These were all amygdaloid lodes. The war has reopened some of them, and as one passes through the locations about the shafts, the bright-colored roofs, lintels and window frames of freshly painted Finnish houses, and the smell of new wood used in remodeling the houses tell of wages being received once more after lean years, especially the years of the Great Depression, when much of the Copper Country was on relief.

One other form of copper mine needs to be mentioned, the conglomerate. To most Americans the Copper Country for years meant the Calumet and Hecla, whose spectacular dividends over many years aroused the interest of the world. In the dim ages of Long Ago a party of prehistoric men apparently had a cache of mass copper, cut perhaps from the great Ontonagon boulder, or mined in the pits of Isle Royale, in a hole dug some twelve miles north of Portage Lake. Perhaps disaster overtook them; perhaps they were not able to find their cache again. At any rate, it lay there till 1859, when Edwin Hulbert, a civil engineer of the Cliff Mining Company, stumbled upon it. He did not realize that there was no mass copper in the vicinity and supposed the cache to be representative of what lay beneath.

By pure accident the buried copper lay over a lode of very rich conglomerate. When the Calumet Mining Company was founded in 1865 with Boston capital and began operations the lode was unearthed. The Hecla Mining Company was formed in 1866 to mine the area to the southwest of the Calumet's land. In May 1871 the Hecla, Calumet, Portland and Scott mining companies were consolidated to form the Calumet and Hecla Mining Company. In 1900 the charter was renewed, and in 1905 it was amended to make the corporation a securities-holding company as well as a mining and smelting company. It then began to secure mineral rights, mines and timber holdings until it brought under its control a large part of the Copper Country. It also became a great landed corporation, with 100,000 acres in Keweenaw County and another 100,000 in Ontonagon and Houghton counties. The mine proper, usually referred to as the Calumet and Hecla, occupies 2,750 acres.

Its center is the city of Calumet. It attained its maximum production about 1906, just when copper mines in the Far West were taking the ascendancy from the Copper Country. As the shafts went farther and farther underground, the yield per ton decreased, but the vein spread. Even by 1890 the product had dropped below sixty pounds per ton. The steadily decreasing yield per ton was offset by careful management and constant improvement of method so that dividends were kept up even when the grade dropped below thirty pounds per ton. After about seventy-five years of operation, however, this bonanza mine ceased operation—except for a probably temporary reopening to meet the demand of war production.

About 18,000,000 feet of timber were used annually underground in the Calumet and Hecla Mine. The company found it economical to have its own timber supply and its own axmen. Since the mine started, it is estimated that 1,000,000,000 feet of timber have been placed in it.

As the Second World War started, there were very few copper mines producing in the Copper Country—the Ahmeek in Keweenaw County, and the Champion, Isle Royale, and Quincy in Houghton County. The northern peninsula in Michigan was one of the areas most disastrously hit by the depression of the 1930's. In December 1934 one-third of the total population was on relief. During the First World War the copper-mining industry employed about 16,000 workers in Houghton County alone. As late as 1923-1924 the copper mines employed 10,000 to 12,000. By 1933 less than 2,000 were regularly employed.

Besides the Cornish settlers, there were many Scandinavians and Finns in this part of the Upper Peninsula, as well as many Canadian French. In the Civil War period it was difficult to get miners. An association of the mining companies was formed in the winter of 1863-1864 to secure immigration from Northern Europe. It brought about four hundred men into the country. Others followed. Nearly every mining community soon had its "Swedetown." Of the Finns who came at this time Louis Adamic has this to say:

"But what started the Finns America-ward in a big way was the shortage of labor in the newly opened copper country in the far reaches of Michigan's Upper Peninsula, which became acute about the middle of the Civil War. Several came over with the Norwegian contract laborers imported by the Quincy Mining Company of Hancock. They showed themselves to be exceedingly strong, hard-working people who took in their stride the sub-zero temperature that reigns over the Upper Peninsula for four months out of the year. So more were sent for, not only by Quincy but other companies. . . .

"Most Finnish immigrants of that period [wound] up on the Upper Peninsula, and as a beginning the majority went into the mines. The towns of Hancock, Houghton, and Calumet drew them by the thousands, as did the iron camps in northern Michigan. And almost simultaneously they spread to Minnesota's Iron Range and other mining regions in the Northwest. Owing to their background as woodsmen in the old country, they were at their best erecting safety props in the pits, but excelled too as actual miners. Many found work in the new mills and smelters, on ore docks, or building railroad embankments through the virgin forests of Michigan, Wisconsin, and Minnesota with pick and shovel and wheelbarrow.

"But, in spite of their competence in it, industrial work did not satisfy the Finns; or, rather, it dissatisfied them more than it did the Irish and Slavs, also numerous in the Michigan and Minnesota mines and smelters. Traditionally, the Finns are farmers, woodsmen, trappers and fishermen, with a passion for the open, silent places, and disposed to go into difficult enterprises without a boss over them; and so a large proportion of them got out of the mining and smelter towns and camps as soon as they saved enough to go on the land. Some did this by way of the woods, where they worked temporarily as timberworkers, or by acquiring, with a small down payment, a piece of land near the mines or smelter plants while still working in them.

"Off and on, back in the eighties and nineties, a great elemental impulse seemed to seize entire groups or colonies of Finnish immigrants in places like Hancock or Calumet or Ishpeming, Michigan, or Ely or Hibbing or Eveleth, Minnesota, and they left the towns for the backwoods of those states to go into farming in cutover areas. . . . I know a man, now very old, who once told me he had left the mines for farming in 1896 because underground he could not recite to himself as he worked a bit of *Kalevala* which he specially fancied:

"Then the aged Väinämöinen
Spoke aloud his songs of magic,
And a flower-crowned birch grew upward,
Crowned with flowers, and leaves all golden,
And its summit reached to heaven,
To the very clouds uprising.
Then he sang his songs of magic,
And he sang a moon all shining,
Sang the moon to shine forever
In the pine-tree's emerald summit,
Sang the Great Bear in its branches."*

It must have pleased the Finns in their new homes to realize that *Hiawatha,* metrically like the *Kalevala,* had its setting in their new home about the great lake.

The presence of Finns in the Lake Superior area, especially in the Upper Peninsula, is inescapable for anyone who reads signs over shops or recognizes Finnish architecture, especially that of the *saunas,* or steam bathhouses. Probably no other group could take over stump land, perhaps also burned over, and make successful farming country of it. Their penchant for co-operatives is well known. They have started all sorts of co-operatives in America. They are also eager for education. In Hancock is the excellent Suomi College, a Finnish institution founded primarily to educate their Lutheran pastors, but also serving many non-Finns.

When the depression of the thirties was at its lowest, a road-building program under WPA auspices was instituted on the Keweenaw Peninsula. The famous scenic drive over Brockway Mountain is the splendid result. Anyone who has loitered along its heights will rejoice, not that there was a depression, but that someone had the vision to recognize a highway opening up the fine scenery of the peninsula could be the solution of the Upper Michigan Peninsula employment problem. Copper mines are exhausted, timber stands are denuded, the fish of Lake Superior can be depleted, but the old earth, with her rocks, remains, and Lake Superior cannot be altered

---

* Louis Adamic, *From Many Lands* (New York: Harper & Bros., 1940), pp. 84, 85.

very much by man. With peacetime driving restored, the tourist trade can be the solution to the unemployment problem.

The region immediately west of the Copper Country is known for its Porcupine Mountains and for the Ottawa National Forest. This area has the last virgin hardwood forest of any size in the Lake States—that is, if it is still left when this is published. The ax and saw are being applied so fast under the plea of war emergency that there may not be a giant maple or yellow birch left when this gets into print. Fifty years ago northern hardwoods covered 7,000,000 acres in the Lake States. By 1937 the main remnant in the Porcupine region still covered 170,000 acres. By 1941 it had shrunk to 140,000. As one conservationist says:

"The sugar maple is as American as the rail fence or the Kentucky rifle. Generations have been rocked in maple cradles, clothed from maple spinning wheels, and fed with maple-sweetened cakes served on maple tables before maple fires. Yet the demise of the maple forest brings us less regret than the demise of an old tire."

He reminds us that maple trees take time to grow.

"Few laymen realize that the penalties of violence to a forest may far outlast its visible evidence. I know a hardwood forest . . . covering a mountain on the north flank of the Alps. Half of it has sustained cuttings since 1605, but was never slashed. The other half was slashed during the 1600's, but has been under intensive forestry during the last 150 years. Despite this rigid protection, the old slashing now produces only mediocre pine, while the unslashed portion grows the finest cabinet oak in the world; one of those oaks fetches a higher price than a whole acre of the old slashings. On the old slashings the litter accumulates without rotting, stumps and limbs disappear slowly, natural reproduction is slow. On the unslashed portion litter disappears as it falls, stumps and limbs rot at once, natural reproduction is automatic. Foresters attribute the inferior performance of the old slashing to its depleted microflora, meaning that underground community of bacteria, molds, fungi, insects, and burrowing mammals which constitute half the environment of a tree."*

He explains that selective logging makes it possible to cut a third of a hardwood forest every twenty years without robbing it of its ability to maintain itself, for the standing trees make the shade necessary for the stripling maples and associated species, along with the requisite microflora which grows only in that shade.

The Porcupine Mountains have the only steep topography available to the public in the snow belt of the Lake States, and their slopes offer fine possibilities for ski trails. Some advantage is already being taken of the terrain for winter sports. All the year round, tourists and vacationists are coming to this region. Fishing is excellent, both on inland lakes and on Lake Superior, where trout trolling has become an important business and sport in recent years, just as elsewhere on much of the north and south shores.

Gogebic County's western limit is also the terminus of Michigan's boundary. Wisconsin's short strip of lake shore comes next, as one goes westward. This is the strip of coast that edged a great pine belt in days gone by. It heard the call of "Timber!" through the snow-laden forests, and witnessed the spring freshets with their annual drives. Here on La Pointe Indian Reservation is one of the old and well-studied groups of natives, whose history is full of human interest. Next comes Chequamegon Bay, the oldest settled area on Lake Superior. On its shores are a big modern city, Ashland, and lesser towns like Washburn and Bayfield. Protecting the bay from the fiercest lake storms are the Apostle Islands. Another Indian reservation stretches here along a shore that is still little changed from earliest days. Finally comes the great city of Superior with its twin, Duluth, occupying the head of the lake.

Ashland is the port for the iron ore that is mined on the Gogebic Range. The range occupies a narrow belt about eighty miles long, extending in a westerly direction from eastern Gogebic County, Michigan, to the Wisconsin state line, and thence through Iron and

---

* Aldo Leopold, "The Last Stand," *The Living Wilderness*, December, 1942.

Ashland counties into Bayfield County, Wisconsin. The ore bodies vary greatly in size and shape. They are soft red, partly dehydrated hematites, with subordinate amounts of hard blue hematite. For the ten years prior to 1937 the average annual shipment was about 4,500,-000 tons. The deposits were known early, but the first shipment, through Marquette, occurred in 1884. Ashland is connected with the range by two railroads, the Chicago and Northwestern and the Minneapolis, St. Paul and Sault Ste. Marie. It ranks fourth in ore-shipping ports on the Great Lakes, with Superior, Duluth and Two Harbors ahead of it. Coal returns in the emptied ore boats and is distributed to parts of Wisconsin, Michigan, Minnesota, North and South Dakota and Iowa. Two additional railroads are concerned in shipping coal out of Ashland—the Chicago, St. Paul and Omaha, and the Northern Pacific.

Ashland was founded in 1854 by Asaph Whittlesey. The panic of 1857 and then the Civil War nearly overcame the little settlement completely, but one family remained, and in 1870 when a railroad line headed in that direction, it made a new start. In 1877 the first railroad, the Wisconsin Central, reached it. The years 1886 and 1887 saw a boom, caused by the realization that Ashland would be the port of the newly opened Gogebic iron range. In the eighties and nineties Ashland was also a great sawmill town.* In the same period it was exporting Lake Superior brownstone, with which public buildings and residences were constructed in Milwaukee, the Twin Cities, and many other places. There were several quarries on Chequamegon Bay and the Apostle Islands. The depletion of the pines, and the use of cement instead of stone in building houses ended both trades. But the ore has continued. Today the mainstay of the city is the ore it ships, but a pulp mill and a large black gabbro polishing plant add considerably to the city's industrial life. Its bay and harbor are among the finest on the Great Lakes.

Bayfield, nestled in hills, lies across the bay from Ashland. It was established largely by St. Paul capital in 1857, apparently in the belief that the new town would be the end of a railroad from St.

---

* See chapter 9, page 197.

Paul to the lake. Henry M. Rice, territorial delegate from Minnesota, and recently connected with the canal survey at the Sault, was the leader in the St. Paul group. He had a road cut between the two villages, which followed a long established Indian trail up the St. Croix Valley, along a tributary of that stream, through the barrens, to the bay. After Superior was founded in the 1850's, another route ran from that place to Bayfield. Over these trails went the mail, first by Indian or half-breed carriers, later by stage. Two of the mail carriers on these routes, Antoine Gordon (Gaudin) and Antoine Denis, were still living in 1943 and were interviewed by the author. Both had become nonagenarians, who had been acquainted with the region between Duluth and Ashland for almost a century. They had known the original Indian residents intimately, spoke their language to some extent at least, and had watched the primeval forest disappear. It is hard to comprehend the changes that have taken place in the area during their lifetimes.

Bayfield was named for a man to whom little credit has ever been given in the Lake Superior region, Admiral Henry Wolsey Bayfield. He was born in Hull, England, in 1795 and had little formal schooling. In the Royal Navy, which he entered as a volunteer during the Napoleonic Wars, he borrowed books from his better educated associates and completed his education. In this way he rose gradually, becoming a lieutenant in 1815 and a commander in 1826. While his ship was in Quebec in 1815, Captain Owen, then making a survey of Lake Ontario, was so much taken by Bayfield's notebooks that the young man was ordered to accompany him. Bayfield helped survey the Canadian shores of all the Great Lakes, and the entire coast line of Lake Superior. His manuscript map of Lake Superior is magnificent in its scope and detail. With it are filed several others of lesser scope, all relating to Lake Superior. One shows merely the north shore, another only Isle Royale. One is his assistant's "Track Survey of the River St. Louis." The big map of the entire lake shows among many other details: "Wreck of the Schooner *Invincible*" just off Whitefish Point, the types of trees along all sections of the lake shore, the site of the American Fur Company's trading post on Madeline Island, detail of the Thunder Bay area, and geological data for the entire lake coast. Bayfield deserves to be remembered as the lake's first modern cartographer.

Something of the early life in Bayfield has been given in extracts from Peet's diary. It has always been an important fishing village. At one period, in the eighties and nineties, it was a great lumbering center.* Today it is one of the centers for lake trout trolling. It is estimated that in normal peace years 5,000 tourist fishermen go to Bayfield to enjoy the trolling. In addition, there are many commercial fishermen who make Bayfield their headquarters. A large commercial company has branch headquarters there and sends out its launch to fishing villages on the islands of the Apostle group every day except Sunday. On Monday, Wednesday and Friday it picks up the fish of the islands to the west of Bayfield; and on the other days it visits the eastern islands, including the largest, Madeline Island.

The Apostle Islands have been misnamed since very early days. Instead of twelve, as one would expect, there are over twenty. They are unusually picturesque islands, both in formation and in the life that goes on among them in the season of navigable water. Only three have human inhabitants during the winter. Take the little boat, the *Apostle Islands,* that serves the commercial fishermen and sit up on deck as Bayfield on its wooded terraces recedes. The route follows the coast line to the northeast until Red Cliff Point is passed, with Bass Island on the right. The Red Cliff Indian Reservation is well named. The coast is high, with red sandstone cliffs underlying the thick stands of deciduous trees. As in all this region, including the islands, the cliffs have been modified greatly by wave action, and present interesting and often grotesque shapes, as well as caverns and arches. Bass Island is heavily timbered, and Oak Island, the next on the right, was until the late summer of 1943. Then it was almost completely burned over, despite great efforts to stop the fire. Oak Island, along with Raspberry and York, is at the end of the blunt point of the mainland. Sand Island begins the turn to the southwest and is the outermost island in that direction to be served directly by the launch. On Raspberry Island is a lighthouse, standing

---

* See page 197, the chapter on lumbering activities on Lake Superior.

out white and high on its shelf of cleared land, its red roof enhancing the dark green of the forest behind it.

Pound nets are visible here and there along the coast and near some of the islands. They can be distinguished immediately by the pole supports that project above the water. This region is one of the best on the lake for pound fisheries, having shallow water close to shore, with very deep water in the immediate vicinity.

There are few houses visible on the shore after leaving Bayfield until Cornucopia is reached on the other side of the point, since the entire point is an Indian reservation. The Indians here and their relatives and friends on the other side of Ashland are the remnants of the numerous Chippewa who once formed the proud La Pointe band. They have suffered, like most of their tribe, from the effects of the United States General Allotment Act of 1887, which was repealed in 1934. For twenty-five years after 1887 the land of the reservation was held in trust by the government; then individual ownership was allowed. The result was the logging of the real assets off the land during the period of government ownership and the passing on of a denuded area to individual Indians thereafter. This, in turn, has been sold, or divided and subdivided in families until little remains to any one person.

In recent years the government has purchased nearly a thousand acres to add to the reservation. Originally there were 14,142 acres at Red Cliff set aside for Chief Buffalo and his tribe under the provisions of the Treaty of 1854, the long-remembered La Pointe Treaty, which alienated from the Indians most of the Chippewa holdings along the north shore and provided for reservations about both shores. After this treaty became effective white men might legally settle along the north shore of Lake Superior. It did not take long for the onrush to start, and the Indians displaced had little in return for the land they lost.

But to return to the Apostle Islands. Sand Island is the first stop of the trip. There is a fairly large summer settlement here, as well as the homes of fishermen. There are two stops on this island. The second stop serves several groups of fishermen, who bring in their catch even as the launch is at the dock. As the captain waits for them, he chats familiarly with the people of the island, practically all of whom—tourists and fishermen—come down to witness the one big event of every other day, the arrival of the boat. Like all the captains of launches that pick up fish on the lake, he is not addressed by his last name. He is "Captain Eli" to everyone. And like most of the fraternity, he is Norwegian. He has Norwegian cookies of a special kind, *fattigmand,* in his boat, which he shares with some of his acquaintances as he waits. Practically all of the fishermen and their wives are also Norwegian or of Norwegian descent. The fishing boats that are tied up at the rickety little dock bear Norwegian names, the *Dorthea,* the *Eversund* and so forth.

While waiting for the fishing boats, the passengers explore the little fishing community, peering into unpainted sheds, where dry nets are hanging in big rolls from the rafters, and where trays of floats and sinkers are kept; examining the great wooden reels outside, on which the wet nets are spread to dry; and picking the raspberries that are so thick on the islands in the latter part of summer.

Finally two fishing boats arrive and pass their catch up to the waiting launch. In midsummer there is not much chance of getting whitefish or trout in any quantity, so the captain gets mostly suckers. Though some are very large and there are many of them, he indicates his contempt for this low-grade fish, which brings only two and a half cents per pound. It is used primarily by fox farmers and to some extent by mink farmers. The trays of fish are hauled onto the deck of the launch with big gaff hooks. Other great trays containing floats, nets and sinkers are left on the fishing boats.

At the back of the fishing boats, which are usually thirty-five-foot launches, are great metal drums, and machinery by which the loaded nets are hauled into the boats. The dry nets are usually played out by hand, and some fishermen both take in and set their nets by hand. Over the center of the boat is a decked area. The skipper of the little craft stands in the undecked stern to guide the boat, his eyes just in position to read the marine compass resting on the edge of the deck before him.

The launch waits while some of the fish are cleaned, for the fishermen have had just enough time to get to the launch without finishing their cleaning. Gulls hover in the offing, anticipating the meal that they know awaits them. The fishermen are very dexterous in slitting and disemboweling their catch. The liver and roe are saved, for they bring good prices. Trout's cheeks are also cut out and saved.

The launch now passes on up the shore of the island to pick up more fish and perhaps take on a few tourists who have been trolling. The shore is rocky and wave-worn. Caves and arches abound. Above hovers an occasional bald eagle, his white head and tail gleaming in the brilliant sunshine against the dark green of the forest wall. Wherever there are fish and solitude about Lake Superior, one may look for eagles and, usually, ospreys (fishhawks). The two are inseparable, since the eagle uses the osprey as his fisherman. As soon as the osprey has dived into the lake and secured his fish, the eagle pursues the hawk and takes it from him. Other wild life is abundant on the islands, but deer, mink, beaver, otter, muskrats and bear are only infrequently seen in daylight from the launch. Loons and mergansers are common on the water, and thousands of herring gulls may be seen. A fortunate observer may catch a glimpse of other kinds of gulls, a Caspian tern or a godwit.

After leaving Sand Island, the launch turns northeastward and passes between York and Raspberry Islands, then between Bear and Otter, touches at South Twin and at two or more places on Rice Island, behind which lies Devils Island. One of the most famous lighthouses of the lake is here. Its alternating red and white flashing light may be seen gleaming from as far away as Castle Danger on the north shore on a clear evening. There is also a radiobeacon. The island is famous for its rock formations, especially its arches.

On the return trip the launch passes between Otter and Oak islands on the right and Manitou Island on the left. The last is high and heavily wooded, with one lone fishing establishment under the hill at its southern end, where an Indian and his dog lead a lonely existence.

Hermit Island is the next on the left. It has its tale of a wealthy recluse who lived there and supposedly hoarded his money. After his death men hurried over with picks and shovels and dug all about his establishment, but with no success. So the island is still supposed to have its buried treasure.

The rest of the way is similar to the outward journey, but with Bass

Island now on one's right. The passengers leave the boat as the summer evening shadows are lengthening, and the crew begin unloading their fish, which will now be sent to all parts of the continent. The launch has traveled sixty miles today among the westerly islands. Tomorrow it will cover as many more around Madeline, Presque Isle, and Michigan Islands to the east. In all, it will pick up the catch of some seventy-five fishing boats in the islands.

Madeline Island deserves to be considered by itself, not only because it is the largest island of the Apostle group but also because it has been the focus of settlement in the entire Lake Superior region since 1659. We have seen how Radisson and Des Groseilliers came to the area in 1659 and were followed by Allouez and Marquette. They found that it had but recently been abandoned by the Chippewa. Years later, about 1850, a descendant of the Chippewa of the region, William Whipple Warren, told the story of native occupation thus:

"We have gradually traced the Ojibways from the Atlantic coast, to their occupation of the surrounding shores of Lake Superior. Computing their generations as consisting of forty years each, it is three hundred and sixty years since the main body of this tribe first reached Pt. Sha-ga-waum-ik-ong on the Great Lake, where for many years they concentrated their numbers in one village. . . . At every step of their westward advance along the southern shores of the Great Lake, the Ojibways battled with the Foxes and Dakotas; but they pressed onward, gaining foot by foot, till they finally lit their fires on the sand point of Sha-ga-waum-ik-ong. On this spot they remained not long, for they were harassed daily by their warlike foes, and for greater security they were obliged to move their camp to the adjacent island of Mon-ing-wun-a-kaun-ing (place of the golden-breasted woodpecker, but known as La Pointe). Here, they chose the site of their ancient town, and it covered a space about three miles long and two broad, comprising the western end of the island. . . . While hemmed in on this island by their enemies, the Ojibways lived mainly by fishing. They also practised the arts of agriculture to an extent not since known amongst them. . . . They manufactured their nets of the inner bark of the bass and cedar trees, and from the fibres of the nettle. They made thin knives from the rib bones of the moose and buffalo. . . . From the thighbone of a muskrat they ground their awls. . . . In those days their shirts and leggins were made of finely dressed deer and elk skins sewed together with the sinews of these animals. They made their wigwam covering of birch bark and rushes; their canoes of birch bark and thin strips of cedar wood, sewed together with the small roots of the pine tree, and gummed with the pitch of the pine, balsam, or tamarac. They made kettles from clay and pulverized stone. . . . Copper, though abounding on the lake shore, they never used for common purposes; considering it sacred, they used it only for medicinal rites, and for ornament on the occasion of a grand Me-da-we. . . . During this era in their history, some of their old men affirm that there was maintained in their central town, on the Island of La Pointe, a continual fire as a symbol of their nationality. They maintained also, a regular system of civil policy, which, however, was much mixed with their religious and medicinal practises. The Crane and Aw-ause Totem families were first in council, and the brave and unflinching warriors of the Bear family, defended them from the inroads of their numerous and powerful enemies.

"The rites of the Me-da-we-win (their mode of worshipping the Great Spirit, and securing life in this and a future world, and of conciliating the lesser spirits, who in their belief, people earth, sky, and waters) was practised in those days in its purest and most original form. Every person who had been initiated into the secrets of this mysterious society from the first to the eighth degree, were imperatively obliged to be present on every occasion when its grand ceremonies were solemnized. This created yearly a national gathering, and the bonds which united one member to another were stronger than exist at the present day, when each village has assumed, at unstated periods, to perform the ceremonies of initiation. . . .

"For the space of three generations, or one hundred and twenty years, the Ojibway remained congregated on the island of La Pointe, in one extensive town.

"At the end of this period, we come to a dark chapter of their history, on which the old men dislike to linger. They are loth to tell the causes which led to the complete and sudden evacuation of their great village, and scattered them in bands and smaller villages on the adjacent shores of the Great Lake, and sent many families back on the track of their former migration to resettle the almost deserted villages of We-qua-dong and Bo-we-ting (Ance-ke-we-naw and Sault Ste. Marie)."*

This "chapter" was a period of cannibalism. Warren then continues:

"When my maternal grandfather, Michel Cadotte, first built his trading post and resided on the island of La Pointe, seventy years ago, not an Indian dare stop over night on it alone, for fear of the Che-bi-ug, which were even then supposed to haunt it. . . . Mons. Cadotte located on the site of the ancient Ojibway town, and at this time the ground on which had stood their numerous wigwams, and waved their fields of corn, was covered with a comparatively young growth of trees, and the stumps of the ancient pines which they had cut down, were in one spot still plainly discernible."

He then tells of how the first white men ever seen by the Indians of the region were discovered one winter day in the middle of the seventeenth century by means of the smoke from their cabin on the island. This event and the subsequent establishment of a permanent fur-trading post led the Chippewa back to their "home" island. He continues:

"Soon after the location of the trading post at Grand Portage, the same company of traders built a 'fort' on the island of La Pointe, at the mouth of a small creek or pond midway between the present location of the 'American Fur Company's' establishment, and the mission house of the 'American Board of Foreign Missions'. Strong palisades of cedar are said to have been planted around this post, and a cannon mounted for its defence. The Ojibways who had resided on this island, and who occupied the surrounding shores of the lake, now traded at this establishment, and they learned to pitch their lodges once more on the spot which they had on a previous occasion so suddenly evacuated. . . . The first old French 'Fort' at La Pointe was not maintained many years before a bloody murder was enacted

* William Whipple Warren, *History of the Ojibway Nation*, in *Minnesota Historical Collections* (St. Paul, 1885), 5:95-108.

within its walls, which resulted in its final dismantling and evacuation. . . . The site of this old post is still plainly discernible from small mounds of stone and rubbish which once formed the chimneys of the dwellings. . . . I learn from Michel Cadotte . . . that this event occurred just one hundred and thirty years ago, in the year 1722."

Earlier in this book the rest of the story of La Pointe under the French regime has been told, with an account of the several officers who were in command until almost the close of the Seven Years' War. Then came Alexander Henry, the settlement of the Cadotte family on the island, John Johnston, and the period of the North West Company's activities. All of these events have been recounted. In 1824, just after the North West Company ended its rule there, two well-known traders, the Warren brothers of Vermont (Lyman and Truman), came to La Pointe and married the daughters of Michel Cadotte. The son of one of them was William Whipple Warren, the historian of the Chippewa, from whose book the preceding quotations about his tribe have been taken. He was born at La Pointe, and from earliest boyhood studied it and his race then living there. His book is one of the most authoritative accounts of the Chippewa on Lake Superior.

In 1830 a Protestant mission was established at La Pointe by Frederick Ayer for the American Board of Commissioners for Foreign Missions. The following year the Reverend Sherman Hall was placed in charge of it and remained there until 1853. Father Baraga came in 1835 and remained till 1843. Father Otto Skolla was there from 1845 to 1853. He was followed by Father Angelus Van Paemel, the resident missionary until 1859. Then Father John Chebul ministered at La Pointe and in its vicinity.

C. D. O'Brien, who later became a familiar figure in St. Paul, recalls his early experiences in La Pointe in 1857, when his father became the teacher there:

"At the time we came to La Pointe, it was a busy, hustling little place. The dock was a large structure, furnishing the safest possible landing for all boats. It had upon it a large warehouse, and on the shore adjoining it, there extended along the lake shore, towards Pointe De Fret, quite a little row of houses; some occupied as stores, some as warehouses and others as cooper shops. There was quite a large building which was used as a hotel on the left hand side as you passed up from the dock, and on the right, another large one, or at least large as I recollect it, which was used as a store by Julius Austrian. Behind this building was a grass plot, and fronting on that, a long row of one-story houses which had been the offices of the American Fur Company. Behind this row of buildings was quite a large garden, surrounded by a high stockade fence, and in my time, that garden produced apples, cherries and currants, besides all the ordinary vegetables.

"Behind the garden was the old church, standing in the church-yard where, at that time, the dead were buried on the surface of the ground, the coffin being laid upon the ground and surrounded by a little frame-work of logs which was filled with sand from the lake shore. . . . The school-house stood in the church yard, and there must have been an average attendance of from twenty to forty pupils of both sexes.

"The town proper consisted of clusters of houses built on each side of a road-way running east and west, close to the lake shore, terminating on the west [at] Pointe De Fret, and on the east at Middle Fort, which was either an episcopalian or a presbyterian mission, but at which no missionary was stationed during my time. Still farther to the east was what was called Old Fort, consisting of a clearing on the eastern side of the island, from which all of the buildings had been removed, but which had grown up to grass and second growth timber.

"There were about three or four white families on the island; the people were mostly half-breeds, the descendants of intermarriage between the old voyageurs and the Indian women, and nearly all the men of middle or beyond middle life were Canadian-French and had been voyageurs or *coureurs des bois,* and had evidently settled upon the island to pass their old age there with their families. In addition to the groups of houses at La Pointe proper and Middle Fort, there was a settlement upon the western side of the island, at a distance of one or two miles.

"The people were a most innocent, affectionate and happy people.

They made their own boats and nets, and the barrels, half-barrels and quarter-barrels in which they packed their fish. During the winter they went out trapping. They raised potatoes and other root crops, and one or two of the white men occasionally raised wheat and oats, but very little of it. There were only two or three horses in the entire settlement, and one or two cows. In winter nearly all the hauling was done with dog teams; nearly every family owning from three to four dogs. These animals were fed upon fish heads taken from the fish in the fall, filled frozen into barrels and kept during the winter for dog food. . . .

"The great events were the arrival of the first steamboat in the spring. Payment time in the fall, when everybody went to Bad River on the Reservation to attend the payment. Christmas day, when we had midnight Mass, and New Year's day, when visits were exchanged, and everybody who had a house kept it open.

"In the spring and fall great flights of migratory birds used to light upon the island and were killed for food; in June pigeons were particularly numerous. The berry season included strawberries, raspberries and blueberries, and altogether the life, while perhaps monotonous, was of great simplicity and singular beauty. From the time navigation ceased until it opened, we were an isolated community. Provisions were stored and provided for in the fall, precisely as if one were going on a voyage, and the first boats used to bring small packages of meat and sausages in their ice-chests, which were sold to such of the inhabitants as could pay for them, and were considered rare delicacies. The old voyageurs were a singularly interesting class of men; uneducated, perhaps, but of a singular dignity of manner and speech and of the utmost morality, scrupulous in the performance of their duties both to God and man. On Sundays, in the little old church, the head of the family always sat with stately dignity on the outside of the pew, and while they indulged in chewing tobacco during the service to a very large extent, yet the habit was conducted in such a simple and dignified way that it ceased to surprise or annoy anybody. The choir in the church included four or five of these old men who sat within the chancel and sung the responses and all of the hymns. I can almost see them now, clad in their white surplices and red shirts, intoning with the utmost dignity all of the responses."*

---

* Quoted in Chrysostom Verwyst, *Life and Labors of Rt. Rev. Frederic Baraga* (Milwaukee, 1900), pp. 289-293.

One still sees dusky faces in and around La Pointe. Today one reaches it by a ferry from Bayfield. In 1943 the old Protestant church was blown down in a severe windstorm. It is said that the church's inner walls were lined with pieces of birch bark, cut and fitted as accurately as wallpaper. The mission property has long been a fashionable summer resort of many cottages and a central Old Mission Inn. The old burying ground may still be seen near some of the cottages, on the hill, with blackened stones telling simply the story of the dead, mostly Indians and half-breeds. A child of Dr. Charles W. W. Borup is buried there. Borup was long a leading trader at La Pointe. He practiced medicine there to some extent, having been educated in Copenhagen. Lists of medical journals that he ordered from New York and Philadelphia are still in existence, as well as scores of his letters from La Pointe. One stone marks the resting place of a child of the Reverend Sherman Hall, a promising lad who died just as his father was leaving La Pointe to take up his work on the upper Mississippi after the La Pointe Indians had sold their land to the United States.

For many years Madeline Island has had palatial summer residences. Yachts may be seen at its wharves or out in the bay near by. The island's beauty is not of the grand type, but quiet and restful. The woods back of the edge of houses are dense and have an interesting carpet of flowers and plants. One can readily understand why the island was so long the favorite residence of most of the Chippewa Indians.

Westward beyond La Pointe and Red Cliff there is no community of any size until one reaches Superior. Cornucopia and Port Wing are both fishing villages on the way. Boat-making is also a specialty. Cornucopia in 1938 had eighteen fishing boats operating out of it and as far away as Isle Royale. This stretch of coast is inhabited largely by Finns. Beyond Port Wing as one travels to Superior, he crosses the Brule River, named for Champlain's intrepid interpreter of the early seventeenth century. Up and down this famous trout stream have passed men of great fame, as they journeyed between the Mississippi and Lake Superior: Brulé, Duluth, Le Sueur, Carver,

Cass, Schoolcraft, Houghton, Crooks, Boutwell and Joseph N. Nicollet, as well as many missionaries and simple voyageurs. It has been and still is a popular summer resort, for the trout fishing is excellent and canoeing is still a joy over its deep pools and around its fascinating twists and turns. Many luxurious houses have been built along its shady banks.

The way to see this stretch of shore, however, is from the lake. A young missionary's wife passing along it in 1842 reveled in its beauties. She was Florantha Sproat, wife of Granville T. Sproat, a missionary of the American Board at La Pointe. She wrote a sort of diary as she traveled to Fond du Lac with her husband, Dr. Borup and his family, Mrs. Borup's sister, six Canadian voyageurs, and two Indians, all in a bateau.

"After our dinner, and commencing our journey the scenery grew more and more grand and beautiful, the shore made for the most part of high precipitous rocks surmounted by evergreens covered with moss of every kind and colour, and assuming strange shapes. . . . At about 5 in the evening we passed some of the most stupendous of God's works—an arched rock extending someways into the lake, supported by pillars perfect and beautiful, bearing on its summit trees of every size and of many kinds, evergreens entwining their roots in every crevice, mosses growing of every color—the whole enchantingly sublime. We sailed our large batteau between the pillars and beneath the rock and forest above. After passing this we came to that which was still more grand—a large mass of rock with forest above supported by innumerable pillars, extending as far as the eye could reach, the water dashing among them, sounding like deep and heavy thunder—the whole certainly aweing. One of the boatmen, who knew not a letter, said 'It is certain the builder of this knew what he was about.' The shores of the lake for miles showed something of like scenery, caverns worn by the water, pillars supporting the rocks, and at times the rocks assuming the form of mighty buildings."

Chapter 12

Queens of the Unsalted Sea

There is a romance about iron. . . . I wonder if the courageous men who seek it in the bowels of the earth realize their big part in the life of the world?

—CHASE S. OSBORN

SUPERIOR IS the last settlement on our westward trek along the south shore. Its modern life as part of the twin port of Duluth-Superior has been discussed in connection with Lake Superior's ore, coal and grain trade. This is the great port on the Great Lakes, and one of the greatest ports in the world. Although residents will say to the contrary, it is practically impossible to separate the life of the two modern cities. As in most twin cities, the people of one place work or play frequently in the other. If an observant stranger tried to state the situation succinctly, he might say something to this effect, though liable to the charge of oversimplification: A resident of the "twins" prefers to say that he *lives* in Duluth; it has the greater social prestige; actually, the commercial and industrial life of the twins is probably greater in Superior. Superior certainly has the advantage in one respect. It has in view the magnificent sight of Duluth across the bay, climbing its rocky heights.

A stranger's first reaction to the entire settlement at the head of the lake, the old Fond du Lac (to be carefully distinguished from the place of that name today), undoubtedly is: How can any business be carried on in a city so precariously perched on rocks and steep hills as Duluth? Marvels have been achieved, however, in making the hillsides usable, despite Nature's lack of co-operation. To bring in railroads and highways it has been necessary to blast away some of the great hillsides. Rock must be terraced to make room for houses. Streets run generally parallel with the shore line. They are few in number because of the great difference in height between each one and the next. Even these can seldom run uninterruptedly along their entire length because of deep gorges that have never been spanned by bridges. In the other direction avenues climb the hills. Since they are spaced along the whole shore line of the harbor, which is large, there are many of them, but because of the hills they climb, most of them are short.

Superior, on the other hand, lies on relatively low and level ground. It lacks Duluth's great scenic beauty, but has decided compensations in its freedom from the problems that face anyone building a residence or business block in Duluth. Its harbor possibilities are probably even greater than its twin's. It was a well-established community while Duluth, or what was to become Duluth, was still a mere collection of unpretentious houses. Yet in recent years Duluth has become a city of over a hundred thousand people, whereas Superior has less than forty thousand.

Superior had its origin as a speculative project in the mind of Henry M. Rice. We have noted him at Bayfield, the energetic Minnesota politician interesting Southern congressmen in the region that the Sault Ste. Marie canal was opening to investors of the United States. Both copper and iron ore were suspected to lie on Lake Superior's northern and western rim. He who got the land first would doubtless reap the benefit which a good ship canal out of Lake Superior now made possible. Therefore Rice urged the acquisition of the region from the Indians. The site of Superior had been acquired in the treaty of 1842, but the site of Duluth and all the Arrowhead Country, as it is now called, to the north and northeast of Duluth, were still closed to individual ownership. The treaty of La Pointe of 1854 secured the desired results: both Superior and its hinterland could now develop.

Actual settlement of Superior began in 1853, when Rice's associates and other groups of speculators from St. Paul and Ontonagon arrived almost simultaneously on the ground. Backing Rice's venture with money and congressional influence were John C. Breckenridge, United States senator from Kentucky; Stephen A. Douglas, United States senator from Illinois, and Rice's personal friend; William Wilson Corcoran, a Washington banker; and several others. They undertook to promote a railroad between the new town and St. Paul, and a wild land boom ensued. Douglas, who had started the pernicious practice of making great gifts of public lands to railroads with the grant of 1850 to the Illinois Central, sponsored a bill in the Senate for a similar grant for a railroad to run from the west end of Lake Superior southward through St. Paul to Dubuque. Scandal of a particularly virulent kind developed in the process of getting the bill through Congress, however, and finally outraged public opinion killed it.

All speculation, including railroad plans, was ended effectively by the panic of 1857, which struck hard at the little settlements on the shores of Lake Superior. From a figure of nearly three thousand, the population of Superior fell to about a thousand. Then came the Civil War, followed by the panic of 1873. Superior had hoped to be the terminus of the first railroad to the head of the lake, but when one came, in 1870, its terminal was Duluth rather than the other twin. In 1884 iron began to be shipped almost simultaneously from the Gogebic and Vermilion ranges.

This time the boom that resulted was justified by something more than hope. Superior began to grow, chiefly through the vision of one man, General John H. Hammond, representing a corporation, the Land and River Investment Company, composed of New York and St. Paul financiers. This was the period when West Superior was platted, and lots were given away in order to draw settlers, and when the commercial end of the town began to prosper. It is the part of the city that now holds much of the shipping, railroad and industrial life of the community. It lies adjacent to Duluth on St. Louis Bay, and also fronts on Superior Bay.

In 1881 the Northern Pacific Railway built into Superior on its way to Ashland. This was the first railroad to reach Superior and it had the foresight to buy terminal facilities in West Superior. Over this road goes much of the coal that is brought to the city, and back over the same tracks from regions as far west as Montana, comes much of the wheat that makes the port so prominent in the grain markets of the nation. The railroad was used to carry lumber, also, when Duluth and Superior were still lumber centers.

Superior became a city in 1889 and by 1900 it had become the second city in population in the state of Wisconsin. The Great Northern, the Duluth, South Shore and Atlantic, and the Chicago, St. Paul, Minneapolis and Omaha railroads now have lines into the city. The grain elevators are among the largest in the world. The Great Northern's Elevator S rises 243 feet above the ground and has a working storage capacity of 2,500,000 bushels. The Great Northern ore docks, on Allouez Bay, in the east part of the city, form the largest group of ore docks in one location in the world. At night their lights can be seen twinkling brightly across the bay, where the people of Duluth call them collectively "The Necklace."

Superior is an important center of the co-operative movement in the United States. The Central Co-operative Wholesale has its office and warehouse in the city and serves more than a hundred retail co-operatives in Minnesota, Wisconsin and Michigan. Here too is the office of the Cooperative Publishing Association, which publishes the *Cooperative Builder* and the *Työvaen Osuustoimintalehti* (the Finnish Co-operative Weekly). The volume of business done by the wholesale co-operative amounts to about three million dollars annually. Its trucks may be seen all through northeastern Minnesota, northern Wisconsin and parts of Michigan.

Duluth lies at the junction of Lake Superior's north and south shores. One of its suburbs is Fond du Lac, which was the mother community for all the settlements at the head of the lake. The Fond du Lac, or St. Louis River, is found on the earliest French maps. It was part of the canoe route leading from Lake Superior to that part of the Mississippi Valley which lies above the Little Falls, where the city of the same name now stands. The St. Louis River was scenically beautiful with deep gorges, dashing rapids and great pine trees before white men began to cut the timber in the later nineteenth century. It is still worth seeing, especially that part which runs through Jay Cooke Park, a state park of great appeal.

Sieur Duluth was almost certainly at the site of either Fond du Lac or Duluth late in the seventeenth century. He may even have passed a winter there. The first actual trading post of which we now have definite knowledge belongs to the following century. In 1784 Jean

Baptiste Perrault found a man named Dufault located on Rice's Point, near the end of Garfield Avenue in present-day Duluth. In 1785 Perrault was back in Superior Bay, where he was detained for a week because of ice in the harbor. In 1789 he was at Fond du Lac, this time with six other traders. Lots were drawn to determine who should stay here and who should go on to posts in the interior. We do not know which one drew the lot for the St. Louis River, but the next fall the same group reassembled and again drew lots for their posts. The Nemadji River, now in the city of Superior, was assigned to Bella Harris; and the St. Louis River was given to another trader. Harris did not do well on the Nemadji, but the others were exceptionally successful in their trade.

Indeed, the success of the ventures between 1784 and 1792 around Fond du Lac was so great that in the summer of 1793 John Sayer, a partner of the North West Company, engaged Perrault to go to Fond du Lac and build a trading post that should serve as the depot for the entire Fond du Lac department. Perrault and ten workmen arrived at Connor's Point, in what became West Superior, and he has left us an interesting account of the building of the fort:

"The Next Day The men prepared for Work and the 18th I gave them rough estimates of dimentions of the timbers and put them in the Wood-yard to Build 2 houses, of 40 feet each and a shed of 60 feet. . . . I set 2 men to sawing, 6 to squaring, Two I kept with me. The 12th of September mr. Sayer arrived, and took up his quarters in his house, half of which Was finished. It was not Long before he was enjoying The other half, which was finished the 24th of September. After this, we Began The second house to shelter ourselves and went into it towards all-saints [November 1]. In the Course of The autumnn, winter, and spring we built the warehouse and stockade. All was ready on The arrival of mr. M'Kenzie, who came to fond du Lac in la Loutre [the *Otter,* the North West Company's schooner], commanded by Capt. m'xwell, and bringing the merchandise for the outfits sent out from Fond du Lac."

The chief who arrived was doubtless Alexander Mackenzie, who had recently completed his trip across the continent from coast to coast. This post was named Fort St. Louis and was occupied by the North West Company until shortly after the close of the War of 1812. The municipal gas plant in Superior stands on or close to the site.

Many reports of Hudson's Bay Company posts about Lake Superior prior to 1821 can be found in books and pamphlets that have been carelessly written, but the truth is that probably only at Fond du Lac and Fort William was there ever a Hudson's Bay Company fort on the lake prior to the union of the North West and Hudson's Bay companies in 1821. Then several former North West Company posts, like the Sault, the Pic, Michipicoten and Fort William, became Hudson's Bay Company posts. During the troubles between Lord Selkirk of the Hudson's Bay Company and the North West Company, which resulted in the seizure of Fort William by the Earl in 1816, an expedition was sent by him to Fond du Lac. Twelve canoes and fifty traders went into the Fond du Lac department to secure the trade of 1816-1817. How much they accomplished we do not know. Only the vaguest references to the entire affair are extant.

When John Jacob Astor's men built a post at the end of the lake, they chose a site at Fond du Lac, the head of navigation on the St. Louis River. The post stood on the north side of the river. It was maintained till nearly 1850, and remains were still visible in recent times. At present there is a modern reproduction of a more or less typical trading fort in a park at Fond du Lac.

Fond du Lac was the center of missionary activity at the head of the lake. Catholics, Methodists and the men and women of the American Board had stations there, and some of them had schools. Some of the outstanding resident missionaries were Edmund F. Ely, William T. Boutwell, Mrs. Ely and Mrs. Boutwell, all American Board missionaries; and Samuel Spates, Peter Marksman, Eri H. Day, Enmegahbowh (John Johnson) and Joseph W. Holt, of the Methodist contingent. Though Father Pierz started a chapel, it was never completed, and the Catholic mission was an itinerant one. It was served from La Pointe, Superior or Crow Wing by Baraga, Skolla, Pierz, Van Paemel and Chebul. A voyageur, Pierre Coté, should also be mentioned, though he was only a sort of lay Catholic teacher during Skolla's time.

Fond du Lac was surveyed and platted in 1856; at that time there were six white families and fourteen buildings. Oneota was surveyed and platted in 1856; a post office was established; and a public school was organized in a private home. There were three dwellings, three huts for work shops, a store, a dock, a steam sawmill, and about twenty inhabitants. Other places, now part of Duluth, as are Fond du Lac and Oneota, were platted and surveyed in 1856, such as Portland, Endion and Bellville. Duluth proper started on Minnesota Point, where George Stuntz built a trading post in 1852. The area near the present ship canal was platted in 1855 and 1856 and a house was built in the latter year. No one could get legal claim to land until that time. In 1857 the town sites of Duluth, Portland and Endion joined and became the town of Duluth. It was given a post office in that year. By that time there were about a hundred buildings from Lester River on the east to Fond du Lac on the west. These places are the present limits of the widely spread city, some twenty-four miles in length.

The village got into its stride just in time to be overtaken by the disastrous panic of 1857. The Civil War followed the panic and the settlement decreased rather than increased in population. With the construction of the Lake Superior and Mississippi River Railroad, in which Jay Cooke was interested, population began to increase. Duluth became a city in 1870 and in the same year the first grain elevator was built. Jay Cooke had indicated his intention of making Duluth the terminus of the Northern Pacific railroad, and one of the railroad's big immigrant houses was built in Duluth; but the panic of 1873 caused Cooke's financial failure. Duluth's interests were bound up with his. It began to decline once more, and even lost its status as a city, becoming the village and district of Duluth.

When the Northern Pacific was revived, late in the 1870's, Duluth also began to take on new life. Soon the Vermilion Iron Range was opened. It shipped its first ore in 1884, but to Two Harbors—a community about thirty miles east of the head of the lake on the north shore—and not to Duluth. Nevertheless, it was certain that Duluth would profit by this boom, especially as lumbering operations were also beginning to center at the village. It became a city once more in 1887. In 1890, when the Mesabi range was being opened, the population had reached 33,115.

The story of the opening and development of the Minnesota iron ranges is one of the most dramatic in American industrial history. The present status of the industry has already been indicated in an earlier chapter. Something of the discovery of mines and the men who were responsible for it needs to be given at this point.

From Duluth, up over the gabbro outcropping, went the Vermilion Indian trail to the large lake of the same name near the international boundary. This had long been an important trail for traders and for Indians going to annual payments. In the middle 1860's two Eames brothers, Richard and Henry H., were appointed to survey the north shore in a geological reconnaissance that was then in progress. In the course of their work they went to Vermilion Lake, where they reported iron ore exposed from fifty to sixty feet in thickness; but as they made little of it and much of some supposed gold discoveries, the immediate result was what is still known as the Vermilion Lake Gold Rush. Duluth profited by the trek of prospectors and others who necessarily had to make the town their outfitting point.

Though this boom soon failed, there were men involved in it who noted the indications of iron ore in the lands they passed over, and later made use of their observations. Among them were George Stuntz, who had built a trading post on Minnesota Point some years earlier; and George C. Stone, also a Duluth resident. Stone, after some difficulty, interested a Philadelphia capitalist, Charlemagne Tower, in the ore possibilities of the district. A surveying party was sent out in 1875 under the charge of Professor Albert H. Chester of Hamilton College, New York. Although he found ore, he was not enthusiastic about it, and suggested further investigation.

Meantime Professor Newton H. Winchell, the state geologist, in 1878 reached the Vermilion area in his survey. His report was enthusiastic about the ores. Chester was sent back by Tower and an associate in 1880. This time he, too, was enthusiastic, and in December 1882 the Minnesota Iron Company was incorporated. The charter members were Charlemagne Tower, both the senior and the junior of that name, George Stone, George R. Stuntz and two others. Using a charter of an earlier railroad that Stone had been connected with, the new company began a railroad, called the Duluth and Iron Range.

The earlier charter had specified that Duluth was to be one terminal, but the new road was actually built to Two Harbors, probably because of its closer proximity to the ore. By 1884 it was completed to Two Harbors, and the first shipment of ore left the dock in midsummer. It was some years later that the railroad was extended to Duluth. In the building of these facilities the company imported Michigan miners and other workmen, chiefly Cornishmen and Swedes.

The Mesabi Range had been given attention by Chester, but Tower and his associates did not think the indications of ore sufficient to warrant outlay until Winchell in 1888 persuaded his former guide of the geological expedition, John Mallmann, to interest the Minnesota Iron Company. A deposit was found, not large but big enough to encourage further exploration. Prospecting was carried on simultaneously by many persons, notably by the seven Merritt brothers of Duluth. The family had been one of the earliest in Oneota, and Peet's diary is full of references to its sons, who were all upstanding members of his small congregation. These men were superb timber cruisers, and in the course of their explorations for pine stands, they watched for the ore which they felt certain was to be found eventually. In 1889 the Minnesota legislature made it possible for a person to lease land on which to prospect. In 1890, therefore, Leonidas Merritt took out 141 such leases and took up prospecting on a large scale. In November 1890 one of the brothers' exploring parties found ore where the Mountain Iron Mine was later to be opened, near the present-day Virginia. Soon after, the Biwabik Mine and the mines at Eveleth and Hibbing were also discovered and worked. Mine after mine was now opened.

A railroad was necessary. The Merritts tried to interest the Northern Pacific and the St. Paul and Duluth in extending track to the region, but to no avail. So they incorporated their own railroad, the Duluth, Missabe, and Northern Railway Company, which at first connected with the Duluth and Winnipeg Railroad at Stony Brook, now Brookston. The first shipment arrived at Superior in 1892.

The ore from the Vermilion Range was mostly hard and required shaft mining; that from the Mesabi was largely soft and could be taken out of the earth by so-called open pit mining. By 1896 the Mesabi mines had shipped 2,882,079 tons of ore; by 1901 the figure stood at 9,004,890. The entire output of Minnesota mines for the decade since the Mesabi made its first shipment was 40,404,967 tons. Thus Minnesota had become the largest producer of iron ore in the United States, and most of it was being marketed by way of Lake Superior.

In 1901 the United States Steel Corporation was organized. Before then, through the panic of 1893 and lack of experience in the intricacies of high finance, the Merritt brothers had lost control of their railroad and much of their mining property to Rockefeller interests. A connection with Duluth had been made by the railroad, and ore docks had been constructed in Duluth harbor. The Rockefeller interests were now acquired by the new corporation. In addition, it became the owner of the ore property, railroad, and ore fleet of the Carnegie Steel Company (which had acquired its property from Henry W. Oliver and others), and of the Federal Steel Company's properties. The United States Steel Corporation now merged the Federal Steel Company, the Lake Superior Consolidated Iron Mines Company (the Rockefeller property), and the Carnegie-Oliver company into a subsidiary, which was given the name of the Oliver Iron Mining Company with offices in Duluth. It has remained the big figure in the mining operations of the two ranges since that time, though there are other important companies and many individual owners, usually referred to as "fee owners."

Duluth entered upon a new era in its history with the opening of the Mesabi range. Its port boomed and its population increased greatly. Attempts were made to smelt the ores close to the mines. Coal was brought to the head of the lakes and a furnace was built. The first failed, but the Zenith Furnace Company took over the plant of the defunct concern and has operated it since that time. Then, in 1907, the United States Steel Corporation, through its subsidiary corporation, the Minnesota Steel Company, bought 1,500 acres of land on the St. Louis River in Duluth and in 1916 opened its own smelting plant. Around it the company has developed a model village, called Morgan Park, for its employees.

Miners and furnace operatives were brought in by the company or came of their own initiative, many from earlier mining centers on the south shore. South Europeans were relatively new in the Lake Superior region, but they became numerous after the Mesabi range began to produce. Finns and Scandinavians also arrived and took up their abode in the range towns and in Duluth and Two Harbors. In 1930 the foreign-born population of Duluth numbered 24,929 out of a total population of 101,463. The two largest groups were Scandinavians, 10,976; and Finns, 3,040.

Newspapers, churches, schools, and other foreign-language institutions were a part of the city's unique life. Today it maintains a symphony orchestra, whose director is a Finn. Much creative ability and genius in many lines are prophesied for a city and its range hinterland that has already indicated so much appreciation of the cultural contributions of its varied population. Here South meets North in a cultural union that has been very happy, Yugoslav joining with Finn and Scandinavian to weave a new and striking pattern into the tapestry of a region already interesting in its design. Credit must also go to the genuine statesmanship of great corporations, which have had the vision in this area to give their best in the way of planning for the future as well as for the immediate present, for the community as well as for themselves.

Duluth is served by eleven railroads. The ship canal, which now admits the ore boats and other craft to Duluth Harbor Basin in Superior Bay, through the width of Minnesota Point, is operated by the Federal government. When cut in 1871, it caused great anger and concern in Superior, hitherto closer to The Entry, or natural entrance to the magnificent harbor, than Duluth was. A lawsuit developed, Superior charging that her harbor would be ruined by the diversion of the waters of the St. Louis River and the consequent filling of the channel with silt. The case dragged on for years and was finally decided in Duluth's favor in 1877 by the Supreme Court of the United States. The Federal government took over the canal in 1873 and later reconstructed it. There is no more popular place in the twin port for tourists than the banks of that canal when the great lake boats are passing through, hour after hour. The sightseers like

to listen to the deep-throated calls from the boats to the bridge operators above the canal and the answers from the bridge. Formerly
there was a unique "aerial" bridge for traffic to and from Minnesota
Point over the canal, a big metal basket that passed on an overhead
trolley line from one side of the canal to the other. Now the traffic
is carried by a regular bridge, the floor of which lifts to let the lake
boats pass freely beneath the high arches of the sightly structure.

If one wants to oversimplify, he can sum up the development at the
head of the lake as one of transportation. Grain needed to be shipped
cheaply, and, later, ore posed the same problem. Water-borne commerce is cheapest, and so grain and ore were brought to Duluth for
shipment by boat to lower lake ports and even beyond. To provide a
return freight, coal was sent back in the boats; and the cars that had
brought the grain went back to the West loaded with coal. Duluth's
contribution to the traffic was the providing of extraordinarily efficient docks and other facilities for handling cargo.

In doing this she made use of the genius of one of her foreign-born
sons, Captain McDougall. McDougall's ingenuity brought other
commerce to Duluth. About the head of the lake lies the great dairy
and egg center of the continent. Before 1913 distributors of butter
and eggs at Duluth had to ship their products by rail in refrigerator
cars to eastern markets. The cost of the products in the East was too
high when rail transportation rates had to be paid for such a long
distance. The Western Transit Company now furnished refrigerator
equipment on four of its package freighters and reduced the cost so
much that the eastern demand for midwestern dairy products and
eggs increased notably.

Facilities for handling these products and those of truck gardeners
were now all that was necessary for perfect success. In 1923 the Mc-
Dougall Terminal opened in Duluth, with 350,000 square feet of general storage space and 1,000,000 cubic feet of cold-storage space. Ten
railroads and two steamship companies delivered freights to and
from the terminal. The Minnesota-Atlantic Transit Company had
been formed and had built its "Poker Fleet" of refrigerator boats:
the *Ace, King, Queen* and *Jack*. Later the *Ten* was added.

After a time the McDougall Terminal Warehouse Company

AERIAL VIEW OF DULUTH HARBOR

DULUTH, AERIAL BRIDGE AND MINNESOTA POINT
BY MOONLIGHT
The lights of the Allouez Bay docks, Superior, may be seen across the harbor.

HULL-RUST MINE AND PART OF HIBBING, MINNESOTA

Before the recent great excavations were made.

merged with the Terminal and Transportation Corporation of America, with warehouses in Chicago, Detroit and Buffalo, as well as Duluth. By 1925 fourteen refrigerator package steamers were serving dairy and agricultural producers of the Northwest. The package steamers to and from the great port have become, in peacetimes, a very important part of the city's life.

McDougall's services to his city also included boat-building, as mentioned in an earlier chapter. During the First World War he greatly increased his boat-building facilities and turned out forty-five vessels for the United States Shipping Board. In the Second World War, both Superior and Duluth have turned to boat-building even more effectively.

One further point in the Lake Superior phase of Duluth's life needs to be mentioned: the provisioning of the great boats that come and go so constantly throughout seven or eight months of the year, staying in the harbor for only a few hours. Here again, everything is done to keep the traffic moving quickly and smoothly. The city does an immense volume of trade, all told, in supplying the food and other needs of the crews of the vessels, who seldom have time to shop in town. So "bum boats," as they are called locally, put out to the vessels as they lie at dock, tie up alongside, and supply everything called for, from sides of beef to thimbles, needles, the latest magazines, medicine and cigarettes.

Part IV

AN ARC OF ROCKS

Chapter 13

The Watershed of a Continent

Behold the rocky wall
That down its sloping sides
Pours the swift rain-drops, blending, as they fall,
In rushing river-tides!
. . . .
From the same cradle's side,
From the same mother's knee,—
One to long darkness and the frozen tide,
One to the Peaceful Sea!
                                    —Oliver Wendell Holmes

WHEN Americans speak of the north shore they usually mean the stretch of lake shore between Duluth and Pigeon River, although the term is frequently elastic enough to include the beautiful region between the international boundary and Fort William. Canadians mean by the same expression the stretch of lake shore between Port Arthur and Heron Bay. The entire curve from southwest to southeast is rock-ribbed for the most part, with practically no natural harbors save at Grand Marais and Thunder Bay. As far as Two Harbors there is a cement road and also a railroad. Thereafter, until Fort William is reached, the whistle of a railroad locomotive is never heard, and all communication is either by water or by an excellent, hard-surfaced bituminous road, which clings to the edge of the shore in most places.

The scenic drive is one of the greatest attractions of the region. Beyond Big Bay, near Grand Portage, the highway turns inland and crosses the Pigeon River between high falls. It does not emerge on the shore again till well beyond Port Arthur. Even then the main lake is seldom in full view, for numberless islands diversify the

291

scenery with their great rocks and dark evergreen trees. Some of the finest views are obtained in the stretch between Nipigon and Schreiber. Beyond the latter a road is being constructed but is not yet opened to the public. From Jackfish on there is no shore road, and between Heron Bay and Michipicoten there is little likelihood that there will be one in the immediate future. The eastern shore of the lake presents such cliffs and crags that the engineering problem of building a road within sight of the lake is terrific. Nevertheless, a beginning has been made between Sault Ste. Marie, Ontario and Batchawana Bay.

Soon after the highway was constructed on the Minnesota part of the shore, an excellent descriptive and geological survey book, entitled *A Guidebook to Minnesota Trunk Highway No. 1,* was written by Professor G. M. Schwartz of the geology department of the University of Minnesota. The geology of this stretch of shore is unusual, and with the little book in hand one can spend a profitable time traveling along the highway, now called Highway No. 61, looking not only at geological displays but also at plants and animals, for space is given to them and to many other phases of life along the coast, all in a pleasant, readable style.

Though the entire shore from Duluth to Grand Marais and beyond has a general similarity, every little section has its unique qualities— and its boosters among both residents and tourists. Some prefer to be within sight of the busy lanes of steamer traffic and to hear the hoarse greetings of the ore boats, and the threefold groans of the fog-horns at Two Harbors and Split Rock. Others prefer to be beyond sight and hearing of anything that reminds them that people are near by. So they go beyond Beaver Bay, to Cross River, Tofte, Lutsen and Grand Marais. Everywhere as far as Big Bay, except for short stretches, the lake is in full view. Most of the homes and tourist cabins are on the lake side of the highway, many of them so close to the water that the pound of surf on the rocks sounds in one's ears throughout the night, a lullaby that has a great attraction.

It is a region of interesting vegetation. Besides the evergreen trees, there are both white and yellow birch, two kinds of poplars, two of mountain ash, and a few others. Gnarled old white cedars are not infrequently to be found, the tree so useful to the old fur traders and voyageurs. With its stringy bark they made the roofs of their forts; and with its wood they constructed the *lisses,* or frameworks, of their birch canoes. Today it has another interesting use: the sprinkler, or *vasta* of the Finnish *sauna* or steam bath, is a branch of this tree.

The balsam grows luxuriantly along this coast. Its towering steeples provide just the necessary shading for the light green of poplars, birches and mountain ash. In early July the two kinds of mountain ash are in bloom, along with the red osier, the mountain maple and the raspberry. Beneath the trees and on the rocks of the shore are smaller plants. Back on the sandy ridges the trailing arbutus may be found in April and early May. By July 1 the Virginia cowslips are coming into bloom. They are abundant in this part of Minnesota, though regarded generally as a much more southern variety. Near them, but out on the shore ledges in clefts and crannies, bloom the still more fragile and much smaller harebells, which sway with every breath of lake air. Certain cinquefoils, saxifrages, ferns and other rare plants are there, too. Though said to grow only as far south as Grand Marais, the butterwort is to be found in the vicinity of Split Rock and Castle Danger, and it is fairly abundant on Isle Royale.

Everywhere in early July in this shore country may be found the twinflower trailing its vine under the evergreens. It is fitting in this land of Scandinavians that the favorite flower of the great Swedish botanist, Linnaeus, should grow here in such profusion. Here, too, these sons of the north find another familiar flower, the *clintonia borealis.* In bloom it may easily escape notice, for its inconspicuous three-belled flower of pale yellow comes early and seems to hide itself; but in midsummer and early fall three or more large berries of midnight blue cannot be overlooked.

In early July a very common sight near the twinflowers is great beds of white bunchberry flowers, which later become shining red berries. Masses of pink and of white clover climb the shoulders of the highway and spread up its banks and into the meadows. Great stalks of white cow parsnip stand in the grass as high as a man. Beds of wild strawberries grow everywhere. Whole meadows of buttercups and daisies gleam in the sunlight. Great stretches of purple selfheal are found here and there, and thousands of green orchids hide away in the drainage ditches along the highway.

Birds are as varied as the plants. One July the author kept a record of the kinds of birds she saw and heard in the region of Castle Danger during the first two weeks of the month. The number was forty-two. For the first week they sang almost continuously from about four in the morning until the last faint daylight had retreated. The second week they were beginning to be a little less vigorous in their singing, and some species were ceasing during the middle of the day.

Nesting in the vicinity were many warblers that are merely passing migrants in most parts of the United States: the parula, the chestnut-sided, the Blackburnian, the black-and-white, the black-throated green, the Canadian, the myrtle and the mourning.

By the second week the whitethroats were whistling their sad, sweet notes much more infrequently than in the opening days of the month. The olive-backed thrushes went right on, however, especially as the cool of the long northern evenings descended. Many sparrows were noticeable: the chipping, the song, the clay-colored, the vesper, the savannah and the pine siskin.

The loons were frequent, but not numerous nor very vocal visitors in the near-by coves. As storms approached, they could be seen in majestic passage inland, uttering their weird flight cries, so different from their mad laughter on the water. Only a few mergansers were in evidence so early in the season, and no grebes, though these are to be seen at many places on the shore. Gulls there were aplenty, riding the air currents up and down shore and screaming whenever they spied food or thought that some boat was turning toward shore with possibilities of refuse for them. A marsh hawk could also be seen now and again enjoying the effortless rides that the air currents afforded over the edge of the land.

Butterflies flitted aimlessly everywhere. The banded purples were especially abundant on the rocky ledges alongshore. Farther back fritillaries, especially commas, could be seen, with numerous little blues and several kinds of moths, one with a long proboscis and tiger markings. In spots, ferns grew luxuriantly, especially the lady, the woodsia and the beech ferns. In other places along the shore ferns are very much in evidence and of many varieties.

Deer are abundant and can scarcely be overlooked even by the least observant tourist. They come down to natural or artificial meadows for hay. In the writer's experience these deer seem to resent intrusion more than most of their kind, or else they are more vocal. When disturbed they stamp and whistle to show their displeasure. Moose are seen infrequently; bear more often.

One October day, as the author was motoring along a shady road to Silver Islet near Thunder Cape, a sudden turn in the road revealed a half-grown bear in the middle of the road. That same day I saw many ruffed grouse and a few porcupines, but no caribou, though they are supposed to be fairly numerous east of Port Arthur. Ruffed grouse are very numerous throughout the northern part of the lake basin and can be heard drumming everywhere in the spring; their cousin, the spruce grouse, is less uncommon than formerly. When encountered on a side road, it is not shy. If it will spread its great tail turkey-fashion for you, you will do well to photograph it, for it is a sight worth preserving.

Only the most observant and silent tourist has much chance of seeing mink, otter and beaver, though all are to be found in this region. Freaks of fortune come to everyone, however, and one of them must account for the beaver that the author recorded at length in color movies in full daylight and within sight and hearing of Highway Number 61 one June day in 1942. He dived, spanked the water in resounding whacks with his tail, ate green algae on the bottom of a pool in the little river, using his front paws like little hands, swam about fearlessly while eying the movie-camera operator, and otherwise showed his emancipation from the conventions and customs of beaverland. Beaver hunting for a short season in the early spring has been permitted again in recent years. The beaver has come back a little, after a century of depletion that had made the animal nearly extinct.

The treaty of 1854, which opened the north shore to settlement, was negotiated in the interest of mining groups or persons who believed that the copper boom of the 1840's and 1850's on the south shore could be duplicated on the north. Even before news of the ratification of the treaty had reached the new town of Superior. men were there ready to depart for the north shore in order to pre-empt land. One man who explored it at this time, Robert B. McLean, writes thus of a trip made in September 1854:

"I found that my associates on the work were preemptors. As I became better acquainted with the people I found they were nearly all preemptors. What conversation I heard around me all turned toward copper and copper claims. There were rumors of great masses of pure copper and large veins full of copper that could be traced for long distances, but they were all on the North Shore and that was Indian territory, white men were not allowed to enter it. About the 15th of September, as I left the old hotel I met Mr. [Thomas] Clark on the sidewalk, he told me to get my blanket and ax and go with John Parry who was an old miner and explorer. Late in the day I met Parry, he asked me if I was going with him; I told him that was my orders, 'where are we going.' 'Well,' he said, 'you must not tell any one what I tell you, but we are going to sneak over onto the North Shore and try and find where those masses of copper and that big vein that we have heard so much about are.'"

With much secrecy they made their explorations as far as Knife River and returned to report to the men who had sent them out:

"R. B. Carlton, George and William Nettleton, Vose Palmer, W. H. Newton, Major Watrous, and Indian agent, Ben Thompson and Major Hatch of St. Paul. . . . This company was later known as the R. B. Carlton company. . . . We returned to Superior after an absence of several days and I went back to my work on the survey. It was but a few days later, on a Saturday afternoon, as we came in from work I heard it whispered around that some halfbreeds and indians had just returned from La Pointe, saying the treaty had been made and signed with the Indians for all the lands on the North Shore, reserving only a small reservation at Grand Portage for the Indians. Later in the evening I was tapped on the shoulder by Mr. Clark. I followed him into his office, he told me to get my blanket and axe and be down at the boat landing about 10 o'clock. . . . Not a word was spoken above a whisper until we were some distance away from shore where we could not be overheard. Oars were taken in and our sails hoisted. I was selected to take the helm and be sailing master. I asked them where they were bound for. 'Head for the entry, we are bound for the North Shore.'"

Thomas Clark's diary of the expedition is still in existence, written in neat pencil script, with exquisite little drawings and explanations of the entire coast line from The Entry to Grand Marais. He mentions houses at Copper Creek, French River, Encampment Island, Waginokaniny [Two Island] Creek, Little and Grand Marais, and a few other places. Near Two Island River on October 22 the little party was caught, apparently, by a nor'easter, common at that season of the year.

"2 o'clock P. M. The wind continues. We are pretty well locked up—the lake before us in a slight foam—a little mad—the rocks in our rear 50 f perpendicular or nearly so & if the wind continues to freshen up our canoe must be elevated above the reach of the surf—& we must climb the wall for camp ground. . . . 4 P. M. We are done for a three days storm—this if possible is the worst place we could have been driven into. We are not only wind bound, but rock & wood bound. The forest is a perfect mat of entwined underbrush—cedar & savin boughs. . . . Mr. Godfrey tells me it is the same sort of coast rocks all the way to the British line (Pigeon River) Baptiste having prepared a snug camp in the side hill—the wind increasing & the lake surf upon the rocks and rugged coast roaring equal to seven Niagaras—thankful we are all safe we retire. . . . About 4 P. M. [next day] the wind ceased, & anxious to have another chance for trout we put out for the creek. . . . One however accustomed to heavy weather with steamers and other large craft, feels quite uneasy in a bark canoe 500 f from a rock bound shore with the seas running 5 or 6 f high, & occasionally an 'old one' letting him down in the trough out of sight of land, & then up as upon a haystack—but with such men as I have, little Bob at the helm & Baptiste at the oars, all are as safe can be, with a half inch of birch bark between one and Davy's Locker, which along here is said to be below 'no soundings.'"

Clark started on foot at one place near Two Island River and records:

"Much of the way where I have walked through the woods (where the shore is impassable) I have observed the remains of a trail—now overgrown with underbrush, moss &c—it not having been used for 10 or 20 years. Along it are frequently old camp grounds—stumps nearly decayed—& perhaps what have been potato patches."

At Grand Marais, McLean found "five Frenchmen from Detroit, Michigan, who were in possession, had some timber cut and carried out for their cabins. They had joined with H. H. McCullough at Sault Ste. Marie in chartering a small vessel there to take them to Grand Portage where Mr. McCullough had his trading post. There they got canoes and reached Grand Marais two days ahead of us." This Grand Portage trader has escaped history except in Mr. Mc-Lean's reminiscences.

Within two years, north shore settlements began to take on stability. McLean's pamphlet describes one step.

"Some time in July [1856] a monthly mail route was established from Superior to Grand Portage. Thomas Clark had the contract for carrying the mail. Postoffices were established at French river, Henry Smith, postmaster; at Beaver Bay, R. B. McLean, postmaster; at Grand Marais, H. Godfrey, postmaster; at Grand Portage, H. H. McCullough, postmaster. I had the honor of taking the first mail through on the route."

The missionary, Peet, went on that trip and published an article about his experiences.

McLean also tells of the near-starvation of the people of Superior in 1856 and of his learning that McCullough had flour in quantity at Grand Portage. So he went by boat to McCullough's post.

"After passing French river we saw no one until we reached Grand Marais. H. Godfrey, with two other young men, whom I had seen there in October, 1854, were still living there. At Grand Portage Henry Elliott, his wife and family were the only white people to be found. Mr. Elliott was in charge of H. H. McCullough's trading post, and had been in charge for three years. After saying 'Bijou, Bijou,' a few times, we asked him if he had any flour that he could spare. He said: 'Yes, I have a hundred barrels over there in the warehouse, you can have all you want.' 'What are you asking for flour down here?' 'Sixteen dollars a barrel.' We bought four barrels, that was all we could get into our boat and leave room for rowing. We were invited to take dinner with them which invitation we readily accepted. Mrs. Elliott gave us a good square meal, such as we hadn't seen for a good many days. After spending an hour or two with them we loaded our flour and started on our return trip. I learned from some Indians before leaving there that he was selling flour to them for $8.00 per barrel."

Thus Grand Portage, far in the wilderness in 1856, fed the coming metropolis of Superior!

A little more of this forgotten czar of the wilderness may be recorded here. McLean continues:

"H. H. McCullough who was postmaster at Grand Portage was not a resident of Minnesota, his home was at Newark, New Jersey, where his family resided. He established his trading post at Grand Portage in 1849 or 1850. . . . About the first of August, 1853, I crossed from Eagle Harbor to Isle Royale for the purpose of meeting Mr. McCullough and to find out if salt and barrels could be bought from him for the season's fishing at Siskowet bay. I met him at the Rock Harbor mine, which was then working with a large force of men. I found that I could get all the salt and barrels we wanted, and with five others I spent two months at Siskowet bay fishing. At that time he was largely interested in the fishing industry; he had one large warehouse and dock at Siskowet bay filled with salt and barrels, another on the north side of the island. He was also largely interested in lands on the north side of the island. My next meeting with him was at Grand Portage in 1857. In September, '61, I was employed by him to go to the Lake of the Woods and take charge of his trading post for the winter. On my way to that point I found he had trading posts at Mountain Lake, Sagana Lake, Basswood Lake, Vermilion Lake, Lac La Croix, Black Bay on Rainy Lake, and the one at Lake of the Woods. In 1863 he disposed of all his interests at Grand Portage and his fishing interests at Isle Royale to P. E. Bradshaw of Superior."

McLean tells a little of a forgotten town in this area: "Asa A. Parker, Charles Kimball, Charles Kingsbury and others were located at Pigeon river." Somewhere, many years ago, the author of this book read a fascinating account of "Parkersville" near the mouth of the Pigeon, as told by a relative of the founder—perhaps his daughter. No amount of searching will turn up that account today, and so we must rely on a dim memory of what was read. It represented a little Eden in that far retreat, with access only by boat, and with beautiful flower gardens. As long afterward as 1874 the hamlet still survived for it is described thus in a guidebook to the Great Lakes published that year:

"Parkersville is a small settlement situated at the mouth of the [Pigeon] River, where also is to be seen Indian huts and wigwams constructed of birch bark. This place, no doubt, is soon destined to become a place of resort during the summer months."

Today one hears at Grand Portage that certain flowers of exotic origin in the postmistress' garden are descendants of plants in fur traders' gardens. More likely they come from Parkersville or Father Pierz' mission on the same river. Unusual trees are reported today on Pigeon Point. Pierz was a horticulturist of note, and, as already remarked, imported plants, shrubs and seeds from Austria and the eastern part of the United States for his garden and orchard. Traders and missionaries depart and their dwellings are no more, but the plants that they set out persist and multiply.

By studying the shipping ledger of the American Fur Company at Sault Ste. Marie for 1846, 1847 and 1848, one may tell to no inconsiderable extent what was going on in the region of the north shore and Isle Royale. On April 30, 1846, the schooner *Swallow* is listed as under the command of Captain Jno. J. Stanard and bound for

Dead River, Copper Harbor and Grand Portage with a large cargo of provisions and supplies addressed to Messrs. Rankin and Company. There were seven passengers in the cabin and two in the steerage; and one fishing boat, one canoe and one large boat aboard. On May 22 the propeller *Independence,* A. J. Averill master, left the Sault for Isle Royale; on July 8 the schooner *Chippewa,* Captain F. Clark master, left for the same destination; on August 29 the *Independence* departed once more for Isle Royale, this time with provisions for the Ohio and Isle Royale Mining Company, care of "L. Ransom, Ile Royale"; and on September 29 the *Julia Palmer* left for Spar Island, Fort William and Point Ignace, care of Thomas Childs, Princes Location. The instructions read, "Jno Ballenden and H. Pierce Esqrs with their party to proceed to Fort William, & to the Locations of the Montreal Mi[ni]ng Co. as designated by Mr Ballenden, touching on way back if practicable at Michipicoten." Ballenden was a Hudson's Bay Company factor, who had served in the Red River country and then had been given the joint management of the Sault Ste. Marie and Lake Huron districts in 1840. Michipicoten at that time was the site of a Hudson's Bay Company trading post.

To resume the record of vessels touching along the north shore and on Isle Royale in the period between 1846 and 1848: On October 16, 1846, the *Ocean,* probably a schooner, with N. W.[?] Randall master, sailed for Isle Royale, and on the 19th the *Florence,* under Captain Angus, left for Baie de Gris and Isle Royale, carrying a cargo destined for Robert Johnson and Captain Smithwick at Rock Harbor on the eastern tip of the island. Navigation closed about November 12 and reopened on May 17, 1847. On July 16, 1847, the propeller *Independence,* with A. J. Averill again captain, left the Sault bound for "Prince's Location North Shore Lake Superior" with the cargo "care owner on board," who appears to have been Thomas C. Childs. On May 6, 1848, the *Swallow* likewise sailed, with Thomas Clark captain, for "Prince Bay" loaded with a cargo for the British North American Mining Company.

It is obvious from these many references to mining on the north shore east of Grand Portage that attempts were being made by Canadians to duplicate in that region the boom that was progressing so astonishingly on the south shore. Success did not come for some time. Meanwhile a first, uncertain attempt at town-building on the American north shore continued.

Peet's article on his trip along the shore in 1856 mentions the beginning of settlement at the site of Two Harbors and Beaver Bay. Today Two Harbors is the only city between Duluth and Fort William. Its history is closely linked with the discovery of ore on the Vermilion and Mesabi ranges, and thus belongs to the generation since 1884. Even earlier Beaver Bay had been quite a thriving little settlement, the nucleus being a group of Germans who operated a sawmill there. For years it was the county seat, but in 1888 it yielded that honor to Two Harbors.

Two Harbors, a city of over four thousand inhabitants, takes its name from the fact that it is located on both Burlington and Agate bays. Its history until 1884 is very slight. Then it became the terminus of the Duluth and Iron Range Railroad, as already mentioned, with railroad shops and ore docks, which stimulated growth. Its population in the first years of development was largely Scandinavian. For a number of years, when the north shore was being cut over, lumbering was important also. Today the city has a big coal dock, as well as three large ore docks, all owned by the Duluth, Missabe and Iron Range Railroad, the successor of the original railroad. Coal received at this port goes largely to Iron Range towns and cities. There is also a United States Coast Guard base here, with year-round service.

The only other settlement of any size between Duluth and Grand Portage is Grand Marais. A general knowledge of French would lead one to suppose that the words meant "Large Swamp." French-Canadian voyageurs, however, had their own special vocabulary, in which the word "Marais" on a coast referred to a harbor of refuge, or a placid, protected cove or bay. It is worth a comment that there are two spots of this name on Lake Superior. The Minnesota village has less than a thousand inhabitants, the Michigan one even fewer.

There is more North Woods flavor to Grand Marais than to any other town on the shore. One can actually see stagged pants, calked boots, and Chippewa complexions there. It still ships pulpwood—mainly to the Hammermill Paper Company at Erie, Pennsylvania.

The harbor is often afloat with logs, which finally are fed into the hold of a boat by means of a great spout.

This is the entrance to the last great canoe wilderness of the country. Up over the high rim of the lake from Grand Marais runs the Gunflint Trail, ending dramatically at the water's edge of Saganaga Lake, some fifty miles northwest on the boundary line. In all this Arrowhead Country there is only one through highway, one running from Little Marais, forty-five miles west of Grand Marais, to the iron ranges. It is the glory and attraction of this part of Superior National Forest that it is a true, not a sham, wilderness.

At Grand Marais are the North Superior Coast Guard station operating twenty-five boats, a Federal forestry office and warehouse, a state forestry station, and offices of the state game and fish department. This is a center of commercial and other fishing. It has an excellent harbor and, in summer, airplane service.

At one time a new industry was undertaken at Crystal Bay near Little Marais. In 1902 the Minnesota Mining Company began to ship from the hillsides there what was believed to be corundum, an abrasive used for grinding wheels. A plant was established first in Two Harbors and, in 1905, in Duluth. At the latter place sandpaper was made, for it had been discovered that the deposit was not true corundum. In 1910 the company moved to St. Paul, where its success in making abrasives and other products has been outstanding.

By the seventies and eighties of the last century it was already becoming popular to take a north shore cruise. Guidebooks featured it and such nationally read magazines as *Harper's* were publishing articles about it. The guidebook of 1874 which has already been quoted has a section devoted to the trip from "Duluth to Isle Royale and Pigeon River." It begins:

"The trip along the North Shore of Minnesota to the mouth of the Pigeon River and Isle Royale, which lies opposite, is one of great interest. The harbors, headlands, islands, and objects of interest are numerous."

It goes on to discuss, briefly, Knife River, Agate Bay, Encampment Island, Beaver Bay, the Palisades, Baptism River, Little Marais,

Temperance River, Good Harbor Bay, Terrace Point, Rock Island, Grand Marais, Grand Portage, Waus-wau-goning Bay and Pigeon River.

About the same time a photographer from Ishpeming took the trip in his own small sailboat, making wet plates in numbers as he went. These he preserved, and nearly seventy years later they were discovered in Ishpeming by a Minnesota artist, Mr. Dewey Albinson, who recognized their value both historically and artistically. Part of them he presented to the Minnesota Historical Society, and the rest he secured for that institution. They form an almost complete album of the scenic grandeur of the north shore before it had been denuded of its forests, and before settlements or the tourist invasion had altered the wilderness in any way. Some of the pictures appear as illustrations in this book.

In the Chicago *Tribune* in August 1870 appears a long item on the north shore. Approaching it, the author was moved to the following raptures:

"The North Shore is in view, an unending range of hills and mountains, indented here and there with beetling crags and frowning precipices on their summits. . . . Here are caverns which might shelter the Titans, gorges which seem fathomless. . . . The beauty of this North Shore is the beauty of sublimity. Nature here is not in her pretty moods, toying with water, playing with flowers. . . . She is in her stern moods. She has piled up Ossa on Pelion. She frowns at you from stupendous crags. Her music is the thunder. Her attire is the sombre green of the pine. Her play is the everlasting wash of the waves against solid granite walls."

From Schroeder northeastward Highway Number 61 runs through the great Superior National Forest till the Grand Portage Indian Reservation is reached. Earlier the highway takes one through the scenic Gooseberry State Park. A little before reaching Mineral Center the main road turns inland, but those who like to see historic spots will do well to turn to the right at Mineral Center and go down the little road that winds to old Grand Portage and on crystal-clear days affords a view of the distant lighthouse and the cliffs of Isle Royale.

Here at Grand Portage is the site of one of the largest fur-trading posts and inland hamlets of the old days. There is little now to tell of its former appearance, though a replica of its fort and stockade has been attempted. Just how early the spot was a trading center is not known, but in 1768 John Askin of Mackinac had ground cleared there and soon afterward established some kind of fort. There is good evidence pointing to an even earlier occupation by French traders.

From 1768 to 1804 this spot teemed with activity. With the formation of the North West Company about the time of the American Revolution, Grand Portage, at the end of a nine-mile portage around the falls of Pigeon River, became the inland headquarters of the great Montreal fur-trading organization. Here the big *maître* canoes from Montreal met the smaller North canoes from the interior, exchanged cargoes and some of the paddlers and passengers, and returned, each to its place of origin. In the eastern canoes came trade goods: blankets, strouds, tobacco, kettles, guns, ammunition, tomahawks, knives and high wines. In the western canoes were pelts of beaver, marten, muskrat, raccoon, fisher, bear, wolverine, fox, mink—but chiefly beaver. These furs and skins the porkeaters, as the novice paddlers were termed, took back to Montreal, via Lake Superior's hazardous waters as far as the Sault, across the portage at the Sault, along a bit of Lake Huron and through Georgian Bay to the mouth of French River, up that stream and across Lake Nipissing, down the Mattawa River into the Ottawa, and finally to the St. Lawrence.

In the western canoes leaving Grand Portage fort were the *bourgeois* and clerks of many posts, either returning to old scenes or going to new ones at the command of the *bourgeois* meeting in annual conference at Grand Portage. These partners and their assistants— *bourgeois* and clerks, or *commis,* were the only expressions ever heard for them in those days—made their way along the lakes and streams that now form the boundary between Minnesota and Ontario as far as the Lake of the Woods. Thence they passed with speed down the

Winnipeg River, with its many falls and portages, to Lake Winnipeg. At that point they divided. Some went far to the western side of the continent; others passed up the Red River of the North to the plains country of modern Minnesota, the Dakotas and Manitoba.

With them, of course, went their paddlers. As partners, clerks and men passed over the rim of the Lake Superior basin between North and South lakes and entered the Hudson Bay basin, they were made Nor'westers if this was their first journey beyond Lake Superior. The voyageurs took this occasion to get a dram of liquor by going through a ceremony of initiation with the novices, requiring certain promises from them and filling the air with the reports of musket shots. Thereafter the initiates might take the title of Nor'-westers, the Gascons of the trade, and claim its privileges, one of which was the right to wear plumes in their hats.

In 1793 there were sixteen buildings within the North West Company's stockade at Grand Portage, besides a pier near by for the schooner. There were also the forts of rivals. Here in early July gathered many hundreds of men. During the annual rendezvous the porkeaters slept under their overturned canoes, the winterers in tents, and the clerks and *bourgeois* in the buildings. There was great feasting and hilarity, besides many conferences and official gatherings. It was the one annual contact with civilization for some of the men. Then, when the last canoe had departed over the long portage or along the north shore of the lake, the peace of the wilderness settled down once more over the bay and its shores. A few red-sashed voyageurs remained for the winter, a *bourgeois* and perhaps a clerk would be there, and the neighboring Indians were not far off.

So Grand Portage continued for about forty years. Meantime the American Revolution was fought, a treaty of peace was made which defined the boundary line in ambiguous terms, and competition with the old Hudson's Bay Company became increasingly sharp. British troops of the Eighth Regiment of Foot under Lieutenant Thomas Bennett were stationed at the fort during a part of the war. With peace re-established, ownership of the post was all important. It was considered vital to the success of the North West Company's fur-trading ventures farther to the west and every effort was made to construe the treaty of peace in such a way as to hold it for the British. The treaty remained in dispute for almost sixty years. Both sides claimed the right to interpret certain phrases and expressions according to their own wishes. By it the boundary line was said to lie through Lake Superior, running northwest of Isle Royale to "the Long Lake." The map used by the peace commissioners, Mitchell's map of North America, published in 1755, shows "Long Lake" as a sort of estuary where the mouth of the Pigeon River lies. No such name for a topographical feature in that vicinity was known.

Here was a talking point for the disaffected fur traders and the men in government who represented their interests. Since no one knew where Long Lake was, how could one define a boundary line running through it? Therefore a reconsideration of the boundary line should be made, the British fur interests said. There were many other points of dispute, but in the reopened negotiations on the boundary line, frequent after 1793, the identity of Long Lake became the chief stumbling block to an amicable settlement of the entire boundary question from New Brunswick to the Lake of the Woods.

Soon after the turn of the century, it appeared to the fur traders that the Americans, by charging customs duties, were going to insist that the portage trail at Grand Portage lay on American soil. Duty payments would have been disastrous to the profits of the company. Therefore it moved its inland headquarters from Grand Portage to the mouth of the Kaministikwia River, about forty miles up the north shore. The new depot was named in honor of a prominent member of the company, William McGillivray. It has persisted, first as a trading center and then as a hamlet and city, to this day, and has been known throughout the years as Fort William.

The fort still had access to the interior by way of a river, but the voyageurs and traders did not like the route as well as that by way of Grand Portage. After 1821 neither route was used to anything like the former extent, for in that year the Hudson's Bay and the North West companies coalesced under the charter and name of the older group. It had the monopoly of the cheaper and easier route to the interior, which Radisson and Des Groseilliers had been instrumental in opening, the sea route through Hudson Bay and thence up the Hayes River to Lake Winnipeg. After 1821 heavy goods were usually shipped that way, and only on special occasions and at infrequent intervals did the new company make use of the old canoe route through Lake Superior. Fort William lost much of its prestige after 1821, and did not regain it until after 1870 when wheat began to pour in from the prairies of western Canada.

Meantime Grand Portage almost disappeared as a center of white man's civilization. David Thompson, the great surveyor and map maker, had recorded bustle and business in 1798. In 1822 he found red clover blooming over depressions in the soil that marked the site of former buildings. In 1822 he was traveling with the British part of the boundary commission, appointed as a result of the Convention of 1818 between the United States and Great Britain, which settled much of the boundary dispute. Both that year and the following one saw him at Grand Portage with men who were trying to iron out the difficulties in interpreting "Long Lake" of the Treaty of Paris.

They were not successful. In 1827 both parties to the Convention turned in reports of what had been accomplished. The British agreed to let "Long Lake" be recognized as the mouth of the Pigeon River, with the boundary line passing up that stream, provided that the line should pass through the portages, including the Grand Portage, on the water communication between Lake Superior and the Lake of the Woods. The Americans rejected both this compromise and another that was then substituted, namely, that a provision be included in the agreement to the effect that the portages on the route should be free and open to the use of both parties. Thus in 1827 Grand Portage was still regarded as of vital importance, though by that time it hardly existed.

All efforts at agreement failed and it was not until 1842 that the boundary line was actually agreed upon, through the ratification of the Webster-Ashburton Treaty. That document placed the boundary line through the Pigeon River's course, but stipulated:

"It being understood that all the water communications and all the usual portages along the line from Lake Superior to the Lake of the Woods, and also Grand Portage, from the shore of Lake Superior to the Pigeon River, as now actually used, shall be free and open to the use of the citizens and subjects of both countries."

Thus the portage trail through Grand Portage village of today is actually the common property of two countries.

By 1842 there was little left at Grand Portage. Indians still considered it their home, but even the fishing venture of Ramsay Crooks and the American Fur Company was coming to a close just then, and Father Pierz' mission was soon to move. In 1838 Pierz had written thus of his post there:

"Grand Portage, my present mission post, is the most beautiful and, since earliest times, the most famous spot on the north shore of Lake Superior. It has a good harbor for landing and good fishing. The soil is well adapted to farming, but thus far has not been used for that purpose. I have made a beginning of agriculture by laying out a beautiful kitchen garden, a large cultivated field, and a little nursery planted with fruit seeds from Carniola. . . . My house for the present is a small cabin of huge unhewn logs, chinked on the outside with mud plaster and whitewashed on the inside with white earth. It is provided with windows and a stone fireplace. . . . My church is made of cedar bark, thirty feet wide and forty feet long and displays real workmanship."

He had seventy-five pupils enrolled in his school on August 1, 1838: thirty-nine were Indians and five were French children; thirty-one were adults.

Pierz was recalled from this mission field in 1839, after baptizing sixty-four persons at Grand Portage and others at Fort William, but in 1842 he was back long enough to start a mission on Pigeon River. He started an orchard, planted gardens and kept stock and poultry there.

Father Otto Skolla, who made itinerant missions from La Pointe, described the region thus in 1846:

"Grand Portage is on the bay of Lake Superior. The position of this place is very pleasant, the ground fruitful and level, although surrounded by rather high mountains. A great deal of black slate is found here and in many places a sort of white earth which was used for filling the crevices between the logs while there were houses here. At present there are no houses, only poor Indian huts. The number of savages is about eighty, including children. They live very meagerly. . . . Six miles from Grand Portage is Pigeon River, a very wild spot between two thick forests. . . . I visited that place also. Here several years ago the honorable Mr. Pierz had begun a church which is still without a roof. . . . Besides the church . . . Mr. Pierz had built a small house of one room and another building where church supplies were kept. The soil is much better and more productive here than in Grand Portage."

In 1848 and 1849 the Pigeon River mission was in charge of the Jesuits under Father Pierre Choné of the Grand Manitoulin Isle mission. He visited Grand Portage in 1847 but did not begin his work till the following year. Then he chose to continue the undertaking at Pigeon River. With him were two other missionaries of his order, Father Nicolas Frémiot and Brother de Pooter. It was called the mission of the Immaculate Conception. A house was constructed, which served as chapel, storeroom, living room, kitchen, refectory and school. Twelve Indian boys and ten girls were instructed in the school kept by Frémiot. In 1849 the mission was removed to Fort William and the house at Pigeon River was burned to the ground shortly after.

Thus permanent religious organization at Fort William began from adjacent American territory, just as the British post itself had started first south of the border. The ties between Canada and the United States are strong here, historically as well as actually. For many years the priests at Fort William served also the Grand Portage-Pigeon River area. Meantime the Chippewa Indians sold their rights in the soil of northeastern Minnesota to the United States by the Treaty of La Pointe of 1854—getting in partial return a reservation in the extreme northeastern tip of the state. The usual reservation arrangements were made, including a government school at Grand Portage. The master was sent by Bishop Baraga in 1855 in the person of Eugene Benoît. The bishop himself visited the place in 1856, and confirmed fifty-three persons. The second teacher was Timothy Hegney. Late in the century this reservation was broken up, allotments were given to the Indians, and most of the remainder of the land was sold for lumbering purposes or opened up to homesteading. A number of settlers took up claims.

There is still an interesting Indian settlement at Grand Portage. Within very recent years the so-called chief still had in his possession the British flags, a silver gorget, two silver arm bands, and some silver medals of George III's time, which his ancestors had received and cherished. The natives maintain themselves, as much as is feasible, by fishing and a little trapping. The tourist business is excellent.

In the middle 1930's a WPA archeological party excavated the site of the former North West Company post. Remains of cedar pickets and many pieces of glass, crockery and other furnishings were recovered, as well as beads, flints, nails and similar objects. Today a sort of fort building stands on the site, surrounded by a stockade, as an attempt to recover some of the spirit of the past.

The beginnings of white settlement at the mouth of the Kaministikwia River, first by the French in the seventeenth century, and later by the North West and Hudson's Bay companies, have already been described. The area was the scene of dramatic struggles between the two British companies in the second decade of the nineteenth century, with such well-known characters as Lord Selkirk and John McLoughlin playing the leading roles. After 1821, when the companies amalgamated, the Kaministikwia settlement enjoyed a period of quiet broken only by occasional canoes arriving from Canada, carrying traders, Red River settlers, explorers, artists of adventurous turn and missionaries.

Another lively chapter in the settlement's history began with the opening of the Sault lock. Steamers and other ships could then come from the eastern regions. We have already noted the arrival of the first steamer in Thunder Bay in September 1846—the *Julia Palmer,* bound for "Spar Island, Fort William, and Point Ignace, care of Thomas Childs, Princes Location." Other vessels that were on the lake in the 1850's and that may have taken cargoes along the north shore after 1855 were those mentioned in Peet's diary: the steamers *North Star, Superior, Lady Elgin, Illinois, Collingwood, Plow Boy, Arctic, Seabird, City of Cleveland, Rescue, Forester* and *Planet;* the propellers *General Taylor, Mineral Rock, Napoleon, Monticello, Montgomery, Iron City, J. E. Eagle, Burlington* and *Manhattan;* the schooners *Fanny and Floy,* the *O. B. Lyon, Mary B. Hale, Sargent, Midnight, James Leslie, Isabella, St. Paul, Twin Brother, Kangaroo, William Case, Rebecca* and many others.

On board the steamer *Rescue* in 1859 was the young naturalist, Robert Kennicott of Chicago, who has left us a diary and many letters telling of Fort William, the boundary country between Minnesota and Ontario, a trip across the prairies to Lake Athabaska and down the Mackenzie River, and more than two years spent in Hudson's Bay Company forts in the Far Northwest. Though it was May 11 when he reached Fort William, he noted plenty of snow on Isle Royale; and the last leg of the trip was made on sleds across the ice of the bay.

On the *Chicora* in 1870 came General Garnet Wolseley and his headquarters staff, bound with troops for Manitoba to quell the first Riel Rebellion. On the same passage the ship carried the men who were to mark out the line of the railroad that was to bind British Columbia to the rest of Canada. In the union that had just taken place, British Columbia had made a through railroad the condition of her joining the federation of Canadian provinces. At first the construction was attempted under government supervision, but that proving a failure, the road was actually built by a private syndicate and became the Canadian Pacific Railway.

The year 1870 was thus an eventful one for the lake town. The troops were landed at the eastern end of the old Dawson Trail. When General Wolseley inquired the name of the little settlement there, he was told that it was called Prince's Landing. Because of the prominence at the moment of Prince Arthur, Duke of Connaught, in the British Empire, Wolseley gave it the name of Prince Arthur's Landing, and this it retained till it was incorporated as Port Arthur in 1884.

Kennicott found "Governor" McIntyre (John McIntyre) in charge of the Hudson's Bay Company post at Fort William when he arrived in May 1859. He was the last factor of note, for the fort ended its career as such in 1881. He was a native of Glenorchy, Scotland, and came to Canada in 1841. That was the year of Governor George Simpson's nineteen months' journey across Canada and around the world, which resulted in a book, *Journey Round the World,* by a ghost writer, and knighthood for the "Little Emperor." Accompanying Simpson on this tour was McIntyre.

Some years later McIntyre returned to Canada, where in 1849 he was appointed to have charge of Brunswick House near James Bay. There he remained for six years. In 1855 he went up Lake Superior to Fort William by canoe, accompanied by his wife and their four small daughters. He remained there, first in charge of the post and later of the whole district, till 1878, the bicentennial of the establishment of a white man's post there. Even after his retirement from the company's service, he remained as a resident of Fort William till his death in 1899, at the age of almost eighty-two years. He aided Wolseley in the difficult task of getting his men and supplies across the Dawson Trail under the pilotage of Donald McKellar; entertained such notables as Chief Factor Donald A. Smith, later Lord Strathcona; Viscount and Lady Milton, who spent the winter of 1872-1873 at Point Meuron up the Kam River; the Earl of Dunraven; Archbishop Machray of Rupert's Land; Lord and Lady Dufferin and their son, Lord Clandeboye; and doubtless many others. As he spoke not only English but also Indian, French and Gaelic, he was a very useful man in the district and came easily by his title of "governor."

McIntyre's first white neighbors outside of company employees were the McVicars and the McKellars. Robert McVicar had had a long and eventful career as a company factor in the Far North when he settled on Thunder Bay in the early 1860's. To his posts on Great Slave Lake and at Fort Resolution had come Sir John Franklin, the great and unfortunate polar explorer. It was Franklin who married McVicar to Miss Christie McBeth, having the legal right to do so because of his position in the expeditionary force.

The McKellars were a numerous tribe, also from Scotland, headed by Captain Duncan McKellar. After a sojourn in Canada, they had been lured to Ontonagon by the copper boom, where not only the father, but also two of the sons, Peter and John, had learned much of mining and geology. In 1863 the three men arrived in Fort William, and in 1868 the rest of the family followed. Two other sons, who became men of importance in the frontier area, were Donald and Archibald. It was the former who guided Wolseley's expedition across western Ontario at the time of the Riel Rebellion. Peter was a prospector and miner, who did much to open up the mines around Fort William and Port Arthur.

About the time these two families arrived, another well-known character in Fort William history came on the scene. He was John McLaurin, an independent fur trader. He, like the McKellars, came by way of the north shore, having spent some years in Duluth and Grand Portage. It would appear that he followed McCullough as a fur trader at Grand Portage. McLaurin became the first merchant in the Thunder Bay area.

A little later—in the middle 1860's—the McKellars explored the Black Bay region for mineral resources—and found them. A syndicate was formed which backed the explorers and allowed them to prospect the Nipigon area, where they found deposits of galena, zinc and copper. A few days after the initial discovery Peter McKellar found an enormously rich lode of similar mineral content, which later became the Enterprise Mine. A little later Peter McKellar also discovered silver ore on the headwaters of the Current River—the Thunder Bay Mine—which gave the first impetus to silver mining in the district. Out of this discovery undoubtedly grew the prospecting that resulted in the discovery of the Silver Islet silver mine, whose story is related earlier in this volume. Encouraged by his success thus far, Peter McKellar prospected westward from Fort William and in 1871 found gold about a hundred miles from Fort William on the shore of Jackfish Lake, south of Shebandowan Lake. It was sold to American capitalists and named the Huronian mine. Finally, the McKellars found the Atikokan iron deposit, which they also sold to American interests. In 1943 it was being developed because of the need of iron ore for armaments, despite many difficulties of mining and a high transportation cost.

Though mines were thought to be the promise for the future in the development of the Thunder Bay country, agriculture proved to be the basis of its success. One may say that about 1870 Fort William and Port Arthur began their modern life. The reason was confederation and the establishment of the Dominion of Canada in response, in part at least, to certain events and conditions of the West. The rule of the Hudson's Bay Company in Rupert's Land—roughly speaking, the Manitoba of today—ended at this time, with compensation to the company from the imperial government. Uncertainties over the place which the area would hold in the new governmental scheme, especially with relation to local government and land titles, and some peculiar local conditions of the half-breed settlers in Rupert's Land, led to the first Riel Rebellion.

With peace re-established in the fertile prairies to the west, and settlers pouring in and taking up land along the right of way of the new railroad designed to bind together East and West in the Dominion, it soon became apparent that Fort William and its twin port would profit greatly by becoming the transshipment harbor for the golden wealth of the prairies. In brief, that is what they have become.

The first sod for the new railway was turned at Fort William in 1875; the government effort proved a failure and the Canadian Pacific, a syndicate, took its place in the development of the railroad. Construction to Vancouver was completed by 1885. In 1881 the first trickle of grain reached Fort William and was put aboard a lake steamer by wheelbarrows. From that small beginning dates the significance of the Twin Ports as the first grain port of the world. An official document of the Corps of Engineers of the United States Army, published in 1937, on *Transportation on the Great Lakes* reports:

"The twin ports of Fort William and Port Arthur are situated on Thunder Bay on the north shore of Lake Superior. Fort William is at the mouth of the Kaministiquia River. The river has three entrance channels. . . . These channels have been dredged to a depth of 25 feet. A turning basin has been built at the junction of the McKellar Channel with the main river.

"Port Arthur adjoins Fort William on the north. It has an artificial harbor protected by an extensive breakwater system. . . .

"The business of this port [the two cities are considered one port in the document] consists mainly of the tremendous volume of grain which funnels to this point from the prairie Provinces of the Dominion. Unlike the grain centers of the United States, a large part of the Canadian grain territory has but one outlet to the sea. The greatest production of the Dominion is in the Provinces of Manitoba and Saskatchewan, and the grain market of Winnipeg is located directly in the path of the easterly flow to the head of the Lakes. Not until recent years have the Pacific coast ports participated in handling the rapidly increasing surplus grain production of the Dominion. The task has fallen almost wholly upon the twin ports of Fort William and Port Arthur. This has led directly to the most phenomenal development of modern elevator facilities to be found at any grain-shipping port on this or any other continent. . . .

"Bulk grain . . . began to arrive before any elevator had been constructed to receive it. The steamer *Erin* took the first cargo of bulk grain in the fall of 1883. The vessel was placed at the dock and the car brought alongside. Spouting was first tried with the spouts resting on top of the grain door and extending to the hatch of the vessel, but this was not successful and runways from the car to the hatches and two-wheel carts were tried.

"With the bulk wheat arriving in increasing quantities, it became necessary to make provision for its storage during the winter months, and sheds were constructed for this purpose. At this time the first elevator had just been completed, but it was not operated until the following year.

"This elevator had a capacity of 250,000 bushels, and the ships whose visits to the port marked the beginning of the grain flow had a carrying capacity of less than 20,000 bushels, while the cars which brought grain to the port had a capacity of only 12 tons and were handled in drags of only 14. The shipments of grain in 1884 reached a total of 1,500,000 bushels. In 1885 they amounted to 2,500,000 bushels and in 1886 to 3,000,000 bushels. . . . The second elevator of the port was constructed at Fort William and was known as Elevator A. It has a capacity of 1,250,000 bushels. This additional elevator temporarily rendered useless the sheds which had been provided for grain storage, but in 1887 on account of the great crop of that year, these sheds had to be again utilized with the addition of a still larger shed holding approximately 750,000 bushels. Two-wheel carts and barrows were used on runways to carry the grain from the cars into the sheds. By 1889 the flow had become so great as to require the construction of an additional elevator known as Elevator B, followed by Elevator C in 1890. Elevator D was the first so-called fireproof structure. By 1902 Elevator E had been completed, thus giving the port five elevators. In 1903 the so-called fireproof steel Elevator D was destroyed by fire, and the plans were then prepared for the construction of one of reinforced concrete and tile. These materials have been used in all terminal elevator construction at this port since that time.

"By 1911 the total storage capacity of the port had risen to approximately 26,000,000 bushels. The crop of 1912 was exceptionally large and with the cessation of the building of elevators during the preceding years, owing to the agitation to have the Government take over all elevators, the facilities at the port were inadequate for the grain which poured in from the West, and congestion resulted. The traffic backed to the western elevators and caused great losses to the western farmers. Part of the overflow was loaded into 59 vessels which had gathered in the harbor previous to the closing of navigation. At the opening of navigation on April 19 of the following year, these vessels moved out of the harbor in practically one unbroken line, constituting probably the greatest commercial fleet ever seen on the Great Lakes. Their cargo aggregated 12,000,000 bushels of wheat, oats, barley, and flax.

"The situation led to a governmental announcement of its policy to allow private ownership of terminal elevators. Construction was thereupon resumed, and the storage capacity of the port was doubled within a few years. By 1935 there were 30 elevators, with a total capacity of 92,615,000 bushels."

By the end of the decade there were thirty-two.

Instead of unloading grain cars with scrapers as is done at Duluth-Superior, one sees here the actual seizure of the grain car in a sort of vise, and the tilting and shaking of it in an iron grip until its contents are emptied into bin hoppers preparatory to being transferred to the elevators. In normal peacetimes it is possible to watch the process, as well as the loading of the ships by spouts, in the same manner as in the other twin port. In one day in 1928, there were unloaded at Fort William-Port Arthur elevators 2,748½ cars, or 3,736,574 bushels. In a single day 6,344,808 bushels of grain were shipped in vessels.

During the navigation season of 1939 a total of 1,229 cargo vessels entered the port of Fort William, of which 815 were Canadian vessels from Canadian ports, 294 were Canadian vessels from foreign ports, and 111 were American vessels. Seven were from Norway, one from Sweden, and one from Estonia.

Another type of cargo that is of considerable importance at the twin port is forest products, especially newsprint paper. At Fort William there are two paper mills, a sawmill with a production rating of 30,000,000 feet of lumber per year, a box factory, and six wood-working factories. Port Arthur has two paper mills and three pulp mills. It also has a 700-foot dry dock owned by the Port Arthur Shipbuilding company, which has constructed many vessels, including the *Noronic,* flagship of the Northern Navigation Division of the Canada Steamship Lines.

There is much to attract the visitor about the Thunder Bay region. About fifteen miles back on the Kaministikwia River are the far-famed Kakabeka Falls, the Niagara of the Lake Superior region. They are 119 feet high. Major Delafield in 1823 felt he must view them on both his outward and inward trip, and writes in his diary on August 19:

"At the falls the banks again diverge, and this fortunate position gives us a view more picturesque and beautiful than in my mind even the great Niagara can afford. The fall is 125 feet high, in one unbroken sheet. . . . Mr. Whistler takes a sketch of this most beautiful of all cataracts, the impression of which will always be foremost in my mind when contemplating the beautiful and the grand of nature's convulsions."

Paul Kane, the Canadian artist, wrote of Kakabeka in his reminiscences of May 1846:

SPLIT ROCK LIGHTHOUSE, NORTH SHORE, MINNESOTA

A PALISADE TEN MILES NORTH OF THE INTERNATIONAL
BOUNDARY, NORTH SHORE

"After pulling our canoes up a rapid current, we arrived about 8 o'clock at the mountain portage, whose falls surpass even those of Niagara in picturesque beauty; for, although far inferior in volume of water, their height is nearly equal, and the scenery surrounding them infinitely more wild and romantic. Whilst the men were engaged in making the portage, I took advantage of the delay to make a sketch."

A painting by him based on the sketch is still in the museum in Toronto.

There are many legends and traditions among the Indians who still reside on their reservation near the twin ports. Some have been gathered and recorded. One that is told nearly every day to tourists in Fort William or Port Arthur accounts for the Sleeping Giant, the great mesa guarding the harbor.

Long ago, in the days when the gods roamed the earth, Nanabazhoo lived with his spouse on distant shores of the lake. Evil days came upon the world; the mighty hunter could find no game in the woods, and the fish did not enter his nets. His squaw, tormented with the agonizing pains of hunger, chided and scorned him, until, enraged beyond control, he smote her with his great war club and she fell lifeless at his feet. Horror-stricken, he fled the wigwam and into the night. The wailing wind shrieked accusations in his ears; the spirits of the rocks and trees rebuked him. Before his horrified eyes rose the specter of his murdered wife, haunting him as he sped onward. Finally, half-crazed with terror and remorse, he staggered and fell backward into the waters of the lake. The Great Spirit took pity upon the Giant and conferred the boon of rest by turning him to everlasting stone.

Chapter 14

Isle Royale

Tow'rd the realm of Shahwondahzy,
Tow'rd the region of the South-Wind,
Stretch'd a sun-lit azure island,
Worthy of her title royal.
—JOHN HOSKYNS-ABRAHALL

WITHIN sight of the twin ports of Fort William and Port Arthur, and lying along the horizon like a blue haze, is the largest island in Lake Superior, Isle Royale. It is about fifty miles long and nine or ten wide at its broadest point, and is really not an island at all, but a miniature continent, surrounded by its own islands. It is not of volcanic origin like most islands. It has its own heights of land, drainage systems, and numerous lakes and good bays for navigation purposes. Its French name shows that it was discovered early. Indeed, it is mentioned in Pierre Boucher's *Histoire du Canada,* which was published in Paris in 1664, the earliest history of Canada; and probably it is referred to in Sagard's narrative of 1632. It may have been visited by some of Champlain's men in the 1620's.

The knowledge of a copper-bearing island in Lake Superior was the cause of early exploration in that lake. How long the mines were worked by prehistoric Indians we do not know, but the natives of the seventeenth century told the French about them. The earliest known French map of Lake Superior, made about 1658, shows two islands; the Jesuit map of 1672 shows it as Isle Minong; Hennepin's map of 1683 shows it in a general sort of way; and Franquelin's map of 1688 gives an excellent representation of it, also calling it Isle Minong. By that name it was known for many years.

Near it, on later maps, and especially on charts of the Revolutionary period, appears a second large island, Isle Phelipeaux. This fictitious island caused a good deal of trouble when England and the United States tried to arrive at a boundary line through Lake Superior after the Treaty of Paris of 1783 and before the Webster-Ashburton Treaty of 1842. Perhaps the idea grew up that there was an island in the region because mariners ran on the shoals a little east of Isle Royale. It may have been on a reef here that two mine sweepers, the *Cerisoler* and *Inkerman,* built for the French navy during the First World War, foundered in 1918 and were never heard of again.

The little that is known of the early history of the island has been recounted: the concealment of a British ship in McCargo Cove during the War of 1812, the superb delineation of the island by Captain Bayfield in his admiralty chart of the 1820's, the fishing stations of the American Fur Company in the 1830's and early 1840's and the mining ventures that were started now and again. Probably not all of the attempts to find copper on the island have been recorded, but it is known that miners were working there at least three times. It was from the island that the tremendous mass of copper exhibited in the Centennial Exposition at Philadelphia in 1876 was taken.

Botanists and other scientists have been as zealous as mining men in visiting Isle Royale. The island is a fascinating study for them. Douglass Houghton visited it in 1840, but his diary of the trip has never been published. In 1847 William Ives conducted a rectangular survey of the island, some four years after it was purchased from the Indians by the United States Government. Many geologists came in 1847, including J. W. Foster and J. D. Whitney, whose joint report on their findings has become famous.

Thomas C. Porter, a botanist from Pennsylvania, came there in 1865 along with Charles E. and Aubrey H. Smith and Joseph Leidy. Dr. A. E. Foote and a party of botanists gathered plants for the herbarium of the University of Michigan in 1868—to the number of 560 species, including the rare fern *Allosaurus achrostichoides* and the *Aspidium fragrans.* Henry Gillman made collections in 1873 for the Gray Herbarium and the herbarium of Columbia University. Between that date and 1900, at least eight botanists collected specimens on Isle Royale. The devil's-club was studied in detail by W. A. Wheeler of the University of Minnesota in 1900 and a short article was written by him on this plant rare in areas east of the Rockies. In 1901 the University of Wisconsin had its botanists in the field. Their collection numbered about 1,500. Dr. Bruce Fink collected lichens in 1902, and two other men lichens and fungi in 1904. In 1904 and 1905 it was the turn of the University of Michigan. Both botanists and a museum party made studies. In 1909 and 1910 W. S. Cooper spent the summer on the island and published five papers on the flora.

In 1928 the Milwaukee Museum sent an investigating party which resulted in the publication of a book on the copper mines.

There have been many other visitors, who have made more or less scientific observations on the birds, fish, mammals, trees, ferns, orchids, geology, insects, butterflies and moths, the weather, bird migrations and other phases of the ecology of the island.

No one who has even a slight interest in plant life can go over the island without becoming enthusiastic about the great variety of plants and the rare specimens to be found. Late June and early July find the swamps full of magnificent pitcher plants, sundews and orchids in bloom; the forest floor is dotted with flowers of many kinds, pyrola or shinleaf, the twinflower, the lovely little "chicken on the wing" or fringed polygala, and the rattlesnake plantain; and the rock shores abound in red wood lilies close to the forest, hedgerows of ninebark a little nearer the water, and rare butterworts with delicate violet blossoms nodding over pools left by the last big wave. Everywhere as one wanders through the woods floats the hymn of the olive-backed thrush.

There is mystery how some forms of animal life have reached Isle Royale, which has been separated from the mainland since glacial times. Up to 1904 practically nothing was known of the cold-blooded vertebrates of the island. Research since that time has revealed eighteen fish species, one toad, one tree toad, three frogs, the mud puppy, and two snakes. Dr. Alexander G. Ruthven, President of the University of Michigan, has this to say about their presence on the island:

"Most of the fish obtained on the island occur both in the inland waters and in the bays and coves about the shores. Since they are, moreover, forms of general distribution in the Great Lakes drainage system, occurring also in Lake Superior, their presence on Isle Royale is easily explained. To account for the presence of the inland, brook-dwelling forms, however, another explanation must be sought; for such species as the common stickleback, nine-spined stickleback, black-head minnow and *Leuciscus neogaeus* can hardly be conceived as able to cross the fifteen miles of open lake intervening between the island and the nearest mainland. At present we have no data that throw light on this problem. The same difficulties arise in attempting to account for the origin of the amphibian and reptile faunas. As in the case of the fish, the species are all of general distribution in northeastern North America, but, with the exception of the mud puppy, none of the species recorded from the island are aquatic, and, as they also belong to groups which are very sensitive to cold, they could neither reach the island through the water in summer or over the ice in winter. The theory of involuntary transportation thus seems to be the only tenable one. At present the most plausible explanation for the presence of the reptiles and amphibians (with the exception of the mud puppy, which might swim across) found on the island is that they have been transported on driftwood."

Bear, porcupine, deer, wolves and several hibernating rodents have never made their appearance on Isle Royale or have disappeared because of unfavorable living conditions. Moose, coyote, lynx, mink, beaver and snowshoe rabbits are common, however. Caribou were once abundant, but have disappeared in recent years. Their place has been taken by moose, which became so abundant in the twenties of this century that the island could not sustain them. At present they are less numerous, but still not infrequently to be seen there. It is believed that the caribou, moose and other mammals crossed the ice from the mainland in order to establish themselves. Occasionally ice of sufficient depth to bear the weight of moose does form between the island and northeastern Minnesota and adjacent Ontario.

Isle Royale was never as heavily wooded as the near-by shore line. Pine existed, however, and spruce, hemlock, fir and tamarack, though not of large size, were fairly abundant until forest fires swept through them. One of the most disastrous fires occurred as recently as 1936. Since then, especially since 1940, fire-prevention methods have been improved. Emergency conservation work was begun by the Federal government in 1935. Today there is a heavy cover of thicket and trees in most places, but the lushness of the forest is rather that of the floor than of the ceiling.

In 1940 plans were completed to keep the wild beauty of the island from ever being spoiled. One hundred and twenty-one thousand acres of privately owned lands were acquired; and on April 3 the Secretary of the Interior accepted the deed from the State of Michigan—though Isle Royale is much closer to Minnesota, it is a part of the State of Michigan—to 133,225 acres of land, which together with the public domain set aside by the President of the United States, constitute Isle Royale National Park, the most recently established among the national parks.

Besides the fishing and quaint fishing establishments, a lush flora and rich fauna, the beauty of rocky shores, long inlets and protecting reefs of islets or skerries, Isle Royale is of interest to the visitor for remains of old copper mines. Many are to be found, but the richest locality for them is the shores of McCargo Cove. Here prehistoric Indians worked the mines for centuries before the earliest French explorers learned of them in the seventeenth century. Alfred Merritt, well known as one of the "Seven Iron Men" of the Mesabi Iron Range in Minnesota, says that from personal experience in 1873 and 1874 he never knew a place on Isle Royale where copper was found by whites but that the red man had been there before them. Many stone hammers, usually broken, have been found in or near the old pits.

Copper was found in mass form and as "barrel copper." The latter occurred in small pieces that could be thrown into a barrel and thus easily transported. The mass copper presented problems to the early native miners and they favored the smaller pieces, just as succeeding white miners did until adequate modern machinery was devised to cope with the difficulties of cutting and transporting great bulks of solid metal. As mentioned earlier in this book, the Indians of much of central North America had and treasured pieces of this copper, and remnants are found now and again in burial places, on sites of old villages, and in nets that have encountered subsurface obstacles in fishing. A friend of the author has a beautiful spearhead of this copper that was pulled up in a fishnet.

In the report of the Smithsonian Institution for 1873 the statement is made that "the amount of mining on three sections of land at a point on the north shore of the island is estimated to exceed that on one of our oldest mines on the south shore of Lake Superior, a mine which has been constantly worked with a large force for over twenty years."

The tradition persists, and may well be correct, that the United States owes its present possession of the island to the foresight of Benjamin Franklin, who knew of its mineral resources and insisted in the treaty negotiations preceding the Peace of Paris of 1783, that Isle Royale must be a part of the United States. Though some grumbling was heard from the other side, the American desires were met in the finished treaty, which states explicitly that the boundary line must pass to the north of the island, well above the center of the lake at that point.

Many years later, about 1915, a British major in his cups (it is recounted by those who recall the incident in the Twin Ports) tried to restore the lost portion, as he conceived it, of the British Empire to its rightful owner. Landing on the northeastern part of the island with a companion or two, he planted the Union Jack securely on the rocks and returned to Thunder Bay well satisfied with having re-established justice in that part of the world. The incident was reported in Duluth by the captain of a vessel, a British consul got hold of the story, and soon it was being referred to on the floor of Parliament. Fortunately for the peace of a great continent, it evoked laughter rather than applause in London, and the major was long tormented by his friends' and acquaintances' jeering references to it.

There are no roads on Isle Royale. Travel is entirely by water or trail. It is reached by semiweekly steamboat from Duluth, by weekly visits of the *South American,* by motor launch from Copper Harbor on semiweekly trips, and by daily motor launch from Grand Portage.

Island headquarters of the park are on lovely Mott Island, on the south shore of Isle Royale. On the mainland the offices are at Houghton.

Formerly there were many private summer homes, but some were given up at the time the national park was established. For many years, notably during the first quarter of the present century, the island had its devotees. Season after season entire families would journey to Duluth in early summer, take the *America* up along the north shore to Port Arthur, stopping here and there at settlements and fishermen's coves, and arrive in due time at Belle Isle, Duncan Harbor, Tobin's Harbor, Rock Harbor, or Washington Harbor or some other cove or bay. There idyllic summers were passed in clear air and solitude till schooltime for the children arrived in early September. Fishing was the chief sport; boat trips along the shore were the main entertainment.

The coast line is almost unbelievably cut up into bays, harbors and coves, with sometimes an outer as well as an inner reef of islets guarding the shore. There are numerous inland lakes; brooks which are the paradise of the trout fisherman; heights, or mountains, from which magnificent panoramic views are obtained both of the island and the mainland, particularly of the Thunder Bay area and adjacent headlands and islands; and good-sized islands near by, some with lighthouses, such as the one on Passage Island, and Rock of Ages beyond the westernmost tip of the little continent. Today there are three centers where accommodations for guests are available: Rock Harbor Lodge, Windigo Inn on Washington Harbor, and Belle Isle Camp on Robinson Bay. Some private cottages are still maintained by their former owners, under arrangement with the National Park Service.

A very beautiful and poetic appreciation of Isle Royale was published by T. Morris Longstreth in his *Lake Superior Country* in 1924. Written still more recently, but recounting events of sixty years before, is Sarah Barr Christian's *Winter on Isle Royale.* As the nineteen-year-old wife of an acting superintendent at the copper mine on Siskiwit Bay, Mrs. Christian spent the winter of 1874-1875 there. Her memories of the island are nostalgic. She tells of the mine itself, of the "location" in the pines, of the Cornish miners, the Scandinavian surface workers, and the Finnish woodsmen employed. Indians were then living on the north shore of the island and came uninvited to listen respectfully to the young wife's attempts at playing the piano. There were sleigh rides on the harbor ice, a great forest fire, dramatics, church service with fine Cornish hymn-singing, picnics at the old lighthouse on Rock Harbor and elsewhere, journeys to "Greenstone" beaches, and to prehistoric copper-workings, and perilous journeys to and from the island in autumn storms. It brings to life a forgotten chapter in Lake Superior's history.

Part V

RED AND WHITE ART

Chapter 15

Nanabazhoo and His Followers

From his pouch he took his colors,
Took his paints of different colors,
On the smooth bark of a birch-tree
Painted many shapes and figures,
Wonderful and mystic figures,
And each figure had a meaning,
Each some word or thought suggested.
—HENRY WADSWORTH LONGFELLOW

LAKE SUPERIOR entered belles-lettres when *Hiawatha* was published. However far that poem may fall short of genius, it holds a unique place in Anglo-American literature. It is one of the few pieces of American literature that English children and adults know and read. And most Americans know at least a line or two of it. Ask even a semiliterate what Gitchee Goomee refers to, and he will reply, "Lake Superior." He will also know who Minnehaha was and possibly a few other characters, places, or incidents in the poem.

Longfellow might conceivably have made a great epic out of the Nanabazhoo cycle of Chippewa mythology, in the manner of Wagner's treatment of the Nibelungenlied, but he was hardly the man for that. Instead, he took the folk tales current about Lake Superior among the natives, was generally quite faithful to them, but softened and tenderized them till they became palatable to the immature taste of Victorians.

Nanabazhoo was the combined Messiah, Puck, Prometheus and Loki of the Chippewa. They felt on very good terms with him. Much of their humor comes out in their tales of his cunning ways. Again, he is their aid and protector, the role that Longfellow gives him almost exclusively. He was not their chief god. Indeed, in many respects he appears as a demigod. Far above him was the Kitchi

331

Manito, or Gitchee Manito, the supreme being for good, who was always represented as the developer rather than as the creator. Another powerful being was the Evil Spirit, Matchi Manito, who took the form of a great fish or two-tailed merman, the Great Lynx or something evil living in the lake. Thus the Great Spirit lived high above mortals, the Evil Spirit dwelt below, and the other four chief spirits (four is the magic number among the Chippewa) were the East, West, North and South winds. There were many lesser spirits, and the "Little People," comparable in some respects to brownies, pixies or gnomes.

J. G. Kohl, a German traveler around Lake Superior about the middle of the last century, published a book of his experiences among the Chippewa, which has been abridged and published in an English form called *Kitchi-Gami: Wanderings Round Lake Superior*. In that work he has much to say about Nanabazhoo, whose name takes many forms in different accounts according to the hearing of the writer. Kohl usually refers to him as Menaboju. Thus he writes of him:

"As far as I have myself noticed, or learned from others, the mighty Menaboju, the Indians' favourite demi-god, is never named in their religious ceremonies. This is strange, and almost inexplicable to me, for they ascribe to him the restoration of the world, the arrangement of paradise, and so much else. Nor did I hear that they ever prayed to Menaboju, or sacrificed to him. And yet, all along Lake Superior, you cannot come to any strangely formed rock, or other remarkable production of nature, without immediately hearing some story of Menaboju connected with it. He is also the legislator of the Indians, and the great model or ideal for all their ceremonies, customs, and habits of life. Nearly all their social institutions are referred to him. It was Menaboju who discovered that the maple-tree could produce sugar. . . . Menaboju taught the Indians hunting, fishing, and canoe building, and, as we have seen, discovered kinni-kannik, at considerable expense to himself. The same god seems also to have invented the art of painting the face."

Fortunately the Nanabazhoo tales were collected in their original form before it was too late. William Jones, under the auspices of the

Carnegie Institution, interviewed many Chippewa about Lake Superior in the years from 1903 to 1905 and prepared for publication much of what he learned. Five informants in particular gave him the Nanabazhoo stories, which were later published in a full volume of the American Ethnological Society, with literal translations. Several stories appear more than once, so that the reader can judge how widespread the tales were. Another volume tells legends and myths not part of the Nanabazhoo group.

Nanabazhoo was cunning right from the start, for while the three other unborn infants, the deer, the chickadee and the Sun, were squabbling in their virgin mother's womb as to who should be firstborn, Nanabazhoo spied a gleam of light and slipped out. Then he addressed his grandmother impudently with, "Do you know who I am? Why, I am Nanabazhoo." His mother having died, his grandmother brought him up.

One of the first things he did was to persuade his grandmother to let him try to get fire. Changing himself into a hare he let himself be captured by the daughter of the owner of fire, who took the "cute little bunny," all wet from being in the lake, and placed him before the fire to dry. Soon a spark fell on him and his fur began to burn. In this state he fled home, pursued by the owner of fire, who was unable to overtake him. Thus the Chippewa got fire, and the hare turns brown in summer. Nanabazhoo is the Great Hare in the Chippewa mythology.

Kohl, in the passage quoted, refers to the discovery of kinni kinnick, or Indian tobacco, by Nanabazhoo "at considerable expense to himself." As this is a typical story in the cycle, and also relates how tripe-de-roche, the hard, ill-looking lichen growing on rocks about the lake, was created and why the loon's back is flat and her feet at the rear of her body, it may be advisable to tell it here, though it is not for squeamish readers. Hardly any of the cycle stories is without portions that can offend them. Indians accepted the several parts of the body and their functions as they did other facts in life and did not hesitate to mention them. This is one of the least objectionable stories from the point of view of the prudish.

Tripe-de-roche, the origin of which the story explains, has saved many an Indian and voyageur from starving. It can be boiled into a gluey concoction that keeps breath in a man's body, though persons who have tasted the dish say they would almost as readily die as eat the porridge. The lichen can be seen almost everywhere north of the forty-seventh parallel. It resembles burned human skin as much as anything else.

Nanabazhoo went hunting, found some goslings far out in the lake, enticed them to shore by promising to teach them new dance steps and got them into an enclosure. As he called the steps, he made them dance with their necks all together and their eyes shut. Then he began quietly to wring their necks. A loon who had joined the party heard something odd, opened her eyes, saw Nanabazhoo wringing the necks of the unfortunate goslings, and fled, squawking that the goslings had better look out, for Nanabazhoo was killing them.

For her pains she got a swift kick in the rear which flattened her out and caused all loons since that time to have a flat back and legs at the rear of the body.

Nanabazhoo killed all the goslings and put them in the ashes to roast, with their legs sticking out to guide him back to them. He decided to sleep while they were roasting. Afraid that enemies or thieves would steal his dinner, he told his bottom, which was in the best position to see, to keep watch. Several times the bottom warned him that someone was coming around the point in the lake, but every time, when Nanabazhoo got up to investigate, the intruders had retreated and he could see no one.

He began to say uncomplimentary things to his bottom and finally to strike it and scratch it for awakening him needlessly. The bottom's feelings were hurt, and it said to itself that it would not warn Nanabazhoo again. This time the intruders really came, saw the goslings' legs protruding from the ashes, ate all the meat but carefully stuck the legs back in the ashes.

Finally Nanabazhoo awoke and prepared eagerly for his feast. He pulled up the first pair of legs but found nothing beneath. As he pulled up one pair after another, he began to guess what had happened, and he vowed vengeance on his bottom. In his wrath and hunger, he piled wood on the fire and then stood over it, in order to punish the bottom. When he heard strange crackles and groans, he decided that his bottom was punished enough and started to move back from the fire, only to discover that he could not walk.

The Bois Fort Indian, Wasagunackank, who told the story to Jones, continues thus:

" 'Wonder what may be the matter with me!' he thought. And so he was without strength when he tried to walk. So this he thought: 'I am curious to know what it is that prevents me from being able to walk.' And when he had sought for a place where there was a very steep cliff, then down from the cliff he slid. When he alighted, he looked back (and) saw nothing but the sore of his bottom along where he had slid. And this was what he said: 'Oh, lichens shall the people call it as long as the world lasts!' Then he continued on his way again. Now, while he was walking about, he saw a dense growth of shrub. Now, as he walked through their midst, he then looked behind, and all the way was the shrub reddened [from his blood]. 'Oh, red willows shall the people call them till the end of the world! The people, when they smoke, shall use them for a mixture (in their tobacco),' he said."

Another Nanabazhoo story tells how he was swallowed by the great sturgeon, canoe and all—a myth strangely reminiscent of the Jonah story in the Bible. Then there is the account of how he injured the great Evil Spirit, or water lynx, as the latter lay sunning himself on a sandy beach of the lake. In revenge the world was flooded by the wounded god. Nanabazhoo saved himself and his grandmother by climbing on to a great pine on a high headland. When the water began to recede, he sent down the muskrat and other animals to find earth, but it was only the beaver that succeeded in bringing up some grains of soil in his paws. From them Nanabazhoo restored the world and its inhabitants. In return for helping him slay or injure the great water lynx, the kingfisher, which had instructed him in the art of camouflage, was painted in bright colors by Nanabazhoo.

One legend relates to the outlet of Lake Superior. To understand it one must remember that the fisher was formerly a common animal about the lake, and that in Chippewa language the Great Dipper constellation is the Great Fisher star. As Nanabazhoo was out walking one day, he heard a pleasing song. Hastening to the spot whence it came, he reached the shore of Lake Superior and saw a Great Fisher holding the shores together by leaping back and forth from shore to shore while he sang:

> The shores of the sea meet together,
> The shores of the sea meet together.

Nanabazhoo watched and listened in rapt admiration for a time and then exclaimed, "Would that I could do that, too!" So the Great Fisher allowed him to take his place, warning that Nanabazhoo must do exactly what he had just seen and heard and that never by any chance must he sing:

> The shores of the sea draw apart,
> The shores of the sea draw apart.

The Great Fisher went off and Nanabazhoo leaped back and forth singing:

> The shores of the sea meet together,
> The shores of the sea meet together.

The shores were held together and all went well until a day or two had passed. Then Nanabazhoo began to weary and finally to wonder what would happen if he sang the other song. So he began to sing:

> The shores of the sea draw apart,
> The shores of the sea draw apart.

Forthwith he fell into the lake and when he came to the surface, not a piece of shore line could he see. He began to struggle and to call on the Great Fisher for help. The latter heard him and returned, singing the original ditty and leaping back and forth. The shores drew together once more and Nanabazhoo was saved.

There is story after story telling how some wild creature got his present form or habits; how some headland, like the Sleeping Giant at Thunder Bay, originated; how some custom started among the Chippewa; and how Nanabazhoo played the buffoon. As you go about Lake Superior, you find the tomb of the Great Hare, his bathtub, the boulders with which he and his father fought near the Sault, his workshop near the Eau Claire Lakes in Wisconsin, his anvil or *ishpeming,* his hammer or *pewabik,* and a thousand other relics of the great god Pan of the Chippewa. He was the first raconteur, the first Paul Bunyan, the first creative artist about the lake. In his wake have followed many others of more modern time.

The origin of the Sault rapids and the whitefish in them is explained by other Indian legends. A certain brave decided to keep the beaver from escaping out of the lake. So he built a dam of rocks at the outlet and left his wife to watch it. He then departed. In his absence Nanabazhoo came by the dam chasing a deer, which leaped into the water. Nanabazhoo called to the woman to head off the deer. So she left the dam to assist Nanabazhoo. Meantime all the beaver which her husband was driving before him down the lake leaped over the dam, scattering the rocks and thus producing the rapids. The angry husband killed his wife in rage and it is her voice that one hears wailing over the din of the Sault.

The whitefish is also the result of a marital tragedy. Finding his wife guilty of infidelity, an Indian murdered her, leaving her two small children motherless. Her spirit came back to haunt the two little ones, who fled hither and thither, trying to escape it. Finally they came to St. Marys River, where a crane ferried them across. Behind them came the wailing spirit of their mother. She implored the crane to take her across also, but in midpassage she fell into the rapids, where she was transformed into a strange new fish. Since that time the whitefish has been the mainstay of Indians about the Sault.

There are many legends about the Thunderers, who rumbled and flashed fire from their abode on Thunder Mountain and Mount Mackay near modern Fort William. They took the form of great birds. There were also little people, water fairies, who appeared on the lake between Isle Royale and Thunder Bay. They were very fond of tobacco. Once a canoe of them was intercepted near the foot of Thunder Mountain, and as the human beings who saw them tried to engage the shy creatures in conversation, the cliff opened and canoe and occupants vanished within it. For a long time their laughter and the sound of their paddles could be heard.

Of all the legends current in the Lake Superior country, perhaps the oddest is the merman story. The sea serpent and the mermaid have long been accepted as inhabitants of the ocean, but who ever dreamed that Lake Superior was so akin to the Mighty Deep that it could boast such rarities? Yet read the testimony of a reputable voyageur of the North West Company before the Court of King's Bench in the District of Montreal, who on November 13, 1812, swore on the Holy Evangelists that he and others had seen a merman near Pie Island of Thunder Bay!

This man was Venant St. Germain of Repentigny, and he swore that on May 3, 1782, as he was traveling from Grand Portage to Mackinac in a canoe carrying, besides himself, three other men and an old Indian woman, he made camp for the night at the south end of Pie Island. As he landed from setting his nets, he saw, not very far away, a creature shaped like a man, though only the size of a child of seven or eight years. The merman was half out of water and was regarding him and his companions curiously but with some uneasiness. St. Germain tried to shoot, but the Indian woman in great alarm prevented him, seizing him violently and warning him that this was the God of the Waters and Lakes and predicting that now all of the human witnesses to the sight would infallibly perish. Meanwhile the merman sank and was seen no more. The Indian woman was so sure of impending danger that she climbed the steep bank near by to avoid the fury of the inevitable storm. About ten o'clock that night it burst upon them in much violence and continued unabated for three days. St. Germain goes on:

"That it is in the knowledge of the deponent, that there exists a general belief diffused among the Indians who inhabit the country around this island, that it is the residence of the God of the Waters and of the Lakes, whom in their language they call *Manitou Niba Nibais,* and that he had often heard that this belief was peculiar to the Sauteux Indians. He further learned from another voyageur, that an animal exactly similar ... had been seen by him on another occasion" when passing from Pie Island to Thunder Cape, "and deponent thinks the frequent appearance of this extraordinary animal in this spot has given rise to the superstitious belief among the Indians, that the God of the Waters had fixed upon this for his residence."

Other Lake Superior myths are of more modern origin. The Dick Buller legends center in the Copper Country. Dick was a Cousin Jack of Central Mine, gifted with such a fine basso voice that he won all the singing contests of that vocally musical community. His voice could penetrate ten levels underground and ten to fifteen miles on the surface. Many are the extraordinary feats that he performed, as recounted for years in the columns of the Portage Lake *Mining Gazette*.

Lake Superior's vast proportions are reflected in other legends, such as the *very* modern Paul Bunyan yarns. These stories of the mighty lumberjack and his Blue Ox appear to have originated in the pineries just back of the lake. Indeed, one may be more specific. The first of them seem to have been the brain children of a certain resourceful and canny resident of Rhinelander, Wisconsin. Meeting with approval among the lumberjacks of that logging area, they spread quickly and were increased remarkably, till the world at large believed that they actually were the spontaneous product of Michigan, Wisconsin and Minnesota lumbering camps. How little that is the case can be judged from the fact that not one of the many lumberjacks interviewed by the author had ever heard of Paul Bunyan until books of his legends began to appear early in the twentieth century.

On more solid basis rests the story of Mott Island. Today it is the local headquarters of Isle Royale National Park, and is located on the outer island fringe of Rock Harbor. Toward the middle of the last century a French-Canadian voyageur, Charles Mott (the name is probably corrupted from La Motte), was taken to the island late in the autumn on the *Algonquin*. He was to hold a certain mining claim for a prospector, and the schooner was to return with a cargo of provisions for him and his Christianized Indian wife, Angélique. For some reason the schooner failed to return. The Motts had very little food and nothing with which to secure the few animals, birds and fish that could be obtained on the island. Mott finally succumbed, and Angélique was left alone with his frozen body. She was indeed in bitter plight. To keep herself alive she pulled hairs from her own head and set snares for snowshoe rabbits. She also contrived a fish net from an old coffee sack. So hungry did she become that at times she cast longing eyes on her husband's frozen body. Only the lessons learned from her religious instructor on the south shore kept her from turning cannibal. Finally, with the spring, a vessel came and rescued her. Her story became a classic on the south shore and is met again and again in its printed records.

Lake Superior has produced no piece of art of greater genius than *Hiawatha*. When that is said, it is obvious that nothing of immortal worth in poetry, prose, sculpture, painting or music has come from the great lake and its setting. This is not to say that the greatest body of fresh water in the world, with its overawing arc of rocks and its unique history, will not eventually produce something for the ages; the fault is not with the subject matter but with the creative artists. Many writers, painters, musicians and poets have done their best, but that best is not sufficient.

The best in writing that has been inspired by the lake is to be found in the artless efforts of travelers and the faithful recording of the natives' legends, mythology and customs. Most of the important travel accounts have been cited and sometimes quoted in this book. Schoolcraft's, Warren's and Jones's monumental works on the Chippewa have been described. One other fine recorder of the Chippewa way of life needs to be mentioned, Miss Frances Densmore. Her works on the customs and music of these natives must be consulted by all who would know the Indians of Lake Superior.

Novels aplenty have been written, but none has attained the heights. The great novel on the fur trade and the Chippewa has yet to appear, though one would suppose that that topic of all in American history would have inspired something effective. Several novels may be mentioned as being worth the reader's time: *The Invasion*, a story of the Johnston family at the Sault, by Janet Lewis; *Black Feather*, a novel of trade and travel on Lake Superior in the early nineteenth century, by Harold Titus; *Forbidden Ground*, an attempt to depict trade in the Grand Portage area in the time of the North West Company, by Neil H. Swanson, who has also written *The Phantom Emperor*, a much better turned novel, dealing with the filibuster, James Dickson, on Lake Superior and elsewhere; *Les engagés du Grand Portage*, by Leo P. Desrosiers, written in the voyageurs' own language and with a genuine appreciation of them; *Joe Pete*, by Florence E. McClinchey; and boys' adventure stories by Ethel C. Brill and Dietrich Lange.

For lumbering days there is *Holy Old Mackinaw*, by Stewart Holbrook; *Peter Good For Nothing*, by Darragh Aldrich; *Come and Get It*, by Edna Ferber; *The King Pin*, by Helen Finnegan Wilson; *Glory of the Pines*, by William Covert; three short stories by Ernest Hemingway in *In Our Times; Fireweed*, by Mildred Walker Schemm; *The Blazed Trail*, by Stewart Edward White; and several books of lumberjacks' songs, including Earl Clifton Beck's *Songs of the Michigan Lumberjacks* and Franz Rickaby's *Ballads and Songs of the Michigan Lumberjacks*. A very recent novel of the North Woods is *Trouble Shooter* by John D. Voelker.

Of Copper Country novels the most successful is probably *The Long Winter Ends*, by Newton G. Thomas, a faithful representation of the Cousin Jack of Keweenaw Peninsula, written largely in his own quaint dialect. There are also: *Where Copper is King*, by James North Wright; *In the Sight of God*, by Dr. Jacob Wendell Clark, formerly of the Calumet and Hecla's medical staff, who also wrote *White Wind;* and the historical and descriptive work of considerable merit, *Boom Copper*, by Angus Murdock. Perhaps Walter Gries's poem, *The Michigan Cornish Miner*, should also be mentioned here.

The resort country of Michigan is the locale for Edith Roberts' *Tamarack* and Sigrid Woodward's *Kathleen*.

For Lake Superior legends there is a slight work, full of inaccuracies and sentimentalities, George Francis Thomas' *Legends of the Land of Lakes;* and *The Eagle of Thunder Cape*, W. S. Piper's interesting collection of Thunder Bay legends united by a narrative of his own unusual experiences among the Chippewa of that area.

Biography is represented by *Seven Iron Men* by Paul de Kruif, an account of the Merritt family of Duluth and the Iron Range; and *Iron Pioneer,* by Henry Oliver Evans, which is the record of Henry W. Oliver, for whom the Oliver Mining Company is named.

Histories and novels of the iron ranges are fairly numerous: *Red Mesabi,* by George R. Bailey; *The Iron Mountain,* by Phil Stong; *The Iron Will,* by Margaret Culkin Banning; and *Iron Brew,* by Stewart Holbrook, who has also published recently *Burning an Empire,* dealing with the devastating forest fires that swept the lumber country during and after the height of logging there. Like *Iron Mountain,* a story of the Mesabi Range, Leonard Cline's *God Head,* a novel of the Gogebic country, deals with racial and national groups. Mrs. Banning's novel, like other works by her, reflects her intimate knowledge of Duluth and its mining hinterland.

Paul Bunyan has had so much written about him that already there is an extensive printed bibliography of works about him. Two of the early books are *Paul Bunyan,* by Esther Shephard, and *Paul Bunyan,* by James Stevens.

Three books which defy classification but which should not be omitted in any list relating to Lake Superior are Florence and Francis Lee Jaques' *Canoe Country;* Chilson D. Aldrich's *The Real Log Cabin;* and Holling C. Holling's *Paddle-to-the-Sea.* The first is not only a very readable appraisal of the recreational values of the region lying between Lake Superior and Lake of the Woods along the international boundary, but also a gallery of inimitable pen sketches of the region's wild life. Mr. Jaques is recognized as one of the ablest bird artists of our day. Much of his apprenticeship was spent in the Lake Superior country, where he doubtless learned the unique lines of every water fowl's movements, the faithful delineation of which is the special quality of his artistic sketches. Mr. Aldrich's book, which is the classic of its kind, was the result, in part at least, of his own log-cabin-building near Grand Marais. He is a Minneapolis architect. The third book is an ingenious device for teaching young people the geography and general characteristics of the Great Lakes, especially of Lake Superior. It is the record of a toy canoe and its carved Indian occupant on an adventurous trip down the lakes from Lake Nipigon. It is superbly illustrated. Much of the story and many of the pictures represent the wild life and commerce of Lake Superior.

Midway between literature and art stands the picture writing of the Chippewa. Though this form of self-expression is by no means confined to the Lake Superior region nor to the Chippewa Indians, it seems to appear most frequently among the natives of that area. Today as the canoeist travels along the waterways of northeastern Minnesota and southwestern Ontario, he lifts his eyes now and again to some cliff towering above him to perceive figures of animals, canoes, men and unrecognizable objects or ideas painted in red pigment on the face of the rock. They are high above the reach of the tallest man, and one of the several mysteries connected with them is how anyone managed to get up to their level long enough to paint them. Another puzzle is the chemical analysis of the paint, which has outlasted practically every pigment that modern man has succeeded in concocting. Who painted these stories, if stories they are? And what do they mean? As late as the summer of 1943, a Duluth subscriber to the magazine of the Minnesota department of conservation wrote to the editor inquiring whether anyone could explain this mysterious picture writing and showing plainly that he believed it had no message to convey.

The Chippewa Indians used picture writing for several purposes, most of them connected with the Mide, or great religious fraternity of that tribe, which had affiliated secret societies, notably the Wabeno and the Jeesukawin lodges. The names of these three organizations are spelled variously. The Chippewa painted hieroglyphics on gravestones, on blazed trees, or rolls or pieces of birch bark, and on cliffs. Schoolcraft mentions these three uses and then continues:

"It remains only to consider their use in an historical point of view, or in recording, in a more permanent form than either [sic] of the preceding instances, such transactions in the affairs of a wandering forest life as appear to them to have demanded more labored attempts to preserve."

Thereupon he describes rock writing, or Muzzinabikon. He does not solve all the mysteries associated with the art, accounting in no way for the enduring quality of the pigment and saying only this in relation to the location of the inscriptions:

"There has been noticed a striking disposition in the persons inscribing these figures, to place them in positions on the rock, not easily accessible, as on the perpendicular face of a cliff, to reach which, some artificial contrivance must have been necessary. The object clearly was, to produce a feeling of surprise or mystery."

He fails, however, to point out that the level of most of the lakes was higher formerly than at present, and that the deep snow of winter could raise the painter still higher by several feet.

The picture writing seen by the author, all in the area of the Quetico Provincial Park of Canada and the Superior National Forest of Minnesota, has been produced by the use of red pigment, but there are two other known methods of inscription. We have already noted these in the quotations from early travelers on Lake Superior. Agassiz' party and other explorers noted Les Ecrits on the north shore, near modern Schreiber, and Les Petits Ecrits farther to the east. These were made, according to Agassiz, by removing lichens from the cliff's face. Peet, the missionary at various places between Ashland and Duluth, records carvings on the sandstone rocks near Bad River. Other explorers mention inscriptions, without details of the form they took, at Thunder Cape and Pigeon Point, besides many found inland from the shores of the lake.

Contrary to many modern statements, these inscriptions were intended to convey definite messages. Fortunately a few of them have been interpreted for us by Indians, half-breeds and the indefatigable Schoolcraft. George Copway, a native missionary, includes quite a discussion of Indian writing and inscriptions in his now rare book, *The Traditional History and Characteristic Sketches of the Ojibway Nation*. He concerns himself mostly with the sacred writings of the Mide, generally inscribed on rolls of birch bark, which were hidden in secret spots, guarded by appointed initiates, and renewed periodically, usually about every fifteen years. Some of these scrolls have been found by white men and are now preserved in modern museums. "These records are written on slate rock, copper, lead, and on the bark of birch trees," writes Copway. "The record is said to be a transcript of what the Great Spirit gave to the Indian after the flood, and by the hands of wise men has been transmitted to other parts of the country ever since. Here is a code of moral laws which the Indian calls 'a path made by the Great Spirit.'" He then shows the hieroglyphics of several inscriptions and songs and interprets them, giving also a page and a half of general expressions or characters. Thus a circle with a dot in the center means "spirit." A plain, empty rectangle means "great." The human foot means "passed." An empty circle means "life"; a black circle means "death." The symbol for "land" resembles a turtle with head and tail extended.

Schoolcraft explains two actual inscriptions on cliffs on the north and south shores of Lake Superior and tells how they came to be. One is at Les Ecrits, already mentioned; the other was made near the site of modern Marquette. Near the latter place lived a chief called Myeengun, or Wolf, of the merman totem. He was skilled in the Mide and so knew the sacred hieroglyphics, and was invested with much power. It should be added here that to a Chippewa Indian the important thing in life was power: power usually supplied by manitous, genii or spirits of natural forces and objects. Hence a man undertaking some great venture always called on his spirits or manitous for power to accomplish his end.

Myeengun decided to raise a war party and cross Lake Superior, a fearful undertaking in a canoe. When he started he called upon his genii to assist and guard him, inscribing his plea to them on a cliff a little west of Carp River and about a half-day's march up that stream. Schoolcraft does not state the form the inscription took, but his reproduction of it is in black and white, probably signifying that lichens were cut away. This is the more likely because the representation of the north shore inscription, which is definitely stated to have been painted, is reproduced in colors on the same page.

The south shore pictures represent Myeengun with his totem, the merman, and his clan, the wolf, as well as the gods or spirits upon which he relied. These were: the fabulous panther or lynx, Misshibezhieu, the god of the waters; Mong, the loon; Mukwah, the black bear; Mooz, the moose; the horned serpent with two feet; and another snakelike creature. The loon represents the power of foretelling the weather, certainly a desirable quality for anyone navigating Lake Superior in a canoe! The moose signifies wariness, the bear strength and sagacity, the two snake creatures swiftness and power over life. About the shores of the lake then as now roamed the mysterious lynx, which to the Chippewa Indian represented the special god for evil associated with the lake. He must therefore be on the suppliant's side or all would be in vain.

The inscriptions at Les Ecrits, or Wazhenaubikiniguning Augawong, were painted in red, blue, black and yellow, if Schoolcraft's colored plate is a faithful copy of the original. Just why Agassiz reports them as lichen-cuttings and Schoolcraft as paintings is for anyone to explain who can. Perhaps when Schoolcraft learned about them they were still paintings, which lichens later overgrew. By Agassiz' time they could then have been lichen-cuttings indeed.

These inscriptions were made following the success of Myeengun's venture, and so tell the story of how it was accomplished. Five canoes, carrying fifty-one men, are depicted in red color. Three suns in red and blue show that the crossing took three days of fair weather. Triumph is shown by the black and yellow turtle, which represents land, *i.e.,* the success of reaching land on the opposite shore. A horse in red is shown, incidentally dating the inscription insofar as it reveals that it was painted after the advent of white men on the continent. A blue eagle represents the courage required for the undertaking. The great lynx and the serpent appear once more, indicating that their aid, after invocation, had been forthcoming.

The substance used for painting rock inscriptions is unknown, but the red symbols which remain—if other colors were used, they seem to have disappeared—may have been fired. There are some indications of that process. A chalky earth, found in certain places in the Lake Superior region, might conceivably have been used. A "quarry" of it is reported today from the north shore of Basswood Lake west of Lake Superior. We have already noted Johnston's statement that the black dye of the Chippewa was found in rocks on Presque Isle near Carp River.

A very successful red dye was made by the Chippewa from the red alder. Joseph Norwood, who conducted a United States geological survey of the Lake Superior country and adjoining regions in the middle of the last century, reports "vermilion" painted on rocks at Namakan Narrows east of Rainy Lake.

Few examples of actual carving in rocks have been reported. Peet does not go into detail in writing of the inscriptions he found carved in the sandstone near Bad River. The Bois Fort band of Chippewa employed actual carving for some of their inscriptions. As recently as 1923 these inscriptions were to be seen on a rock in Nett Lake in northeastern Minnesota.

Still fewer remains of lichen-cuttings are known today. Within the memory of living men, however, examples of this art were to be seen on the northward-facing cliffs on the south shore of Gunflint Lake in northeastern Minnesota, but recent searching for them has been in vain. South of that lake and north of Duluth, there are still to be seen some lichen-cuttings in the tripe-de-roche on a cliff on the south bank of a little river, according to information given to the author by the United States Forestry Service. By the very nature of things lichens grow again and obliterate the Indians' cuttings. Therefore it is not strange that the only reported inscriptions of this sort come from an area still inhabited by the Chippewa.

Lake Superior's contributions to art are rather better than what she has given to literature. Peter Rindisbacher, though he did not live or travel about Lake Superior, painted some of the Chippewa and Cree Indians of the region about 1820. He was a young Swiss immigrant to the Red River country, who later went to St. Louis. His western canvases and water colors were in much demand about 1830. Eighteen of his water colors hang in the Ordnance Museum in West Point, and others are in Toronto and Ottawa, along with many of his oils and sketches. Seth Eastman, Paul Kane and George Catlin were also painters of merit in the Indian field. Eastman illustrated Schoolcraft's monumental work on the Indians of the United States, and is represented in McKenney and Hall's *Indian Tribes of North America*. An early woman painter of voyageur and Lake Superior scenes was Mrs. F. A. Hopkins, a seasoned traveler in canoes of the 1850's, whose husband was Sir George Simpson's secretary. Her "Voyageurs Crossing Lake Superior" is perhaps the outstanding thing of its kind. She has several other excellent canoe scenes. Arthur Heming is another who has given the spirit of the region, both in his paintings and in his writings.

An American artist, however, came closest to making Lake Superior famous through pigment or pencil, the genre painter, Eastman Johnson, whose life extended from 1824 to 1906. He was born in Lovell, Maine. Success came to him early, in Washington and Boston, where he made portraits of the famous of the day—Mrs. Alexander Hamilton, Dolly Madison, Robert Winthrop, John Quincy Adams and Henry W. Longfellow. After a period of study in Europe, he returned to America in 1855, and the following year found him in Superior, Wisconsin, where his brother-in-law owned a sawmill. He made himself a log-cabin studio on the north shore, and, after a short visit in the East, he spent some time making sketches and paintings of the Indians at Pokegama Bay near Duluth and at Grand Portage. He also did a few landscapes during his stay. His biographer says:

"It was on this second trip to Superior that Johnson did, in fact, most of his paintings and drawings of the Indians. . . . Stylistically, these Indian paintings and drawings are valuable documents, for they show a greater freedom and a brighter color range in the oils than anything previous. They seem, however, to have been more in the nature of sketches, done for his own satisfaction, than as finished pictures for the market. Even so, they forecast surprisingly the work which he was to do some ten years later rather than the tighter style of the large genre paintings which followed immediately."

Some thirty-five of these sketches and paintings have been preserved in the St. Louis County Historical Society in Duluth. Johnson became one of the most famous American painters of his day. His works are eagerly sought by collectors.

Another artist, very well known in his own day and now practically forgotten, was Gilbert Munger. His work must have been *de rigueur* about the time the iron barons were arriving socially, for nearly a dozen of his great oils now hang in hotels and other public buildings in Duluth and on the iron ranges, many of them with no American, not to say Lake Superior, interest. One of his smaller paintings hangs in the Duluth Public Library and shows the city in 1871. Something of the genius of the man is apparent in it through the majesty he has managed to impart to the panorama of bay, peninsulas and open lake, which he viewed from the heights of the city.

More recently the artists who have succeeded best with Lake Superior topics are Dewey Albinson and Carl Rawson of Minneapolis, David Ericson of Duluth, Lowell Bobleter of St. Paul, and the Swedish painter, Leon Lundmark. The last has done some notable representations of the lake itself. One, "A Nor'easter, Lake Superior," in a private collection, is full of dashing spray on basaltic rocks defying a typical storm. For those who prefer a level horizon of blue lake with only slight surf, there is "A Breezy Afternoon, North Shore, Lake Superior." The qualities of near rocks and distant headlands, with dashing spray midway, are to be found in "Shore of Lake Superior" and "Morning, Lake Superior." Many critics compare the artist's work very favorably with that of Winslow Homer, remarking that it has some of the same marine qualities. His list of Lake Superior canvases is a long one.

Another Swede has made a gigantic onyx Indian the vehicle for his philosophy of peace. Whether or not Carl Milles had a Lake Superior Indian in mind when he designed the Peace Memorial Statue in the St. Paul courthouse is not certain, but the chances are that any European in representing a noble savage would be tremendously influenced by his conception of Hiawatha. Certainly most of the thousands of tourists who view the great piece of magnificent sculpture, the artist's chief work by his own admission, speak of it as the Hiawatha statue.

A poem, known chiefly for its seventh stanza, and occasioned by the gift of an eagle feather from Lake Superior in 1846, may fittingly close this book. It is John G. Whittier's "The Seer" and obviously was written for the most part in a facetious mood, and in some haste.

There are several editions, some much longer than others. The one given below is an early form. It may be conjectured that William Cullen Bryant, who was at the Sault in 1846, or some miner friend, presented Whittier with the eagle feather. The poem has been almost forgotten and lives only because of the genuine artistry of the seventh stanza.

> I hear the far-off voyager's horn,
>   I see the Yankee's trail—
> His foot on every mountain pass,
>   On every stream his sail.
>
> He's whistling round St. Mary's Falls,
>   Upon his loaded train;
> He's leaving on the Pictured Rocks
>   His fresh tobacco stain.
>
> I hear the mattock in the mine,
>   The axe-stroke in the dell,
> The clamor from the Indian lodge,
>   The Jesuits' chapel bell!
>
> I see the swarthy trappers come
>   From Mississippi's Springs;
> And war-chiefs with their painted brows,
>   And crests of eagle wings.
>
> Behind the scared squaw's birch canoe,
>   The steamer smokes and raves;
> And city lots are staked for sale
>   Above old Indian graves.
>
> By forest, lake, and water-fall,
>   I see the peddler's show;
> The mighty mingling with the mean,
>   The lofty with the low.
>
> I hear the tread of pioneers
>   Of nations yet to be;
> The first low wash of waves where soon
>   Shall roll a human sea.

BIBLIOGRAPHICAL NOTE
AND
ACKNOWLEDGMENTS

BIBLIOGRAPHICAL NOTE

For the period of French exploration and occupation there is an excellent study by Dr. Louise P. Kellogg entitled, *The French Régime in Wisconsin and the Northwest* (Madison, 1925). She bases it upon original manuscripts and such printed documents as a series of journals and reports, or *Relations,* which the Jesuit missionaries published for many years of the seventeenth century. Reuben Gold Thwaites republished them in seventy-three volumes and with translations as *The Jesuit Relations and Allied Documents* (Cleveland, 1896-1901). Still another collection of original French documents is Pierre Margry's six-volume *Découvertes et établissements des Français dans l'Ouest et dans le Sud de l'Amérique Septentrionale* (Paris, 1879-1886). Louis Karpinski has published reproductions of many of the manuscript maps of the period in his *Historical Atlas of the Great Lakes and Michigan* (Lansing, 1931). Grace Lee Nute's *Caesars of the Wilderness* (New York, 1943) is a joint biography of Des Groseilliers and Radisson.

The great English and colonial explorers of Lake Superior are represented by Daniel W. Harmon's *A Journal of Voyages and Travels in the Interior of North America* (Toronto, 1911); Alexander Henry's *Travels and Adventures* (Boston, 1901); L. R. Masson's collections of letters, diaries and similar material which he published in two volumes as *Les bourgeois de la compagnie du nord-ouest* (Quebec, 1889); and David Thompson's manuscript diaries, maps and other papers in the possession of the Department of Public Records and Archives of the Province of Ontario at Toronto. Thompson's reminiscences have been edited by J. B. Tyrell and published by the Champlain Society as *David Thompson's Narrative* (Toronto, 1916).

Later travelers on Lake Superior during the British period were Dr. John Bigsby, who published two volumes of reminiscences of his travels along the boundary waters as *The Shoe and Canoe* (London, 1850); and Major Joseph Delafield, whose diaries and other documents of the American boundary commission's survey party have appeared recently as *The Unfortified Boundary,* edited by Robert McElroy and Thomas Riggs (New York, 1943).

Discussions of the activities of the several great trading companies may be found in Gordon Davidson's *The North West Company* (Berkeley, 1918); Harold A. Innis' *The Fur Trade in Canada* (New Haven, 1930); Louise P. Kellogg's *The British Régime in Wisconsin and the Northwest* (Madison, 1935); Arthur S. Morton's *A History of the Canadian West to 1870-71* (New York, 1939); Wayne E. Stevens' *The Northwest Fur Trade, 1763-1800* (Urbana, 1928); and Kenneth Porter's two-volume biography, *John Jacob Astor* (Cambridge, 1931). Grace Lee Nute's two books, *The Voyageur* (New York, 1931), and *The Voyageur's Highway* (St. Paul, 1941), relate not only to the voyageurs but also to their employers. In Charles M. Gates' edition of the diaries of *Five Fur Traders of the Northwest* (Minneapolis, 1933) is included one by John Macdonell of Lake Superior interest. A novel of considerable historical veracity is Kenneth Roberts' *Northwest Passage* (New York, 1937).

Trowbridge's journal of Cass's expedition of 1820 may be found in three issues of *Minnesota History*, the magazine of the Minnesota Historical Society published at St. Paul, during the year 1942. McKenney's trip of 1826 is recorded in his *Sketches of a Tour to the Lakes* (Baltimore, 1827). Schoolcraft's *Narrative Journal* of his trip with Cass appeared in Albany in 1821; and his *Narrative of an Expedition through the Upper Mississippi* was published in New York in 1834. Louis Agassiz' *Lake Superior* is a record of his trip in 1849 and was published in Boston in 1850. English and Canadian travelers to Hudson's Bay Company posts on the lake were Nicholas Garry, whose *Diary* was published in Ottawa by the Royal Society of Canada in 1900; Paul Kane, who published his log soon after his journey of 1846 and 1847, and which has been republished as *Wanderings of An Artist* (Toronto, 1925); and Frederic Ulric Graham, whose diary still awaits general publication, only a few privately printed copies having been published by his family in London in 1898.

The most authentic account of the Hudson's Bay Company is Douglas MacKay's *The Honourable Company* (Toronto, 1936).

Much of the material which tells the story of missionaries about Lake Superior has never been published, though great numbers of their letters, diaries and reports have been copied for the Minnesota Historical Society under the direction of the author. A volume of the earliest of these modern documents appeared as *Documents Relating to Northwest Missions, 1815-1827*, edited by Grace Lee Nute (St. Paul, 1942). John H. Pitezel's *Lights and Shades of Missionary Life* (Cincinnati, 1883) is based on his three diaries, now owned by the Carnegie Public Library in Sault Ste.

Marie, Michigan. Sister Mary Aquinas Norton devotes considerable space to Lake Superior in her *Catholic Missionary Activities in the Northwest, 1818-1864* (Georgetown, 1930); and Antoine I. Rezek in his two volumes of the *History of the Diocese of Sault Ste. Marie and Marquette* (Houghton, 1906-1907) tells the story of Baraga, Pierz, Skolla and several other Catholic missionaries. Evans' diary has never been published; it is owned by the University of Western Ontario.

For vessels and shipping on the lake there are many accounts, few of which have great merit. The best are A. P. Swineford, *History and Review of the Copper, Iron, Silver . . . of the South Shore of Lake Superior* (Marquette, 1876); James C. Mills' *Our Inland Seas* (Chicago, 1910); George A. Cuthbertson's *Freshwater* (New York, 1931); and official publications of the United States Department of War, such as *Transportation on the Great Lakes,* the revision of 1937. The Canada Steamship Lines, Limited, of Montreal has published several well-illustrated booklets. Alexander McDougall's *Autobiography,* published privately in 1932, is good source material. The Carnegie Public Library in Sault Ste. Marie, Michigan, has Franchere's and Livingston's manuscript records of shipping accounts of the American Fur Company, as well as other manuscript data. For the Canadian side of the picture a manuscript, "Early Ships and Pioneer Captains" by W. Russell Brown, and newspaper articles by Captain James McCannel in the Port Arthur *News-Chronicle* were of great service to the author. Martin McLeod's diary is printed in *Minnesota History* for August and November 1922.

One of the most satisfactory volumes available for the geology of the iron ranges and for modern figures and facts about iron mining and shipping is the Lake Superior Iron Ore Association's *Lake Superior Iron Ores* (Cleveland, 1938). Brief but authoritative accounts are Helen M. Martin's *Ne-saw-je-won* (Cleveland, 1939) and John H. Hearding's *Mining in the Lake Superior Region,* published in the bulletin of the Robert Morris Association in August 1929. Douglass Houghton's famous report was the fourth annual report of the geological survey of Michigan (Lansing, 1841). James Fisher of the Michigan College of Mines wrote an excellent summary of mining activities in the Copper Country for the annual *Keweenawan,* 1924, of his college. Specialized brochures are: *The Geology of the Rove Formation . . . in Northeastern Minnesota* (Minneapolis, 1933) by Frank F. Grout and George M. Schwartz; and Elfric Ingall's *Report on Mines and Mining on Lake Superior* for the annual report, 1887, of the Geological and Natural History Survey of Canada. The classic volume on the geological history of the lake is Charles R. Van Hise and Charles K. Leith's *The Geology of the Lake Superior Region,* published by the United States Geological Survey in 1911. A biography of the Merritt family of Minnesota, iron prospectors and mine owners, is Paul De Kruif's *Seven Iron Men* (New York, 1929).

For the fisheries of the lake there are good technical accounts but practically nothing on the fishermen. The only books that devote any space to them are George Brown Goode's *The Fisheries and Fishery Industries of the United States* (U. S. Commission of Fish and Fisheries, Washington, 1887, part 2), which also contains a good general account; Knut Gjerset's *Norwegian Sailors on the Great Lakes* (Norwegian-American Historical Association, 1928), which mentions briefly the Norwegian fishermen on the stretch of shore between Duluth and Port Arthur; and Webb Waldron's *We Explore the Great Lakes* (New York, 1923). For the earliest chapter in commercial fishing the only account is Grace Lee Nute's "The American Fur Company's Fishing Enterprises on Lake Superior," in the *Mississippi Valley Historical Review* of March 1926. Federal government publications, in addition to the one already mentioned, are: R. H. Fiedler's *Fishery Statistics of the United States, 1940;* Walter Koelz's *Fishing Industry of the Great Lakes* (1926); and the International Board of Inquiry for the Great Lakes Fisheries, *Report* and *Supplement* (1943). Anna Jameson rhapsodizes over the Sault's whitefish in her *Winter Studies and Summer Rambles in Canada* (New York, 1839).

There is an almost endless list of books on the history, development and scenery of the south shore. Besides those already mentioned as relating to topics already covered, there are specialized works that need a mention. Guy Burnham's *The Lake Superior Country in History and in Story* (Boston, 1930) is more specialized than its title indicates, for its chief topic is Ashland and Chequamegon Bay. Edward H. Capp's *The Story of Bawa-ting* (Sault Ste. Marie, Ont., 1904), on the other hand, deals almost exclusively with the Canadian Sault; and Otto Fowle's *Sault Ste. Marie and its Great Waterway* (New York, 1925), while devoted largely to the Michigan city at the rapids, has a wider scope. Unfortunately, it is marred with errors and was never completed by the author. Stanley Newton's *Story of Sault Ste. Marie* (Sault Ste. Marie, 1923) is better and more nearly up-to-date.

James Hargrave's Correspondence, 1821-1843 was edited by C. P. Glazebrook for the Champlain Society, which published it in 1938. Manuscript maps and charts by Henry Bayfield are to be found in the Hydrographic

Service of Canada, Department of Marine, Ottawa. *A Narrative of the Captivity and Adventures of John Tanner* was edited by Edwin James and published in New York in 1830. *John Long's Voyages and Travels in the Years 1768-1788* has been edited by Milo M. Quaife (Chicago, 1922). William Cullen Bryant published his *Letters of a Traveller* in New York in 1850. Gabriel Franchere published his *Narrative of a Voyage* in New York in 1854.

Florantha Sproat's letters appeared in the *Wisconsin Magazine of History* (State Historical Society, Madison) as "La Pointe Letters" in September and December 1932. C. D. O'Brien's reminiscences of La Pointe occur in Chrysostom Verwyst's *Life and Labors of Rt. Rev. Frederic Baraga* (Milwaukee, 1900).

Chase S. Osborn and Stellanova Osborn discuss Schoolcraft's life on Lake Superior, as well as the origins of *The Song of Hiawatha* in their *Schoolcraft-Longfellow-Hiawatha* (Lancaster, Pennsylvania, 1942).

Very little of worth has been published on the growth and individualities of cities and towns on the south shore and at the western end of the lake. The best are R. N. Cunningham and H. G. White's *Forest Resources of the Upper Peninsula of Michigan* (U. S. Department of Agric., Misc. Pub. No. 429, Washington, 1941); Frank A. Flower, *The Eye of the North-West: First Annual Report of the Statistician of Superior, Wisconsin* (Milwaukee, 1890); Duluth Board of Education, *The Story of Duluth* (Duluth, 1923); and Dwight Woodbridge and John S. Pardee, *History of Duluth and St. Louis County,* two volumes (Chicago, 1910). Ralph D. Williams' *The Honorable Peter White* (Cleveland, 1907) is reasonably accurate and full for the Marquette district.

For the north shore, data are scarcer. Thomas Clark's manuscript diary is in the possession of his daughter in Superior, Wisconsin. Kennicott's diary appears in James Alton James' *The First Scientific Exploration of Russian America* (Chicago, 1942). Accounts of Grand Portage occur in Solon J. Buck's *The Story of Grand Portage,* which appeared privately in Minneapolis in 1931; and in Grace Lee Nute's "Grand Portage" in *Indians at Work* (U. S. Office of Indian Affairs) for April 15, 1937. Robert McLean's *Reminiscences of Early Days* is an undated booklet which is full of authentic but unorganized data on the earliest days of settlement. An unpublished manuscript by Lloyd L. Smith, Jr., and John B. Moyle is *A Biological Survey and Fishery Management Plan for the Streams of the Lake Superior North Shore Watershed,* which was prepared for the Minnesota Department of Conservation, Division of Game and Fish. It contains the best available material on logging and forest fires. James A. Merrill's *The Wonderland of Lake Superior* (Minneapolis, 1936) is a small book published by offset process and especially good for the geography of the lake and the north shore.

Isle Royale's history is given best in scientific monographs such as Charles C. Adams' *An Ecological Survey of Isle Royale, Lake Superior,* (Lansing, 1909); Clair A. Brown's *Ferns and Flowering Plants of Isle Royale, Michigan* (U. S. Dept. of Interior, 1940); George R. Fox's *The Ancient Copper Workings on Isle Royale* (*Wisconsin Archaeologist,* volume 10, No. 2, July-October 1911); Adolph Murie's *The Moose of Isle Royale* (Univ. of Mich. Museum *Publication,* No. 25, 1934); and George A. West's *Copper: Its Mining and Use by the Aborigines of the Lake Superior Region* in the Bulletin of the Public Museum of the City of Milwaukee, volume 10, 1929. Mrs. Sarah Barr Christian's *Winter on Isle Royale* was privately printed in 1932. Several good bibliographies of the island's history, particularly of recent magazine stories and accounts, are to be had at the Duluth Public Library.

For the lumbering history of the region nothing adequate is available. The best material for the north shore has already been mentioned. For the south shore and Duluth-Superior the only book of any worth is George W. Hotchkiss' *History of the Lumber and Forest Industry of the Northwest,* which was privately printed in Chicago in 1898.

Nanabazhoo is the subject of many paragraphs in John Hoskyns-Abrahall's *Western Woods and Waters* (London, 1864) and J. B. Kohl's *Kitchi-Gami: Wanderings Round Lake Superior* (London, 1860). Frances Densmore has published much on the Chippewa but her outstanding works are *Chippewa Customs* and *Chippewa Music,* both published by the Bureau of American Ethnology (Smithsonian Institution, Washington, 1910, 1911 and 1929) in one volume for the former and two for the latter work. Vernon W. Kinietz' *The Indians of the Western Great Lakes, 1616-1760* is weak on the Chippewa. The Nanabazhoo legends occur as volume VII, parts 1 and 2, *Ojibwa Texts,* collected by William Jones, of the American Ethnological Society's publications (Leyden and New York, 1917, 1919).

John I. Baur has published a booklet on *An American Genre Painter, Eastman Johnson, 1824-1906* (Brooklyn Institute of Arts and Sciences, 1940). J. W. Young is the author of a similar biography and appraisal of Leon Lundmark, *The Rise of Lundmark Marine Painter* (Chicago, 1924).

ACKNOWLEDGMENTS

I AM indebted to many persons for helping me assemble material and obtain illustrations for this book. Several libraries and their staffs have helped me immeasurably, notably the Duluth Public Library, the Carnegie Library in Sault Ste. Marie, the Peter White Library in Marquette, the St. Louis County Historical Society in Duluth and the Minnesota Historical Society in St. Paul. Individuals who have assisted me and to whom I give my especial thanks are: Miss Jane Morey, Miss Alice Clapp, Miss Phyllis Rankin, Miss Leona Geismar, Mr. Stanley Newton, Mr. John Fritzen, Dr. Lloyd Smith, Jr., Dr. Richard Bardon and Mrs. Bardon, Mr. Theodore Thompson, Mr. Tolov Thompson, Mr. Oliver Isaacson, Mr. Wallace Lawrie, Mr. Edwin Brown, Miss Lois Fawcett, Mrs. Irene Warming, Mr. J. P. Bertrand, Mr. H. G. Runge, Mr. Samuel Ranck, Mr. Dewey Albinson, Mr. Frank B. Hubachek, Mr. John Hearding, Mr. Keith Denis, Mrs. Carol Paul, Miss Elizabeth Bachmann and Miss Elizabeth Ellison.

G. L. N.

INDEX

INDEX

NOTE: All vessels are indexed under the general heading of Vessels.